TOURISM MANAGEMENT

Sara Miller McCune founded SAGE Publishing in 1965 to support the dissemination of usable knowledge and educate a global community. SAGE publishes more than 1000 journals and over 800 new books each year, spanning a wide range of subject areas. Our growing selection of library products includes archives, data, case studies and video. SAGE remains majority owned by our founder and after her lifetime will become owned by a charitable trust that secures the company's continued independence.

Los Angeles | London | New Delhi | Singapore | Washington DC | Melbourne

2ND EDITION

CLARE INKSON & LYNN MINNAERT

TOURISM MANAGEMENT

AN INTRODUCTION

Los Angeles | London | New Delhi
Singapore | Washington DC | Melbourne

Los Angeles | London | New Delhi
Singapore | Washington DC | Melbourne

SAGE Publications Ltd
1 Oliver's Yard
55 City Road
London EC1Y 1SP

SAGE Publications Inc.
2455 Teller Road
Thousand Oaks, California 91320

SAGE Publications India Pvt Ltd
B 1/I 1 Mohan Cooperative Industrial Area
Mathura Road
New Delhi 110 044

SAGE Publications Asia-Pacific Pte Ltd
3 Church Street
#10-04 Samsung Hub
Singapore 049483

Editor: Matthew Waters
Assistant editor: Lyndsay Aitken
Assistant editor, digital: Chloe Statham
Production editor: Sarah Cooke
Copyeditor: Solveig Gardner Servian
Proofreader: Audrey Scriven
Indexer: Silvia Benvenuto
Marketing manager: Alison Borg
Cover design: Francis Kenney
Typeset by: C&M Digitals (P) Ltd, Chennai, India
Printed in the UK

First published 2012. Reprinted in 2012 (twice), 2014 (twice),
2015 (twice), 2016 (twice) and 2017
This second edition published 2018

Library of Congress Control Number: 2017955622

British Library Cataloguing in Publication data

A catalogue record for this book is available from
the British Library

ISBN 978-1-5264-2388-7
ISBN 978-1-5264-2389-4 (pbk)

To my family: thanks for your love, patience and support during the writing of this book. And for spending your holidays looking for interesting tourism sites and sights to photograph for me!

Clare Inkson

To my husband Pierre: thank you for all your love and support.

Lynn Minnaert

SUMMARY OF CONTENTS

CONTENTS

LIST OF FIGURES

LIST OF TABLES

LIST OF CASE STUDIES

ABOUT THE AUTHORS

Clare Inkson is a Senior Lecturer in Tourism at the University of Westminster in London. She has extensive experience of working in tourism in operational and marketing roles in the UK and overseas, for tour operators, wholesalers and travel agencies. Her research interests include tourism distribution channels, destination marketing and the tourism sharing economy.

Dr Lynn Minnaert is the Academic Director and Clinical Associate Professor at New York University's Jonathan M. Tisch Center for Hospitality and Tourism. Her research specialism is social inclusion and social sustainability in tourism and events: she has conducted research projects into social tourism, the social impacts of the Olympics and social legacy initiatives in the meetings industry. She has lectured in tourism and events management at undergraduate and postgraduate levels in the US, the UK and in a range of different countries – this international perspective is reflected in this book.

ONLINE RESOURCES

The second edition of *Tourism Management: An Introduction* is supported by a wealth of online resources for students to aid study and for lecturers to support teaching, available at https://study.sagepub.com/inkson

FOR STUDENTS:

- Additional case studies and snapshots
- Further readings online for every chapter, including free full-text SAGE journal articles
- Links to interesting videos on relevant topics
- Useful web links
- Flashcard glossary of key terms

FOR INSTRUCTORS:

- Instructors manual
- PowerPoint slides

GUIDED TOUR OF THE BOOK

HOW *TOURISM MANAGEMENT: AN INTRODUCTION* WILL SUPPORT YOUR LEARNING

This second edition of *Tourism Management: An Introduction* offers a range of learning resources within each chapter:

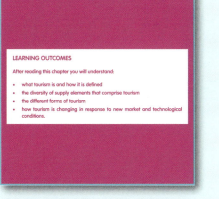

Learning Outcomes at the start of each chapter highlight at a glance the key topics that the chapter will cover and help you to understand.

Glossary Terms in coloured text and defined in the margin enable you to understand and reference key tourism management terminology.

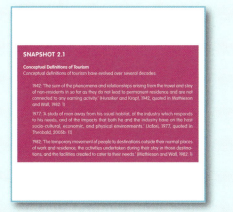

Snapshots throughout each chapter highlight interesting examples of specific issues in practice to help you understand how concepts apply to tourism destinations, business and organisations, tourists or host communities.

Case Studies supported by **Reflective Questions** help you to understand important points covered in each chapter in a practical and international context.

Summaries at the end of each chapter recap on the key topics that the chapter dealt with to help you consolidate what you have learnt from reading it.

Self-Test Questions at the end of each chapter help you check your understanding of the key topics and revise for assessments.

Further Reading and **Useful Websites** provide you with recommendations of useful articles, books, reports and websites to further your study and guide your revision.

PRAISE FOR THE PREVIOUS EDITION

'This book is important – it reminds us that tourism activity does not occur in a vacuum, but rather is shaped by forces linked to globalisation, sustainability, information and telecommunications technology. With its accessible and engaging writing style, it is a must for undergraduate students in their early days of studying tourism management and offers a very welcome addition to the tourism literature.'

Dr Philippa Hunter-Jones, University of Liverpool Management School, UK

'*Tourism Management: An Introduction* provides a refreshing and accessible perspective on key aspects of tourism for those new to the subject. This is something of an achievement as there are some very good books on the library shelves already.'

Rhodri Thomas, Professor of Tourism and Events Policy, Leeds Metropolitan University, UK

'Tourism is an exciting and dynamic sector which affects so many lives in many different ways and in this foundation text the authors bring that to life for students who are starting their tourism studies and require a succinct and comprehensive introduction. Students will find the self-test questions and recommended reading lists particularly valuable.'

Professor Nigel Morgan, Welsh Centre for Tourism Research, University of Wales Institute, Cardiff, UK

'This is a hugely readable, accessible and clearly structured introduction to the broad, diverse and complex dimensions of tourism. It is perfect for first and second year undergraduates as the authors clearly explain the issues that affect the success of tourism in destinations, and the management of tourism's impacts on destination economies, environments and communities. Students will like the inclusion of snapshots and case studies to demonstrate how theory applies in practice and the definitions of specialist terminology.'

Professor Annette Pritchard, Director of The Welsh Centre for Tourism Research, University of Wales Institute, Cardiff, UK

'This book provides a detailed discussion on a wide range of issues affecting tourism. Easy to understand, well-structured and a particularly useful book for undergraduate courses in Tourism Management.'

Kelly Maguire, Business and Humanities, Sligo Institute of Technology, Ireland

'A great book for undergraduates new to the subject area as well as those with more advanced knowledge of tourism. The book provides an excellent overview of the main areas of discussion within the subject for those studying it.'

Dr Sarah Snell, Marketing and Enterprise, University of Hertfordshire, UK

'The success of *Tourism Management: An Introduction* lies mainly in its ability to connect management concepts with broader issues such as globalisation, responsibility and sustainable development. I highly recommend this book ... The plain language, case studies and snapshots used by the authors make the book perfect for non-native English-speaking first-year undergraduates.'

Dr José Carlos García-Rosell, Faculty of Social Sciences, University of Lapland, Finland

'A good introductory text that introduces students to the wider issues relating to tourism management. Useful case studies bring the topics to life and offer points for discussion.'

Alan Marvell, Department of Leisure, Tourism, Hospitality and Events, Gloucestershire University, UK

PART I
TOURISM OVERVIEW

CONTENTS

1

INTRODUCTION

'If our lives are dominated by a search for happiness, then perhaps few activities reveal as much about the dynamics of this quest – in all its ardour and paradoxes – than our travels.'

A. de Botton, 2002: 9

Santa Monica, California

Source: Lynn Minnaert

ABOUT THIS BOOK

Tourism is an exciting and dynamic sector that is constantly changing. It can affect people's lives in many different ways: for tourists it can be a source of lifelong memories, joy and fulfilment, and for businesses and destinations it is a source of income and employment. As tourism has grown and become an ever more prominent activity, tourism studies as an academic field has also developed. When studying tourism, you will find that it is a broad and diverse topic area that encompasses several business sectors, and draws on a range of disciplines.

When one of the authors of this book studied tourism in the late 1980s, tourism textbooks were notable by their absence – the library shelf for tourism consisted of five or six textbooks only. Since then, tourism as an academic study has evolved considerably, and now hundreds, if not thousands, of tourism texts are available that consider tourism in a variety of contexts, and focus on specialist forms of tourism activity. This text is intended to provide a solid starting point to your learning about tourism – to give you a strong understanding of the dimensions of tourism, the industries of which it is comprised, the issues that affect the success of tourism in destinations, and the management of tourism's impacts on destination economies, environments and communities.

This text has been written for students who are starting their tourism studies and require a succinct yet comprehensive introduction to the broad, diverse and complex dimensions of tourism. It consists of 14 chapters, each of which focuses on a discrete tourism topic; the book can be read from start to finish in the conventional order, or you can pick individual chapters to read in any order, as and when you need to. The book has been designed to provide a foundation in tourism in line with the Quality Assurance Agency (QAA) recommendations for the structure of tourism degree programmes, and has been written particularly for first and second year undergraduates, so that they will have a strong overview of tourism before they start to specialise in a particular form of tourism or in a particular tourism issue.

The book is broadly structured along three main themes: the demand and supply of tourism, the impacts of tourism, and management and marketing. In the second chapter we explain the concept of tourism, how an understanding of tourism has evolved, and the theoretical framework that underpins its study. In Chapters 3 and 4 we consider the factors that influence the demand for tourism by identifying the conditions within an individual's usual environment that enable them to engage in tourism activities, and the forces that motivate tourists to choose tourism as an activity. Chapters 5, 6, 10 and 13 consider the supply of tourism: the industries that supply tourism products in destinations and their common operating characteristics, the role of intermediaries in making these products available for sale to tourists, and the destination itself, common development patterns, and the role of the public sector. The remaining chapters of the book consider the impacts of tourism on destination economies (Chapter 7), communities (Chapter 8) and environments (Chapter 9), and how these impacts can be managed to reduce their negative effects and optimise the benefits that tourism can bring to destinations (Chapter 12). Chapter 11 considers how marketing is applied in tourism, and we end the book with a consideration of the future (Chapter 14) – the future of tourism in general and your future as a young graduate in the tourism sector.

TOURISM IN THE TWENTY-FIRST CENTURY

As you develop your knowledge about tourism, you will notice that it is a dynamic sector that is often strongly influenced by changes that take place in society – tourism is very much a part of how we live today. It is important to remember that tourism as an activity, as an economic sector and as an area of study, cannot be separated from the wider external environment within which it operates. Tourism is influenced by external issues that have a significant impact on the nature of its development, on the ability of tourism businesses to operate successfully, and on tourism's potential to benefit or damage destinations. Throughout this book, we consider tourism in the context of contemporary forces that shape the economy and operating environment in general and to which successful tourism enterprises and destinations must be able to adapt and respond effectively. Three of these forces are of particular importance for tourism, and make their influence felt in every chapter of this book: globalisation and global conflict; sustainability and climate change; and developments in information and communications technology (ICT). In the remainder of this chapter, we explain the context of contemporary tourism in regard to these forces.

GLOBALISATION AND GLOBAL CONFLICT

Globalisation, at its simplest, means crossing borders. Globalisation is not new: goods, people and ideas have traversed the globe for millennia. In recent times

SpongeBob SquarePants advertisement in Iran

Source: Lynn Minnaert

however, globalisation has increased at a rapid pace: new technologies, like jet planes and the Internet, have led to global economics, politics and communications (*Economist*, 2001: ix). Wahab and Cooper (2001: 4) say globalisation is 'an all-encompassing term that denotes a world which, due to many politico-economic, technological and informational advancements and developments, is on its way to becoming borderless and an interdependent whole.' This means that any occurrence anywhere in the world can, in one way or another, have an impact somewhere else: in another country, in another continent. If for example the cotton crop in India is devastated by floods or a pest, this could mean that clothing prices may go up in North America. Political conflicts in Russia, a major exporter of natural gas, can lead to higher gas prices in Europe. Globalisation describes the process by which events, decisions and activities in one part of the world come to have significant outcomes for communities and individuals in quite distant parts of the globe.

Because it has become easier for goods, ideas and people to cross borders, certain products and cultural phenomena are now readily available almost everywhere. Brands like Coca-Cola, McDonald's and Nike are sold almost everywhere in the world, and popular music and Hollywood films can reach worldwide audiences via global distribution and the Internet. Globalisation has also led to multicultural communities, where a range of cultures co-exist and come together (Micklethwait and Wooldridge, 2004). Even though there are still cultural differences between the regions of the world, there is a growing body of products and phenomena that these regions have in common – Beynon and Dunkerley (2000) argue that this marks the emergence of a new 'world culture'.

Albrow (2004) summarises that globalisation can be seen as a combination of four phenomena:

- The values and daily behaviour of many groups in contemporary society are influenced by the state of other parts of the world, and its inhabitants.
- Images, information and products from any part of the world can be available anywhere and anytime for ever-increasing numbers of people worldwide.
- Information and communication technology make it possible to maintain social relationships and direct communication with people all over the globe, across time and distance.
- International laws and agreements ensure that people can move across national boundaries with the confidence that they can maintain their lifestyles and their life routines wherever they are.

Although there may be benefits attached to globalisation, such as the opportunities for communication between people in different parts of the world and the sharing of information, there are also those who claim that globalisation has a series of disadvantages. Examples are that globalisation reduces the power of national governments; that it reduces cultural differences and fades national identities; that it is a source of environmental degradation; and that it increases the gap between rich and poor.

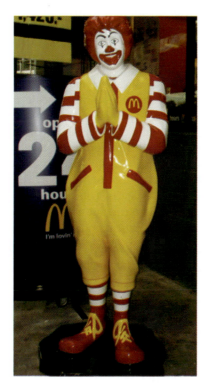

Ronald McDonald figure in Bangkok, in typically Thai pose

Source: Lynn Minnaert

Tourism can be seen as part of the process of globalisation – it is a sector with globalised supply and demand, and it is also a social phenomenon that can influence communities around the world. Many tourism suppliers, such as hotel chains and tour operators, have expanded across borders – tourists can, for example, stay in Hilton hotels in destinations ranging from Japan to Jamaica, confident that the level of service and comfort will be the same across the globe. In developing countries, foreign-owned tourism companies may reap the economic benefits from tourism; many people in the host communities, however, are often excluded from the profits tourism can bring. Globalisation has also resulted in a growth in international tourism demand: cross-border travel is on the increase and continental and intercontinental travel is growing fast (OECD, 2008b: 12). Visitors have an increasing number of destinations to choose from – they can find out about them via 'a globalised world of communications and advertising' (Macleod, 2004) and travel to them via extensive transport routes. This has led to an intense competition between destinations, and pressure on certain destinations as they suffer from an excess of visitors.

While a global sector like tourism may seem to benefit from globalisation, it is heavily dependent on political stability in the destination. Bianchi (2006: 64) states that

> [i]nternational tourism represents the apotheosis of consumer capitalism and Western modernity, based on an apparently seamless harmony between the free movement of people, merchandise and capital. However, as the growing insecurities engendered by the globalisation of terrorism and military interventionism, as well as targeted attacks on foreign tourists in certain parts of the world illustrate, the liberal calculus of unhindered mobility, political stability and the unfettered expansion of the market, which underpins the 'right' to travel, is increasingly mediated by heightened concerns of risk and security.

Geopolitical conflict and terrorism have affected many destinations in recent years, and it is not uncommon for tourists to be the specific target of attacks. In 2015, Tunisia was rocked by two attacks: one in the Bardo National Museum in Tunis, killing 22 tourists; and one three months later, at a beach resort near Sousse, killing 38 tourists. In 2016, a MetroJet flight from Sharm-El-Sheikh, Egypt, to St Petersburg, Russia, was downed by ISIS, killing all 224 passengers and crew on board. That same year, two bombs were detonated in Brussels Airport, Belgium, claiming 16 lives. Additional attacks in Nice, Istanbul, Paris, London and other destinations have had a profound impact on the tourism sector, and safety and security play an ever more important role in destination development and management.

The globalisation of tourism affects the different aspects of tourism that are discussed in this book. The characteristics of global tourism demand and supply will be discussed in Chapters 3, 5, 6 and 12. Globalised tourism also has far-reaching economic, socio-cultural and environmental impacts on host communities: these will be discussed in Chapters 8, 9 and 10. The potential to reach a global market has brought about changes in the way many companies market themselves (Chapter 13). Finally, crisis management for destinations will be covered in Chapter 12.

SUSTAINABILITY AND CLIMATE CHANGE

'Sustainability' is a term for which many definitions exist. Rogers et al. (2008: 5) describe sustainability as 'the term chosen to bridge the gulf between development

Grand Canyon National Park

Source: Lynn Minnaert

and environment'. Dresner (2008: 69) explains that 'the starting point of the concept of sustainable development was the aim to integrate environmental considerations into economic policy. More profoundly, it was conceived as an attempt to bring environmentalist ideas into the central area of policy, which in the modern world is economics'.

Originally the term was applied to forestry, fisheries and groundwater, to answer questions like 'How many trees can we cut down and still have forest growth?' and 'How many fish can we take and still have a fishing industry?'. Today, 'sustainability' is applied more widely to a variety of sectors and aspects of development. The problem is that this makes the term hard to define. At its core, sustainability balances environmental concerns with an allowance for economic growth: this means that development and growth are not blocked, but the way in which growth is achieved is considered closely. There is, however, not one particular way in which sustainability needs to be achieved: a wide range of actions can be classed as aiming towards this goal. Because the term can be interpreted in many different ways, one could say it has become rather vague – some even say it has become almost meaningless (Dresner, 2008).

Even if there are many different definitions for sustainability, there is a general consensus that it has three aspects:

> *Economic*: maximising income whilst maintaining a constant or increasing level of capital.
>
> *Environmental/Ecological*: maintaining and maximising the robustness and resilience of the natural environment.
>
> *Social/Socio-cultural*: maintaining and maximising the robustness and resilience of social systems and cultures. (Rogers et al., 2008)

Sustainability and sustainable development came to prominence in 1987, when the United Nations World Commission on Environment and Development, chaired by

Norwegian Prime Minister Gro Harlem Brundtland, published its report 'Our Common Future' (United Nations, 1983). The central recommendation of this document, usually known as the Brundtland report, was to balance the competing demands for environmental protection and economic development through a new approach: *sustainable development*. The Commission defined it as development that 'meets the needs of the present without compromising the ability of future generations to meet their needs' (Dresner, 2008: 1).

Further UN Conferences on Environment and Development included the 'Earth Summit' in Rio de Janeiro in 1992, where Agenda 21 was produced. The 40 chapters of Agenda 21 offered an action plan for sustainable development, integrating environmental with social and economic concerns, and articulating a participatory, community-based approach to a variety of issues, including population control, transparency, partnership working, equity and justice. Local Agenda 21 was not binding but many countries included it in policy making, with municipal governments often taking a strong lead (Blewitt, 2008: 17).

Another milestone for sustainable development was the 1997 Kyoto Protocol, a UN treaty that was signed by over 140 states. The Kyoto Protocol, like many other climate change agreements however, concentrated almost exclusively on reducing greenhouse gas emissions, largely ignoring the other aspects of sustainable development (Blewitt, 2008: 18).

The 2015 *Paris Climate Accord* takes a different approach from the Kyoto Protocol. Rather than binding emission limits for each country, the new climate agreement requires all parties to set their own emission targets. The goal is to keep a global temperature rise this century well below 2°C above pre-industrial levels. The agreement does not provide a concrete mechanism for carbon trading on a global level but reaffirms the role of carbon markets in achieving its climate goals (United Nations Framework Convention on Climate Change, 2017).

The three determinants of sustainable development are consumption, production and distribution (Rogers et al., 2008):

Consumption: in sustainable development, it is the aim not to use resources beyond the reasonable limit set by nature through regeneration.

Production: sustainable development recognises the need for new production patterns that take into account not only the economic benefits of production, but also the social and environmental benefits.

Distribution: sustainable development aims to reduce poverty and inequality – the socio-economic aspects of sustainability are particularly important here.

Several authors distinguish between strong and weak sustainability. A strong sustainability approach emphasises that resources need to be used in restrained ways as humankind cannot substitute them, and they must be preserved for future generations (Munier, 2005: 15). This is a more hard-line approach, which advocates using resources at the rate they are produced. For example, we currently consume oil a million times faster than it is produced (Dresner, 2008: 3) – a strong sustainability approach would advocate that we need to reduce our consumption of oil to one-millionth of its current level. A weak sustainability approach regards resources as a commodity that supports humankind (Munier, 2005: 15): although humankind needs to use them wisely, it allows for a responsible use of them. A weak sustainability approach would seek to reduce the dependency on oil with gradual reduction targets (Dresner, 2008). Blewitt (2008: 29) refers to these terms as 'deep' and 'shallow' ecology.

A major sustainability challenge that affects all aspects of life, including tourism, is climate change. Human activity, in particular the burning of fossil fuels, has increased the 'greenhouse effect': warming that results when the atmosphere traps heat radiating from Earth toward space (NASA, 2017). As a result, extreme weather events increase in frequency: for example droughts, heatwaves, cyclones and hurricanes. Global warming can also lead to rising sea levels, threatening human and wildlife habitats. The extent to which tourism as a sector is prepared for the impacts of climate change is a concern for many stakeholders: destinations are seen to be adapting to climate change, rather than pro-actively considering how it could affect their very nature. The European Environment Agency (EEA) has mapped how climate change will likely affect this region of the world, home to some of the most popular global tourist destinations (see Figure 1.1).

Arctic region
Temperature rise much larger than global average
Decrease in Arctic sea ice coverage
Decrease in Greenland ice sheet
Decrease in permafrost areas
Increasing risk of biodiversity loss
Some new opportunities for the exploitation of natural resources and for sea transportation
Risks to the livelihoods of indigenous peoples

Atlantic region
Increase in heavy precipitation events
Increase in river flow
Increasing risk of river and coastal flooding
Increasing damage risk from winter storms
Decrease in energy demand for heating
Increase in multiple climatic hazards

Mountain regions
Temperature rise larger than European average
Decrease in glacier extent and volume
Upward shift of plant and animal species
High risk of species extinctions
Increasing risk of forest pests
Increasing risk from rock falls and landslides
Changes in hydropower potential
Decrease in ski tourism

Coastal zones and regional seas
Sea level rise
Increase in sea surface temperatures
Increase in ocean acidity
Northway migration of marine species
Risks and some opportunities for fisheries
Changes in phytoplankton communities
Increasing number of marine dead zones
Increasing risk of water-borne diseases

Boreal region
Increase in heavy precipitation events
Decrease in snow, lake and river ice cover
Increase in precipitation and river flows
Increasing potential for forest growth and increasing risk of forest pests
Increasing damage risk from winter storms
Increase in crop yields
Decrease in energy demand for heating
Increase in hydropower potential
Increase in summer tourism

Continental region
Increase in heat extremes
Decrease in summer precipitation
Increasing risk of river floods
Increasing risk of forest fires
Decrease in economic value of forests
Increase in energy demand for cooling

Mediterranean region
Large increase in heat extremes
Decrease in precipitation and river flow
Increasing risk of droughts
Increasing risk of biodiversity loss
Increasing risk of forest fires
Increased competition between different water users
Increasing water demand for agriculture
Decrease in crop yields
Increasing risks for livestock production
Increase in mortality from heat waves
Expansion of habitats for southern disease vectors
Decreasing potential for energy production
Increase in energy demand for cooling
Decrease in summer tourism and potential increase in other seasons
Increase in multiple climatic hazards
Most economic sectors negatively affected
High vulnerability to spillover effects of climate change from outside Europe

FIGURE 1.1   Forecasted impacts of climate change on Europe

Source: EEA (2012) © European Environment Agency

Annual average land temperatures over Europe are projected to continue increasing throughout the twenty-first century, with the largest temperature increases projected over eastern and northern Europe in winter, and over southern Europe in summer. Annual precipitation is projected to increase in northern Europe and to decrease in southern Europe, enhancing the differences between currently wet regions and currently dry regions. The intensity and frequency of extreme weather events are also projected to increase in many regions, and sea-level rise is projected to accelerate significantly (EEA, 2017). The impacts of a rise in sea levels could be disastrous for a low country like the Netherlands, where one-third of the country is below sea level.

Tourism has not escaped discussions about sustainability: as a transport-intensive sector that has seen dramatic growth over the last decades, tourism has been accused of being inherently unsustainable. Some of the key challenges for tourism are the coordination and cooperation between different stakeholders, the limitations of the efforts of the industry (many being voluntary), and the fact that many small-scale businesses operate in tourism (Harris et al., 2002). The challenge of making tourism more sustainable is a key theme throughout this book. Chapter 7 discusses the extent to which tourism should be allowed to dominate destinations and change it. Chapter 9 specifically examines the environmental impacts of tourism on destinations, and proposes measures that can limit environmental damage. Chapters 7 and 8 consider how the economic and social impacts of tourism for host communities can be optimised.

INFORMATION AND COMMUNICATIONS TECHNOLOGY

Developments in information and communications technology (ICT) have been transforming tourism's competitive environment since the 1950s and continue to do so still; indeed, ICT developments since 2010 have had very significant effects on tourism. ICT is the use of computer hardware, software, mobile and fixed telecommunications, internet and satellite technologies, to store, process, retrieve and transmit information electronically. ICT is used by organisations to collect and record data, to process information efficiently and accurately, to communicate internally within and between departments, and externally with partners and with existing or potential customers, to connect users through virtual communities, and most recently, to connect objects electronically via the Internet of Things (IOT).

Egger and Buhalis (2008: 459) suggest that 'ICTs support the globalization of the industry by providing organisations with tools for developing, managing and distributing offerings worldwide'. ICT has revolutionised the ways in which consumers research, purchase and communicate about products and services. In tourism, for example, the handling of vast amounts of data relating to availability and reservations, prices, and the production of travel documents, is an extremely complex process, which, until ICT became widely used, was time-consuming, labour intensive and vulnerable to errors (Middleton et al., 2009).

Buhalis (2003) identifies four stages over which the use of ICT has evolved:

> *Data processing (DP)* – from the 1950s, operational efficiency was increased through the automation of information-based processes using mainframe and mini computers. The costs of hardware and programming excluded all but the largest organisations from using them, and in tourism major airlines began using computers to process reservations data, with systems known as computerised reservations systems or CRS (Inkpen, 1998; Sheldon, 1997).

Magnetronic Reservisor – the first electronic reservations system, introduced in 1952 by American Airlines

Source: Z22 (Own work) [CC BY-SA 4.0 (http://creativecommons.org/licenses/by-sa/4.0)], via Wikimedia Commons

Management Information Systems (MIS) – from the 1970s, data processing was linked to internal information sources such as accounting or inventory to improve management effectiveness and decision making. In tourism, global distribution systems (GDS) were introduced by the airline industry to provide a platform for travel agencies to access the CRS of several airlines, hotel and car rental companies through one system, for instance Sabre and Apollo (Sheldon, 1997).

Strategic Information Systems (SIS) – from the 1980s, management information systems within an organisation could be integrated into ICT networks. Managers were able to customise information to their own needs to produce their own management reports using personal computers to forecast, budget and plan using past data and simulation models. This development enabled more precise decision making and enhanced an organisation's performance. Buhalis suggests that 'SISs were primarily used to support or shape the competitive strategy of an organisation and their ability to gain and maintain competitive advantage' (2003: 12).

The network era – from the late 1990s, the use of local area networks (LAN) and wide area networks (WAN) as well as the Internet, intranet and extranets has revolutionised communication, allowing for greater collaboration within and between organisations and between consumers. This era is particularly important because in theory it has reduced the significance of location and size as a competitive advantage. For example, very small and remote tourism organisations can now use ICT to communicate with a global audience, and the audience itself is partly connected through membership of social networks. Consumers' access to information about tourism products in any destination is available instantly through search engines; this information may be provided by organisations or even by other consumers via platforms designed for C2C (customer to customer) or P2P (peer to peer) communications. In reality, the power and huge budgets of large corporations tend to dictate search results and it has become rather difficult for small organisations to appear on the first page of search results; instead they have to find innovative ways to capture attention, or partner with large corporations to gain access to global audiences online.

The development of networks has transformed the global economy into one in which potentially everyone is interconnected, and organisations can compete on a global scale regardless of their size or location. Social networks have revolutionised the way in which people communicate about their experiences, subsequently reducing the power of organisations to control information about their own products and services. Social media are extremely powerful because they allow any user to post comments about any organisation online that potentially could be read by hundreds, thousands or millions of viewers. These posts may reinforce the positive image that the company seeks to project, or could undermine an organisation's own investment in advertising and branding.

YouTube allows users to upload video content which can be viewed by an almost worldwide audience, and has over 1 billion users across 88 countries; 1 billion hours of video are viewed daily (YouTube, 2017). Facebook had 1.32 billion active daily users in June 2017 alone, and over 2 billion active monthly users (Facebook, 2017). Twitter is a real-time information network that allows its 1.3 billion account holders to create content that can be viewed by anyone who follows them; approximately 500 million tweets a day are added to Twitter (Smith, 2016). The power of these networks was demonstrated clearly in April 2017 when passengers on a United Airlines flight filmed the forceful eviction of a fellow passenger; footage was uploaded to social media by several people within minutes, subsequently shared with thousands of other users and went viral, attracting the attention of the global news media, and making headlines around the world.

The phenomenal speed of new developments in internet and mobile technologies since the beginning of the twenty-first century has far-reaching implications for organisations, particularly those in sectors like tourism that rely on the fast transmission of reliable information. Middleton et al. (2009: 243) state that 'information is the life-blood of tourism'. In order to compete effectively, businesses must adapt quickly to new technology, to changes in the ways in which consumers behave, and to new opportunities to communicate with consumers about their products (Middleton et al., 2009). As the United Airlines example showed, they also need to monitor, manage and respond to social media content.

Buhalis (2003: 7) stresses the role of ICT in organisations' success, enabling them to achieve their objectives and compete effectively. He also stresses the importance of 'humanware' in ICT: that is the intellect, knowledge, expertise and competence that enable an organisation to 'develop, programme and maintain the equipment' (2003: 6). We would add here that recent ICT developments have extended this 'humanware' element to individual users who create and share their own content within their digital social communities or make it publicly available online via social media or review sites. Organisations harness the power of these communities to their own marketing activities by maintaining an active presence on Facebook, Twitter, Instagram and YouTube and other social networking sites, running campaigns encouraging users to add and share content about them, and by responding to reviews.

The transformative impact of ICT on the commercial environment and the operations of organisations cannot be underestimated. It enables:

- greater productivity by reducing the time required to complete tasks and reducing staff costs
- the rapid submission, transmission and sharing of information to speed up processes, and integrate some departmental functions.
- the processing of vast amounts of data very quickly to allow quicker decision making within an organisation and by consumers too.

Since the early twenty-first century, the term 'big data' has been coined to describe the collection and analysis of huge volumes of data in almost real time, to reveal trends, patterns of behaviour and interactions online. Specialised software and algorithms analyse data about an individual's past behaviour online to predict how they will respond to specific information (e.g. the messages that are likely to be most effective) and to tailor offers specifically for that user (O'Neill, 2017). Our online behaviour is tracked and monitored constantly in order to identify the best time to target us with offers and information, and the best prices to offer us. Assumptions are made about us based on how other users with similar characteristics also behave (O'Neill, 2017). Data protection laws are only just catching up with big data: in May 2018, new privacy regulations – the General Data Protection Regulation (GDPR) – will come into force within the EU to strengthen data privacy and consent laws, with fines of up to €20 million for breaches (EU GDPR, 2017).

The Internet itself is not a static technology and continues to evolve. The term 'Web 1.0' refers to websites or internet usage with static content that allows data to be posted, viewed and downloaded; its use is limited to the provision and retrieval of information. Web 2.0 is a commonly used term to describe advanced internet technology and applications that enable users to generate content, for instance blogs, wikis, RSS (Really Simple Syndication) and social networking. Web 2.0 allows web content to be used dynamically through the creation of virtual communities and user-centred design that encourages users to generate content and to connect to other users and content providers (Middleton et al., 2009).

Web 2.0 caused a major shift in power towards consumers (Middleton et al., 2009). In tourism, customer review sites are particularly important to consumers who can check other consumers' opinions and experiences of a supplier before making a purchase decision, and potentially be deterred from making reservations. Tourism businesses and organisations must understand how their customers are influenced by social networks and thereby incorporate social media into their own marketing, using innovative approaches.

Web 3.0 is emerging now. Also known as the 'semantic web', it consists of applications that are capable of understanding the meaning of words, interpreting past searches and personalising data retrieval (Naughton, 2014). For example, search engines analyse a user's key word usage and frequencies to interpret a search request and present the results it deems most relevant to that user. The large technology companies are investing in artificial intelligence (AI) in the form of virtual assistants that respond to voice and provide personalised results, for instance Apple's Siri, Amazon's Alexa, Microsoft's Cortana and Google's Google Assistant. Travel technology companies such as KAYAK use chatbots – computer programmes that mimic humans – to interact with users by asking questions and then personalise search results (KAYAK, 2017). In 2017, FCM Travel Solutions launched a 'pocket travel assistant' app: Sam (Smart Assistant for Mobile) (FCM Travel Solutions, 2017) provides conversational interfaces that track a user's travel patterns and preferences, anticipate needs, make recommendations and take action. The more data the AI has on the user, the more personalised the recommendations and actions are:

> From pre-trip information, such as letting you know your destination weather, to organizing your airport transfers and letting you know where to collect your bags on arrival, you'll find Sam really helpful. Sam will send you travel alerts based on up-to-date information to ensure you don't miss your connection. But if you do, Sam will help schedule you onto the next best option, all within your company travel policy. Sam is always on, so you don't have to be. (FCM Travel Solutions 2017)

In the five years since the publication of the first edition of this book, developments in ICT have enabled the rapid rise in power of innovative companies, often described as 'disruptors'. In tourism two forms of disruptor in particular have transformed the competitive environment:

- P2P sharing, or collaborative, economy
- online distributors of travel products – online travel agencies (OTAs).

THE SHARING ECONOMY

The sharing economy, also known as the collaborative economy or P2P economy, emerged online in the first decade of the twenty-first century in the form of digital platforms that enabled individuals to exchange, swap, rent or sell their possessions and property to strangers around the world at the touch of a button. The property may include: household goods and equipment, for example a lawn mower or DIY tools; leisure equipment such as skis, surfboards or bikes; leftover food or unwanted used items; and in tourism specifically includes rooms in homes or the entire home, vehicles such as cars, private jets and yachts or seats on these, and guiding, dining, and entertainment services.

The concept of the sharing economy in not a new one in tourism. Centuries ago, before the emergence of a hotel industry in destinations, tourists travelling for health, education, business, and early forms of leisure travel would be introduced to home owners by a mutual acquaintance and may stay with the home owner, or rent their entire property, for extensive periods of time. In the twentieth century, home owners wishing to swap properties, or make their first or second homes available for hire to tourists, would advertise in travel or exchange newspapers or magazines. Homestays with local families have long been used by language schools to accommodate students on short courses, and hitching a ride with car drivers was common until the later decades of the twentieth century. The emergence of digital platforms in the early twenty-first century created a global market for property owners, and made a less common form of tourism easily accessible to users. Often the new sharing economy platforms promote their experiences as unique, authentic or local to suggest a different type of experience to those of the formal tourism industries, and to appeal to more confident and adventurous types of tourist.

In tourism several sharing economy platforms have seen great success: Airbnb is probably the best known sharing economy platform for accommodation but there are several that enable home owners to swap properties temporarily (Love Home Swap), to invite travellers to stay at their homes free of charge (CouchSurfing) or to rent a room or the whole property to tourists (HomeAway, Homestay, Onefinestay). There are also sharing economy platforms for transport (Uber, Lyft, BlaBlaCar, Jettly), and for tours and activities in destinations (BonAppetour, Withlocals, EatWith, Airbnb Experiences). Short-term rental accommodation via sharing platforms such as Airbnb or HomeAway have completely changed the accommodation offer in some destinations, creating entrepreneurial opportunities for some homeowners, but not without unintended negative social impacts on the host community in some cases, and creating new forms of competition for the hotel sector. We consider this phenomenon throughout this book but in particular in Chapters 5, 8, 10, 11 and 13.

Online Travel Agencies

The term 'online travel agencies' (OTAs) is used to describe travel intermediaries that began to emerge at the turn of the twenty-first century and sold exclusively online. They quickly gained market power because they offered the tourism consumer a convenient way of researching, booking and paying for travel products, particularly hotel rooms. In addition, they facilitated access for tourism suppliers to markets worldwide. OTAs such as Expedia, Priceline and Ctrip have grown to dominate online travel commerce and wield huge marketing power over tourism suppliers, hotels in particular, through their leverage of the results of online searches and advertising. They have transformed the way in which travel is researched and booked, and have created many opportunities, but also many challenges, for suppliers. There is also some overlap between OTAs and the sharing economy, for example Expedia owns HomeAway. We discuss OTAs in detail in Chapter 6.

The Internet of Things

The Internet of Things (IoT) is the next generation of the Internet which is currently emerging. The IoT connects devices electronically and shares data between

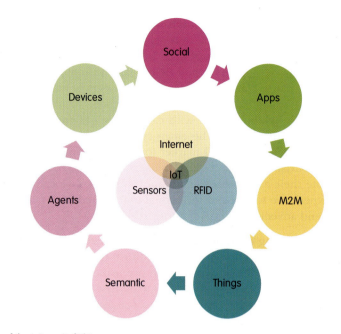

Components of the Internet of Things

Source: Toma Cristian, Cristian Ciurea and Ion Ivan (http://jmeds.eu/index.php/jmeds/article/view/105) [CC BY 3.0 (http://creativecommons.org/licenses/by/3.0)], via Wikimedia Commons

them, for example via mobile enabled sensors, beacons, the Internet, wearables, and apps on smartphones. Many hotel companies use IoT to enhance the guest experience by enabling:

- mobile checking in and checking out
- use of the guest's smartphone as a room key
- viewing of social media and streaming channels via the room's TV
- control of heating, lighting, air conditioning and curtains.

In tourism, destinations are also embracing the power of the IoT and big data to become 'smart'. By encouraging visitors to download apps onto their smartphones or by offering free WiFi throughout a destination, realtime data on visitors' movements around the destination is collected and collated with data from destination suppliers such as attractions and transport, and social media. This data is used to enhance the visitor experience of a destination by providing personalised guides on visitors' smart phones including information about attractions close by, transportation and traffic status, wait-time at attractions, and the weather. The data collected is also useful for tourism organisations and local authorities to learn about visitor behavior in the destination, for example by analysing the flow of visitors around and between sites or how local transport is used. This data facilitates decision making about accessibility, infrastructural needs and so on. The use of such technology could help to improve the sustainability of tourism by suggesting itineraries and routes that disperse visitors away from busy routes or sites, by monitoring when sustainable capacities at sites are exceeded, and by encouraging visitors to use public transport. Sustainability is discussed in more detail in Chapter 9. Smart destinations is a new approach to destination management; indeed, the UNWTO held its first conference on smart destinations in 2017 and the UNWTO Secretary-General concluded that '"Smart tourism" is not a trend, but the future of tourism development' (UNWTO, 2017a).

Immersive Technologies

At the time of writing, immersive technologies are emerging as a valuable marketing tool, particularly in tourism. 'Immersive technology' refers to technology that blurs the distinction between the physical world and the simulated world, creating a digital experience that feels real. Immersive technologies have great potential in tourism because they can inspire a desire to visit a destination or attraction by allowing people to explore and discover experiences and sites whilst still at home. For instance Tourism Australia has produced a range of films that use virtual reality and 360-degree images shot from above and below aquatic and coastal sites to immerse the viewer in the scene and imagine themselves there (Tourism Australia, 2017b). During a visit to a destination or attraction, augmented reality via headsets or apps on smartphones can enhance the visitor's experience by simulating historical or cultural events and scenes, or by making a static site more dynamic and exciting. For example, Discover Moscow Photo App allows users to 'meet' historical figures at relevant sites around the city associated with them, take photos of the site featuring the figure, and even take selfies with them (Destination Think!, 2017).

Blockchain technology

The next significant ICT development to transform tourism is currently considered to be block chain technology. Blockchain is a decentralised database that is distributed among thousands or millions of computers. The database is continually updated in real time, and records can only be added, not removed or amended. Each computer in the chain holds a full or partial copy of the data so any crash, hack or loss of data is highly unlikely. Bitcoin is probably the best known current example of blockchain technology: a digital currency with which online payments can be made. At the time of writing, blockchain technology in tourism is very much in its infancy. Suggestions have been made that it could transform online distribution of travel products such as airline or hotel capacity: transport, accommodation and attraction suppliers could make their capacity available on a public blockchain travel platform that is available to everyone. Each time a reservation was made, availability would be updated on the database in real time throughout the chain, thereby reducing the need for OTAs and GDSs. At the time of writing, one of the largest travel companies in the world, TUI Travel Group, announced that they would adopt a private blockchain database to manage availability across all of their hotels (Whyte, 2017).

ICT has become one of the strongest influences in tourism: recent developments have transformed the way organisations market their products, have facilitated the greater involvement of host communities in tourism supply, have accelerated tourism's role in the process of globalisation, and have the potential to improve sustainability through tools that monitor and manage the negative social and environmental impacts of tourism. Throughout this book, we highlight how ICT can be used to harness operating, distribution and marketing advantages, and the opportunities it offers to small and medium-sized businesses to communicate with potential consumers and collaborate in partnerships.

HOW TO USE THIS BOOK

This book offers you a succinct and clear introduction to the many different aspects of tourism that you will study. It has been designed so that you can read the chapters in the order that is most useful to you and the references between chapters will lead you to other relevant information. Each chapter includes several snapshots and one case study to demonstrate how theory applies in practice, and, where appropriate, we have included definitions of specialist terminology in textboxes in the margin. Each chapter ends with self-test questions to check your understanding and a recommended reading list with references to books, articles and websites that can help you develop your knowledge further. We hope you enjoy studying this fascinating subject!

2

UNDERSTANDING TOURISM

'Tourism is much more than you imagine.'

UNWTO (2016a)

LEARNING OUTCOMES

After reading this chapter you will understand:

- what tourism is and how it is defined
- the diversity of supply elements that comprise tourism
- the different forms of tourism
- how tourism is changing in response to new market and technological conditions.

Galapagos Islands, Ecuador

Source: Claudia Dolezal

INTRODUCTION

Tourism today is a familiar and easily recognised activity that is enjoyed by over one billion people every year. Interestingly though, our understanding of what tourism is and whether it can be described as a distinct industry in its own right, as well as the criteria by which travellers are classified as tourists, is still evolving.

International tourism: Tourism activity by individuals outside their country of residence

Impressive claims are made about the importance of tourism – 'one of the world's largest sectors' (World Travel & Tourism Council, 2017d), 'one of the fastest-growing economic sectors in the world' (UNWTO, 2017b) – underlining its significance as an economic force. Certainly since the mid-twentieth century the expansion of tourism has been rapid, with the growth rates of **international tourism** averaging 6.5 per cent every year between 1950 and 2005 (UNWTO, 2010), and despite slower growth rates as a result of the global economic crisis that began in 2007, international tourist arrivals are expected to reach 1.8 billion by 2030 (UNWTO, 2016b). Tourism is an activity enjoyed by substantial proportions of the populations of industrialised economies, and most countries promote their natural, historic or cultural resources as tourist attractions to earn a share of the US$1,260 billion industry (UNWTO, 2016b).

Tourism is often described as a 'phenomenon', meaning that it is an observable event or occurrence. The occurrence is most observable in the destinations that tourists visit because of the infrastructure that tourism usually requires, and the economic, environmental and social impacts of tourism activities. However, an understanding of tourism requires an appreciation not just of what tourists do and need in destinations, but also of why and how the decision to engage in tourism is taken. Therefore, tourism involves the study of places visited by tourists (i.e. where tourism is consumed) and of the factors and conditions in the places where tourists live (i.e. where the demand for tourism is created).

In this chapter we consider how tourism is described conceptually, the criteria by which travellers are defined as tourists, and the industries that supply the tourism product. We finish the chapter by discussing the main forms of tourism.

WHAT IS TOURISM?

The word 'tourism' is derived from the Greek and Latin words meaning to turn or to circle, and in the context of a journey means a trip that ends in the same place that it began; a round trip (Theobald, 2005b). It may be stating the obvious to say that tourism involves travel, but not all travellers are tourists and this leads us to one of the main problems in understanding tourism – identifying the forms of travel, and the types of activities, that are, or are not, tourism.

Tourism as an activity is often located within the broader framework of leisure and recreation because, traditionally, tourism was understood as holidays and therefore involved recreational activities during leisure time (Mathieson and Wall, 1982). However, while holidays represent one specific use of leisure time, not all tourism is for leisure purposes.

It has been suggested that the focus on holidays has created a perception of tourism as a superficial, fun and pleasurable activity and has delayed its recognition as a serious economic sector and subject of academic study. This has not been helped by slow progress in reaching a consensus on definitions of tourism and classifications of tourists. In addition, even tourism itself is variously described as 'the travel industry', 'the hospitality industry', 'the visitor industry' and 'the holiday industry', thus adding further to the confusion.

Academics, practitioners and governments have struggled to define tourism for many decades. Definitions of tourism and classifications of tourists have been proposed and amended since the 1940s, and have evolved as tourism itself has evolved and changed. As recently as 2008, the UNWTO refined its classifications of tourism and tourists.

Definitions of tourism have evolved into two broad types – conceptual and technical – each with its own rationale and application (Theobald, 2005b):

Conceptual definitions describe what tourism is by providing a holistic theoretical framework that identifies all the elements of tourism and reflects its multi-faceted and multi-disciplinary characteristics.

Technical definitions identify who tourists are and what the tourism industry is, specifying the criteria by which travellers can be classified as tourists and enterprises can be classified as part of the tourism sector. Technical definitions facilitate the collection of data, measurement of impacts and statistical comparisons.

We begin by considering conceptual definitions.

CONCEPTUAL DEFINITIONS OF TOURISM

Several definitions have evolved since the 1940s as our understanding of tourism has been refined and tourism itself has changed (Mathieson and Wall, 1982). Conceptual definitions should capture the whole essence of tourism by recognising the role of tourists' routine environment as well as where they travel to and the impacts of tourism. One of the challenges of defining the concept of tourism is to include all its components without generalising so much that the description becomes vague.

The snapshot below presents some early conceptual definitions of tourism that emerged from the 1940s onwards.

SNAPSHOT 2.1

Conceptual Definitions of Tourism
Conceptual definitions of tourism have evolved over several decades:

1942: 'The sum of the phenomena and relationships arising from the travel and stay of non-residents in so far as they do not lead to permanent residence and are not connected to any earning activity.' (Hunziker and Krapf, 1942, quoted in Mathieson and Wall, 1982: 1)

1977: 'A study of man away from his usual habitat, of the industry which responds to his needs, and of the impacts that both he and the industry have on the host socio-cultural, economic, and physical environments.' (Jafari, 1977, quoted in Theobald, 2005b: 11)

1982: 'The temporary movement of people to destinations outside their normal places of work and residence, the activities undertaken during their stay in those destinations, and the facilities created to cater to their needs.' (Mathieson and Wall, 1982: 1)

These definitions stress that tourism results from individuals' decisions to move temporarily from their usual environments. Note the changes in emphasis to avoid excluding business tourism, and to acknowledge the impacts on destinations. The more recent term 'sustainable tourism' reinforces aspirations for tourism as a force for inclusive and equitable development, environmental protection, poverty reduction and sustainable economic growth (UNWTO, 2015). All tourism should be sustainable of course, but this has not yet been achieved. We discuss sustainability in detail in Chapter 1 and refer to it throughout the text.

In 1993 the United Nations endorsed the World Tourism Organization's proposed definition of tourism as 'the activities of a person travelling to a place outside his or her usual environment for less than a specified period of time whose main purpose of travel is other than the exercise of an activity remunerated from within the place visited' (UNWTO, 1991, cited in Theobald, 2005b: 16). The specified period of time was defined as one year, and the purposes of tourism travel included leisure, business, visiting friends and relatives (VFR), health treatments, religious pilgrimage and 'other' purposes, specified by the WTO's technical classification of tourists.

The definition of business tourism excluded travellers who were directly employed and paid by an employer located in the destination. The 1993 definition of tourism was widely adopted by academics, practitioners and governmental organisations. However, definitions of tourism have evolved again more recently.

In 2008 the UNWTO refined their description of tourism further: 'tourism is a social, cultural and economic phenomenon related to the movement of people to places outside the usual place of residence' (UNWTO, 2008a: 1). The 'usual place of residence' is interpreted as the geographical location of an individual's routine work and life activities, and individual nations determine the distance that must be travelled for a trip to be described as tourism.

This description reflects a more holistic approach to the concept of tourism, recognising that the effects of tourism are not limited to economic interests. From an economic perspective, tourism is defined as 'the actions and behaviours of people in preparation for and during a trip in their capacity as consumers' (UNWTO, 2008a: 106), recognising the significance of tourist spending for tourism within their usual environment, as well as within the destination visited.

The tourism activities for a single trip therefore occur in at least two locations – the tourist's usual environment and the place or places they visit during the trip – and occur over several stages – before departure, during the trip, and after the return home. Additionally of course, in order for tourism to occur, these locations must be connected by transport and infrastructure. Tourism therefore involves a number of separate elements.

Mathieson and Wall (1982: 14) illustrate this well by describing tourism as a 'composite phenomenon' comprising a range of components and relationships that together form a coherent conceptual framework (see Figure 2.1).

Mathieson and Wall's Conceptual Framework of Tourism

Mathieson and Wall (1982) identified three basic elements to tourism:

The dynamic element: representing demand for and forms of tourism, which are fluid and subject to change.

The destination element: originally called the static element, representing the tourist and the characteristics of their behaviour, the characteristics of the destination, and its static capacity and environmental and social threshold.

The consequential element: representing the economic, environmental and social impacts that occur as a result of the interaction of the dynamic and destination elements, and their measurement and control.

These elements are incorporated into the conceptual framework to illustrate the inter-relationships between them (see Figure 2.1).

The framework identifies tourism as the interaction of demand and supply, and shows how each affects the other and creates impacts in the destination. These impacts must be managed and controlled by measures implemented within the destination. The framework illustrates how change in one element influences and changes the other elements. The framework illustrates well that the study of tourism requires an

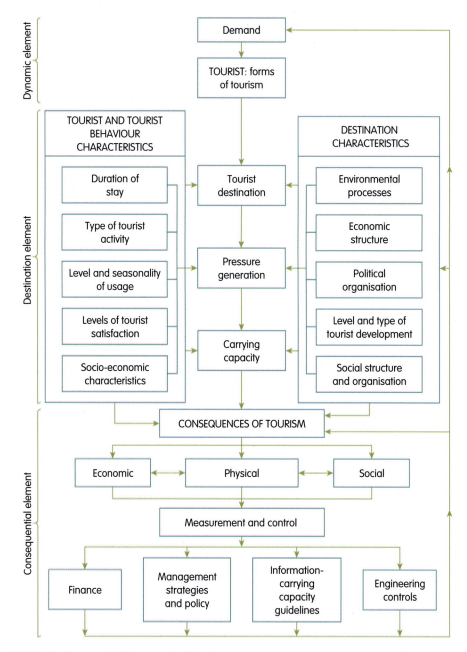

FIGURE 2.1   A conceptual framework of tourism

Source: Tourism: Change, Impacts and Opportunities, Wall and Mathieson, Pearson Education limited. © Pearson Education Limited 2006. Reprinted by permission

understanding of a broad range of discrete subject areas and issues: marketing is used to manage and influence the dynamic element; economics, sociology, ecology, planning, development processes and business management influence the destination element; while destination, business and environmental management influence the consequential element.

Conceptual definitions tell us what tourism is, but they do not specify any technical characteristics such as the distance from the usual place of work or residence that must be travelled in order for a trip to be recognised as tourism.

TECHNICAL DEFINITIONS OF TOURISM

Technical definitions specify the criteria by which travellers are recognised as tourists, and businesses and organisations are recognised as being part of the tourism sector. This may appear to be an easy task but in reality it has proved difficult.

Clear and standardised technical definitions are important because:

- they facilitate the collection of statistical data about the size of tourism and its economic value to enable governments to measure tourism and understand its influence on their economies

- they help tourism suppliers to identify trends and anticipate changes in demand in order to respond effectively

- internationally and nationally standardised definitions of tourists enable countries, regions of countries and individual destinations to compare tourism performance in terms of the number of arrivals and their economic contribution through expenditure in the destination.

These comparisons cannot be achieved unless each destination uses the same definitions to identify the travellers that are tourists, the businesses and organisations that are tourism enterprises, and the forms of expenditure that count as tourism expenditure. The process of standardisation has been slow because a number of organisations have researched and proposed technical definitions independently of each other, and reaching a consensus, particularly internationally, is not straightforward. In the meantime, individual states have defined tourists and tourism enterprises using their own criteria.

The need for clear and standardised criteria to identify tourists and tourism enterprises increased during the 1980s as governments recognised the economic potential of tourism and its interdependence with other industry sectors. The ability to compare tourism's contribution with the performance of other industry sectors in a national economy (e.g. construction or agriculture) required the use of the same measurement criteria and classifications. During the 1980s the WTO and the United Nations Statistics Division began a review of the definitions and classifications used for tourism statistics in order to improve their compatibility and consistency with other national and international statistical systems. At the same time, a number of other international agencies were investigating methods for harmonising classifications of tourism and collection of data. In 1995 the EU initiated legislation to harmonise and improve the tourism statistical data collected by member states, and in 1997 the OECD proposed classifications to be used in its members' national accounts (UN, 2010).

Tourism is often considered from one of two perspectives – the demand side, and the supply side:

Demand-side perspectives consider tourism consumption and identify the characteristics of tourists and their behaviour and expenditure in destinations. Technical definitions of tourism have traditionally focused on the demand side.

Supply-side perspectives examine the businesses and organisations that supply tourism products. Many authors claim that the supply-side understanding of tourism has been neglected (Cooper and Hall, 2008; Theobald, 2005b), and the evidence considered later in this chapter seems to support this view. It should be noted, however, that the UNWTO has been taking steps for some time to improve definitions and classifications of tourism supply, but this is a particularly challenging task.

Demand-side Definitions

Demand-side definitions identify the characteristics that distinguish tourists from travellers for other purposes, and specify purpose of visit and duration of stay. Definitions have evolved since the 1930s, but at the time of writing the most recent revisions were proposed in 2008.

In 1937, for statistical purposes the League of Nations defined an international tourist as one who 'visits a country other than that in which he habitually lives for a period of at least 24 hours' (Theobald, 2005b: 12). In 1945 the UN endorsed this definition and added a maximum duration of six months. Note that this definition refers only to international tourism and does not recognise travel to another country for less than 24 hours as tourism. Additionally, it does not define the purpose of the visit.

Significant refinements to this definition were proposed in 1963 at the UN Conference on International Travel and Tourism (IUOTO, 1963), which recommended the use of the term 'visitor' to describe 'any person visiting a country other than that in which he has his usual place of residence, for any reason other than following an occupation remunerated from within the country visited' (Theobald, 2005b: 13). The conference identified two broad purposes of travel for tourism and included activities beyond the traditional understanding of tourism (Leiper, 1979):

* Recreation, holiday, health, study, religion and sport.
* Business, family, mission or meeting.

Visitors would then be classified as either:

* tourists, if they stayed in the country visited for at least 24 hours, or
* excursionists, if they stayed less than 24 hours in the country visited, and not overnight. This was to include cruise ship passengers who stayed overnight on-board ship (IUOTO, 1963, in Mathieson and Wall, 1982: 11).

These definitions were endorsed by the UN Statistical Commission in 1968 and approved in 1976 as the provisional guidelines on statistics of international tourism (UN, 2010). They only referred to international tourism, however; the value of **domestic tourism** was recognised in 1980 by the WTO's Manila Declaration that extended the terms 'visitor', 'tourist' and 'excursionist' to include domestic tourism too. Individual countries' own statistical definitions continued to define the distance from home, purpose of travel and length of stay (Mathieson and Wall, 1982).

Domestic tourism:
Tourism activity by individuals within their country of residence

In 1991 the WTO and the Canadian government jointly hosted the International Conference on Travel and Tourism Statistics in Ottawa. The conference recommended coordination of statistical definitions of domestic and international tourism with other international statistical standards, for example the balance of payments, international migration statistics and the System of National Accounts (UN, 2010).

The recommendations specified the purposes of tourism travel more explicitly as:

- Leisure, recreation and holidays
- Visiting friends and relatives
- Business and professional
- Health treatment
- Religion/pilgrimage
- Other.

In 1993 these recommendations were approved by the UN as *The Recommendations on Tourism Statistics* (UN, 1994). This was the first international agreement to provide a uniform system for tourism statistics with common interpretations of tourism concepts, definitions and classifications (UN, 2010).

In 2004, the WTO was integrated into the UN as a specialised agency to coordinate all the organisations that were involved in proposing how tourism statistics should be compiled. In 2010 the UN's statistical division published new recommendations on technical definitions and classifications of international tourism in order to:

- make them applicable to developing and developed economies worldwide
- make them consistent with definitions and classifications used by other national and international organisations that collected economic, household and migration statistics; for example the International Labour Organisation (ILO), the International Monetary Fund (IMF), the European Union (EU), the Economic Commission for Latin America and the Caribbean (ECLAC)
- make them applicable at **sub-national** as well as national levels
- consider destinations at a regional, municipality or other sub-national level
- make them conceptually precise
- be measurable.

Sub-national: A region within a nation

The *International Recommendations for Tourism Statistics 2008* (UN, 2010) confirmed the 1963 interpretation of visitors as either tourists or same-day visitors (excursionists), and revised the purposes by which trips are classified as tourism to two broad types – personal and business/professional – with further sub-classifications as outlined in Table 2.1. Of course, on one trip a visitor may undertake a variety of these activities. To avoid confusion, the classification recommends that trips are classified by their main purpose, without which the trip would not take place.

It is clear from the conceptual and technical definitions that tourism involves the temporary and voluntary movement of people to places away from their usual environment for personal or business and professional purposes, and the supply of particular products and services before and during their visit. We will now consider tourism from the supply side.

Supply Elements in the Tourism System

The term 'tourism supply' refers to the businesses and organisations that produce the products and services that tourists consume. Leiper (1979: 400) defines tourism supply as 'the firms, organisations and facilities which are intended to serve the specific

TABLE 2.1   The UN's classification of the main purpose of a tourism trip

Classifications of tourism purpose	Examples
Personal Holidays, leisure and recreation	Sightseeing, visiting natural or man-made sites, attending sporting or cultural events, recreational sports activities (skiing, riding, golf, tennis, diving, surfing, sailing, climbing etc.), using beaches, swimming pools and any recreation and entertainment facilities, cruising, gambling, attending summer camps, resting, honey-mooning, fine dining, well-being and fitness (spas, therapies), staying in a vacation home owned or leased by the tourist
Visiting friends and relatives (VFR)	Visiting friends and relatives, attending weddings, funerals or other family events, short-term caring duties
Education and training	Formal or informal short-term courses or study programmes, professional or other special courses, university sabbatical leaves
Health and medical care	Receiving short-term hospital, clinic, convalescent services, health and social institutions, visiting health resorts for medical treatments
Religion and pilgrimage	Attending religious meetings and events, pilgrimages
Shopping	Purchasing consumer goods, for personal use or as gifts
Transit	Stopping at a place without any specific purpose other than being en route to another destination
Other	Volunteer work, investigative work, temporary unpaid activities not included elsewhere
Business and professional	The activities of self-employed and employees not linked to direct employment in the destination region: attendance at meetings, conferences (congresses), trade fairs and exhibitions, giving lectures, performing concerts, shows and plays, buying and selling goods or services on behalf of non-resident producers, diplomatic, military or international government missions (except when stationed on duty in place visited), NGO missions, scientific and academic research, professional sports, formal or informal on-the-job training courses, crew member on private transport

Source: IRTS (2008)© United Nations, reproduced with permission.

needs and wants of tourists.' However, identifying tourism supply is not as simple as it may at first appear because, as Table 2.1 demonstrates, the products that tourists consume are extremely diverse:

- Tourism is often described as heterogeneous because it is not a single product, but an amalgam of separate products and services. These products and services are provided by companies and organisations that are part of separate industry sub-sectors, for instance transport and accommodation, which are studied and measured separately.

- The products and services for a single tourism visit may be produced in a number of separate locations, for instance in the tourist's place of residence and in different parts of the destination region, and as a result can be described as 'spatially fragmented'.

- Some tourism products and services are used solely by tourists, but in reality many are also used by other types of user too. For example, hotel meeting rooms or restaurant and banqueting facilities may be used by the host community or local businesses, while a transport service may be used by migrants and commuters as well as to transport freight. Therefore, identifying the extent of tourism activities of businesses and organisations can be very difficult.

- The public sector has a significant role in tourism, either directly through the provision or management of attractions for tourists or services to the commercial sector, or indirectly through statutory services such as planning or environmental health, but are often ignored in considerations of tourism supply (Litteljohn and Baxter, 2006). We discuss the role of the public sector in Chapter 13.

- Tourists also often consume products and services that are not part of the traditional tourism sector, for example high street shops and petrol stations that primarily serve the local community. In some destination regions tourism's contribution to their revenue may be substantial.

These problems in identifying tourism supply were recognised by the UN in 2010, which defined tourism supply more broadly as 'a set of productive activities that cater mainly to visitors or for which an important share of their main output is consumed by visitors' (UN, 2010: 2). This recognises that tourists use a range of suppliers, some of whom may not be traditionally tourism related.

This diversity has created great challenges in defining what tourism supply is composed of, in measuring the value of tourism activities, and in creating a holistic image of what tourism is. Despite the difficulties in recognising the range of businesses and organisations that form tourism supply, and in identifying the extent to which tourism contributes to their revenue, a supply-side view of tourism is becoming increasingly important because governments need to:

- analyse the economic value of tourism and understand its links to other economic sectors by measuring its size, its revenue, and the number of jobs it creates

- anticipate how policy and planning decisions will affect tourism, and the legislative requirements of the sector

- consider the effects on tourism of changes in the external environment.

Litteljohn and Baxter (2006) suggest that tourism supply can be considered from either a functional or an income approach.

Functional Approach to Tourism Supply

The functional approach groups tourism supply according to its function in tourism; that is, by the type of product it produces or by the nature of its interaction with tourists.

Holloway (1985) identifies the function of tourism supply as producers, intermediaries or support services:

Producers, known by industry as 'suppliers', provide the product consumed by tourists and consist of passenger transport operators, accommodation, venues and attractions.

Intermediaries create links between producers and consumers by selling some or all of the producer's capacity. Intermediaries are travel agencies, tour and MICE operators and wholesalers.

Support services provide products or services to the businesses and organisations that supply the tourist product, or to tourists direct. Private sector support services include guiding services, training providers and travel insurance providers, while public sector support services include visa and passport services and national, regional and local tourism organisations.

Suppliers and intermediaries interact directly with tourists, either in person or digitally, during the decision-making, purchasing or consumption stages. Suppliers and intermediaries can be subdivided by industry, for example the airline, hotel or tour operator industry. We discuss suppliers in detail in Chapter 5 and intermediaries in Chapter 6.

Complementarity:
Together forming a whole entity

Each category of supply function provides a portion of the tourist's experience and is dependent on the other categories for the provision of the remainder. The quality, availability and value of one category will affect demand for the others. For instance, the success of accommodation suppliers in a destination depends on the availability of quality attractions to draw tourists to the destination, and efficient and affordable transport routes to the destination. This interdependence is known as **complementarity** (Middleton et al., 2009) and implies a need for a close working relationship between different types of supplier.

Within a destination, the cooperation and coordination of suppliers is often facilitated by public sector or not-for-profit tourism support services, which also often have a substantial role in providing tourist information, destination marketing, and the commissioning of research to understand the characteristics of visitors to a destination.

The functional approach to tourism supply is useful in simplifying the fragmented nature of tourism and showing how its individual elements are complementary. It also recognises the network of interdependence, relationships and interactions that exists in tourism. The snapshot below illustrates these concepts in relation to the UK.

SNAPSHOT 2.2

Tourism in Great Britain

'Few British industries are as strong as travel and tourism, and few have such growth potential'.

VisitBritain (2017a)

Great Britain benefits from a strong tourism infrastructure that is spatially fragmented across four countries, hundreds of thousands of suppliers and several industries:

- 620,170 hotel rooms (PwC, 2016) in over 40,000 hotel and similar accommodation establishments (Eurostat, 2015)
- diverse attractions – ancient monuments; historic towns; world-class museums; National Parks and protected coastline; and cultural, sporting and business events
- 20+ airports handling over 1 million passengers annually (CAA, 2017)
- 10+ cruise ports (Cruisemapper, 2015)
- domestic and international rail links
- national and local tourism destination organisations.

Edinburgh during the Festival Fringe

Source: Clare Inkson

Inbound tourism demand to Britain is usually highest in July–September and lowest in January– March: 10.66 million compared to 7.55 million respectively in 2016 (VisitBritain, 2017c). However, political, economic and terrorist shocks have caused significant annual fluctuations: following the 2007 global financial crash, inbound demand to Britain did not recover to 2007 levels until 2014 (VisitBritain, 2017c).

TOURISM INCOME APPROACH

To assess the size and economic contribution of an industry, it is necessary to have a clear understanding of which enterprises form the industry in question. All governments classify enterprises by type and code them to identify their role in the national accounts and to measure employment. To encourage consistency in classification and coding, and comparability between individual countries, the UN introduced international standard industrial classifications (ISIC). However, tourism wasn't recognised as a distinct activity in ISIC; instead figures measuring tourism's contribution to an economy were derived from figures on accommodation or catering. This has important implications for the measurement of tourism supply, as it excludes many parts of the tourism sector from statistics on tourism employment and revenue (Cooper and Hall, 2008).

In 1990 the WTO revised ISIC to make it more applicable to tourism and recommended a standard international classification of tourism activities (SICTA). SICTA distinguished between enterprises whose source of revenue was mainly tourism (T), or partially tourism (P), and coded enterprises accordingly.

This approach considers the value of tourism to businesses and organisations, and identifies the extent to which suppliers rely on tourism financially. A tourism income approach enables a more comprehensive understanding of the economic impacts of tourism because it considers all types of businesses and organisations that derive an income from tourism, whether or not they are typical of tourism supply.

The EU used this approach in 1998 to measure tourism employment and identified three types of businesses: core tourism businesses derived 50–100 per cent of their income from tourism; complementary and ancillary services derived 25–50 per cent of their income from tourism; and the remainder derived less than 25 per cent (Litteljohn and Baxter, 2006). However, the reliability of the approach depends on the ability to differentiate between tourism income and other types of income, which is not always possible.

In 2010 the UN recommended describing tourism supply in one of two ways:

- Tourism characteristic products are supply that would be unlikely to exist without tourism, and for which statistical data can be obtained.
- Tourism connected products are supply that would still exist without tourism, or supply that depends on tourism but is not recognised as such globally, for example hospitals, clinics or language schools.

Table 2.2 lists the type of supply that is identified by the UNWTO as tourism characteristic and demonstrates the fragmentation of tourism supply across several industries. This fragmentation has raised doubts about whether tourism can be described as an industry at all.

TOURISM AS AN INDUSTRY

A question occupying many academics and economists is whether tourism should be regarded as an industry in its own right. Lobbyists for tourism refer to tourism supply as 'the tourism industry' to highlight its economic value, to compare its value with other industries, and to give credibility to a phenomenon that has struggled to be taken seriously by governments (Davidson, T. L., 2005).

There are two definitions of an industry. The traditional economic view of an industry is of a collection of competing enterprises that produce the same product. According to this view, tourism cannot be described as an industry because it includes enterprises producing different types of product that complement each other (Davidson, 2005).

Alternatively, the standard industrial classification (SIC) regards an industry as a group of establishments with the same primary activity whose size is statistically significant (Davidson, T. L., 2005). Tourism as a whole does not fit into this description either, because the primary activities of transport, accommodation and attractions are clearly not the same.

We have seen that tourism results from a combination of the activities of several separate industries producing different but complementary products. Within each individual industry such as the hotel industry or the airline industry, suppliers produce the same product and compete with each other, but it is not possible to identify tourism as a single industry (Davidson, T. L., 2005; Leiper, 1990b). Leiper (1990b) suggests that tourism should be described as a sector that impacts on a diverse range of industries.

In practice though, the term 'tourism industry' is widely used. The UN's 2010 revision of technical definitions recommended using the term 'a tourism industry' to describe a set of enterprises with the same principal activities as are listed in Table 2.2, that collectively are known as 'the tourism industries'.

TABLE 2.2   Tourism characteristic supply

Products	Activities
Accommodation for visitors	Hotels, resort hotels, pensions, guesthouses, B&Bs, apartments, bungalows, cottages, youth hostels, mountain shelters, cabins, university halls of residence, sleeping cars, boarding houses, campsites, recreational vehicle parks and caravan parks, second homes, timeshare properties
Food and beverage serving services	Restaurants, cafes, food and beverage services in hotels or on ships and trains, self-service and fast-food, mobile food services, bars, nightclubs, bars in hotels, ships and trains, beverage-serving activities
Railway passenger transport	Sightseeing services by rail, interurban railway services
Road passenger transport	Taxis, airport shuttle services, car rental, man- or animal-drawn vehicles, non-scheduled bus and coach services, cable cars, ski lifts, sightseeing by coach, scheduled bus, coach, trams
Water passenger transport	Rivers, canals, ferries, inland cruises, water taxis, ocean cruises
Air passenger transport	Sightseeing flights by plane or helicopter, scheduled and chartered plane and helicopter services, space transport
Transport equipment rental services	Car and light van hire
Travel agencies and other reservation services	All reservation services for transport, accommodation, cruises, package tours, events, entertainment and recreational services, tour operators, tourist guides, visitor information services
Cultural services	Theatre, dance and music performances, museums, historical sites and buildings, gardens and zoos, nature and wildlife reserves
Sports and recreational services	Stadiums, ice rinks, sports fields, golf courses, bowling alleys, scuba diving, hang-gliding, casinos, horse riding, ballrooms, dance halls, ski hills, beach and park services, fireworks, sound and light performances, amusement parks
Country-specific tourism characteristic goods	Retail trade: duty free shops, specialised retail trade in souvenirs, handicrafts
Country-specific tourism characteristic services	Other country-specific tourism characteristic activities

Source: Adapted from United Nations (2010) © United Nations 2010. Reprinted with permission.

We have seen so far that tourism is a complex phenomenon that is composed of a variety of elements in different locations and different industries and comes in a variety of forms. Many tourism theorists (Cooper and Hall, 2008; Gunn, 1972; Leiper, 1979; Matley, 1976) suggest that tourism is most easily understood as a system.

TOURISM AS A SYSTEM

A system is a collection of individual components that when combined will create a particular phenomenon. In a tourism context the system consists of tourists, geographical regions and the resources required for tourism production and consumption. Each element of the system requires different types of production and consumption, but crucially, these are interrelated and interdependent; change within one element will cause change in the other elements.

Leiper first proposed a systems framework for tourism in 1979 with subsequent amendments in 1990. His model recognises 'how tourism (the behaviour of tourists) gives rise to tourism systems' (1990b: 601) and has made a major contribution to our understanding of tourism (Figure 2.2).

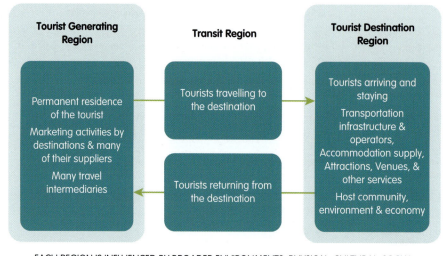

EACH REGION IS INFLUENCED BY BROADER ENVIRONMENTS: PHYSICAL, CULTURAL, SOCIAL, ECONOMIC, POLITICAL, TECHNOLOGICAL, LEGAL

FIGURE 2.2   Leiper's tourism system

Source: Adapted from Leiper (1979: 404). Reprinted from *Annals of Tourism Research*, 6(4), 1979. Reproduced with permission from Elsevier.

The system identifies how the behaviour of people as tourists creates 'arrangements of people, places and organisations in certain roles' (Leiper, 1990b: 604) with five basic elements: tourists; generating regions; transit routes; destination regions; and the tourism industries. These elements operate within, and are influenced by, broader physical, cultural, social, economic, political and technological environments.

Tourists are the human elements of the system who temporarily and willingly move beyond their routine environment through the discretionary use of time and money. Leiper (1990b) includes business travel if it is not part of the travellers' usual work routine. He describes tourists as the behavioural element of the system.

Generating regions are the usual place of residence for tourists and the source of demand for tourism. Conditions here, particularly economic and political conditions, influence the ability of residents to engage in tourism, and cause fluctuations in demand levels.

The generating region is the location of the tourism decision-making process and is usually where tourism is planned, booked and paid for, in advance of departure. Subsequently, the generating region is the focus of promotional activities to persuade consumers to engage in tourism and to purchase particular travel products. The travel trade has a major presence in generating regions in the form of travel agencies, wholesalers and tour operators.

Transit routes are the journey that must be made to reach the destination region. Transit routes determine the destinations that are accessible from the generating region.

The available modes of transport such as air, sea, road or rail, and the necessary infrastructure for their operation, determine the routes available and travel time, while political, economic and technological conditions influence their cost. Transit routes are particularly important in determining the volumes of tourist flows between generating and destination region as it determines a destination's accessibility to potential tourism consumers.

Destination regions are the location of the resources that attract tourists (Leiper, 1990b). This region is the focus for most tourism studies because the consequences of tourism activities are felt most strongly here and affect the local economy, environment and society in a positive or a negative way. Within the destination, planning and management strategies that influence these impacts are required.

The tourism industries comprise the businesses and organisations that provide experiences, services and facilities for tourists. Leiper (1979: 401) describes the tourism sector as 'a linked chain' because it is located in the generating, transit route and destination regions, is fragmented across a number of industries, and involves the commercial and the state sector.

Leiper describes tourism as 'partially-industrialised' because tourists' experiences often include non-industrial resources, for example natural attractions, private homes or private transport (Leiper, 1979), and also often include the consumption of products that are not directly associated with tourism (Leiper, 1990b). The extent of industrialisation of tourism varies between different tourist markets (e.g. international tourism is often more industrialised than domestic tourism).

Broader environments are the conditions outside of tourism that influence the tourism system by affecting conditions in the generating, transit and destination regions. Leiper (1990b) identified a range of broader environments including socio-cultural, economic, technological, political and legal.

The tourism system cannot control the broader environment but must be able to respond to it effectively to ensure that the system continues to function. The first decades of the twenty-first century have been particularly tumultuous for tourism as it has been struck by one catastrophic external event after another: 9/11; wars in Iraq, Afghanistan, Syria and Yemen; SARS, swine flu, ebola and the zika virus; global financial crisis and economic recession; the continuing terrorist threat in European, north African and Middle Eastern destinations; the refugee crisis; and instability and political tension in the Far East. Each of these has affected either the ability of residents in some generating regions to engage in tourism, the safety and cost of transit routes, or the appeal of particular destination regions.

The inter-relationship of elements of the tourism system means that the system is dynamic: change in one element is felt across the whole system, creating instability and constant change. This change can be positive or negative. For instance, the Chinese government's relaxation of controls over the tourism activity of its citizens has transformed international tourism since the 1990s. The case study below describes changes to China's tourism system.

CASE STUDY 2.1

China's Tourism System

Tiananmen Square, Beijing in 1990

Source: Clare Inkson

Between 1949 and the early 1980s China was isolated. After Mao's death in 1978, China's new 'Open China' policy targeted inbound tourism as a route to foreign currency earnings. In 1982 the new China National Tourism Administration (CNTA) began promoting China to international visitors and investing in infrastructural development (Mintel, 2004). Additionally, controls over Chinese citizens' tourism activity were gradually reduced (Nyiri, 2006). By 2016, China had become the world's fourth most visited destination country, and the largest tourist-generating region (UNWTO, 2016b).

China offers numerous world-class heritage and natural attractions (e.g. the Great Wall, Forbidden City, Terracotta Warriors), however, initially it lacked hotel and transport capacity. Relaxation of foreign investment restrictions in the 1980s allowed foreign hotel companies into China (Mintel, 2004), and government investment stimulated rapid growth of the road, high-speed rail, and airport infrastructure (Mintel, 2004). Today major hotel companies offer properties in China: InterContinental Hotels Group (IHG), Marriott and Wyndham Worldwide. In 2014, China attracted 55.6m international tourists; its main inbound markets are Hong Kong, South Korea, the USA and Russia; 2014 also saw almost 100 million day visitors from Hong Kong and Macau, and in 2015, 4 billion domestic trips (Mintel, 2016a).

In 2016, domestic and inbound travel and tourism contributed US$1,000.7 billion to GDP – 9 per cent of the total economy – supporting almost 70 million jobs (WTTC, 2017c). Leisure tourism dominates tourism expenditure (80.8 per cent) and domestic visitors' contribution is 82 per cent compared to 18 per cent from international visitors (WTTC, 2017c).

The International Air Transport Association (IATA) estimates that by 2029, China will be the world's top passenger airline market (cited in Mintel, 2016a), but until the 1980s, tourism was seen as a Western activity (Nyiri, 2006). Government attitudes to tourism have relaxed gradually: Chinese outbound tourism was permitted for business or VFR, although each trip required government approval (Nyiri, 2006). In 1997 the CNTA began encouraging domestic tourism (Li, 2007), and China officially recognised outbound leisure tourism and established regulations requiring countries seeking to attract Chinese leisure tourists to enter into bilateral tourism agreements with the Chinese government, known as approved destination status (ADS) (Li, 2007). By 2014 more than 146 ADS agreements had been signed with destinations around the world.

Initially, outbound leisure tourists had to travel on organised group tours operated and sold by CNTA-approved tour operators and travel agencies. While group travel is still significant, a new type of Chinese tourist, known as free independent travellers (FITs), is being targeted by many destinations. FITs are young, educated and experienced travellers who seek adventure and unique experiences. They enjoy researching and planning trips and tend to book online; in response to this, Chinese online travel companies such as Ctrip have become very powerful – Ctrip is the fastest-growing OTA, and the third-largest by booking value after Expedia and Priceline (Rossini, 2016).

China, the world's largest generating region, ranked first for outbound visits in 2015 (127.9 million) and for spending on international tourism (US$292.2 billion) (UNWTO, 2016b). In many countries China is already the first or second most important generating region.

Reflective Questions

1. How did the broader environment influence China as a destination region for international tourism, and as a generating region for outbound tourism by Chinese citizens?

2. How did destinations in China develop the supply necessary to transport and accommodate international tourists?

A systems approach to tourism provides a simple and flexible framework to understand a complex phenomenon:

- It can be applied at a variety of levels, for example nationally to consider tourism flows between two countries, or sub-nationally to identify tourism flows between two regions or two local areas.
- It can be considered in the context of a range of disciplines such as geography, economics, anthropology or marketing.
- It illustrates that tourism is an amalgam of products and experiences that are fragmented across a number of stages and suppliers.

We have seen that tourism occurs when an individual travels temporarily from their routine environment for a range of personal or professional reasons. Tourism includes a variety of separate elements – demand, supply and impacts – and is experienced across three geographical regions – the generating, transit and destination regions. Tourism supply is fragmented across these three regions as well as over a number of separate industry sectors. The external environment in the generating, transit and destination regions, over which tourism suppliers have no control, is extremely significant in influencing demand and the impacts of tourism.

We will now complete this chapter by identifying the main forms of tourism.

FORMS OF TOURISM

Tourism can be described in numerous ways to distinguish its many forms. Indeed, the term 'adjectival tourism' has developed to demonstrate the ability to add a particular adjective to the word tourism to denote a specific type of tourism destination, activity or market (Ashworth, 2003). The main distinctions between types of tourism are based on:

- the geographical setting of the destination
- the type of activity engaged in on the trip
- the location of demand and its relationship to the destination from the national perspective of a country
- the characteristics of the trip including how it was organised and the number of tourists.

THE GEOGRAPHICAL SETTING OF THE DESTINATION

Forms of tourism are often characterised by the geographical characteristics of the destination:

Urban tourism: tourism in cities and towns using the resources that are provided primarily for local residents and businesses as attractions for tourists; for example museums, theatres, markets, shops, restaurants, nightclubs, sports and cultural facilities, events and meeting facilities. Transport links to and within urban destinations are usually well developed (Page, 2005).

Rural tourism: tourism in small towns and villages or to remote natural areas. Attractions may be natural, cultural or based on specific physical activities (e.g. rock climbing, hiking, cycling) and resources may be spread over a wide area. Demand is heavily influenced by the weather. Rural tourism destinations mainly attract holiday, leisure and recreational visitors. Access to and within rural destinations may be limited, and require the use of private vehicles by tourists (Lane, 1994).

Resort tourism: tourism in a place that attracts large volumes of tourists, and where the economy and services are dominated by tourism. Resort tourism may develop in an existing village or town, or be purpose built. Resort tourism is often located in coastal or mountain regions.

The distinction between tourism types based on the geographical setting of the destination is useful because the type and scale of resources in each type have particular implications for the destination's ability to attract certain types of tourists, the nature of the impacts of tourism, the management of the destination and its ability to market itself effectively. Chapter 10 focuses on destination management and marketing,

The Type of Activity Engaged in on the Trip

A further way to describe forms of tourism is by the main type of activity engaged in on the trip. Table 2.3 identifies some of the common types of activity. Descriptions of tourism by type of activity are useful because the activity often identifies the main motivation for the tourism trip, the type of destinations and attractions likely to be visited, and the resources required to attract this form of tourism.

Destinations often promote their tourism resources and identify broad market segments by the type of activity. In addition to types of activity, descriptions of tourism can be further refined according to the location of demand and its relationship to the destination.

TABLE 2.3   Types of tourism by activity

Heritage tourism	Visits to sites of cultural, historical or ecological importance in a destination – monuments, buildings, geographical features
Eco tourism	Visits to rural or wilderness environments to actively learn about the natural environment and with a focus on positive impacts for the local environment, economy and host society
Sun, sea and sand tourism	Visits to coastal destinations for relaxation where climate and beaches are the main attraction
Cultural tourism	Visits to enjoy the cultural resources of a destination, for example art galleries, museums, architecture, religion, local lifestyle, language and traditions, and cultural events
Sport tourism	Visits for the specific purpose of taking part in a particular sport such as skiing, surfing or golf, or to spectate at a sporting event
MICE tourism	Visits for meetings, incentive, conferences and exhibitions. Customers may be companies, associations or individual tourists travelling for business or professional purposes
Event tourism	Visits to participate in or spectate at a particular organised event, which may be cultural or sporting
Dark tourism	Visits to sites associated with significant sinister events, for example battlefields, prison camps or murder sites
Cruise tourism	Travel and stay on board a marine vessel for ocean or river journeys, often with visits to multiple destinations
VFR tourism	Visiting friends and relatives

THE LOCATION OF DEMAND AND ITS RELATIONSHIP TO THE DESTINATION FROM THE NATIONAL PERSPECTIVE OF A COUNTRY

From a national perspective types of tourism can be described as domestic, inbound or outbound:

Domestic tourism is tourism activity by residents within their own country. For example a Thai resident engaging in tourism in Thailand, or a Canadian resident in Canada.

Inbound tourism refers to tourism arrivals of residents from other countries. For example in Australia, tourists from Japan, the USA and Europe are inbound tourists.

Outbound tourism refers to the tourism activity of individuals outside their country of residence. For example Australian residents travelling to Japan, the USA or Europe represent outbound tourism for Australia, but would be inbound tourism for the destination countries (UN, 2010).

Most industrialised economies that do not restrict the mobility of their residents experience domestic, outbound and inbound tourism, although the extent of each varies significantly between individual countries.

The implications of inbound and outbound tourist flows are discussed in detail in Chapter 7, and the snapshot below describes the types of tourism flows experienced by Cuba.

SNAPSHOT 2.3

Tourism Flows in Cuba

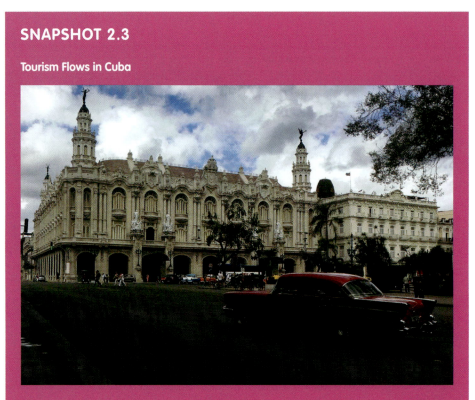

Havana, Cuba

Source: Iain Lanyon

Cuba's tourism has been shaped significantly by politics. Located just 150kms from Florida, since 1963 the US has strictly controlled its citizens' visits there (US Department of State, 2017b), forcing Cuba to seek alternative generating regions.

During the 1960s domestic tourism increased, along with inbound tourism from the Soviet bloc (Bleasdale and Tapsell, 1994, cited in Spencer, 2016: 14). In 1975 Canada was also targeted and remains an important generating region. Following the Soviet bloc collapse in the 1990s, Cuba's economic strategy focused on tourism and the expansion of the Canadian and European markets. By 2002, Canada and western Europe provided 68 per cent of all arrivals (Mintel, 2005). Until 2013, when outbound travel restrictions were eased, Cuban nationals required an exit visa to travel internationally (*Guardian*, 2013).

Power transferred to Raul Castro in 2008. In 2014 President Obama restored US/Cuban diplomatic relations and in 2016 reopened transport links (Mintel, 2016b). Until June 2017 the US allowed 12 categories of travel to Cuba including education, family visits by Cuban-Americans, and people-to-people (cultural exchange); leisure tourism to Cuba remains outlawed (US Department of State, 2017b).

In 2015, international arrivals reached 3.5 million. Rapid expansion of 100,000+ new tourist rooms by 2031 and extensive airport expansion by 2020 are planned to supply the forecasted growth in demand (Mintel, 2016b). In June 2017, President Trump reversed the people-to-people category and tightened the regulations on US travel to Cuba.

Finally, tourism can be described by the characteristics of the trip.

CHARACTERISTICS OF THE TRIP

The characteristics of the trip including how it was organised and the number of tourists. In practice, tourism is often described using certain trip characteristics relating to the composition of the travel party, the method of organisation or the scale and impacts of the trip. The main distinctions between trip characteristics are outlined in Table 2.4. In reality, there is an overlap between these different ways of describing tourism; for example one tourism trip could be described as outbound, independent, cultural tourism.

TABLE 2.4   Types of tourism by trip characteristics

Independent travel	Tourists not travelling with an organised group. The tourist researches, makes reservations and payments direct with suppliers, or via a travel agency or wholesaler. Demand for independent travel has increased considerably in some regions since internet technology has improved, and as a result of the growth of low-cost airlines.
Inclusive travel (package travel)	A pre-arranged combination of transport, accommodation and/or other travel services, sold at one price, to groups or to individual tourists, and usually organised by a tour operator or travel agency. Usually associated with holidays, leisure and recreation but could also be used for conference and incentive travel.
Group travel	Tourists travelling with an organised group of tourists on the same trip. They may or may not know each other. The trip may be for personal or business/professional purposes. Often group travel is also an inclusive tour.
Corporate travel	Tourism for business or professional purposes that is organised and paid for by companies. Travel agencies and tour operators may specialise in providing tourism services to corporate customers.
Mass tourism	Large-scale holiday tourism offering standardised products and experiences, requiring major infrastructural development in destinations, and with general appeal to broad tourist markets. Often equated with outbound inclusive travel to coastal resort destinations. Often associated with negative environmental and social impacts in the destination, although this is not necessarily true.
Alternative tourism	Often used to describe specialised forms of tourism that attract low volumes of tourists. Often associated with tourism that actively benefits the host economy, environment and society. May also be described as soft tourism, slow tourism, eco tourism, sustainable tourism, responsible tourism or green tourism.

Source: Beaver (2002)

Since the 1990s, tourism has changed radically as a result of changes in the external environment. These changes have created a 'new tourism' that was notably researched by Auliana Poon.

POON'S NEW TOURISM

In 1993, Poon published an important text identifying how tourism was being transformed. She argued that the rapid growth of tourism demand and supply between the 1950s and the 1970s had produced a form of tourism that was 'mass, standardised and rigidly inflexible' (Poon, 1993: 4). This mass tourism used the principles of mass production from the manufacturing sector to produce identical holidays in large volumes in the most cost-effective ways. The emphasis on achieving the lowest operating costs led to large-scale development, often in fragile locations, and created a number of negative environmental and social impacts in destinations. Tourists consumed their holidays 'with a lack of consideration for the norms, cultures and environment of the host countries visited' (Poon, 1993: 4). By the 1980s, mass tourism had become the business model for tourism development in many destinations.

Poon argued that mass tourism would not, and should not, survive the four key forces that were beginning to emerge at the end of the twentieth century:

- New consumers
- New technologies
- Emergence of a new global best practice
- Limits to growth.

NEW CONSUMERS

Poon differentiated between 'new tourists' and the 'old tourists' of mass tourism. For 'old tourists', tourism was motivated by a break from routine; travel was a novelty and the specific destination was less important. Old tourists were not experienced travellers, were cautious and felt more comfortable travelling in groups on pre-arranged and pre-paid inclusive tours. In contrast, 'new tourists' are experienced travellers who are independent, flexible and more demanding. They want to be in control of their tourism experiences and use tourism to stand out from the crowd and demonstrate their individuality. They also want to experience something different and are spontaneous, adventurous and flexible. New tourists are happy to research and book their own travel arrangements, and unpredictability may be part of the attraction of the tourism experience.

Poon suggested that the emergence of the new tourist would require that tourism suppliers provided products and services that were customised to the needs of specific market segments, and that suppliers would have to understand how tourism consumers thought, felt and behaved in order to provide satisfactory experiences. In the twenty-first century it seems that Poon's prediction has been fulfilled in some generating regions, for instance Case Study 2.1 shows that Chinese FIT tourists are now a significant market. The emergence of low-cost airlines (LCAs) and the sharing economy is partly in response to these new types of tourist. We discuss different types of tourists in more detail in Chapter 4.

NEW TECHNOLOGIES

Poon described tourism as an 'information-intensive industry' for which information technology (IT) was an indispensable tool. Despite writing in the early 1990s, before the Internet was widely used, Poon recognised the value of IT in the processing, storing, retrieval and distribution of information. She suggested that IT would be a key tool in transforming mass tourism into new tourism because it would facilitate the provision of high-quality, flexible tourism experiences to new tourists. In Chapter 1 we explained how technology has evolved in the twenty-first century, probably with capabilities beyond Poon's expectations.

EMERGENCE OF A NEW GLOBAL BEST PRACTICE

Poon suggests that the developments in IT and the information age of the late twentieth century have created a new understanding – a new paradigm – about ideal patterns of production. In all sectors the emphasis on mass production as a production model is diminishing to make way for flexible production. Mass production reduced costs and generated profits through the production of large volumes of identical products, allowing producers to compete on price. In contrast, flexible production emphasises product quality, the need to respond to, and satisfy, customer needs through the development of customised products for specific market segments.

Poon suggested that tourism was an ideal candidate for flexible production because of the desire for individuality from new tourists and the information intensity of the sector. New tourism embraces the flexible production paradigm by providing quality tourism experiences that closely match the needs of particular market segments, continuously striving to improve customer satisfaction levels to maintain customer loyalty and innovating in the development of new products. Poon used the term 'holiday-makers' to describe tourism companies that produced quality tourism experiences at prices that compared favourably with mass, standardised and packaged alternatives. She suggested that Disneyland, Club Med, Sandals and the cruise sector were examples of flexible tourism production because their products could be customised to meet the needs of specific market segments while also maintaining low production costs. In the twenty-first century, competition between destinations and between suppliers has intensified, leading several suppliers and destinations to develop attractions and services that stand out – and that will attract positive word-of-mouth recommendations and loyal customers – perhaps by offering unique experiences, providing high levels of satisfaction, or actively seeking to reduce the negative impacts of their activities on the host community, economy and environment. The emergence of big data, the IoT and mobile technologies is enabling greater customisation of products or services. We discuss these developments in Chapter 1.

LIMITS TO GROWTH

> Mass tourism destroys exactly what it seeks – such things as quiet, solace, pristine cultures and landscapes, unpolluted waters, intact reefs, fishes, turtles, mountains, ski slopes, wildlife and virgin forests. (Poon, 1993: 6)

Concerns about sustainability and climate change have questioned the wisdom of unlimited tourism growth. Poon suggested that mass tourism methods of production and consumption that were environmentally intensive could not continue, and that environmentally sound tourism had to be adopted for tourism to survive, and for the negative impacts of tourism to be reduced.

New tourism requires environmentally sound tourism production and consumption, for instance through environmental planning and management in destination development, environmental sensitivity in tourism suppliers' operations, and through changes to consumer behaviour in their choice of suppliers and their activities in destinations. Poon argued that new tourism must be sustainable tourism; sustainable tourism is now a key topic in tourism studies. In the twenty-first century, concern about climate change, damage to eco systems and loss of biodiversity is becoming more pressing. Some tourism businesses actively seek to prevent the negative environmental impacts of their activities, and some destinations and attractions seek to educate tourists about the impact of their behaviour. Interestingly, limitations to tourism growth emerged as a pressing issue in several urban destinations with resident protests about overcrowding and price inflation in their cities (i.e. in Venice and Barcelona). Indeed, the term 'overtourism' has been used since 2012 (Responsible Tourism Partnership, 2017) and seems to have become mainstream in the media in 2017. Limits to growth is likely to remain an urgent issue as tourism demand increases.

SUSTAINABLE TOURISM

A comprehensive understanding of tourism requires awareness of how tourism industries and tourist activity can affect places, people and the economy. The term 'sustainable tourism' had developed to describe forms of tourism that take 'full account of its current and future economic, social and environmental impacts, addressing the needs of visitors, the industry, the environment and host communities' (UNEP and UNWTO, 2005: 11–12). Sustainable tourism is an aspiration for all forms of tourism and all types of destination, but even in 2017 some tourism development occurs that does not comply with the principles of sustainable tourism.

The three pillars of sustainability are people, planet and profits, known as 'the triple bottom line'. In a tourism context this requires tourism development and activities that: conserve natural resources, biodiversity and ecological processes; respect the values and traditions of host communities; increase understanding and tolerance between cultures; provide fair distribution of socio-economic benefits to all stakeholders; ensure viable operations in the long term; provide stable employment and business opportunities to host communities; and help to reduce poverty. Sustainable tourism also provides strong tourist satisfaction and creates meaningful experiences that raise tourists' awareness of sustainability issues (UNEP and UNWTO, 2005).

In addition, the UNWTO designated 2017 the Year of Sustainable Tourism for Development to highlight the power of tourism to contribute to the UN's Sustainable Development Goals (SDGs) – to be achieved by 2030. Tourism is sometimes claimed to be a force for good because it can stimulate rapid economic and social development, and provide an incentive for protecting vulnerable natural, historic and cultural resources. Its success in achieving these depends on the degree of sustainability that is achieved.

The snapshot below describes an operator of guided walking tours in the Dhavari slum, Mumbai, which in 2015 won the World Travel & Tourism Council's 'Tourism for Tomorrow Community Award', recognising its contribution to sustainable tourism (WTTC, 2015).

SNAPSHOT 2.4

Reality Tours & Travel

Slums are popular attractions in some destinations but slum tourism is very controversial. Critics claim that it is exploitative, intrusive and voyeuristic, with limited benefits for residents. Supporters claim that slum tourism can reduce poverty by creating employment and business opportunities for residents, and by educating tourists about the reality of poverty (Tourism Concern, 2013). In fact the objectives and management of such tours determine their impact on slum communities.

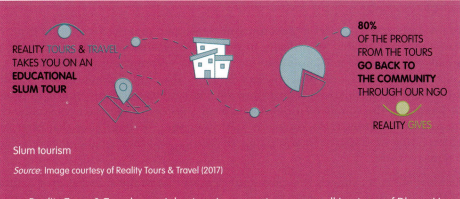

Slum tourism

Source: Image courtesy of Reality Tours & Travel (2017)

Reality Tours & Travel, a social enterprise, operates group walking tours of Dharavi in Mumbai. Its mission is to 'provide authentic and thought-provoking local experiences … and to use the profits to create change in our communities' (Reality Tours & Travel, 2017). To achieve this, their tours are carefully planned to protect the privacy and dignity of the residents and to ensure that they benefit too:

- Maximum group size of 6
- Strict dress code for tourists
- Strict no photography policy
- Guides are recruited from the local community
- Regular consultation with the community to identify problems caused by the tours
- Donation of profits – 80 per cent from tours and 100 per cent from merchandise sales – to their charity Reality Gives to deliver healthcare, education and youth empowerment programmes for residents.

Source: Reality Tours & Travel (2017)

TOURISM AND THE EXPERIENCE ECONOMY

In 1999, Pine and Gilmore coined the term 'experience economy' to describe a new phase of economic development that appeared to emerge in the 1990s (Pine and Gilmore, 1999). In the experience economy, businesses compete on the type and quality of experience that they create for their customers: the more unique and memorable the experience, the more successful the business is likely to be. Although this idea applies to the economy in general rather than tourism in particular, we can see links to Poon's prediction of a new global best practice for tourism that we explained on page 44. Tourism companies offering distinctive and highly managed experiences, often in purpose-built resort developments, are able to charge premium prices and command customer loyalty. Interestingly, many destinations also seek to create unique and memorable experiences for visitors through the staging of business or leisure events such as literary or music festivals, mega sporting events or trade shows and conferences, or by animating public spaces. The desire for unique experiences has been embraced by some tourism suppliers and destinations, which have created unusual attractions whose appeal is sometimes their incongruousness or their faked reality. Some academics have coined this type of tourism as 'post-tourism'.

POST-TOURISM

In the early 2000s, the term 'post-tourism' developed to describe tourism experiences that are created specifically to provide entertainment, fun or thrills in a simulated, sanitised and controlled environment – often creating an imitation to celebrate a theme, a fantasy or an event (Smith et al., 2010). Examples cited include attractions or destinations which draw on fictional associations linked to films or literature, the commercial development of sites of atrocity such as accidents, massacres or battles (also known as 'dark tourism'), heritage sites that offer an entertaining or sanitized interpretation of history, and theme parks that recreate a fantasy world.

Smith et al. (2010) suggest that post-tourists are aware of the manufactured nature of their experience and embrace it in an ironic manner. Some destinations offer experiences that could be described as post-tourism and their extraordinary nature seems to be their appeal. Macao, Las Vegas and Dubai epitomize this with resort hotels or attractions that simulate an entirely different destination. The Venetian Macao describes itself as 'an incredible, immersive hotel experience. 350 world-class shopping choices line a masterfully reconstructed Grand Canal, bridges spanning each bank, just as they do in Venice. An incredible array of dining options, from the food court to the Michelin-starred Golden Peacock to room service, bring guests the best of global cuisines no matter their appetite' (Sands Resorts, 2017). Dubai has created a massive indoor ski resort, Ski Dubai, with a 'Penguin Encounter' experience, all located in the middle of the desert, and marketed as 'extraordinary'.

SUMMARY

This chapter has considered what tourism is, how it is defined, how tourism suppliers are identified and the ways in which tourism can be described. It is important to remember that our understanding of tourism is still evolving and that some of the conceptual and technical definitions we have discussed have been developed as recently as 2008.

Tourism is a massive sector that consists of a diverse range of purposes of travel, an extensive variety of suppliers and destinations, and numerous forms. It has spawned the development of destinations worldwide and demand continues to grow. Tourism is now studied widely at undergraduate and postgraduate level because of its potential to bring economic, environmental and social benefits to destinations, and to ensure that its impacts are positive rather than negative. The complexity of tourism, its vulnerability to external shocks, its economic significance and its potential detrimental impacts on destination communities and environments have created a need for in-depth understanding of all elements of the tourism system and for professional management to direct the future growth of tourism sustainably.

SELF-TEST QUESTIONS

1. Draw Leiper's tourism system and locate within it your most recent tourist visit. Within in each region, note down the types of supply that you used.

2. Reflect on your most recent experience as a tourist – do the characteristics of your trip equate with 'old tourism' or 'new tourism'?

3. Find out from your friends how important sustainability is to their own tourism experiences.

FURTHER READING

Leslie, D. (ed.) (2012) *Responsible Tourism: Concepts, Theory and Practice*. Wallingford: CABI.

McLaren, D. (2003) *Rethinking Tourism & Ecotravel*. Boulder, CO: Lynne Rienner.

USEFUL WEBSITES

China National Tourism Administration: http://en.cnta.gov.cn/

Cuba Tourist Board of Canada: www.gocuba.ca/en/

Las Vegas Sands Corp: www.sands.com/properties/all-properties.html

Skift – https://skift.com

Travel and Tourism Industry Guide – Mintel Country Reports: academic.mintel.com

United Nations World Tourism Organisation: www2.unwto.org/

VisitBritain: www.visitbritain.org/

World Travel and Tourism Council: www.wttc.org/mission/tourism-for-tomorrow/redefine-tourism/

PART II
TOURISM SUPPLY AND DEMAND

CONTENTS

3

TOURIST GENERATING REGIONS

'Travel and leisure have become an integral part of daily life. These changes in the role of travel and leisure in society as well as changes in the workplace ... all have implications for the travel and tourism industry.'

A. Poon, 1993: 128

LEARNING OUTCOMES

After reading this chapter you will understand:

- the conditions that must prevail within a society to enable the development of demand for tourism
- why some regions of the world dominate as tourist generating regions
- the significance of different purposes of tourist travel in an international context.

Advertising on the London Underground

Source: Clare Inkson

INTRODUCTION

In Chapter 2 we saw that the study of tourism requires an understanding of all elements of the tourism system (Leiper, 1979) or the tourism framework (Mathieson and Wall, 1982). Leiper (1979) refers to the 'tourist generating region' as an essential part of the tourism system, and Mathieson and Wall (1982) identify the crucial role of the dynamic element – demand – in the tourism framework. In this chapter we consider the conditions that enable the residents of a generating region to engage in tourist activity either as domestic or outbound tourists.

Levels of demand from tourists in a generating region are a reflection of the economic, social and political conditions that prevail there. Specific **enabling factors** must exist for an individual to engage in tourism. These enabling factors have emerged, or are starting to emerge, in different world regions at different times and therefore there is substantial variation between the tourism behaviour of residents of different countries. This chapter will help you to understand the factors that influence individuals' abilities to engage in tourist activity, and the significance of holidays, VFR and religious, health and business and professional purposes in international tourism. We end the chapter by considering the most significant generating regions. Please note that many of the statistics used in this chapter refer to outbound tourism rather than domestic tourism, purely because outbound data is more widely available; the enabling factors discussed here also apply to domestic tourism demand.

Enabling factors:
Conditions within a society that make it possible for individuals to engage in particular activities

CONDITIONS THAT FAVOUR THE DEVELOPMENT OF DEMAND FOR TOURISM

Despite descriptions of tourism as the fastest growing and largest industry in the world, tourism activity is engaged in by a minority of the world's population. People who do enjoy tourism activity predominantly reside in regions with specific economic, social and political characteristics.

In order for a country, or region within a country, to become a leisure tourist generating area individual residents there must have:

- leisure time
- discretionary income
- freedom from political barriers to travel
- fast, safe, affordable transit routes
- in some cases, travel intermediaries to organise the tourism experience.

These are known as 'enabling factors' that give individuals the option to engage in tourist activity. Countries where all of these enabling factors are enjoyed by substantial proportions of the population are likely to be major tourist generating regions. We will now consider each enabling factor in turn.

LEISURE TIME

'Leisure time' refers to the part of an individual's time that is not committed to work, caring or any other responsibilities, and can be spent as the individual chooses. The availability of leisure time is a key enabling factor in tourism for personal purposes as defined by the UN (2010) – holidays, leisure, recreation, VFR, education and training, health and medical care, religion and pilgrimage, and shopping. Leisure time is much less significant as an enabling factor for business and professional tourism purposes because this is largely conducted during work hours, during the working week, although it is not uncommon for business travellers to add leisure tourism experiences to a business trip – some travel trade media refer to this as 'bleisure tourism'.

The duration and frequency of an individual's participation in tourist activity for personal purposes will depend on the amount of leisure time available. Overall, levels of leisure time have been steadily increasing in industrialised economies since the late nineteenth and throughout the twentieth centuries, aided by the introduction by governments of:

- public holidays
- the legal right for employees to receive paid annual leave from work
- limits to the working week.

There are significant international differences in leisure time enjoyed by employees; in countries where the other enabling factors for tourism exist but leisure time is relatively low, we would expect the volume of tourist activity generated to also be relatively low. We will now consider the role of national holidays, paid annual leave entitlement and the working week.

Public Holidays

The concept of the public holiday, when most businesses and organisations within a country close down for a day of official holiday, was formalised by the governments of many European countries and in the USA in the mid-nineteenth century. For example, the British government introduced the Bank Holiday Act in 1871 when four specific dates were designated as holidays for banks, and consequently other business sectors that could not operate when banks were closed (Dawson, 2007).

Public holidays celebrate religious and cultural festivals or politically and histori-cally significant events. Inevitably there is much variation between countries in the number of public holidays and the time period that is taken. Colombia and India have the highest number, with 18 a year, whereas the UK and Mexico have the lowest with eight (Mercer, 2014). In eastern Asia, workplaces close for one week to celebrate the Lunar New Year, while in countries with a Christian tradition two or more days of national holiday are usually given at Christmas and at Easter. In Moslem countries three or more days of national holiday are given to celebrate the end of Ramadan, Eid al-Fitr.

In countries where the other enabling factors exist too, public holidays stimulate tour-ist demand; often there is a surge in movement away from main generating regions as large numbers of residents seek to leave at the same time; for example in China, 344 million domestic trips occurred during the week of the Spring Festival in 2017 (CNTA, 2017).

Paid Leave Entitlement

The aim of paid leave is to give workers restorative time away from the pressures of the workplace (ILO, n.d.). Annual paid leave is calculated in working days, calendar days (or weeks), or days excluding paid public holidays. For example, a 4-week annual leave can mean 28 calendar days, or 20 working days (based on a 5-day work week).

Paid leave entitlement stipulates the number of days leave that an employee is entitled to each year, without sacrificing pay. Most national governments stipulate a minimum statutory entitlement, although individual employers may increase this. The snapshot below describes global variations in paid leave entitlement.

SNAPSHOT 3.1

Global Variations in Paid Leave Entitlement

August in Conil de la Frontera, Andalucia, Spain

Source: Clare Inkson

During the early twentieth century, the pressure to provide formalised paid leave for all employees gained momentum through social and trades union movements internationally. By 1937, annual paid leave for all workers was available in 24 countries including Finland, France, the USSR, Chile, Venezuela and Norway (Dawson, 2007).

The International Labour Organisation's (ILO) 1970 Convention No. 132 stipulates three weeks of annual leave for 1 year of service. The EU Working Time Directive (2008/88/EC) provides a 4-week standard across all member states. Globally though there is wide legislative variation on minimum paid leave entitlement as shown below (ILO, 2015):

- Angola: 22 working days
- Australia: 4 weeks
- Brazil: from 12 to 30 days (depending on number of other absences)
- China: based on cumulative years of employment: 1–10 years (5 days), 10–20 years (10 days), 20+ years (15 days)
- Estonia: 28 calendar days
- Indonesia: 12 working days

(Continued)

- Japan: 10 days
- Lebanon: 15 days
- Tunisia: 1 working day per month worked; 1 extra day for each 5 years worked up to 18 in total annual leave days
- UK: 28 days
- USA: 0

Paid leave entitlement can directly affect the demand for tourism for personal purposes because it influences the volume of trips that can be taken in one year, the duration of individual trips, and therefore the distance that tourists can travel.

In addition, institutional traditions have a very strong influence on when paid leave can be taken. School holiday periods determine when families with school age children can take holidays, and in some industrial regions it is common for all factories and offices to close at the same time for holidays.

In addition to paid leave legislation, most countries also limit the number of hours in a week that an employee can work.

The Working Week

Research by the ILO (2010) shows that on a global scale the average limit to the working week is 40 hours, but again there are significant differences internationally:

- Most developed economies, including the USA, Japan, New Zealand, Canada, and most of Europe, impose a 40-hour working week limit.
- Several countries in Asia and the Pacific impose a 48-hour limit, such as India, Vietnam and the Philippines.
- In Africa, several countries impose a 45-hour limit: Botswana, South Africa, Tanzania.

Shorter working weeks increase the levels of leisure time enjoyed by workers, and in areas where the other tourism enabling factors exist, potentially increase demand for short breaks and day trips.

In addition to working hours, typical work days vary internationally. For example, in Israel the typical working week is Sunday to Thursday evening or Friday noon; in Egypt, Syria and the United Arab Emirates it is Sunday to Thursday; and in Iran, Saturday to Thursday. In most countries with a Christian heritage, the working week is Monday to Friday. Patterns of demand for business or personal tourist purposes are therefore likely to vary between generating regions.

The factors above indicate that leisure time has a very important role as an enabling factor in the development of demand for leisure tourism activity: it not only determines the amount of time that an individual can potentially use for tourist activities, but also, for some groups, dictates when they can engage in those activities. The variation in levels of leisure time enjoyed by the residents of individual countries suggests that some states are likely to be more significant tourist generating regions than others. However, leisure time alone is not sufficient to generate tourist demand; an individual's ability to pay for tourist activities is a crucial component.

DISCRETIONARY INCOME

'Discretionary income' refers to any personal or family income that remains after all the basics of life, such as housing, food, utilities, tax and so on, have been paid for. Tourism activity for personal purposes is often described as a discretionary purchase – that is, individuals choose to spend their money on tourist activities: it is not an essential part of life, and spending on tourist activity can be substituted by spending on other discretionary purchases. For example, instead of going on holiday, an individual may buy new furniture, or a new car, or choose to save the money.

Income levels and therefore levels of discretionary income vary between residents within the same region depending on the type of employment and subsequent level of pay that an individual earns. Within the same generating region, there will be large variations between individuals' discretionary income. Where an individual's discretionary income is high, and their levels of leisure time are high too, they may decide to take several tourist trips for personal purposes in a year. In some generating regions where the propensity to engage in leisure tourism is high, for example in the UK, second and even third holidays are not uncommon for a large proportion of the population, along with several short breaks and day trips. UNWTO figures for 2015 show that spending on outbound tourism from Germany, the UK and Australia averaged between US$946 and US$978 per head (UNWTO, 2016b).

There is an important link between economic development and tourism demand. The process of industrialisation expands opportunities for the business and professional classes who engage in tourism for business and professional purposes, as well as for holidays, leisure and recreation.

Industrialisation stimulates demand for tourism for business purposes to source new markets and materials for manufacturing, the need for conferences to share knowledge with other professionals, and the demand for exhibitions to display products and expand markets. Industrialisation also increases incomes by creating higher-paid employment opportunities, particularly in professions that require a skilled and educated workforce, such as banking, insurance, shipping and law. Growing demand for tourism in Europe and the USA in the nineteenth century has been partly attributed to the growth of the middle classes within those economies (Weiss, 2004). In emerging economies in the early twenty-first century, the growth of the middle class is stimulating the growth in demand for leisure tourism. Brazil, Russia, India and China (known collectively as BRIC) are becoming increasingly important as generating regions for international tourism as a result of the increase in urban middle-class consumers, stimulated by rapid economic growth in the final decades of the twentieth century.

The USA is one of the wealthiest countries in the world yet its role as a generating region, particularly for outbound tourism, is unusual.

SNAPSHOT 3.2

The USA as a generating region

US passport

Source: Clare Inkson

The USA is one of the world's richest countries, ranked by the OECD as top for housing, income and wealth, and above average in health status, employment and earnings, and education and skills. Average annual disposable income (income minus taxes) per head is US$41,000 – the highest in the OECD – and unemployment rates are low at 5 per cent in 2016. By 2016, the US recovery from the financial crisis was amongst the strongest of OECD members (OECD, 2016a).

The USA is the world's second largest generating region for international tourism expenditure: in 2015, 73 million outbound travellers from the US spent US$118 billion. However, in a population of 322 million, spending on international tourism per capita is relatively low – US$351 (UNWTO, 2016b); the gross propensity to travel outbound is only 22.7 per cent.

US workers are not legally entitled to paid leave although approximately 75 per cent of the workforce is given an average of 8–11 days per year (Bureau of Labor Statistics, 2016). Many of these workers do not use all of their entitlement: in 2016, 54 per cent waived their full entitlement, forfeiting 206 million vacation days in total, worth US$66.4 billion in benefits (US Travel Association, 2017).

Rises and falls in discretionary income in a generating region affect tourist demand from that region and impact flows of tourists to destination regions; when incomes fall, individuals seek cheaper destinations, cheaper accommodation and transport and take fewer or shorter trips. For instance since 2014, outbound demand from Russia has decreased, probably in response to the slowing of the Russian economy (UNWTO, 2016b).

FREEDOM FROM POLITICAL BARRIERS TO TRAVEL

The ability to travel for business or leisure, or indeed any purposes, requires individuals to have the freedom to travel. In some societies, citizens' freedom to travel internationally, and perhaps domestically, is strictly controlled by the government through the requirement to obtain exit visas or certificates, for example in China and North Korea. In 2013, Cuba relaxed its strict exit visa requirements for Cuban citizens (*Guardian*, 2013). In addition, destination countries put in place entry visa requirements for the citizens of many countries.

In countries where outbound travel is not officially regulated and controlled by governments, inbound and outbound tourist flows may be restricted by entry visa requirements, or by diplomatic tensions between governments. This attitude is often demonstrated through the existence, or not, of transit routes between two countries. For example, there are no direct transport links between the UK and northern Cyprus, so outbound tourists from the UK must travel via Turkey. Until July 2008, all flights between mainland China and Taiwan had to be routed via Hong Kong or Macao because of diplomatic tensions between the two states, and until 2016, direct commercial passenger flights between the USA and Cuba were not allowed.

Tourist flows between generating and receiving regions are also influenced by political attitudes to the economic regulation of transport. 'Economic regulation' describes the controls and restrictions that prevent transport operators from responding freely to market demand and competing with each other. Until the late 1970s most states regulated coach, sea, rail and air services, but since the late 1970s a process of liberalisation, led by the USA, has relaxed the government controls of domestic and international transport in many countries. The removal or reduction of economic regulation within the transport sector is often linked to specific benefits for passengers and for tourism. Factors such as the ability of a new operator to enter existing routes or set up new routes, the freedom of operators to plan schedules in response to demand, and to compete on price, often result in greater choice, more convenience and lower prices for passengers. For tourism, these changes are very significant as they stimulate demand from the generating region.

Arguably the deregulation and liberalisation of civil aviation has had the most significant impact on tourism; according to Forsyth (2008, cited in Graham et al., 2008: 74), 'for many countries, aviation policy is tourism policy – if they wish to stimulate the growth of tourism, the most effective single measure they can take is to liberalise their international aviation arrangements, if they can', thus liberalising transit routes to major generating regions. We discuss the liberalisation of transport in detail in Chapter 5.

In addition, residents in generating regions are advised on the safety of destination regions by their own governments; advice to avoid specific destinations due to health or safety threats can have a dramatic impact on flows of tourists from a single generating region. For example the 2015 terrorist attacks on tourists in Tunisia led to a travel advisory from the British government advising British residents to avoid visiting Tunisia; this advisory remained in place until 2017, and displaced demand from British tourists to other countries, notably in southern Europe.

FAST, SAFE, AFFORDABLE TRANSIT ROUTES

'Transit routes are paths linking tourist generating regions with tourist destination regions, along which tourists travel and include stopover points' (Leiper, 1979: 397). Transit routes are a fundamental element of tourism, without which tourism would not be possible. Transit routes create the physical link between generating and receiving regions, determining where, when and how tourists can travel, and the length and cost of their journeys.

Duval (2007) states that the relationship between transport and tourism is determined by a framework consisting of three key components: modes, networks and flows. We will consider each of these in turn.

MODES OF TRANSPORT IN TOURISM

The term 'transport mode' refers to the method used. Page (2005) identifies three main modes of transport (water, land and air transport) and within each mode, a range of types has evolved over time, some of them specifically as types of tourism transport:

Land: private and rental cars, campervans, motorbikes, bicycles and taxis; bus and coach services; intercity and local trains.

Water: cruise ships, passenger liners, canal and river boats, ferries, pleasure craft.

Air: scheduled and charter passenger airline services; scenic flights by hot air balloon, helicopter, light aircraft; space flights.

Advances in transport since the sixteenth century have revolutionised personal mobility and the ability of individuals to participate in tourist activity. The growth in demand for tourism is inextricably linked to developments in transport technology that have made each mode of transport faster, safer and more affordable. Such transformations in travelling time and price have significant implications for tourism demand from residents based in generating regions that are connected to routes and services which are faster and more affordable.

Technological advances that developed new types of transport or invented new engine technologies increased speed and therefore reduced journey times, expanding the range of destinations that could be reached from a generating region within a specific travelling time. For example, the development of the railway in the late nineteenth-century USA transformed travel times between New York and San Francisco from six months to one week in 1869, and between New York and Chicago from three weeks to 72 hours (Weiss, 2004). Those distances can now be travelled in 6 hours and 2 hours 20 minutes respectively by air. The impact of the railways in England and Wales between 1840 and 1870 was also spectacular: passenger volumes by train increased 20-fold and in the mid-1830s, it was anticipated that on a new route, passenger numbers would be at least double the volume of people who would previously have travelled the same route by road (Bagwell, 1974).

The invention of the jet engine and its application to passenger aviation transformed the speed of flight; for instance, the cruise speed of the Britannia 310, a turbo-prop airliner, which came into service in 1956, was 571km/hour, but was surpassed three years later by the Caravelle VI R, a turbo-jet airliner, whose cruise speed was 816km/hour (Doganis, 1991). Currently the world's fastest commercial passenger jet is the Boeing 747 8i, with an average cruising speed of 1062 km/hour (Boeing, 2017). In addition to improvements in speed, technological advances that increase the seat capacity of vehicles have been particularly important in making some transit routes more affordable.

Increases in seat capacity allow the total cost of operating a service to be divided among more passengers, thereby reducing the unit cost of each seat. A good example of this has been the regular introduction of larger wide-bodied aeroplanes since the late 1960s that have provided significant capacity increases. For instance in 1968 the passenger payload capacity of a Douglas DC-8-63 was 259 passengers; in 1969 the Boeing 747 was 493; in 1983 the Boeing 747-300 was 660; and in 2007, the Airbus A380 was 882 (Doganis, 2009). When the unit cost of each seat is reduced, operators have the opportunity to reduce the sale price of seats; if this does happen, routes on which the larger planes operate become more affordable to more residents of the departing generating region.

The most popular mode of transport in tourism is land, specifically road transport, but this does vary between countries, depending on the level of infrastructure provision, and on the distance tourists travel from their generating region. However, aviation's share of international tourism is growing and in 2016 accounted for over 50 per cent of all international tourist trips (UNWTO, 2016b).

High-speed rail travel is becoming particularly important as a mode of transport for tourism. Towards the end of the twentieth century interest in rail travel re-emerged with the introduction of high-speed train networks connecting major urban centres, which compete favourably in terms of travel time with flights. The first was in Japan in 1964 on the Tokyo–Osaka route, known as the 'Shinkansen' or 'Bullet Train' (Arduin and Ni, 2005), and more countries have subsequently revitalised their railways by investing heavily in rail infrastructure and high speed trains; for instance Trains à Grand Vitesse (TGV) in France, Intercity Express (ICE) in Germany, Pendolino trains in Italy and Alta Velocidad Espana (AVE) in Spain, all travelling at speeds of between 280 and 350kph. On many routes, high-speed trains have replaced air travel and road transport as the most popular mode of transport. AVE trains on the Madrid–Barcelona route, launched in 2007, can achieve speeds of up to 350kph and reduced the airlines' share of passengers on the route from 88 per cent to 40 per cent within two years. Indeed, research suggests that rail could capture between 60 and 90 per cent of traffic on journeys of two to three hours, suggesting that rail travel provides a feasible alternative to air travel on such distances (Steer Davies Geave, 2009).

The ability of individuals to engage in tourism, and their choice of destinations to travel to, are determined by the transport networks that link generating and destination regions.

TOURISM TRANSPORT NETWORKS

Networks are the pattern of transport services that are operated either by a particular mode of transport or by a particular operator.

Geographers refer to networks as the routes operated within a mode or by a type of transport (Duval, 2007), for example a rail, ferry, cruise, road or air network. The development of networks linking generating and destination regions requires the provision of appropriate infrastructure, for instance airports, railway track, port facilities or maintained roads. Often the provision and quality of transport infrastructure are a reflection of economic development. MacKinnon et al. suggest that wealthy regions and nations enjoy superior transport infrastructure and a greater choice of services than less developed ones: 'modes of transport are better connected, their geographical reach is greater and fewer places are inaccessible' (2008: 10). Involvement in tourist activity is therefore likely to be easier for residents of wealthy countries who enjoy access to a range of well developed transport networks. The growth in demand of air travel has put pressure on aviation infrastructure in many generating regions. The snapshot below describes challenges facing airport infrastructure in the UK.

SNAPSHOT 3.3

Airport expansion in the UK

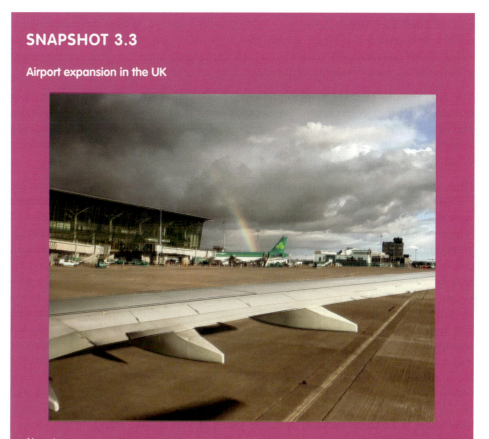

Airport

Source: Jade O'Brien

London is an important generating as well as destination region for international tourism. Its population of nearly 8.7 million is well served by airport infrastructure: six international airports are located within 40 miles/64km of central London: Heathrow, Gatwick, Southend, Stansted, Luton and London City.

For several decades, airport runway capacity in the south-east of England has been under pressure. The Airports Commission (2013) identified when each airport will be full: Heathrow 2010; Gatwick 2020; City 2024; Luton 2030; Stansted 2041.

The UK Government established the independent Airport Commission to investigate expansion options at Heathrow and Gatwick with a full public consultation; in 2015 the Commission recommended a third runway at Heathrow and in October 2016 the UK government announced its support.

Expansion at Heathrow is controversial: new construction will destroy swathes of rural land and homes, increase the number of residents exposed to noise and air pollution and increase Heathrow's contribution of aviation carbon emissions to more than 50 per cent of the UK total (Campaign for Rural England, 2015). In February 2017 the government launched a 16-week public consultation on its draft Airports National Policy.

In a liberalised environment, individual transport operators operate networks made up of their own routes, and determine frequency of departure and capacities based on forecasts of demand. Commercial operators constantly evaluate the effectiveness of their networks and make modifications in response to changes in demand. The decision to stop operating a route, or to increase the frequency of departures on a route, will directly affect the volume of tourist flows between a generating and destination region. Transport networks determine the choice of destination regions to which tourists can travel from the generating region and when they can travel. The cost of particular transit routes determines their affordability to different social groups.

TOURISM TRANSPORT FLOWS

A 'transport flow' is the volume of demand for a network. Transport flows may comprise different types of user who use the transport network at the same or at different times; for example rail and air services or road networks may be used by commuters, the local community or freight operators, as well as tourists.

Tourism flows themselves may consist of different types of tourist, for example business, leisure and VFR tourists, who will exhibit different seasonal patterns and different purchasing characteristics and abilities to pay. Transport operators will use pricing mechanisms to manage flows of demand to ensure that those tourists who have no choice about when to travel, for instance business tourists travelling during periods of peak business demand, and leisure tourists travelling during peak holiday periods, pay the highest fares, while fares for the least popular departures will be deliberately low to stimulate demand. We discuss this in more detail in Chapter 5.

Transit routes create the physical link that enables individuals to move between generating and destination regions. However, the distance between generating and destination regions creates difficulties for suppliers of tourist products in promoting to, and communicating with, potential customers, and has created a role for companies acting as intermediaries.

TRAVEL INTERMEDIARIES

Tourists usually need to research, reserve and pay for transport and accommodation, and sometimes attractions too, in advance of their departure; therefore tourism suppliers need to find effective ways to enable this within the generating region. Internet technology has, in theory, transformed their ability to do this, but before this became possible many suppliers relied on intermediaries to do this on their behalf. In fact, some online intermediaries, known as OTAs, currently wield great market power and dominate online travel sales. We discuss OTAs in Chapter 1 and in Chapter 6.

Intermediaries, in the form of wholesalers, operators and agencies, create a link between suppliers in destinations and their potential customers while they are still in their usual place of residence. Intermediaries provide a channel by which individuals in generating regions can research, book and pay for tourist products before departure. Agencies provide points of sale in the generating region for the suppliers of tourist transport, accommodation and attractions, while tour operators sell pre-arranged packages of trips that provide assistance during the trip in the form of a local representative or a tour manager. Often these points of sale are now online, in the form of the intermediaries' websites, although many do also have physical offices or shops.

Tourism intermediaries have existed since the mid-nineteenth century in generating regions where the development of enabling factors increased tourist demand. In the early twenty-first century new forms of intermediary developed in response to changes in tourist consumer behaviour in generating regions. The snapshot below describes how sharing economy platforms developed from these changes.

SNAPSHOT 3.4

Peer-to-peer tourism platforms

Consumer and technology trends are transforming tourists' purchasing behaviour in many generating regions. In countries where a high proportion of residents are confident and experienced travellers, a market for unusual and unique experiences has developed (OECD, 2016b). This, combined with easy access to online and mobile technologies and high levels of connectivity through social media, has created a market for P2P or sharing economy platforms which link residents in generating regions to accommodation, transport, tour and activity hosts in destinations.

Tourism sharing economy platforms are a twenty-first century phenomenon that appeals to tourists seeking adventure. Many of these P2P platforms stress the benefits of experiencing the destination 'like a local', meeting local people and discovering neighbourhoods that are 'off the beaten tourism track'. Tech start-up companies responded to growing demand for this type of travel experience by setting up websites showcasing peer-to-peer accommodation to markets in generating regions around the world. These companies are very young and are expanding very quickly: CouchSurfing was set up in 2004, Airbnb in 2008, onefinestay in 2009, Homestay in 2013 and UnderTheDoormat in 2014.

The role of intermediaries in stimulating and facilitating tourism cannot be overlooked. Operators have made outbound tourist trips more accessible and affordable for tourists and are often associated with the rapid growth of destinations (sometimes very controversially), particularly on the Spanish Mediterranean and the Caribbean coasts during the 1960s and 1970s. Agencies have provided a convenient source of travel advice, reservations and payment for tourists within their home towns, in advance of their trip. Without intermediaries, the ability to research, organise and reserve tourist products and plan trips would be much more complex.

However, the Internet has transformed the ability of suppliers to communicate with potential customers directly, and as a result the role of intermediaries has reduced in some generating regions. In the late twentieth century, in generating regions with large numbers of residents who were experienced in buying tourism products and confident travellers, a process of 'disintermediation' occurred, whereby growing numbers of tourists began to research, reserve and pay for tourist trips independently of operators and agencies. The tourist markets for intermediaries in Europe and the USA matured and stopped growing, and in some cases shrunk. In response, powerful intermediaries such as Thomas Cook, the TUI Travel Group, American Express and Kuoni have expanded into Brazil, Russia, India and China to exploit opportunities in these newly emerging generating regions. We discuss the role and characteristics of intermediaries in detail in Chapter 6.

This section of the chapter has discussed the role of enabling factors in creating tourist generating regions. It is worthwhile remembering that no two generating regions have experienced identical patterns of growth in tourist activity by their residents: some have experienced consistent growth for two centuries, some generating regions emerged in the late twentieth century, whereas others are still experiencing very low levels of demand that show no significant growth. The penetration of tourism demand within a generating region is known as 'travel propensity'.

TRAVEL PROPENSITY

Travel propensity measures the penetration of tourist activity within a generating region's population during a stated period, usually a year, and is measured as either gross or net travel propensity.

Gross travel propensity is calculated by measuring the number of tourist trips that occur from a generating region as a percentage of the population (Bowen and Clarke, 2009).

Calculations using UNWTO's 2015 data show great variation in gross outbound travel propensities between generating regions: UK 99 per cent; Canada 90 per cent; Australia 40 per cent; South Korea 38 per cent; Russian Federation 35 per cent; USA 23 per cent; and China 9 per cent (UNWTO, 2016b).

Net travel propensity measures the percentage of the population that takes at least one tourist trip and identifies the proportion of the population in a generating region that participates in tourism. Net travel propensity will never be 100 per cent because there will always be some individuals who do not engage in tourist activity, even in generating regions where all of the enabling factors exist; Cooper et al. (2008) suggest that the maximum net travel propensity in a developed country will be between 70 and 80 per cent. To understand the demand for tourism it is useful to break this down into three basic elements:

Effective or actual demand: describes the number of tourist trips from a generating region. Tourism statistics measure this form of demand.

Suppressed demand: describes the number of individuals within a generating region who would like to engage in tourist activity but are unable to. Suppressed demand can be further broken down to either potential demand or deferred demand. Potential demand refers to those who are unable to engage in tourism because of their personal circumstances – perhaps they have limited leisure time or disposable income, or responsibilities that prevent them from engaging in tourism. Deferred demand refers to those who are prevented from travelling by external factors: for example because of political restrictions on freedom of movement or poor access to, or high cost of, transit routes. If the factors that suppress demand are removed, this form of demand will become actual demand.

No demand: within a generating region there will always be individuals who do not wish to engage in tourism.

Changes to an individual's leisure time, income or freedom to travel, or the development of a new transit route, may transform suppressed demand into actual demand. It is not uncommon, however, for actual demand to fall in a generating region and become suppressed demand in response to external events, for example when economic conditions reduce or threaten the level of individual disposable income available.

Mathieson and Wall (1982) describe tourism demand as dynamic because it is unstable and liable to change in response to changes in personal or external conditions. The extent to which demand changes is described by economists as 'elasticity of demand'.

ELASTICITY OF DEMAND

Elasticity of demand measures the sensitivity of demand to changes in consumers' income or to price changes in the destination, for example as a result of exchange rate fluctuations.

The relationship between demand and price is usually inverse; that is, the higher the price of a product the lower the demand, and vice versa. Price elasticity varies between tourist markets: for instance business tourists are often described as less price elastic than leisure markets because demand for business travel tends not to increase when prices fall, whereas demand from leisure tourists is often stimulated by lower prices. Price elasticity also seems to vary between different generating regions. Research conducted by Becken and Schiff (2011) investigated the impact on visitor arrival numbers of exchange rate fluctuations between the New Zealand dollar and currencies in 16 generating regions. Their findings suggested that Asian market segments are more price sensitive than European and US segments; for instance a 10 per cent increase in the NZ$/Japanese yen exchange rate led to a 15.5 per cent fall in arrivals from the Japanese tour segment to New Zealand.

Income elasticity describes how changes in personal income affect demand; as we have seen, tourism has a positive income elasticity of demand because as incomes rise, tourist demand often increases too, if the other enabling factors are also in place. Durbarry and Sinclair (2002) investigated the impact on visitor arrival numbers in Malta of changes in income in its main generating regions. Their findings suggest that a 1 per cent income rise in its main generating regions would increase the demand for Malta by about 0.7 per cent.

The Russian Federation is a very interesting example of the development of conditions that will stimulate an increase in the propensity to travel. The case study below explains Russia's development as a tourist generating region.

CASE STUDY 3.1

Russia as a generating region

Russian passport

Source: Clare Inkson

Russia's population is 143 million (UNWTO, 2015) and the country is the world's largest by area. Russians' tourism behaviour has changed dramatically since the break-up of the Soviet Union and it has become a significant generating region for outbound tourism.

In the decades prior to perestroika, tourism was highly organised and regulated by organisations including Intourist and Sputnik inbound tourism, and the Trade Union's Central Council for Tourist Excursions for domestic tourism. Travel outside the Eastern Bloc was usually unavailable to Soviet citizens, and allowed only for specific functions, for example sports, culture or politics (Burns, P., 1998).

Tourism for Soviet people was heavily subsidised by trade unions and state enterprises who recognised the opportunity for workforce recuperation and for improved health and

(Continued)

stronger citizenship. Health and wellness tourism was provided by trade unions who organised vouchers from the Ministries of Health and Social Welfare on behalf of their members. Children's holidays were organised to Young Pioneer summer camps in rural areas. Most domestic tourism was for sport or recreation around the Black Sea, Caucasus, and on river cruises, and for culture, heritage and citizenship purposes to Moscow, the Golden Ring, and St Petersburg. In 1990 the Central Council for Tourist Excursions organised approximately 52 million domestic trips (Burns, P., 1998).

After the break-up of the Soviet Union in 1991 and the establishment of the Russian Federation, outbound travel restrictions were reduced. In 1995, 2.6 million Russians holidayed outside of Russia; by 2006 this had grown to 7.7 million (VisitBritain, 2014).

Paid leave entitlement in Russia is generous: 20 working days, plus 9 days from 31 December to 8 January, and 5 more public holidays. Schools have a long summer holiday from June to September (VisitBritain, 2014).

Russia's economy grew by 7–9 per cent in the decade before the global financial crisis, and by 3–4 per cent between 2010 and 2012, creating very strong prospects for outbound tourism. In 2009, TUI Travel Group, recognising the potential for outbound tourism, expanded into Russia through joint ventures with Russian companies: 200+ TUI branded travel agencies appeared, offering travel programmes to 20 outbound destinations (TUI, 2010).

In 2011 there were 136,000 high net worth individuals in Russia, creating demand for luxury tourism, but most Russians have a modest standard of living by Western standards and tend to take one holiday a year, to the coast (VisitBritain, 2014). In 2012, Russia ranked fifth for expenditure on international tourism with US$43 billion expenditure on 36 million outbound visits. Ukraine was the most visited destination (VisitBritain, 2014) and several destination regions actively pursued the Russian market, for example the USA simplified its visa processes for Russians, and Estonia, Poland and Spain conducted promotional campaigns in Russia.

Since 2012 the Russian economy has slowed dramatically, exacerbated since 2014 by international economic sanctions in response to the Russian annexation of Crimea. As a result, some outbound demand from Russia has been suppressed: in 2014, 46 million outbound trips were generated, with US$50 million of expenditure, but in 2015 Russia dropped a position in global rankings to sixth most important generating region in terms of expenditure on outbound tourism, spending US$35 billion in 2015 on 37 million trips (UNWTO, 2016b).

Reflective Questions

1. Consider how the political economy of a generating region influences the tourism behaviour of residents.

2. After the break-up of the Soviet Union in 1991, why was the Russian market attractive to destinations around the world?

We will now consider the most significant tourist generating regions for international tourism.

GENERATING REGIONS FOR OUTBOUND TOURIST VISITS

Demand for international tourism has grown rapidly since the mid twentieth century. UNWTO's numbers, reproduced here as Figure 3.1, demonstrate the rapid speed of this growth in demand since 1950 and its projected continued growth by 2030.

The graph shows that international tourist arrivals grew from about 35 million in 1950 to over 600 million in 2000. Forecasts suggest that in 2030, this will have grown to 1.8 billion. This rapid growth in demand shows that the propensity to engage in international tourism is increasing rapidly, and suggests that the enabling factors for tourism are becoming prevalent in more generating regions, or to substantially more individuals in existing generating regions.

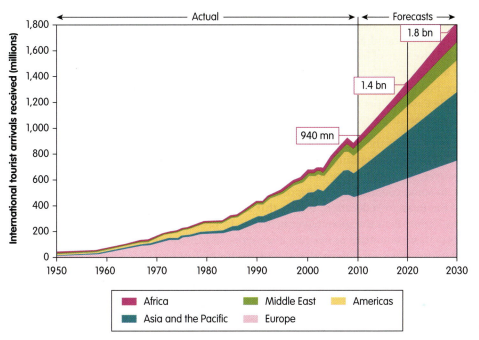

UNWTO Tourism Towards 2030: Actual trend and forecast 1950–2030

FIGURE 3.1   The growth in demand for international tourism

Source: © UNWTO (2016b:14) 92844/36/17

Figure 3.1 identifies the regions of the world that these international tourists visit, but the UNWTO also conducts research into generating regions to monitor changes. Historically Europe and North America have dominated as tourist generating regions for international tourism, but since the beginning of the twenty-first century this domination has been challenged by a very rapid growth in demand from generating regions like China where international tourism is a relatively new activity. The newly emerging tourist generating regions will have a very significant impact on international tourist flows. The importance of these shifts in demand and the emergence of new tourist generating regions cannot be overestimated.

THE MAIN OUTBOUND GENERATING REGIONS

Outbound tourism has been dominated by tourists from Europe since the 1950s because the enabling factors for tourism existed there simultaneously first. In addition, international tourism is relatively easy for Europeans because of the proximity of countries and the availability of efficient transport networks between European states. International tourist visits by residents of one country to another country within the same region are defined as 'intraregional tourism'. High levels of demand for intraregional tourism by Europeans explain Europe's dominance both as a generating region and a destination region.

UNWTO (2016b) data shows the proportion of demand for international tourism by world region: Europe generates the most international tourists (50 per cent) followed by Asia and the Pacific (24 per cent), the Americas (17 per cent), the Middle East (3.0 per cent) and Africa (3.0 per cent). The three most significant generating regions for outbound tourism – Europe, Asia and the Pacific, and the Americas – are a reflection of the number of industrialised economies within each region. In addition, the large share of outbound tourism in Europe and Asia and the Pacific can be explained by the relative ease of intraregional travel within both regions. Interestingly though, average annual growth rates of demand for international tourism between 2005 and 2015 were highest in Asia Pacific (6.6 per cent) followed by Africa (6.2 per cent) and the Middle East (5.4 per cent) compared to 3.9 per cent and 2.8 per cent in the Americas and Europe respectively (UNWTO, 2016b).

Table 3.1 shows the generating regions that spend the most on international tourism, namely the total spending on outbound tourism for the 10 highest spending countries. However, we should note here that the propensity for travel outbound is relatively low in some countries as a proportion of the total population, for example in China and the Russian Federation. Where this is the case, and where demand is growing at rates higher than the global averages (e.g. in China and Russia once again), we can expect those countries to become even more significant as generators of demand for, and expenditure on, international tourism in the future.

TABLE 3.1   International tourism's top spenders

Rank		International tourism expenditure (US$ billion)		Market share (%)	Population 2015	Expenditure per capita
		2014	2015	2015	(million)	(US$)
1	China	234.7	292.2	23.2	1,375	213
2	United States	105.5	112.9	9.0	322	351
3	Germany	93.3	77.5	6.2	82	946
4	United Kingdom	62.6	63.3	5.0	65	972
5	France	48.7	38.4	3.0	64	598
6	Russian Federation	50.4	34.9	2.8	146	239
7	Canada	33.8	29.4	2.3	36	820
8	Korea (ROK)	23.2	25.0	2.0	51	493
9	Italy	28.8	24.4	1.9	61	402
10	Australia	26.4	23.5	1.9	24	978

Source: Adapted from UNWTO (2016b: 13) © UNWTO 92844/36/17

FORMS OF TOURISM

Figure 3.2 illustrates the contribution of each form of tourism to total international tourism demand. The figure shows that global statistics on VFR, health and religious tourism are combined so identifying the growth of each of these separately over time is not possible on the basis of these data. The figure identifies leisure, recreation and holidays as the main purpose of international tourism.

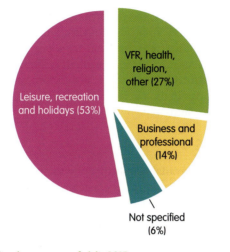

FIGURE 3.2   Inbound tourism by purpose of visit, 2015

Source: UNWTO (2016b: 5) © UNWTO 92844/36/17

However, the purpose of visits to individual destinations varies by generating region. National tourism organisations in destination regions collect data about the purpose of visit from their main generating regions. For example, VisitBritain statistics show that in 2016 the majority of visits to the UK from the Irish Republic were for VFR purposes (around 40 per cent), while VFR demand to the UK from Saudi Arabia was very low (around 5 per cent) but holidays were the main purpose of visits (around 50 per cent). Tourism Australia research shows that in 2016 the main purpose of visits to Australia from China was holiday (55 per cent), with the remainder consisting of VFR (19 per cent), education (13 per cent) and business (7 per cent) (Tourism Australia, 2016). No two generating regions have the same patterns of demand for tourism, nor the same choices of destination regions; if they do visit the same destination, the purpose of the visits may vary considerably. As we have seen, demand is dynamic and constantly evolving too, so the collection of data about the characteristics of demand from each generating region is an extremely important role of national destination organisations; their role is detailed in Chapter 13.

SUMMARY

We have seen that tourism demand grows in response to the development of conditions within a society that facilitate increases in discretionary income and leisure time. For these conditions to have a significant impact on levels of demand for tourism, they must exist simultaneously with the availability of fast, affordable transit routes and the freedom to travel. Additionally, the involvement of travel intermediaries has played a significant role in making almost all forms of tourism more accessible and affordable.

This chapter has shown that Europe has traditionally dominated as the main generating region of the world for international tourism. However, this domination is being slowly eroded with the emergence of new generating and receiving regions in almost each decade since 1950.

Since the early twenty-first century, the conditions that stimulate demand for tourism are prevalent in most developed countries. Tourism has become a multi-billion dollar activity, generating over a billion international trips per year, plus huge volumes of domestic tourism. The projected increase in growth of demand suggests that by 2030 participation in tourism will have penetrated further into emerging generating areas, and consequently current destination areas will expand, and new destinations will be developed, to meet this demand.

SELF-TEST QUESTIONS

1. Using UNWTO statistics available at http://unwto.org/ or market data available at VisitBritain (www.visitbritain.org/markets-segments) select one generating region and calculate the gross propensity to travel outbound.

2. Can you explain this level of demand for international tourism and suggest how it may change in light of economic and social trends within that region?

3. Consider the domestic and international transport networks that exist within your selected generating country. Can you suggest where residents can travel to most easily as tourists?

FURTHER READING

Bagwell, P. S. (1974) *The Transport Revolution from 1770*. London: Batsford.

Becker, E. (2016) *Overbooked: The Exploding Business of Travel and Tourism*. New York: Simon and Schuster, Chs 10 and 11.

Benckendorff, P. J., Moscardo, G. and Pendergast, D. (2009) *Tourism and Generation Y*. Wallingford: CABI.

Weiss, T. (2004) 'Tourism in America before World War II', *Journal of Economic History*, 64(2): 289–327.

USEFUL WEBSITES

Foreign and Commonwealth Office Foreign Travel Advice: www.gov.uk/foreign-travel-advice

London Heathrow Airport: https://your.heathrow.com/takingbritainfurther/

Project Time Off: www.projecttimeoff.com/

Skift: Skift.com

United Nations World Tourism Organisation: www2.unwto.org/

VisitBritain Inbound Markets and Segments: www.visitbritain.org/markets-segments

4

TOURISM DEMAND

'A child on a farm sees a plane overhead and dreams of a faraway
place. A traveller on the plane sees the farmhouse ...
and thinks of home.'

C. Burns, 2008: 6

LEARNING OUTCOMES

After reading this chapter you will understand:

- the different motivators that underlie tourists' desire to travel, and understand the main models of tourism motivation

- the uses and limitations of tourist typologies

- the different models of decision-making processes that apply to tourists
when they select and buy travel products

- the different methods that can be used to monitor and forecast tourism
demand.

Tourists enjoy a summer evening in Nice, France

Source: Lynn Minnaert

INTRODUCTION

In the previous chapter we discussed the conditions that enable an individual to participate in leisure tourism. However, the existence of these enabling conditions is not sufficient to explain why an individual chooses to spend their leisure time and discretionary income on tourist activity. The most basic questions therefore are: Why do individuals engage in tourism in the first place? Why do they spend their money on tourist trips when there are so many other consumer products to choose from? And once they have decided to spend their money on tourism, why do they go to certain destinations and engage in certain activities when there are virtually limitless choices on offer? Furthermore, how do they make these decisions, and what can the tourism sector learn from this?

In this chapter we consider a number of issues related to the demand for tourism. We begin by discussing tourist motivations: the underlying psychological drivers that create the decision to travel and influence the decisions tourists make. On the basis of these decisions, tourists are often categorised into different tourist types, and we consider a number of models of tourist typologies, their usefulness and their limitations. We then look more closely at how these travel decisions are made, before discussing how tourism demand can be measured, monitored and forecasted.

TOURIST MOTIVATIONS

Academics have been interested in the motivations behind tourism behaviour and travel for several decades. Their research has resulted in a wide variety of definitions and models of tourism motivations. This section provides an explanation of the most significant approaches.

DEFINITIONS

The motivation for tourism has been defined in different ways by numerous authors. Table 4.1 contains a number of examples of these.

The different definitions show that tourist motivation is a complex concept to describe and research. Pearce and Lee (2005) point out that tourist motivation is not the same as the purpose of travel: it is easy to identify whether an individual travels for leisure or business, for example. The underlying motivations for tourism though may be **covert**: they may be formed within a traveller's psyche and based on their individual needs and wants. A number of models have been developed over the last decades that have attempted to structure these needs and wants and their relationship to tourist behaviour. The following section discusses a selection of these – it does not refer to all models that are in existence, but introduces the most influential ones.

Covert: Hidden, not openly shown or avowed

TABLE 4.1   Definitions of motivation

A psychological condition in which an individual is oriented towards and tries to achieve a kind of fulfilment. (Bromley, 1990: 264)
It acts as a trigger that sets off all the events involved in travel. (Parrinello, 1993: 234)
A state of need, a condition that serves as a driving force to display different kinds of behaviour toward certain types of activities, developing preferences, arriving at some satisfactory outcome. (Backman et al., 1995: 15)
The cause of human behaviour. (Mook, 1996: 12)
A set of needs, which predispose a person to participate in touristic activity. (Piznam and Mansfield, 1999: 7)
The driving force behind all actions. (Pearce and Lee, 2005: 226)

TOURIST MOTIVATION MODELS

There is no one commonly agreed theoretical approach to understanding tourist motivation (Holden, 2005: 67). Instead, a number of models, each with their own particular focus and emphasis, propose a framework to better understand what motivates tourists. These are usually rooted in social science disciplines such as psychology or sociology. There are similarities and overlaps between some of the models, and in general they complement, rather than contradict, each other. The choice of model for use in a particular study or research project often depends on which aspect of motivation is being studied – and it is not uncommon for researchers to draw on different models in the same text. We have distinguished between models using four themes: tourist motivation as a result of needs; tourist motivation in relation to a 'centre'; tourist motivation as a ladder/career; and tourist motivation as a combination of push-and-pull factors.

Tourism in Relation to Needs

In these models, it is proposed that tourists become involved in tourism to fulfil a need that cannot easily be fulfilled in their own environment. Several tourist motivation models are based on Maslow's (1954) Hierarchy of Needs. Maslow identified five human needs that he then organised into a hierarchy as depicted in Figure 4.1.

On the first level, we find *physiological* needs. These are the most basic needs that have to be met for a human being to survive and function. Examples are food and drink, sleep and sexual activity. If these needs are not met, then human beings start to focus fully on satisfying them, and all other needs disappear into the background.

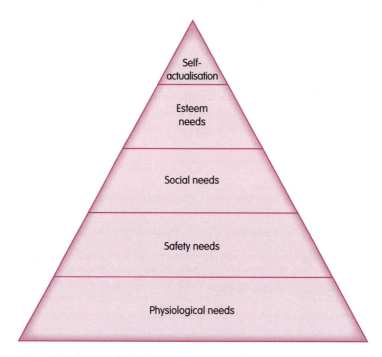

FIGURE 4.1   Maslow's Hierarchy of Needs

Source: After Maslow (1954)

On a second level, we find *safety* needs. Examples of these are security, stability, freedom from fear and chaos, and the need for law and order. Self-protection is a very basic human need, and Maslow argues it will dominate all others if threatened. In extreme situations, such as wars, practically everything can look less important than keeping safe. In non-extreme situations, this can refer to job security or the need for insurance or a savings account.

On the third level, there are *social* needs, also called *belonging and love* needs, which refer to giving and receiving affection. This can involve a partner, family members or friends. When these needs are not satisfied, the person feels lonely, rejected and ostracised. This person's behaviour may then become focused on forging relations via joining clubs, networks, or indeed going on a group holiday.

The fourth level is occupied by *esteem* needs: these refer to the need humans feel to have a stable and high evaluation of themselves. This high evaluation is reached through self-respect, or the respect of others. We achieve this via our achievements and competences, or by accruing fame, glory, prestige and appreciation.

The highest level of needs is *self-actualisation* needs. This level refers to the need humans feel to develop themselves, and to do something they are particularly talented in.

Artists feel a deep need to be involved in their art; athletes find themselves in their sport. The form these needs take will vary greatly from person to person: self-actualisation principally refers to whatever it is that makes people feel they are realising their potential and developing their full capabilities: 'However, the common feature of the needs of self-actualisation is that their emergence usually rests upon some prior satisfaction of the physiological, safety, love and esteem needs' (Maslow, 1954: 22). In other words, before people can develop themselves fully, all other needs will usually need to be met first – it is hard to focus on self-realisation when one feels hungry, unsafe, lonely or unappreciated. An individual is therefore motivated to satisfy needs from the bottom level upwards, and progress cannot be made from one level to another unless the lower levels are satisfied.

Tourism can be seen as a way to meet a number of these needs. Although it is not a basic need, such as food, shelter or safety, it can potentially fulfil love needs, esteem needs and self-actualisation needs. Travelling with family or friends can strengthen personal relationships. Tourists may also forge new relationships on holiday, thus fulfilling social needs. Some holiday types or destinations are prestigious and exclusive – this could gain tourists the respect of others and fulfil their esteem needs. Finally, tourism can be a deep, meaningful experience that makes tourists feel they are achieving their potential – in this case self-actualisation needs are addressed.

Beard and Ragheb (1983) adapted Maslow's model specifically to tourism and leisure needs. They developed a motivational typology of four components to explain people's participation in tourist and leisure activities:

Intellectual component: This motivates people to use tourism to undertake mental activities like learning, exploring, thinking and imagining.

Social component: In this case people undertake tourism and leisure activities for social reasons: to make friends, gain people's esteem or to build inter-personal relationships.

Competence-mastery component: Usually this refers to physical activities: people engage in these to master new skills, compete with others or challenge themselves.

Stimulus-avoidance component: These motivators relate to getting away from stressful or problematic environments, for example at work. People engage in tourism to relax and unwind.

McIntosh et al. (1995) developed a similar model with four categories of motivation:

Physical motivators: These relate to the refreshment of body and mind, health purposes, sport and leisure. They are usually engaged in to reduce tension.

Cultural motivators: These concern the desire to learn about new cultures or the music, art, architecture and lifestyles of a destination.

Interpersonal motivators: These are linked to meeting new people, or visits to friends and family. They can also refer to the escape from the home environment, or spiritual reasons.

Status and prestige motivators: These are concerned with the desire for attention and recognition from others in order to boost personal ego. They may include a desire for the continuation of education, or personal development in the pursuit of hobbies.

Physical motivators answered in Barbados

Source: Lynn Minnaert

Both models link the needs that were highlighted by Maslow to travel and tourism. Beard and Ragheb's (1983) stimulus-avoidance component can be linked to Maslow's physiological needs (rest). McIntosh et al.'s (1995) status and prestige motivators can be linked to Maslow's esteem needs. The main difference is that where Maslow's needs are presented in a clear hierarchy, the other two models do not make one type of motivator dependent on the fulfilment of other needs. They also leave open the option that tourists are motivated by more than one type of need.

Tourism in Relation to a 'Centre'

Cohen's (1979) model was one of the first to look at the sociological motivations of tourists. Cohen regarded the motivations for travel as the search for certain tourist experiences in relation to a 'centre'. The 'centre' is a theoretical concept that refers to values and meanings that are important and valuable for the individual. The centre is what people value, the principles by which they want to lead their lives, aspects that are 'central' to who they are. The centre can be religious, spiritual or cultural, or entirely personal – whatever gives a deeper meaning to someone's life can be part of the 'centre'.

Cohen used this concept to critique a common view of tourism at the time he was writing: that tourism was a frivolous, superficial and trivial phenomenon. He identified five types of tourist experiences and their underlying motivations and relationship to the 'centre'. Together, the five types form a spectrum of motivations for tourism, from the quest for superficial 'mere pleasure', to a search for deep and meaningful, in some cases life-changing, tourist experiences. These five types are:

The recreational mode: In this form of tourism, the motivation of tourists is to take a break from daily life and come back refreshed and positive. A holiday in this sense is a form of entertainment that is similar in nature to the cinema, the theatre or television. With regard to tourism, tourists on a sun-sea-sand holiday, who do not engage with the local culture much and just want to relax, could be seen as being in recreational mode. Tourism is in this case far removed from the 'centre': 'Though the tourist may find his experiences on the trip "interesting", they are not personally significant' (Cohen, 1979: 184). Like other forms of mass entertainment, these forms of tourism may be seen as superficial, shallow and trivial: the tourist may be lured by commercialised, contrived, or even inauthentic tourism products in the destination. But rather than seeing this as a sign that the tourist lacks insight, Cohen argues that the tourists in this category get what they want: the pleasure of entertainment. Authenticity may not be all that relevant to them: tourism can be seen as similar to a movie or a play – even though the spectators know what they see is not real, it is still enjoyable. With regard to motivation for travel, tourism is thus mainly seen as a 'pressure valve' (Cohen, 1979: 185): when real life, and everything related to the real 'centre', become too stressful, a holiday takes the pressure off. From this perspective, tourism plays an important role in modern society: by 'getting away' for a period of time, the tourists can, upon their return, fully focus again on their 'centre'.

The diversionary mode: In this form of travel tourism is seen as a diversion, as an escape from boredom and meaningless routine. This is a rather pessimistic view of travel motivations: it suggests that for some people their professional and personal life is unrewarding, and that tourism is just a way to find temporary oblivion. Whereas in the recreational mode people concentrate fully on their 'centre' after their return, travellers in this mode have lost sight of their 'centre': nothing is important to them any more. The motivation for travel is superficial and non-committed, not thought through: it is entirely a search for meaningless pleasure. This view of tourism often underlies critiques on modern mass tourism: tourism is then seen as 'a symptom of the general *malaise* in modern society' (Cohen, 1979: 186).

The experiential mode: In this form of tourism, people who have lost their 'centre' start looking for meaning in the life of others via tourist experiences. The motivation to travel is thus a search for meaning outside their own society and culture: it is important that tourist experiences are authentic and meaningful themselves. From this point of view, tourism is almost like a religious quest or pilgrimage, with the difference that tourists may be looking at religions that are not their own, usually without necessarily wanting to be converted to this different way of life. The experiential mode is thus more profound than the previous two, but does not generate 'real' religious experiences (Cohen, 1979: 188).

The experimental mode: This form of tourism seeks, just like the previous one, new meaning and a new 'centre' through tourism. In this form though, the trip takes on more of a spiritual significance. The motivation for experimental tourists in this model is to 'find themselves' (Cohen, 1979: 189) via tourism. Often this involves sampling different cultures, different alternatives, in the hope that one will suit their needs perfectly or satisfy their centre. Because of the profound spiritual motivation, the actual tourist activities may take a different form compared to the previous modes: the tourist may spend time in a hippie commune, an Israeli kibbutz, or a small village in a developing country. In some cases, these tourists discover the meaning they are looking for, and for them the experience may become a new way of life. In other cases though, the tourists become drifters, and never find the deep spiritual experience they set out to find.

An Israeli Kibbutz in the 1970s

Source: Rafi Kornfeld

The existential mode: This mode of tourism refers to tourists who have found a new 'centre' through tourism, and for whom the experience has taken on a deep spiritual meaning. This may mean that the tourists move permanently to a destination where they have found this deeper meaning, or it may mean that they visit the destination periodically on a sort of 'pilgrimage', from a place that is, for them, devoid of meaning to their new 'centre'. The motivation to travel is thus profoundly to 'derive spiritual **sustenance**' (Cohen, 1979: 190).

Sustenance: Something that provides support or nourishment

Cohen (1979) concludes that some tourist motivations are much easier to realise than others. Recreational and diversionary tourists, for example, seek entertainment and pleasure, they require little with regard to authenticity – so as long as the trip was pleasurable, the tourists can be seen to have achieved their goal. For tourists in the other categories, authenticity is crucial – travel has a deeper spiritual meaning. There is a much greater risk in these cases that the trip may not meet the expectations of the tourist, and that tourist experiences do not bring the tourist any closer to a 'centre'.

SNAPSHOT 4.1

Lifestyle Travellers or Tourists? Travel as a 'Centre'

For most people, travel can be seen as a break from everyday life, that takes place either at certain times of the year or that marks the transition from one life stage to the next (gap years and honeymoons for example). There are a small minority, however, who see leisure travel as 'a way of life that they may pursue indefinitely' (Cohen, 2010: 64): these people can be seen as 'lifestyle travellers'. For this group, travel is not a way to get closer to a 'centre': travel is the 'centre' itself. As opposed to the 'existential mode' discussed above, they do not tend to relocate to a destination to start a more permanent life – their ideal is to keep moving, to keep exploring. If they take up employment at one of their destinations or in the home environment, they only do this because it allows them to earn enough money to set off again. In each destination, the lifestyle travellers can test a different way of life in their quest for meaning. Lifestyle travellers are usually experienced backpackers who want to distance themselves from the enclaves and routes that are well-trodden by other backpackers in large numbers (Cohen, 2010).

Travel as a 'Career'

The models discussed so far have examined tourist motivations at one particular point in time – these motivations may affect the tourist when deciding to travel, choosing a destination or engaging in certain activities. Pearce (2005), however, discusses tourist motivations over a longer period: he argues that tourists may change their travel motivations over time, as their experience of tourism grows. His model is based on Maslow's Hierarchy of Needs model to show how tourism experiences can change. Pearce proposes that

> many people systematically move through a series of stages or have predictable travel motivational patterns. One pattern proposed is that over time some people may be seen as moving towards more self-esteem and self-actualisation needs, while others may stay at a relationship or stimulation level, depending on contingency or limiting factors such as health and financial considerations. (2005: 53–54)

As people accumulate travel experiences, they may thus be able to move to different travel motivations: from this perspective, tourism may be seen as a 'career'. The state of someone's travel career, like a career at work, may be influenced by several factors: previous experience, travel budgets, lifestyle, family commitments or age. A tourist can be said to reach a higher level in his or her travel career when self-development through tourism becomes more important. Pearce and Lee's (2005) empirical study has shown that it is usually the tourists with more travel experience who see tourism as a form of self-development and self-education, through experiencing different cultures and meeting the local population. This does not mean though that tourists with less travel experience necessarily approach tourism in a frivolous and meaningless way: this group scored more highly in the area of personal development: developing skills and talents, gaining self-confidence, and gaining a sense of accomplishment. A tourist may, for example, learn how to scuba-dive in a holiday resort and gain a sense of personal satisfaction from doing so. It can thus be proposed from this study that as individuals gain more travel experience, it is the motivation to interact with the destination itself which often becomes stronger. The travel career is not hierarchical: tourists with more travel experience may look for self-actualisation on one holiday, but might decide to book a package deal to an all-inclusive resort in order just to relax on their next holiday.

Tourism as a Combination of Push-and-Pull Factors

The models discussed so far suggest a range of different motivations for tourist activity, but they don't show how these motivations influence the choice of destination. Models with 'push-and-pull' factors distinguish between the reasons why individuals participate in tourism at all, and the reasons why they travel to a particular destination.

Dann (1977) describes tourist activity as the result of push-and-pull factors. 'Push' factors are the personal drivers that predispose a tourist to travel, for example a need to escape the daily routine, a need to spend quality time with the family, or the lust for adventure. Dann argues that there were two main push factors for tourism: on the one hand the need 'to get away from it all', to escape the stresses of daily life (he called this an escape from 'anomie'); and on the other hand the search for status and a feeling of superiority (he called this 'ego-enhancement'). 'Pull' factors are the elements that attract a tourist to a specific destination in order to satisfy the push factors. Pull factors could be a sunny climate, a music festival, opportunities for scuba-diving, or a famous art gallery.

Crompton (1979) expanded on this theory by investigating the 'push' factors further. He argued that the tourism industry was too concerned with the attributes of destinations (pull factors), whereas for many tourists, the destination itself can be relatively unimportant. Crompton also argued that in many cases 'respondents did not go to particular locations to seek cultural insights or artefacts; rather they went for socio-psychological reasons unrelated to any specific destination. The destination served merely as a medium through which these motives could be satisfied' (1979: 415). In other words, tourists may decide to travel because they want to relax on the beach with their family or loved ones. Where exactly this activity takes place may be of secondary importance. The beach resort in question may be in Malta, Cyprus, Kenya or Mexico – as long as the needs of the tourist are met, and there are opportunities to relax on the beach, the holiday experience is satisfactory.

The pull of the casinos and entertainment in Las Vegas

Source: Lynn Minnaert

Crompton (1979) distinguishes between seven types of socio-psychological motives for travel, two of which were also identified by Dann. The seven motives are:

Escape from a perceived mundane environment: This motive refers to the escape from boredom and routine, or from an urbanised environment.

Exploration and evaluation of the self: Being in a new environment, and engaging in different activities, can lead to self-discovery – by travelling, tourists can gain a better insight into themselves.

Relaxation: This motive mainly refers to mental relaxation. Some tourists can engage in intense and exhausting sporting activities whilst on holiday, but still feel they have come home 'relaxed'; for others, physical relaxation and 'doing nothing' are equally important.

Prestige: The motivation here is the attainment of status amongst peers by engaging in tourism, or by visiting certain destinations. Crompton argues that in generating regions with a high propensity to travel, the prestige motivation has diminished because participation in tourism is no longer limited to the elite; however, the destination, accommodation type or class of travel can be a source of prestige.

Regression: Tourists can feel free from obligations on holiday, which encourages some to behave in a more irrational and juvenile manner, such as indulging in heavy drinking or drug use, even though they do not do this at home.

Enhancement of kinship relations: This motive refers to spending 'quality time' with family and loved ones, bonding and reconnecting to others. Family holidays or VFR are examples.

Facilitation of social interaction: For some tourists, holidays are an opportunity to interact with others. These contacts can be rather brief, or develop into friendships or relationships. Group holidays or organised tours can facilitate social contacts.

Apart from these socio-psychological motives, Crompton (1979) also refers to cultural motives for travel, such as exploring new cultures and destinations, or learning about these to become a more rounded individual.

When choosing a destination, the tourist searches for a place where the push factors described above can be matched with appropriate pull factors. Tourists for whom the search of prestige is an important push factor may be attracted by the pull of exclusive and luxurious facilities of exotic destinations such as the Seychelles. On the contrary, tourists for whom evaluation of the self is a push factor may rather be attracted to the pull factors of a meditation facility deep in the Scottish Highlands.

Complex Motivations

From the variety of models that exist (of which a number have been described above) it can be seen that tourist motivations are complex and highly personal constructs. What motivates a person to engage in tourism can change over time and even by trip – many individuals will take several short trips per year and the motivations for each of these trips can be very different. A tourist might, for example, go on a two-week holiday to a Turkish beach resort, to relax and spend time with the family, and later go on a fishing trip to the Scottish Lakes with friends. When travelling in groups, each person's motivations need to be taken into account, which may result in a number of compromises. Models are helpful tools for the analysis of motivations, but may not reflect this highly complex combination of motives. The case study below considers research that has been conducted into the tourist motivations of the gay community.

CASE STUDY 4.1

Motivations of Gay Tourists

The models above have shown that tourism motivations can be linked to a range of personal characteristics and personality traits. In recent years, academic tourism literature has shown an increasing interest in the demand and motivations of the gay tourist. This market segment is of particular interest to the tourism industry, as the gay community are generally seen as high spenders – this is often referred to as the 'Pink Pound/Euro or Dorothy Dollar' (Waitt and Markwell, 2006). Understanding the travel motivations and purchasing decisions of gay tourists is therefore vitally important for destinations that want to attract this market.

The gay tourist market is often seen as desirable because of a number of typical characteristics. Gay tourists are usually characterised by high education and income levels, and they tend to spend more on discretionary items such as holidays. Not only is their travel propensity higher, they also tend to spend more on these trips. This can be linked to the fact that gay people are less likely to have children, and thus have more free time. They are also generally seen as more style-conscious and more individualistic in their purchasing decisions (Hughes, 2002; Pritchard et al., 1998; Waitt and Markwell, 2006).

Several authors have indicated that this view of the gay market may not reflect reality completely. Guaracino and Salvato (2017) highlight that there are differences in class and wealth in this segment of the population, just as in any other: not all gay people are affluent and well educated. They have different ethnicities, can be married or single, young or old, parents or childfree and so on. Rather than grouping all gay tourists together, the market needs to be more carefully segmented by tourism businesses and destinations. For example, while there are some similarities between the travel motivations of gay men and lesbian women, there are also differences.

Similarities:

- Both lesbian women and gay men tend to travel to LGBT events like Pride to affirm their sexual identity.

- Both groups tend to support destinations and tour operators that contribute to the LGBT community.

- The travel motivations of lesbian women and gay men tend to become more similar as they grow older or have families. Both groups like travelling with their pets.

Differences:

- Lesbian women are more likely to travel as a couple and do not usually seek to meet other people. Gay men are more likely to look for a sexual experience.

- Lesbian women are more likely than gay men to plan travel around romance: a honeymoon, wedding or anniversary.

- Lesbian women are more likely to feel invested in the political climate and human rights record of the destinations they visit. If a destination has a history of minority oppression or animal cruelty, they might be reluctant to visit.

- Lesbian women tend to value access to nature, whereas gay men tend to prefer access to culture. (Guaracino and Salvato, 2017)

The travel motivations of gay travellers also differ depending on their age. The Community Marketing & Insights (CMI) 'Annual Survey on LGBT Tourism and Hospitality' distinguished the motivators for Millennials, Generation X and Baby Boomers. Key findings include:

- Millennials are much more likely to be motivated by nightlife and 'foodie culture' than Generation X and Baby Boomers.

- Generation X are more motivated by warm weather, and rest and relaxation than Millennials and Baby Boomers.

- Baby Boomers are more motivated by historical attractions and natural scenery than Generation X, but Millennials tend to share these interests. (CMI, 2016)

(Continued)

In brief, gay tourists are a market with many dimensions. Gender, culture, age and family circumstances distinguish travelers and may affect their travel motivations. Sometimes their sexuality will play a role in their travel motivations – honeymoons are an example. At other times, for example for a business trip, their sexuality will not be a key influencer.

Reflective Questions

1. When analysing the travel motivations of gay men and lesbian women based on Maslow's and McIntosh et al.'s models, which differences do you see?

2. Fort Lauderdale is a destination in the USA that has attracted gay tourists successfully for many years. Take a look at their website: www.sunny.org/lgbt/. What makes this destination so successful?

The research into tourist motivations has led to the development of a number of tourist type models. These will now be discussed.

TOURIST TYPES

Since the 1970s, a range of authors has developed typologies of tourists to model tourism demand. These models aimed to group tourists with similar characteristics and connect them to destinations and activities they would be likely to choose. Some models also focus on the underlying values of tourists, and the meanings they attribute to travel. By grouping tourists with homogeneous needs, different market segments can be distinguished – this process is referred to as 'segmentation'. Even though some models are now fairly old, they are well established concepts in tourism theory.

COHEN'S TYPOLOGY

Cohen (1972) was the first scholar who attempted to divide tourists into different categories. He distinguished between four tourist types, and based his model on the relationship of the tourist with the 'novelty' or 'strangeness' of the visited culture. One of the key attractions of tourism is that the tourist spends time away from the home environment, where certain needs can be better met. How familiar or unfamiliar these places are can vary widely; there will be differences in the level of strangeness or challenge that a tourist seeks:

The organised mass tourist: Tourists of this type prefer to stay within a tourist 'bubble', in an environment that has similarities with their routine environment. They tend to travel in groups on pre-arranged trips that are organised by an intermediary (see Chapter 6), often travel on special tourist transport, and are often accompanied by a tour leader or resort representative. They require food that is familiar, and to communicate in their own language or another language the tourist understands. Familiarity is at a maximum, novelty at a minimum (Cohen, 1972: 167).

The individual mass tourist: This type is similar to the organised mass tourist but prefers some flexibility to venture outside of the familiar 'bubble' occasionally during the trip, perhaps by taking local transport to visit a site independently or sampling a local meal.

The explorer: This type of traveller organises the trip independently, and requires comfortable accommodation and a reliable means of transportation. Explorers try to engage with the local community more and will also try to speak their language – they will attempt to break out of the familiar 'bubble' and experience the 'real' destination. Explorers look for novelty, but still maintain certain routines and levels of comfort from their home life.

The drifter: This type of tourist tries to completely immerse themselves in the host culture: live the way the host community lives, eat the food they eat, and fully share their habits. For this type of tourist, familiarity is at a minimum and novelty at a maximum.

PLOG'S TYPOLOGY

Similarly to Cohen, Plog (1974, 1991, 2003) developed a tourist typology on the basis of tourists' willingness to experience unfamiliarity and novelty on holiday. His model additionally connects visitor types to the sorts of destinations they are most likely to visit: it argues that tourism changes destinations, and that very different types of tourists are often attracted to one destination over time.

Astana, Kazakhstan: Venturing off the beaten track

Source: Lynn Minnaert

Plog's typology consists of two main types: venturers (allocentrics) and dependables (psychocentrics). Venturers seek out unique and novel travel experiences and are usually the first to discover a destination. When they feel tourism has 'spoilt' a destination, they will seek alternative 'unspoilt' destinations. Dependables prefer a destination with familiar amenities, such as modern hotels, good transport links and well developed attractions. They usually visit destinations with a tourist infrastructure. In the middle

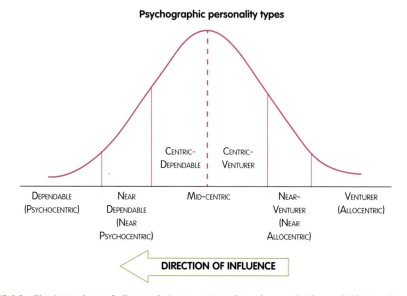

Psychographic personality types

CENTRIC-DEPENDABLE | CENTRIC-VENTURER

DEPENDABLE (PSYCHOCENTRIC)   NEAR DEPENDABLE (NEAR PSYCHOCENTRIC)   MID-CENTRIC   NEAR-VENTURER (NEAR ALLOCENTRIC)   VENTURER (ALLOCENTRIC)

DIRECTION OF INFLUENCE

FIGURE 4.2   Plog's typology of allocentric (venturers) and psychocentric (dependable) tourists

Source: Plog (1991)

of the two extremes are mid-centrics, who are between the two extremes and looking for a destination that is neither wholly familiar, nor wholly unfamiliar.

Table 4.2 summarises the key travel behaviours and characteristics of venturers and dependables.

TABLE 4.2   Venturer and dependable travel motivations

Venturers	Dependables
Prefer non-touristy areas	Prefer the familiar in travel destinations
Engage in lots of new activities	Engage in fewer new activities
Want spontaneity and accept unpredictability in trips	Want structured, routinised travel
Want new destinations for each trip	Prefer returning to the same and familiar places
Spend more money on travel	Spend more money on material goods
Seek off-the-beaten-track hotels and restaurants	Want standard hotels and conventional meals

Source: Based on Plog (1991: 66–67).

SNAPSHOT 4.2

Tourists, Travellers and Holidaymakers

In his book *Welcome to Everytown*, philosopher Julian Baggini (2008) discusses how, in his opinion, there are not only tourists and travellers but also 'holidaymakers'. His categorisation shows a resemblance to Plog's tourist typology, with travellers standing for venturers, tourists for mid-centrics, and holidaymakers for dependables. Baggini pokes fun at these distinctions:

> I have never had much time for the alleged contrast between travellers and tourists, which, according to an old joke, is that tourists go to McDonald's for the food and travellers go there for the toilets. Tourists are the inferior beings in this hierarchy, who follow itineraries set by others and never see the 'real country'. Travellers, in contrast, are free spirits who do what they like and get real with the locals. Of course, this is hogwash. Travellers go where all the other travellers go, following the Lonely Planet Bible. They may stay in more basic accommodation, but that does not make their experience more real, just less comfortable. After all, it's not as though locals live in youth hostels … Travellers are just deluded tourists with pretentions. I realised that there was another, genuinely different category: the holidaymaker. Whereas tourists and travellers travel in order to see new places and try new things, the holidaymaker goes away simply to have a good time where the weather is better and the problems of home are forgotten. (2008: 145–6)

KRIPPENDORF'S TYPOLOGY

Krippendorf (1984) was one of the first authors to typify tourists by their impact on the destinations they visited. As one of the earliest theorists on the topic of sustainable tourism, Krippendorf argued that because tourism was growing at a rapid pace, tourists were also increasingly likely to impact negatively on host communities and environments. He therefore constructed a typology with the 'much maligned tourist' on the one hand, and the 'alternative tourist' on the other.

The 'much maligned tourist' is a combination of all the negative stereotypes that exist about tourists. They are ridiculous with their big cameras and their pale skin. They are naïve and ask dumb questions. They are uncultured, spend whole days at the beach, and show no interest in local culture or food. They are exploiting, polluting, and follow other tourists like sheep. Krippendorf argues that it is easy to poke fun at tourists, because the tourist is always the other person – even if people travel themselves, they do not necessarily identify with this stereotype of a tourist.

At the other end of the spectrum we find the alternative tourist. Even though these tourists show respect for other cultures and people, and do not conform to the negative stereotype, they are not free of negative impacts either: they may have limited negative impacts on destinations, but by discovering new destinations they pave the way for tourism development and the invasion of 'much maligned tourists'.

Krippendorf (1984) concluded that it is too simplistic just to divide tourists into a 'good' and a 'bad' category: he argued for awareness-building and education initiatives that would inform tourists of the consequences of their visit and activities on destinations.

SEGMENTATION IN PRACTICE

Tourist typologies can be beneficial for the tourism sector, but these also have a number of limitations. The concept of tourist types as useful generalisations to differentiate between groups of travellers with similar needs and wants is still of use today. It may be helpful for destinations and tourism companies to know more about the type of tourist they attract or want to attract – this way they can adapt the product they offer to the needs and wants of that particular tourist type.

Nevertheless, there are also several limitations attached to the tourist typologies discussed above. First there is their age to consider – all three models were developed in the 1970s and 1980s and travel behaviours have changed significantly since then. They have also been developed on the basis of evidence from one generating region: for all models these were Western, developed countries. It is thus not necessarily possible to apply them generally to tourists today, and it can be argued that they do not span the full scope of tourist types today. As such they may be useful theoretical concepts, but their practical applicability is less clear. When, for example, one would want to research a group of tourists on the basis of Plog's model, it may be very difficult to judge where on the scale between venturers and dependables they are situated. And in terms of Krippendorf's model, would any tourist ever identify themselves as a 'much maligned tourist'? Most statistics in tourism therefore will use a more standardised typology of tourists, usually one based on purpose of travel, while many companies and organisations will segment the tourist market using a range of demographic, socio-economic and pyschographic factors. These are discussed in detail in Chapter 11.

CONSUMER DECISION MAKING

The previous sections explored what motivates individuals to participate in tourist activity and how this influences what they seek from destinations. We have seen that these motivations can be generalised in a number of models, and that tourists have been categorised into typologies based on their motivations and behaviour. Some questions now need to be asked here: how does an individual turn this motivation into a trip? How do the push-and-pull factors combine to create a purchase decision? How does the tourist make decisions about destination, transport, accommodation and duration? These are addressed by theories about the tourist decision-making process. This section starts by exploring the different steps in tourism decision making, and then discusses the concept of involvement. A number of models will then be presented which will show the different factors influencing this process.

STEPS IN DECISION MAKING

Kolb (2006) identifies five steps in all purchasing decisions, including tourism purchasing decisions. These are as follows:

Need recognition: This is when consumers become aware of a need that they would like to see met. These could be simple daily needs, such as to buy food or pay a bill, or they may be more complex: the desire to develop a new career for example, or the organisation of a wedding. In tourism, needs recognition usually refers to the moment when a person realises that the needs we discussed in the first part of this chapter will be met most easily by engaging in tourist activity. Kolb (2006: 130) adds that 'when consumers decide to travel, they are usually fulfilling an internal emotional desire'.

Information search: Consumers search for information about products because they want to make sure their purchasing decision is correct. If the product they are considering buying is very expensive, such as a car or a house, they will try to minimise the risk by gathering as much information as possible about the product they intend to buy. Products they buy routinely and which do not cost much (such as bread or a newspaper) are usually not researched in similar depth. To gather information, consumers may use documentation provided by the producers of the product or intermediaries; they may ask for recommendations from friends or family members, or read product reviews in the specialised press or online.

Evaluation of alternatives: The consumer will then compare a number of potential products or services. Criteria that can be used here are quality, price, design and brand reputation, to name but a few. When choosing a holiday destination, for example, the tourist will usually compare the destination characteristics they seek with those on offer in different places. Of those characteristics, some may be more important than others: a tourist may, for example, be primarily looking for a sunny destination for a family holiday that offers good value for money and does not require more than 4 hours on a plane. If that destination also happens to offer cultural attractions and a summer festival, this may be an added bonus for the tourist, but it may not have been key to the decision-making process.

Purchase process: The act of purchasing a product or service can be very simple: if you want to buy a newspaper, for example, you can just go to the newsagent and do so. Other products, however, may require a more complicated purchase process: when buying a house, the buyer may need a solicitor or notary to help complete the purchase. In terms of holidays, the purchasing process can be simple when the tourist decides to book a package holiday via a travel agent. In this case, a fixed price is paid, and the accommodation, transport, and in some cases extras like tours or excursions, are all included. When booking independently, however, the process becomes more complicated, as a holiday may include a flight, a hotel and airport transportation. Prices for tourism products can also change very rapidly, so that the tourist may feel under pressure to complete the different elements of the purchase process quickly.

Post-purchase evaluation: This step is where consumers evaluate the products they have bought, and check if these have met their needs and expectations. When buying a holiday, tourists will often only have pictures of destinations and facilities to go on – only on holiday can it be determined if these reflect the reality. The product that was bought can thus not be evaluated after purchase, but only after consumption, and much time may pass between the two activities. The fragmented nature of a holiday, which is supplied by various producers (accommodation, transport, attractions), creates difficulties in evaluating the whole trip. If the expectations of the tourist are met or exceeded, the satisfaction with the purchase will be high, and this may result in repeat business for the destination. If the expectations are not met, this will result in low satisfaction or dissatisfaction.

INVOLVEMENT

In marketing theory, a distinction is made between *convenience goods* (which are low in price and are bought frequently) and *shopping goods* (which are high in price and are bought less frequently). The purchase of convenience goods is an example of routine problem-solving behaviour, whereas the purchase of shopping goods involves more complex decision making (Swarbrooke and Horner, 2007).

The distinction between convenience and shopping goods can be attributed to differences in consumer *involvement*. Consumer involvement in tourism can be high or low depending on the cost, frequency of travel and the significance of the trip to the tourist, and consequently there are significant differences in the decision-making process.

Low-involvement tourism purchase decisions happen routinely and are not emotionally significant. Often little research goes into these purchase decisions, and consumers will choose products on the basis of past experience or price. For example, an individual with a second home may purchase a plane ticket on an impulse, or if an individual is familiar with a destination and with the usual prices for transport and accommodation the trip may require little research or consultation with others (Kolb, 2006).

Swarbrooke and Horner (2007), and Kolb (2006), suggest that high-involvement tourism products are characterised by:

A higher level of emotional significance: A holiday is often something the buyer will look forward to every year and this is therefore seen as an important decision. If the tourist only takes one longer holiday each year, then the risk involved is rather large: if the wrong destination is chosen, they will need to wait another year before they can go on holiday again. The whole family may also have a say in deciding the destination. A honeymoon is another example of a holiday with a high emotional involvement – the newlyweds will only have one chance to have that perfect trip. Moreover, the money that would be spent on the holiday may be compared to other goods such as a car, a designer watch or a luxury handbag.

A higher level of information search: Consumers who make high-involvement purchasing decisions will usually be more likely to spend a longer time researching and comparing products. Particularly when the product is unfamiliar, extensive research may be needed. This may also involve consultations with other people such as friends or product specialists.

Long-term decisions: Many high-involvement purchases are decided a longer time in advance than low-involvement purchases. We will often book a holiday a number of months in advance – we do not decide what we are going to have for dinner for months to come. The consumer is thus predicting what he or she will want in the future; this makes the decision more complex. The purchase decision is also more long term because it is made less often: travel products are bought less regularly than convenience goods. The purchase process is thus a more unique experience that is handled less routinely.

More strongly influenced by other people: This aspect has to do with both the nature of travel and with the higher level of information search. Many tourists travel in smaller or bigger groups: couples, families, groups of friends. The motivations and expectations of different individuals will need to be taken into account before purchase decisions are made. Even when tourists travel alone, the choice of travel dates and destination may be dependent on when they can get time off or be free from other obligations. Moreover, in many cases advice will be sought from product specialists (such as travel agents), friends and relatives, or fellow travellers (on travel blogs or review websites).

DECISION MAKING IN TOURISM

A range of different models of decision making in tourism has been developed that can break down the purchasing process into a number of components or steps. Mathieson and Wall (1982) and Moutinho (1987) are examples of these models. This chapter presents a more recent interpretation of decision making in tourism: the stimulus and response model.

Middleton et al. (2009) compare the human brain to a computer when it makes decisions: when performing a task (making a decision), a computer depends on a certain input of data, from which it presents the user with an output (solution). Simple operations can be carried out quickly, whereas more complex operations, with more input, may take more time to process. The input is referred to as a 'stimulus', and the output as a 'response' (see Figure 4.3).

A detailed exploration of the stimulus and response model can be found in Middleton and Clarke (2001). This can be divided into six steps or 'processes':

Process 1: *Product inputs*: This process refers to the range of products that is available to tourists when they make their decision. These can be travel agents, tour operators, booking websites and businesses.

Process 2: *Communication channels*: This step refers to the different ways a customer can find out about the products on offer. The communication channels can either be 'formal', via brochures and advertisements, or they can be 'informal': buyers may ask the advice of friends and family members, or look for advice from other travellers in online forums.

Process 3: *Communication filters*: In this step, consumers 'make sense' of the wealth of information available to them so that they can make a decision. The brain acts as a mental 'sieve' that filters out information that will be acted upon.

Process 4: *Motivation*: The communication filters in process 3 have strong connections to the personal motivations of travellers in process 4. This step refers to the tourists' needs, wants and goals – these are affected by their socio-economic characteristics (the money they have to spend and their level of education), personality, attitudes and cultural background. All these factors influence the type of tourism product the tourist is looking for and they drive the selection processes that have been made in processes 1–3.

Process 5: *Purchase decision*: This step concerns the actual act of buying a product at a certain price, within a certain brand, and via a certain distribution channel. This step is likely to be monitored closely by service providers, even though it is only the very last phase of the complex processes described above.

Process 6: *Post-purchase and post-consumption feelings*: In this step, the tourist evaluates their purchasing decisions after consumption of the product, service or experience. If the decision is evaluated positively, this may encourage repeat business and positive word of mouth. If the evaluation is negative, the tourist is unlikely to buy the product again and may discourage other travellers (see process 2) from buying it also.

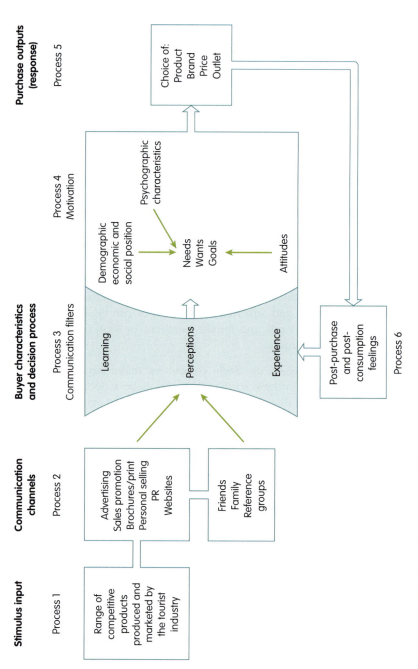

FIGURE 4.3 Stimulus and response model

Source: Middleton and Clark (2001). Reprinted with permission from Elsevier.

MEASURING AND FORECASTING THE DEMAND FOR TOURISM

Measuring and forecasting tourism demand is very important for the tourism industry. This is mainly because many tourism products are 'perishable': if an airline does not sell a seat on one flight, it cannot put two passengers in one seat on the next: the loss of revenue cannot be made up. The same goes for a hotel bed or a seat on a sightseeing bus. Adequate measurements and forecasts of tourism demands can help tourism managers with the planning, marketing and selling of their products.

MEASURING DEMAND

International tourism demand is generally measured in terms of the number of tourists from an origin country who visit a foreign destination, or in terms of tourist expenditures by visitors from the origin country in the destination country (Witt and Witt, 1992: 4). Another way of measuring demand is to count tourist nights in the destination country. These data are collected in a variety of ways. Tourist visits are usually recorded via counts at the border (inbound) or by surveying a sample of travellers (inbound and outbound). Records of accommodation establishments (such as hotels) can be used to count the number of visitors and number of nights at the destination. International tourist expenditure data are usually collected using the bank reporting method, or by conducting specialised surveys with travellers. The bank reporting method is based on a registration by authorised banks and agencies of the buying and selling of foreign currency by travellers (Witt and Witt, 1995).

It is very difficult to compile accurate overviews of tourism demand because there are certain problems associated with each of the methods described above. Counts at the border, for example, cannot always differentiate between transit visitors and visitors to the destination itself. Large airports, for instance, may experience a lot of transit traffic, and tourists may drive through certain countries on the way to their holiday destination without actually staying or spending any money there. The records of accommodation establishments exclude people who stay at friends' or family members' houses and day trippers. Specialised surveys are often expensive to carry out and may be based on a small sample. The bank reporting methods may not be accurate either, because it can be difficult to distinguish a tourism transaction from another transaction, or relevant transactions may not be recorded at all (Witt and Witt, 1995).

An added problem in the measuring of tourism demand is the fact that data are collected differently in various countries. Tourism arrivals may be registered by their country of residence or nationality, for example. In France and Germany, data are collected through personal interviews, whereas in the UK and the USA, this is done via surveys at airports (Witt and Witt, 1992). Tourism Satellite Accounts (TSAs) are often proposed as a method to achieve comparable data for different countries (see Chapter 7).

SNAPSHOT 4.3

The UK Passenger Survey
The International Passenger Survey (IPS) is a survey of a random sample of passengers entering and leaving the UK by air, sea or the Channel Tunnel. Over a quarter of million

(Continued)

face-to-face interviews are carried out each year with passengers entering and leaving the UK through the main airports, seaports and the Channel Tunnel. Interviewing is carried out throughout the year with a sample that represents about one in every 500 passengers. The interview usually takes three to five minutes and contains questions about passengers' country of residence (for overseas residents) or country of visit (for UK residents), the reason for their visit, and details of their expenditure and fares. There are additional questions for passengers migrating to or from the UK. While much of the content of the interview remains the same from one year to the next, new questions are sometimes added or will appear periodically on the survey. The data collected by the UK Passenger Survey are used not only to compile international tourism statistics, but also to calculate the balance of payments (see Chapter 7) and to estimate the numbers and characteristics of migrants into and out of the UK. The survey results can be accessed via the website of the Office for National Statistics (2017a).

FORECASTING DEMAND

'Forecasting' fundamentally refers to the process of organising information about a phenomenon's past in order to predict its future (Frechtling, 2001: 8). Forecasts can have different timescales: short-term forecasts, for example, are needed for scheduling and staffing, whereas long-term forecasts can influence the level of investment in aeroplanes and hotels (Witt and Witt, 1995).

Two types of methods can be used in forecasting tourism demand: *causal* and *non-causal* methods. Non-causal methods start from the principle that 'a variable may be forecasted without reference to the factors which determine the variable' (Witt and Witt, 1992: 7). In other words, non-causal methods look at the past development of a phenomenon, and predict the future of the phenomenon by extrapolating the trend. If tourism has been growing at a certain rate in the past, it predicts tourism demand based on continuous levels of such growth. The benefit of this method is that it is fairly easy to apply at a low cost. The problem is that it presumes that the causes of growth and decline will just stay the same in the future, which may not be the case. Moreover, historical data for tourism demand are often lacking, which means that there is no trend that can just be extrapolated to the future. Tourism demand is also highly volatile and can be severely affected by events such as wars or crises: demand is thus not stable enough to assume that it will just continue to grow or fall (Frechtling, 2001).

Causal methods link forecasting to a set of determining factors. Forecasts are made up of each of these determining factors and factored into the forecast depending on their impact on tourism demand. This is called an 'econometric forecasting' method (Frechtling, 2001; Witt and Witt, 1992). Econometric forecasts take into account the arrival and expenditure of visitors, but also other factors such as, for example, the size of the origin population, the income of the origin country per capita, the price of products and services at the destination, and the price of products and services in comparable destinations (Witt and Witt, 1995). This type of forecasting is more complex, but because it incorporates more factors it should be more representative of the complexity of tourism demand. However, it is also more expensive and it can be difficult to find forecasts for all the determining factors.

SNAPSHOT 4.4

New Zealand Tourism Demand Forecast 2017–2023

New Zealand's tourism forecasts for 2017 until 2023 are compiled on the basis of a variety of data sources. The forecast results cover New Zealand's eight key markets (Australia, China, UK, USA, Japan, Germany, Canada and Korea) and two fast growing markets (India and Indonesia). The model generates annual forecasts for:

- total visitor arrivals
- total visitor nights
- total visitor expenditure
- average length of stay per visitor
- average spend per day per visitor.

The results of this data collection process were then checked via telephone interviews and focus groups with key stakeholders in the industry: this is called a 'Delphi' process.

Figure 4.4 shows an example of how these techniques are used to forecast international arrivals to New Zealand.

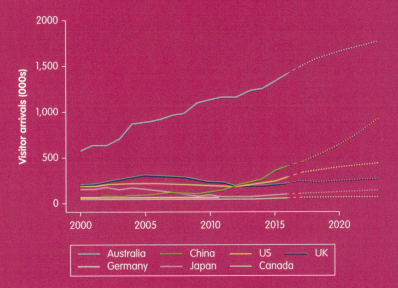

FIGURE 4.4   International arrivals to New Zealand

Source: Statistics New Zealand, MBIE (2017). Copyright protected by Crown copyright.

The dotted lines show the forecasted growth for international tourism to New Zealand. You will see that much growth is expected from the Chinese market: this line shows the steepest upward trend. China was New Zealand's second largest tourism market in 2017 in terms of both arrivals and spend. This market is expected to grow strongly during the forecast period overpassing Australia as the largest contributor in spend. Major events such as Australia–China Year of Tourism 2017 and New Zealand–China Year of Tourism 2019, policy changes extending the duration of multiple-entry visitor's visas to five years, and an increase in airline seat capacity are all expected to support this strong growth (Ministry of Business, Innovation and Employment, 2017).

SUMMARY

This chapter has discussed tourism demand from different perspectives. First it has looked at why individuals engage in tourism activity; at the psychological or social factors that drive them to spend an often considerable part of their income on a product of which they have often little knowledge in advance and thus often includes a certain level of risk. On the basis of motivations, tourists then make a purchasing decision. We have looked at different models that unravel this process, which has been shown to be often complex and time-consuming. Finally, the chapter has explored the measuring and forecasting of tourism demand: it is important for the industry to gain a deeper insight into demand and how it will evolve, so that it can plan its resources effectively.

SELF-TEST QUESTIONS

1. Julian Baggini (2008) says that 'travellers are just deluded tourists with pretentions'. What do you think he means by this?

2. Compare a range of adverts for different destinations. What sort of image are they trying to convey for each destination? Is this image realistic and believable?

3. Forecasting the number of tourist arrivals is notably difficult, and often the forecasts will turn out to be inaccurate. What can be the causes for unexpected surges or dips in tourist arrivals?

FURTHER READING

Kolb, B. (2006) *Tourism Marketing for Cities and Towns: Using Branding and Events to Attract Tourists*. Burlington: Butterworth-Heinemann, Ch. 6.

Krippendorf, J. (1984) *The Holiday Makers: Understanding the Impact of Leisure and Travel*. Oxford: Butterworth-Heinemann.

Swarbrooke, J. and Horner, S. (2007) *Consumer Behaviour in Tourism*. Oxford: Butterworth-Heinemann.

USEFUL WEBSITES

Best Trip Choices: http://besttripchoices.com/

New Zealand Ministry of Business Innovation and Employment: www.tourismresearch. govt.nz/

Official Statistics: www.statistics.gov.uk/ssd/surveys/international_passenger_survey.asp

5

TOURISM SUPPLIERS

'... tourism involves many different suppliers working across
different locations and countries in different industries.'

D. Litteljohn and I. Baxter, 2006: 23

LEARNING OUTCOMES

After reading this chapter you will understand:

- the types of suppliers that provide tourism products
- the main characteristics of each tourism supply sector
- common characteristics that affect all tourism suppliers.

Resort hotel in Los Cabos, Mexico

Source: Image courtesy of Executive Group Travel

INTRODUCTION

Tourism suppliers are providers of the travel products and services that are consumed by tourists during their trip, on transit routes and in destinations. Tourism suppliers can be broadly defined by the sector within which they operate – transport, accommodation, non-residential venues, attractions and cruises – however, each of these sectors is highly fragmented and consists of a broad range of distinct suppliers and products. In addition, the emergence of sharing economy suppliers, which often operate outside the planned and regulated commercial tourism supply, has added a new dimension to tourism supply in many destinations. Sharing economy supply in tourism includes accommodation, transport and attractions, so cuts across all of the traditional tourism supply sectors – it's almost a sector in its own right, and we discuss it separately within this chapter.

We also consider these tourism sectors and the types of suppliers of which each is composed, highlighting significant sectoral issues. We begin by considering the accommodation sector and focus on hotels and the variety of ownership, management and affiliation models that are commonly found. We then discuss non-residential venues, which are often overlooked in discussions of tourism suppliers, and their role in stimulating demand for other tourism suppliers in destinations. We consider the transport sector and the role of government regulation in the airline industry. The visitor attractions sector is then explained, followed by the cruise sector, and finally, the sharing economy. We end the chapter by considering some of the major common characteristics that describe all tourism suppliers.

ACCOMMODATION SUPPLIERS

Accommodation suppliers are based in destinations or on transit routes and offer capacity to tourists for overnight stays, either by selling to the tourist directly or via intermediaries. The tourist accommodation sector is huge and consists of many different accommodation types. Middleton et al. (2009) suggest differentiating between them as serviced and non-serviced accommodation:

Serviced accommodation: Provides rooms in which to sleep plus other services that are provided by staff on site, such as housekeeping and food and beverage services. Serviced accommodation is most commonly, but not exclusively, seen in the hotel and guest house sector.

Non-serviced accommodation: Often called self-catering accommodation, does not provide these services, although it may be possible to arrange them separately.

Serviced and non-serviced accommodation can be broken down further into specific forms of accommodation as listed in Table 5.1.

TABLE 5.1   Serviced and non-serviced accommodation

Serviced sector	Non-serviced sector (self-catering)
Hotels/Motels/Hostels	Aparthotels/Condominia
Guesthouse/Pensions	Gites/Cottages/Villas/Apartments/Hostels
Farmhouses	Timeshare properties
Educational establishments' residences	Holiday Centres/Camps
Local homes via sharing economy platforms	Caravan/Chalet parks/Campsites
Homes of friends/relatives	Second homes for personal or commercial use registered as tourism accommodation
	Educational establishments' residences
	Local homes via sharing economy brands

Source: Adapted from Middleton et al. (2009: 365)

The variety of accommodation types creates difficulties in discussing the sector as a single entity. For instance, cottages, villas and apartments are often owned by private individuals; some may only be used by the owner, and some may be available for rent by tourists. Some providers such as universities and farm owners sell accommodation capacity to tourists in order to supplement income from their main activities but are not full-time tourist accommodation operators. The **sharing economy** has become a major supplier of tourist accommodation in some destinations.

Accommodation providers that operate commercially (i.e. with the objective of making a profit) must manage their capacity and availability very carefully. Two methods of measuring the sales performance of a hotel are occupancy rates and revenue per available room (RevPAR).

Occupancy rate is the percentage of available rooms that were sold during a specific period of time. Occupancy is measured by dividing the number of rooms sold by the number of rooms available (Smith Travel Research, 2011):

Occupancy = Rooms Sold/Rooms Available

For example, a hotel with 100 available rooms on a specific date would have an occupancy rate of 50 per cent if half the rooms were sold. Occupancy rates are a useful

Sharing economy:
Also known as 'collaborative economy' or Peer-to-Peer (P2P) economy' transactions between individuals, usually online, where assets are exchanged or borrowed free of charge or for a price

tool for describing the demand for accommodation, but they do not measure financial performance; for instance a hotel that sells its rooms very cheaply could achieve 100 per cent occupancy regularly but may not be profitable.

RevPAR measures the average income achieved at the property by calculating the total room revenue for a specific date and dividing it by the number of rooms available. For example a 100-room hotel with revenue of £10,000 on one night achieves a RevPAR of £100; this could have been achieved through a 100 per cent occupancy rate at £100 per room per night, or 50 per cent occupancy at £200 per room per night.

For the remainder of this section we will focus on the hotel sector.

THE HOTEL SECTOR

Hotels are serviced accommodation properties that provide guest rooms and other facilities such as meeting rooms, bars and restaurants, as well as banqueting facilities. The global hotel sector consists of a variety of types of property. We list the main types in Table 5.2.

TABLE 5.2   Common types of hotel

Full-service hotels	Properties offering a range of services such as a restaurant, bar, lounge facilities, meeting space, banqueting facilities, porterage, leisure facilities and room service
Limited-service hotels	Properties offering room-only operations with few additional services
All-suite hotels	Properties offering guest units with one or more bedrooms and a separate living area
Boutique hotels	Distinct and unique small properties, often style-led and usually full service
Resort hotels	Properties in holiday destinations with extensive leisure amenities such as pools, spa facilities, sports facilities, restaurants
All-inclusive hotels	A resort hotel for which all services including food and beverages, entertainment and sport are paid for in advance and are not charged for separately
Aparthotels	A property offering hotel services with self-catering facilities in some or all rooms

Source: Adapted from Smith Travel Research (2011)

In addition to describing hotels by type, these can also be categorised according to:

Standard and grading: Many countries use a rating system such as stars or crowns to indicate hotel standard and quality, ranging from one to five. No formal body awards ratings above five stars, yet in the early twenty-first century self-designated seven star properties have opened such as the Burj Al Arab in Dubai and the Pangu in Beijing. There is no international system for categorising and classifying hotels. Hotel chains with properties in several countries often usually describe their properties as luxury, deluxe, premium or budget.

Brand: Hotels can be described as either branded or unbranded. Unbranded hotels are unique properties that operate using their own unique name and individual identity. Branded hotels operate using the identity and format of a nationally or internationally recognised hotel brand, for example Hyatt, Holiday

Inn or W Hotels. Once a brand has more than eight properties it is known as an 'affiliated brand' or 'affiliated chain' (STR Global, 2017). The brand does not necessarily own each property with which it is affiliated.

Hotel brands have grown significantly since the 1980s and many now have a global presence with thousands of hotel properties in the main business and leisure tourism destinations worldwide. Hotel brands design a common format, identity and image for their hotels that is reproduced in all properties that operate under the same name. Currently, many hotel companies are developing so-called 'lifestyle' brands to create a unique and stylish experience for their guests. Knowles (1996) suggests that branding is particularly advantageous for hotels for the following reasons:

- Hotel groups expanded in the 1970s and 1980s through the acquisition of existing properties of diverse standards and quality; it was therefore logical to categorise them into distinct types.

- Hotel classification and star ratings vary between countries and can confuse consumers; branding enables a clear indication of the standard and level of service provided.

- Brands communicate specific messages to customers about the standard and quality of the accommodation product; hotel brands tailor their product to the expectations of certain types of customers, for example the HUALUXE Hotels and Resorts brand is designed by InterContinental Hotels Group (IHG) specifically for Chinese guests (IHG, 2017a).

Table 5.3 presents the largest hotel companies in the world.

TABLE 5.3   Top five largest hotel companies in the world by room count December 2016

	Properties	Rooms	Pipeline properties (rooms)
Marriott International	5,929	1,158,107	2,045 (348,422)
Hilton Worldwide	4,856	790,659	1,774 (274,483)
Intercontinental Hotels Group	5,034	727,820	1,379 (221,281)
Wyndham Worldwide	7,699	675,036	N/A
Accor Hotels Group	3,897	528,369	737 (136,553)

Source: Statista (2017b)

These hotel companies operate a portfolio of hotel brands that appeal to distinct market segments. For example Accor Hotels has 24 brands including luxury brands (Pullman, Sofitel, Raffles), midrange brands (Mercure, Novotel) and economy brands (hotelF1, ibis). The company has recently developed or acquired a number of 'lifestyle' brands (Mama Shelter, JO&JOE, Onefinestay) (Accor, 2017).

Hotel ownership is complex because frequently hotels that operate using a brand may retain their independent ownership. For instance, the Accor Hotel Group only directly owns or leases 22 per cent of the properties that operate as one of its brands (Accor, 2017). Many hotels that operate under a brand name actually retain their independent ownership, but are affiliated to a brand for marketing purposes. This is usually achieved in one of four ways: by contracting the brand to manage the hotel; by leasing the hotel to the brand; by becoming a franchisee; or by membership of a marketing consortium (also known as a 'soft brand').

Management Contracts

Management contracts describe a long-term arrangement where an independent hotel owner contracts a brand to manage and operate the property. The property owner pays a percentage of their total revenue (usually 2–4 per cent of revenue) and a percentage of their profit (usually 5–10 per cent) to the brand, plus fees for centralised reservations, sales and marketing, loyalty programmes and training (Balyozyan et al., 2017). The brand usually provides the general manager and other senior managers but the hotel owner provides all other staff.

Lease Contracts

Lease contracts describe an arrangement where the brand owner leases the hotel building from the owner, usually for a minimum of 3 years, and pays rent, calculated as a proportion of revenue, as well as an annual fee. This model is quite popular in Europe, where 29 per cent of hotels operate in this way, compared to North America where only 2 per cent operate under lease contracts (Collins and Perret, 2015).

Franchises

Franchising is a business model that allows hotel owners (franchisees) to run their own businesses with the marketing support of a brand (the franchisor). The franchisor grants the right to the franchisee to operate using their name, design and image. In return, franchisees pay a fee to join the franchise, plus a proportion of their annual revenue and a percentage of their profit (Collins and Perret, 2015).

Franchising allows independent hotel operators to adopt a brand with a proven track record, established reputation and business strategy. Each franchised property must adopt the brand image, physical appearance and operational procedures of the franchisor, and usually subscribe to the franchise for a period of 15 to 25 years (Balyozyan et al., 2017). They are regularly inspected to ensure compliance with the brand's standards.

The snapshot below describes the franchises offered by Marriott International Inc.

SNAPSHOT 5.1

Marriott International Inc.

In September 2016, Marriott International acquired Starwood Hotels & Resorts and became the world's largest hotel company. In 2017, total properties numbered 6,000+ with 1.2 million rooms in 125 countries and territories, and 100+ million loyalty programme members. The company now offers 30 brands, described as 'Classic' or 'Distinctive':

CLASSIC

JW MARRIOTT · ST REGIS · THE RITZ-CARLTON

LUXURY

MARRIOTT · Sheraton

DELTA HOTELS · LONGER STAYS · Marriott EXECUTIVE APARTMENTS

UPPER UPSCALE

COURTYARD Marriott · FOUR POINTS BY SHERATON · SPRINGHILL SUITES MARRIOTT · LONGER STAYS · Residence Inn Marriott

UPSCALE

PROTEA HOTELS MARRIOTT · FAIRFIELD INN & SUITES Marriott · LONGER STAYS · TOWNEPLACE SUITES MARRIOTT

UPPER MIDSCALE

DISTINCTIVE

RITZ-CARLTON RESERVE · THE LUXURY COLLECTION · BVLGARI HOTELS & RESORTS

W HOTELS · EDITION

LUXURY

WESTIN HOTELS & RESORTS · Le MERIDIEN · AUTOGRAPH COLLECTION HOTELS

RENAISSANCE HOTELS · TRIBUTE PORTFOLIO · GAYLORD HOTELS

UPPER UPSCALE

AC HOTELS MARRIOTT · aloft HOTELS · LONGER STAYS · element BY WESTIN

UPSCALE

moxy HOTELS

UPPER MIDSCALE

Source: Courtesy of Marriott International Inc.

Marriott International operates a business model whereby it owns few of its properties; the majority operate as franchises (53 per cent) or management agreements (44 per cent).

(Continued)

Franchisee properties pay Marriott International various fees including:

- initial application fee
- marketing fees
- 4–6% of room revenue (royalty fees)
- central reservations system (CRS) fees.

In return, franchisees benefit from many advantages that they could not achieve alone, including:

- advice and guidance on brand choice, hotel development and design
- representation by Marriott International's CRS, worldwide sales offices and sales teams
- access to global travel agency network via Marriott's GDS codes
- participation in Marriott's contracts with OTAs
- promotion and reservations via Marriott International's websites and mobile apps, available in 12 languages
- participation in Marriott's loyalty programmes.

Source: Marriott International (2017)

Independent hotels that become franchisees are required to commit to a long-term contract and comply with very specific product requirements, for instance the layout, design, decoration and fitting out of rooms and public areas, food and beverage provision, staff uniforms and operating procedures. However, the owner retains management responsibility for the property unless they negotiate a contract with a third-party operator (TPO), a professional hotel management company, to manage and operate the business. So in practice, a hotel may be independently owned, operate as a franchisee and use the identity of a global brand, and be managed and operated by a TPO!

Independent hotels whose owners prefer to retain their individual style, or whose property cannot be easily adapted to match the product specification of franchisors, can obtain similar marketing benefits by joining a hotel consortium, also known as a 'soft brand'.

Hotel Consortia (Soft Brands)

A consortium can be defined as the collaboration of a number of organisations for a common purpose: 'a kind of mutual self-help organisation' (Knowles, 1996: 304). Hotel consortia, now more commonly known as soft brands, are voluntary collaborations between hotels; each contributes financially to a joint brand and marketing organisation, and achieves marketing benefits that they would be unable to achieve alone. Commonly this gives them access to global marketing, centralised reservations centres in major generating regions; a brand website featuring all member properties, inclusion in the brand's loyalty programme; a sales team who will build relationships with travel agencies, tour and MICE (meetings, incentives, conferences and events) operators, and corporate customers; attendance at travel trade exhibitions promoting the brand; and opportunities to sell via travel agencies worldwide through a GDS presence (Knowles, 1996).

Member hotels benefit from joint purchasing opportunities and access to resources that would be outside their remit individually. Hotel consortia often provide management services too, such as purchasing, HR and training. Consortia provide similar benefits as franchises but allow their hotels to define and deliver their own unique product offer and retain their individuality: 'Consortia usually make an asset out of the individuality of their member hotels' (Knowles, 1996: 305). Examples of long-standing hotel consortia include Relais and Châteaux, Best Western International, and Leading Hotels of the World. Interestingly, the major hotel brands are also now entering this arena by developing soft brands which offer a collection of unique properties: Unbound by Hyatt, Tapestry by Hilton, Autograph by Marriott; these collections offer unique properties that conform to brand service standards but offer diverse and individual facilities and services.

Full service hotels provide venues for meetings and events and these are a very significant part of the tourism supply in destinations, particularly for business tourism. Venues provide facilities for conferences, conventions, meetings, exhibitions and events, and some destinations seek to attract these forms of tourism by building stand-alone, non-residential venues.

NON-RESIDENTIAL VENUES

Non-residential venues are dedicated convention and exhibition centres, exhibition halls, theatres, arenas and stadia that are designed to hold large numbers of people. They provide space for conferences, conventions, exhibitions, meetings and events, concerts, stage shows, product launches, sports and team-building events. Venues are very important suppliers for business tourism, in particular through hosting conventions and exhibitions. They also host events for the public, which may also attract leisure tourists to a destination (Davidson and Rogers, 2006).

The construction and operation of a large venue are capital intensive, and the public sector is often involved in their financing. In many destinations, large venues are owned by the local, regional or national government, and the location of the venue is often selected to regenerate the immediate vicinity and act as a catalyst to attract further investment and development for the benefit of the local economy and community.

There have been three stages to the evolution of venue ownership and management:

1. The first stage was the development of stand-alone dedicated centres that were built and operated under public ownership and management.

2. The second stage required a reduction of state involvement in the management and operation of venues through the development of a model of public ownership and private management; in this situation, state-owned venues are managed and operated by experienced and successful private venue management companies under a management contract.

3. The most recent evolution has seen a move away from standalone venues to developments that integrate venues with hotel, retail or casino developments; the state sells the land surrounding the venue to the private sector in order to finance the construction of the venue, and often leases the venue to a private operator in long-term public–private partnerships (Donaghy, 2007). For example, the STAPLES Centre at L.A. LIVE, London's O2 Arena, Dubai Arena, Oman

Convention & Exhibition Centre, Cairns and Kuala Lumpur Convention Centres, among several more theatres, stadia and convention centres, are managed on a long-term lease and operated by one multinational venue operator: AEG or one of its subsidiaries (AEG Ogden, 2017).

The visual appeal of a venue is becoming increasingly important and recently built venues will often use an iconic design or innovative materials. In addition, venues need to offer a flexible, multi-purpose space that can be used in a variety of ways for different types of event, provide the latest audio-visual (AV) equipment and lighting, and be sound-proof. Venues will usually have a number of rooms for smaller break-out sessions, banqueting, business centres, offices and administration space (McCabe et al., 2000).

The snapshot below presents the largest exhibition centre in the world.

SNAPSHOT 5.2

Hannover Fairgrounds/Exhibition Grounds

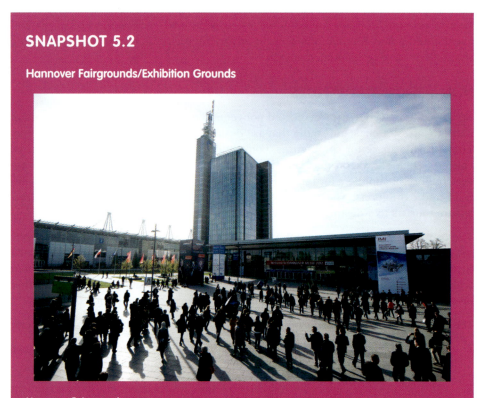

Hannover Fairgrounds

Source: Deutsche Messe (n.d.)

Hannover Fairgrounds, Germany, has been a top exhibition venue for more than 60 years. Following World War II, the British military government's economic strategy focused on building up Germany's exports as a route out of the economic devastation of the war. An exhibition was needed to showcase the potential of Germany's manufacturing. The most appropriate site was a former aircraft factory; the first export exhibition was held in an aircraft hangar. Since then the site has been developed extensively with innovative, architecturally distinctive, purpose-built exhibition and conference facilities. The venue is now named Deutsche Messe and is jointly owned by the State of Lower Saxony, the City of Hannover, and Greater Hannover.

Today, Hannover Fairgrounds is the largest exhibition venue in the world. It offers 466,000 m² of indoor space in 26 halls and pavilions, a Convention Center with 35 function rooms, and park-like areas in 58,000m² of outdoor space. The site can operate up to four mid-sized events simultaneously – with their own entrances, visitor navigation systems and shuttle services.

Deutsche Messe also manages and operates two convention centres in Asia: Shanghai New International Expo Centre and Indonesia Convention Exhibition (ICE).

Source: Deutsche Messe (n.d.)

Accommodation and non-residential venue suppliers are of key importance to the tourism offer of a destination. To attract tourists, however, destinations must be accessible. Transport suppliers provide the necessary links between tourist-generating regions and destinations.

TRANSPORT SUPPLIERS

In Chapter 3 we identified the main modes of tourist transport as land, sea and air, and explained that within each mode were a variety of types of transport. Some of these may be privately owned, like the private car or private jet, and some of these may be a tourist attraction rather than a method of transport, for example hot-air balloon flights. In this section we focus on the transport suppliers that enable tourists to travel to destinations, or within destinations, and that are operated along commercial principles, namely high-speed rail services, scheduled and chartered coach services, ferries, and scheduled and chartered airlines. We consider the main differences between types of service and the impact of regulatory systems on the operations of tourist transport suppliers. Table 5.4 identifies the main types of tourist transport.

There are two key concepts that influence both scheduled and charter transport operators: load factor and yield.

LOAD FACTOR AND YIELD

The term 'passenger' or 'seat load factor' is used in the transport sector to measure sales performance. It refers to the proportion of seats sold as a percentage of the seats available on a departure. For example, if 25 seats of a total capacity of 50 are occupied on a ferry, coach, train or plane departure, the load factor is 50 per cent. Operators seek to achieve as high a load factor as possible but most are unable to achieve 100 per cent load factors on a regular basis. In the airline industry in 2016, for example, average annual load factors ranged between 83.5 per cent in North America and 74.7 per cent in the Middle East (IATA, 2017). Some transport operators calculate seat prices based on the minimum load factor required in order to cover their costs, known as the 'break-even load factor'. However, the number of seats sold is less important than the price paid by passengers for each seat – known as 'yield'.

TABLE 5.4   **Main types of tourist transport**

High-speed rail services: High-speed train networks connect major urban centres. The first was introduced in Japan in 1964 on the Tokyo–Osaka route, known as the Shinkansen or Bullet Train (Arduin and Ni, 2005), and more countries have subsequently revitalised their railways by investing heavily in rail infrastructure and high-speed trains; for instance Trains a Grand Vitesse (TGV) in France, Intercity Express (ICE) in Germany, Eurostar between London, Paris and Brussels, Pendolino trains in Italy, Alto Velocidad Espana (AVE) in Spain, and High Speed Railway (HSR) bullet trains in China, all of these travelling at speeds of between 280 and 350kph.

Coach services: Technological developments have led to the development of larger and more comfortable coaches with a capacity for up to 79 passengers, a sleeping berth for the second driver, air-conditioning, on-board washroom facilities and refreshments, and WiFi, making travel by road faster and more comfortable, and through a higher capacity, cheaper per passenger. Coach services can be either scheduled or chartered:

- *Scheduled coach services*: These provide a network of domestic or international services that are operated to a published timetable, on which seats are available for purchase by the public. For example, Eurolines provides international services across Europe, from Morocco to Finland, and Greyhound operates domestic routes in the UK, Australia and Canada, as well as the USA.

- *Chartered coach services*: These are contracted by a third party, such as a tour operator or the organiser of a group trip, to provide specific journeys. The third party is responsible for filling the seats and the service is not available for sale to the public. Chartered coaches are used extensively for group tours by road lasting several weeks and led by a professional tour manager, as well as for short sightseeing tours within destinations and for transfer services between arrival gateways like airports, ports and railways, to city centres, resorts or specific hotels.

Ferries: Ferries provide services by sea connecting two port destinations on domestic or international routes. Ferries may be passenger only or passenger and vehicle services that can accommodate cars and coaches as well as trucks. The largest passenger ferries are known as superferries, for instance Irish Ferries' *Ulysses* can carry up to 2,000 passengers and crew plus 1,342 cars. The fastest ferries have smaller capacities (i.e. the *Stena Voyager* with 1,500 passengers and 360 cars) but can travel at twice the speed of conventional ferries, at up to 40 knots.

Airlines: Airlines provide flights between airports on domestic or international routes. Airline services are either chartered or scheduled:

- *Charter air services*: Aircraft are contracted by third parties to operate specific routes for specific groups of tourists. For example, tour operators charter aircraft to transport their inclusive tour customers and small, private aircraft can be chartered for luxury business or leisure travel. Charter flight schedules are not published and tickets are not usually available to the general public for sale.

- *Scheduled air services*: These operate to a published timetable and seats are available for purchase by the public, either directly or through travel agencies. There are three types of scheduled airlines: full service, low cost and all business class.

- *Scheduled full service airlines (FSA)*: These operate a comprehensive route network, usually with international and intercontinental services, which follow a published timetable and on which seats are available for purchase by the public. Aircraft are usually configured with two or three classes of cabin – economy, business and first – and seats are usually sold through travel agencies as well as directly. Some airlines (Etihad) offer suites or apartments on certain long-haul routes. Some US airlines have recently added a new basic economy class in order to compete with low-cost airlines. The top 10 airlines by passenger-kilometres flown on international and domestic routes in 2016 are American Airlines, Delta, United Airlines, Emirates, China Southern, South West Airlines, Lufthansa, British Airways, Air France and Ryanair (IATA, 2016).

- *Scheduled low-cost airlines (LCAs)*: These offer a basic no-frills product on domestic or short-haul international routes, although some now also offer long-haul routes (e.g. Norwegian and Level). LCAs often use less popular (secondary) airports and prices do not include in-flight catering or entertainment. Cabins are usually configured as economy class only, and many LCAs only sell direct, although some do now sell through travel agencies too. Southwest Airlines, Ryanair and Easyjet are the largest LCAs by traffic volume (Dunn, 2016). Spirit is a new breed of LCA – a US ultra low-cost airline that promises the lowest fares available.

- *Scheduled all-business class airlines*: These offer direct services on a limited number of routes from Europe to the USA. The cabin is configured as all business class, and offers high standards of comfort and service. A notable example is La Compagnie (Paris/New York). Several all-business class airlines have failed to make a commercial success and closed.

Yield is the term used to describe the average revenue received per passenger kilometre, known in the airline industry as revenue per passenger kilometre (RPK). Transport operators seek to achieve as high a yield as possible; airlines use a complex process of real-time yield management to determine prices and calculate the price for each seat. However, transport operators are not always free to determine the prices they sell their seats at because of regulations that govern their activities.

REGULATION OF TOURIST TRANSPORT SUPPLIERS

The term 'regulation' refers to the framework of laws and rules that affect how transport suppliers operate. Governments regulate the transport sector in order to:

- Enforce minimum standards of safety for passengers and the communities on the routes served, for instance laws determine maximum working hours, qualifications, training and licensing requirements, security procedures at terminals and on board, and the performance and maintenance procedures of vehicles and vessels.

- Influence the level of competition between operators providing specific transport services by regulating the economic conditions that they operate under. Economic regulation may prevent transport operators from setting up new routes, adding departures onto existing routes or adjusting their prices in response to demand. The rail, sea, bus and aviation sectors have a history of government regulation of routes, ownership of operators, control over the number of operators on routes, and controls over frequency of departures and even the prices that can be charged.

Traditionally, the right to operate international services was granted by the government of each state on the route, and therefore the number of transport suppliers operating an international route is often a reflection of government attitudes to the free market. The international passenger aviation industry is a good example of complex economic regulation.

In civil aviation, individual governments traditionally negotiated international air routes over, to and from their territory in a system of bi-lateral agreements that specified the freedoms of the air granted to one or more airlines from each country. The Freedoms of the Air, listed in Table 5.5, were drawn up at the Chicago Convention in 1944. The details of the bilateral agreement between two countries affect the development of routes, the number of airlines offering services on the route, the frequency of departures and therefore the number of seats available, and the degree of price competition between carriers.

Some governments restrict the levels of competition faced by their state-owned national carrier, and usually only grant a maximum of the first four freedoms to treaty partners, specifying which airports can be served, and may specify the frequency and capacity of flights, which airlines can operate on the routes, and even that governments must approve of the fares to be charged. For instance the Canada/India bilateral agreement specifies that Air Canada, Air India and Jet Airways can operate direct routes between the two countries, that each side can operate two routes with 2,100 seats per week on the first route and two frequencies per week on the second route; each treaty party can refuse to agree to fare rises or reductions (Government of Canada, 2011).

More liberal bilateral agreements grant more freedoms to each partner and allow each partner's airlines to respond to market forces with no controls over frequency,

TABLE 5.5   Freedoms of the air

First Freedom of the Air	
The right to fly over territory, granted by State A to scheduled international air services of State B.	Botswana allowing scheduled international airlines of South Africa to fly over its territory.
Second Freedom of the Air	
The right to land in territory, granted by State A to scheduled international air services of State B.	Botswana allowing scheduled international airlines of South Africa to land for non-traffic purposes e.g. refuelling.
Third Freedom of The Air	
The right to transport revenue traffic originating in State B, granted by State A to scheduled international air services of State B.	Japan allowing scheduled international airlines of China to sell tickets on Beijing-Tokyo flights.
Fourth Freedom of The Air	
The right to transport revenue traffic originating in State A, granted by State A to scheduled international services of State B.	Japan allowing scheduled international airlines of China to sell tickets on Tokyo-Beijing flights.
Fifth Freedom of The Air	
The right granted by State A to scheduled international airlines of State B to transport revenue traffic from a third state (C) to and from State A.	The UK allowing scheduled international airlines of New Zealand to sell Los Angeles-London tickets on a flight originating in Auckland. The USA also needs to agree to this.
Supplementary rights *The following 'freedoms' have not been officially recognized by international treaty.*	
Sixth Freedom of The Air	
The right of a scheduled international airline to carry revenue traffic via its home state on routes between two other states.	The UK and India allowing scheduled international airlines of Bahrain to sell tickets between London and Delhi, via Bahrain.
Seventh Freedom of The Air	
The right granted by State A to scheduled international airlines of State B to transport revenue traffic on routes between State A and any third state with no inclusion of territory in State B.	France and China allowing scheduled international airlines of Australia to sell tickets between Paris and Beijing on flights that do not connect with Australia.
Eighth Freedom of The Air (also known as Cabotage rights) The right granted by State A to scheduled international airlines of State B to carry revenue traffic between two points in State A on a service originating or terminating in the home territory of the airline.	Argentina allowing scheduled international airlines of Canada to sell tickets from Mendoza to Buenos Aires on flights originating in Toronto.
Ninth Freedom of The Air (known as stand alone cabotage) The right granted by State A to scheduled international airlines of State B to operate domestic routes entirely within the territory of State A.	Australia allowing scheduled international airlines of Russia to operate flights between Perth and Sydney.

Source: Adapted from ICAO 2004 Manual on the Regulation of International Air Transport (Doc 9626, Part 4)

capacity or prices. Some parts of the world now have 'open skies' aviation policies whereby any airline based in each signatory country is able to operate any route between the territories of each signatory.

Levels of economic regulation vary between individual countries and between transport sectors within each country. Many Western economies since the late 1970s/early 1980s have sought to reduce levels of economic regulation, state ownership and subsidy, and allow market forces to determine routes, the number of operators, frequencies, capacities and prices. At a domestic level this is known as 'deregulation' and can be achieved through government legislation. At an international level the process is known as 'liberalisation' and is a slow and fragmented process that requires a re-negotiation of existing agreements with all other governments on international routes.

The removal or reduction of economic regulation within the transport sector is often linked to specific benefits for passengers and for tourism. The ability of new entrants to operate routes, of new routes to be set up, for demand to determine the frequency of departures, and for operators to compete on price often results in greater choice, more convenience and lower prices for passengers. For tourism, these improvements are very significant as they stimulate the demand for existing and new destinations.

Arguably the deregulation and liberalisation of civil aviation has had the most significant impact on tourism. Until 1978, all civil aviation was subject to strict economic regulation on a national and international basis. However, a slow process of liberalisation started in 1978 with the US Airline Deregulation Act, the impacts of which have promoted deregulation in other parts of the world, and created new opportunities for airlines (Hanlon, 2007).

The case study below describes the process and impacts of liberalisation of passenger aviation.

CASE STUDY 5.1

Liberalisation in International Civil Aviation

The US's Airline Deregulation Act of 1978 removed capacity, frequency and price controls on inter-state routes, with spectacular results: airlines operating interstate routes increased from 36 to over 120 by 1985; market domination by the top five carriers reduced; fares fell; and with increased efficiencies, costs also fell, increasing airline profitability and giving travellers more choice and lower fares (Hanlon, 1996).

The US sought similar impacts on international routes by renegotiating bilateral agreements with other governments. Country by country, US bilaterals were renegotiated, removing fare and capacity controls, and allowing more than one airline from each country to operate the route (multiple designation): with the UK (1977), the Netherlands, Germany and Belgium (1978), and between 1978–1980 with Singapore, Thailand, Korea and the Philippines, and then with Malaysia (1985) and Australia (1989) (Doganis, 1991).

(Continued)

Passengers boarding low-cost airline Ryanair

Source: Jade O'Brien

Some of these countries began to liberalise their bilaterals with other countries: Canada/West Germany (1982), UK/the Netherlands (1984), Singapore/the UK (1989).

The impacts of these renegotiated treaties were dramatic. On North Atlantic routes, demand grew by 23.4 per cent in 1978, and by 15.5 per cent in 1979, and by the mid-1980s airlines operating services had increased from three to 12; load factors increased from an average of below 60 per cent between 1960 and 1975, to 67.4 per cent by 1979 (Doganis, 1991). However, price wars on routes with new entrants threatened airline profitability; between 1979 and 1982, most US airlines made losses on the North Atlantic routes and many airlines collapsed (Doganis, 1991). Since 1992 the US has pursued Open Skies agreements with other countries and in 2017 over 100 of these existed, either bi-laterally (US–St Vincent and Grenadines, April 2017) or multi-laterally (multi-lateral agreement on the liberalisation of international air transportation, or MALITAT) in 2001 with New Zealand, Singapore, Brunei, Chile, Samoa, Tongo, Mongolia) (US Department of State, 2017a).

Within Europe, liberalisation began with deregulation in the UK and Netherlands in the 1980s and 1990s. The 1997 EU-wide Three Packages legislation established the European Common Aviation Area (ECAA), outlawed government subsidies to airlines, and granted all eight freedoms of the air to all ECAA registered airlines, stimulating an expansion of the LCA sector, especially easyJet and Ryanair (Graham, 2009). However, some formerly stable, state-owned airlines suffered from financial instability (Alitalia, Air France), and some collapsed (Swissair). Since 2006, bilaterals between ECAA and non-EU countries have been negotiated; the 2007 Open Skies agreement between the USA and the EU allows market forces to determine routes, frequencies, capacities and prices, allowing US and EU airlines to operate to any airport in either territory. EU-type regional agreements, some retaining some restrictions, have been introduced within trading blocs around the world including CARICOM in 2003 and ASEAN in 2015.

By the early twenty-first century, domestic airline regulation had reduced in most countries (Forsyth, 2008), although some states do still restrict the number of airlines and retain state ownership. Liberalisation of international routes varies: the USA, Singapore,

New Zealand, United Arab Emirates and Chile have liberal attitudes to aviation, but Japan, China, the Philippines, African and South American nations are more restrictive. The remaining countries (Australia, Canada, ECAA and Southeast Asian states) liberalise routes on a case-by-case basis if the advantages are clear, for example stimulating inbound tourism.

Reflective Questions

1. Select three routes that connect your home country by air to destinations around the world. Find out how many airlines operate each route and identify the freedoms of the air that each airline is operating under.

2. Select three domestic air routes within a country of your choice. How many airlines operate each route and in which country is each airline registered?

Accommodation, non-residential venues and transport suppliers provide important supporting roles for tourism in a destination: they allow a visitor to come to the destination and spend time there. The fact that tourists will visit one destination and not another, however, is closely linked to its perceived attractiveness, and this aspect is usually primarily influenced by a fourth type of supplier: visitor attractions.

VISITOR ATTRACTIONS

The term 'visitor attraction' describes a site that is the focus of recreational activity by tourists and excursionists, and may also be used by the host population of a destination (Wanhill, 2008). There is a diverse range of types of visitor attraction and a huge variety of suppliers, making the study of visitor attractions quite complex. Middleton et al. (2009) refer to 'managed visitor attractions', which are resources that have been formally designated as permanent sites 'for the enjoyment, entertainment and education of the visiting public' (2009: 409). They identify 10 different types of managed attraction:

1. *Ancient monuments*: Protected and preserved sites such as fortifications, burial mounds and buildings; for example the Pyramids in Egypt, Stonehenge in England, Machu Pichu in Peru, the Great Wall of China.

2. *Historic buildings*: Also known as 'heritage sites' – castles, houses, palaces, cathedrals, churches, town centres, villages.

3. *Designated natural areas, parks and gardens*: National parks, country parks, long-distance paths, gardens, managed beaches. Often these are owned by the state but managed by a designated agency, for example the National Park Authority or local government.

4. *Theme parks*: Amusement and leisure sites that are based on a particular brand, character, historic period or site. Major theme park suppliers are The Walt Disney Company, SeaWorld Parks & Entertainment, Universal Parks & Resorts.

5. *Wildlife attractions*: Zoos, aquaria, aviaries, wildfowl parks, game parks and safaris, farms.

6. *Museums*: Sites housing significant collections. Museum content may be subject-specific (science, natural history, transport), site specific (The Forbidden City in Beijing, or the Ironbridge Gorge in England); or area-based (national, regional or local collections).

7. *Art galleries*: Galleries with collections built up over many decades. Includes the new wave of modern art galleries in striking new buildings, for example the Guggenheim in Bilbao, Spain. Often state-owned and funded.

8. *Industrial archaeology sites*: Sites and structures identified with specific industrial and manufacturing processes, such as mining, textiles, railways, from the period post-1750.

9. *Themed retail sites*: Speciality retail centres, often located in historic buildings or in purpose-built sites. The largest in the world include The Dubai Mall, attracting over 80 million visitors in 2014 (The Dubai Mall, 2017), New South China Mall in Dongguan, Golden Resources Mall in Beijing and SM City North EDSA in Quezon City, Philippines.

10. *Amusement and leisure parks*: Parks constructed primarily for 'white knuckle' rides (e.g. rollercoasters) and associated stalls and amusements. Major suppliers are the Merlin Entertainments Group, Six Flags Entertainment Corporation and Cedar Fair Entertainment Company.

(Adapted from Middleton et al., 2009: 410)

Visitor attractions are possibly the most important element of the tourism system because they draw tourists to a destination, and stimulate demand for transport, accommodation and other suppliers. Boniface and Cooper (2009: 40) describe attractions as '… the *raison d'être* for tourism; they generate the visit, give rise to excursion circuits and create an industry of their own.'

The visitor attractions sector is polarised between a small number of attractions that draw in over one million visitors a year, and thousands of small attractions that bring in fewer than 30,000 visitors a year and with less than £100,000 in visitor revenue (Middleton et al., 2009). The management and operational challenges faced by different types of attraction, and different sizes of attraction, can vary significantly, and it is therefore useful to categorise attractions that share similar characteristics.

A common approach to categorising attractions is to distinguish between those that are natural and those that are built:

Natural attractions include beaches, forests, woodland, mountains and lakes, and although they may not provide any built services or charge admission, these still need to be managed and to employ staff to maintain the site, particularly in those that attract large numbers of visitors. Management of natural attractions is often concerned with conserving or protecting the site and with managing visitors effectively to reduce environmental pressure (Fyall et al., 2008).

Built attractions include historic properties, museums and galleries, farms, gardens, parks, workplaces, leisure parks and wildlife attractions. Built attractions usually focus on increasing visitor spend by attempting to attract demand to match their capacity, and by developing other revenue sources on site to encourage visitors to spend more, for example through food and beverage facilities and souvenir shops. Built attractions can be further sub-divided into those that have been purpose-built as a visitor attraction and those that were originally built for an entirely different purpose.

Purpose-built attractions include theme parks, water parks, zoos, aquaria, some museums and art galleries. Purpose-built attractions are designed carefully with a consideration of the most desirable and profitable location and capacity, the most effective location of on-site services such as ticket offices and restrooms, and the provision of revenue opportunities such as food and beverage facilities and shops.

Built attractions whose original purpose was not related to tourism include temples, cathedrals, palaces, churches, gardens, farms and workplaces. Some of these may have intentionally developed into visitor attractions as a way of attracting new sources of revenue, while others may be reluctant tourism suppliers. In many cases, these non-purpose built attractions still fulfill their original purpose but have had to adapt in order to provide visitor services as well. Provision must be made for visitors in terms of charging policy, the admissions process, managing visitor behaviour to avoid damage or inappropriate behaviour, control over access to the site, and providing information within the attraction unobtrusively. Some such attractions also exploit revenue opportunities by selling guidebooks or souvenirs on site.

While it can be useful to classify attractions as natural or built, there are several other characteristics that can also be used to differentiate between them. Leask (2008) illustrates the multiple dimensions by which attractions can be classified, as Figure 5.1 illustrates.

The second main approach to classifying attractions is by charging policy; that is, whether admission is free or paid for by the visitor. Admission charging policies are usually a reflection of the management's objectives. Leslie (2001) identifies the main objectives of visitor attractions as:

- education and stewardship
- conservation and preservation
- profit.

FIGURE 5.1   Further dimensions of visitor attractions

Source: adapted from Leask in Fyall et al. (2008).

Attractions whose objective is to safeguard their contents for the benefit and education of the general public will usually charge low entrance fees in order to encourage attendance. For example, since 2001 all UK museums and art galleries that house national collections have charged no admission fee, in order to implement their objective of providing access to the widest possible public.

Attractions whose objective is to conserve and preserve their contents may use admission fees to raise funds to finance preservation, and may also charge high fees to reduce the number of visitors in order to prevent damage to the resource. For example, tourists to the Galapagos Islands, an Ecuadorian national park and World Heritage Site, must pay an entry tax: the amount varies depending on the age and nationality of the visitor, but most international tourists from outside the Mercosur nations aged 12+ pay US$100 each (UNESCO, 2017a).

Profit-seeking attractions charge entrance fees to cover their costs and to generate a return on investment. Many purpose-built attractions, particularly those whose purpose is to entertain, are often, though not always, commercially owned and operated and are therefore required to generate profits. For example, Disney's theme parks and resorts revenue reached almost $17 billion in 2016 (The Walt Disney Company, 2017).

Charging policies are often a reflection of the type of ownership and funding. The model identifies four types of ownership within the visitor attractions sector – public, private, voluntary and charity – and proposes that each operates differently in terms of staffing, priorities, pricing, visitor access and financial resources. We consider ownership in more detail later in this chapter, in relation to all tourism suppliers.

The operating environment of a visitor attraction is influenced by the market that it attracts, for instance whether visitors are mainly local, regional, national or international, or a combination of all of these. The nature of the product, the need to change and update the product regularly, prices that can be charged, the feasibility of additional revenue sources on site, and the way in which information is provided to visitors will vary depending on the source markets attracted (Leask, 2008).

The types of attraction that we have discussed thus far are permanent attractions; that is, they are intended to exist in the long-term. In tourism, there are also a variety of temporary attractions that will have been created specifically for a short period of time – hours, days, weeks or months – that are known as 'events'. Events are a recognised form of tourist attraction.

EVENTS

An event is a non-permanent form of attraction. Events are described as 'an organised occasion such as meeting, convention, exhibition, special event, gala dinner' (Convention Industry Council, 2003, in Bowdin et al., 2006: 14). Getz (2007) stresses that the key principle of events is their temporary and unique nature, and describes events as planned or unplanned activities. Planned events are scheduled, designed and controlled by accountable producers and managers in order to achieve specific outcomes which may be personal, political, cultural, social or economic; unplanned events are spontaneous and unpredictable (i.e. a political demonstration) and are not managed or controlled by a central accountable body. In this section we focus on planned events that are intended to attract tourists to, or encourage them to stay longer in, a destination, or to change the image of a destination.

Events management has become an important field of study in its own right, but it overlaps with tourism when an event is staged that draws in leisure, VFR or business tourists. In this section we consider different types of planned events and their suppliers.

The range of types of events is very broad. Getz and Page (2016) developed a typology of planned events as shown in Figure 5.2.

Type of planned event	Examples
Cultural events	Festivals, commemorations, carnivals, religious events
Business events	MICE, product launches & promotions
Arts and entertainment events	Music, art, and performance activities
Sport and recreation events	Sporting festivals, matches, competitions
Political and state	Displays of power – processions, state visits, military displays
Private functions	Weddings, funerals, parties, personal celebrations

FIGURE 5.2   Typology of planned events

Source: Adapted from Getz (2016)

Further approaches to describing events consider their size or function. Bowdin et al. (2006) differentiate between local/community events and major events:

Community events: Local or community events are organised, usually by volunteers, for local audiences and are staged in public venues such as schools, streets, sports centres and parks. Bowdin et al. (2006) stress the community benefits of local events: for example community pride, participation in sports or arts activities, exposure to new ideas or experiences, and appreciation of diversity and tolerance. Local governments often support local events as part of their community and cultural development strategies, and don't attract tourists in significant numbers unless these become so popular that they evolve into a major event, as the Rio Carnival in Brazil has done.

Major events: These attract large audiences, media attention and economic benefits through visitor spending and a greater awareness of the destination.

Getz and Page (2016) provide definitions for different event types. The main ones are:

Hallmark events: These are staged once or recur at regular intervals and are intrinsically linked to the destination in which they are staged, for example the Munich Oktoberfest, the Rio Carnival and the Glastonbury Festival. Hallmark events form part of the destination's image, brand and identity.

Iconic events: These describe events that have a strong appeal on their own because of their meaning, and can include hallmark events such as the London Marathon, as well as events that could be held successfully anywhere like the FIFA World Cup or the NFL Superbowl.

Premier/prestige events: These are the top event in the activity that they represent and may be staged in the same place or in different locations. Examples include the FIFA World Cup Finals, the NFL Superbowl, the IAAF World Championships or the World Expo.

Mega events: These are events that attract 'extraordinarily high levels of tourism, media coverage, prestige or economic impact for the host community, venue or organisation' (Getz, 2007: 25). Mega events might be staged once or repeated in different destinations, and attract large audiences and media attention, prestige and economic impact. Global events such as the Olympics, the FIFA World Cup Finals and World Expos are usually described as mega events, but Getz (2007) stresses that these can also include smaller events that have a significant impact on the image of the host destination, such as a political conference or a religious or community festival.

Corporate events: These are events produced for a corporation, for example product launches, meetings, conferences, trade exhibitions and grand openings.

SNAPSHOT 5.3

Coachella Valley Music and Arts Festival

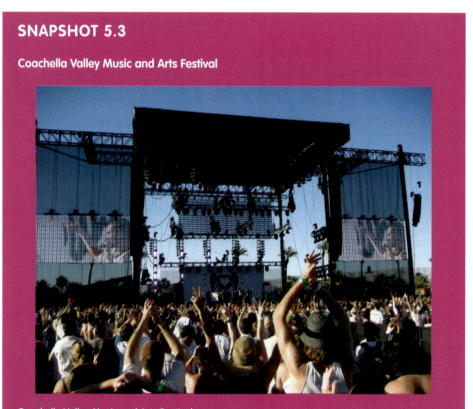

Coachella Valley Music and Arts Festival

Source: Greg Thomas

The small city of Indio, California, hosts one of the largest and best-known music festivals – the Coachella Valley Music and Arts Festival.

Coachella has been staged since 1999 by Goldenvoice. However, its origins can be linked to 1993 when the band Pearl Jam sought venues that weren't controlled by Ticketmaster, in protest at the high service charges added to ticket sales. Goldenvoice staged one of their gigs at the Empire Polo Club in Indio, giving the music entrepreneur Paul Tollett, who worked for Goldenvoice, the idea of hosting a festival in the expansive grounds (Seabrook, 2017).

The first Coachella Festival was held in October 1999 over two days, and, except in 2000, has returned every year beginning in April 2001 as a single-day event. In 2001, AEG bought Goldenvoice, and in 2004 bought 50 per cent of Coachella. In 2002, Coachella reverted to a two-day event, increased to three days in 2007, and in 2012 a second weekend was added; the line-up each weekend is identical (Seabrook, 2017). The festival now attracts 250,000 visitors (City of Indio, 2017).

Events can provide a tourism legacy, which will live on for years after the event has been staged (Robinson et al., 2010). Many of today's major permanent tourist attractions were originally built for events that took place many decades ago. The Eiffel Tower, for example, is one of the most iconic tourist attractions in Europe: the structure was built for the World Expo in Paris in 1889. The Olympic Park in Munich is also a key tourist attraction for the city, and was built for the Summer Olympic Games in 1972.

One type of tourism supplier that combines the characteristics of transport, accommodation and visitor attraction criteria is the cruise sector, which we explore in the following section.

THE CRUISE SECTOR

The cruise sector has experienced rapid growth in demand since the 1980s as a result of technological and operating developments that have increased the capacity of ships, resulting in lower unit costs per passenger.

Until the 1980s, cruising mainly attracted wealthy retired customers because of long cruise durations and high prices. Technological and operating advances have created larger, faster ships, increasing capacity so that the unit cost of each passenger became lower, making cruises affordable to more markets. In 1998 the largest cruise ship ever was launched, Princess Cruises' *Grand Princess*, with capacity for 2,600 passengers. However, by 2008 the capacity on new ships had doubled to over 5,000 passengers; 2016 saw the launch of the world's largest cruise ship, Royal Caribbean International's (RCI) *Harmony of the Seas*, which carries 6,780 passengers and 2,100 crew (RCI, 2017).

These megaships are floating cities, with shopping malls, theatres, ice-rinks, water parks and cinemas, and are almost destinations in their own right – they provide transport, accommodation and attractions together in one product. Their size dictates their itineraries as they cannot sail with passengers in unpredictable waters, so remain within the Caribbean and Mediterranean. They also require specific port facilities to accommodate such large vessels and volumes of passengers, and to process the volume of waste generated on board.

In the late twentieth century, cruise tourism experienced rapid growth in demand, stimulated by lower prices, and the development of cruise products to appeal to a range of market segments, for instance families, singles and young couples, and, in northern Europe, the sale of cruises by tour operators. This growth has continued; according to Cruise Lines International Association (2016), 24.7 million people took an ocean cruise in 2016, compared to 15.8 million in 2007. In 2017, 26 new ocean, river and speciality cruise ships are expected to come into service, with 71 more by 2026.

The cruise industry is dominated by four large shipping companies that own several brands:

Carnival Corporation: Carnival Cruise Line, Fathom, Holland America Line, Princess Cruises, Seabourn Cruise Line, P&O Cruises, Cunard, AIDA Cruises, Costa Cruises.

Royal Caribbean Cruises Ltd: Royal Caribbean International (RCI), Celebrity Cruises, TUI Cruises, Pullmantur Cruises, Azamara Club Cruises, SkySea Cruise Line.

Genting Hong Kong: Star Cruises, Dream Cruises, Crystal Cruises.

Norwegian Cruise Line Holdings Ltd: Norwegian Cruise Line, Oceania Cruises, Regent Seven Seas Cruises.

We now finish the discussion of each tourism sector by explaining sharing economy tourism supply.

SHARING ECONOMY TOURISM SUPPLIERS

The sharing economy, also known as the collaborative or P2P economy, has become a powerful force in some destinations since the first decade of the twenty-first century. Sharing economy platforms enable owners to promote their personal property, for example their home or a room in their home, or their car, private jet or yacht, or to offer services such as guided tours, meals in their homes or other activities, to tourists visiting the destination. The property or services may be offered free of charge, for example CouchSurfing, on mutual exchange, for instance Love Home Swap, or for sale, for example Turo (formerly RelayRides), Catch-A-Ride, VizEat, Withlocals and Airbnb. Some sharing economy accommodation providers, such as onefinestay and UnderTheDoormat, organise stays in local homes that are fully serviced; that is, the company organises housekeeping, linen, toiletries and a concierge service. We discuss the sharing economy throughout this book and introduce it in more detail in Chapter 1.

The rapid growth of the sharing economy in some destinations, particularly in cities, has created new forms of competition for the traditional tourism suppliers, especially the hotel sector. Sharing economy accommodation providers are not subject to the same regulations as hotels, for instance fire or food safety regulations, in many destinations are not inspected or registered, and do not pay for membership to their local destination marketing organisation. Global hotel brands are investing hundreds of millions of dollars to respond to the impacts of sharing economy accommodation (Ahmed, 2017) including:

- Moving away from standardised design of properties and rooms to create a more relaxed and unique experience that conveys the atmosphere of the destination, provides entertainment and opportunities for guests to interact in informal spaces, and creates the feel of an urban refuge; for instance Accor's new hotel brands JO&JOE, Mama Shelter and 25hours (Accor Hotels Group, 2017).
- Acquiring sharing economy platforms to include as part of their portfolio; for example in 2016, Accor bought onefinestay, and in 2017, bought Travel Keys and Squarebreak (Ahmed, 2017).

The full impact of sharing economy tourism suppliers has yet to be felt in full. At the time of writing, the media have reported rumours of Airbnb competing more directly with hotels by launching a premium brand that offers inspected and serviced luxury properties, and local governments in some cities are developing or enforcing the regulation of sharing economy accommodation provision.

The previous sections have provided an outline of the main forms of tourism suppliers. We will now consider the main characteristics that are common to all tourism suppliers.

CHARACTERISTICS OF TOURISM SUPPLIERS

We have seen that the supply of the tourism product is fragmented across several sectors and that within each sector there is also a range of different types of industry. Despite this variety tourism suppliers, regardless of the sector or industry within which they operate, are characterised by the same features. Tourism suppliers are part of the service sector and some of the characteristics that we discuss below are common to all service providers, whether they operate in tourism or not, while other characteristics are unique to tourism suppliers. We start by considering the characteristics of services – intangibility, inseparability, perishability and heterogeneity – and how these affect tourism suppliers.

INTANGIBILITY

'Intangibility' means without physical substance and is used to describe assets that cannot be touched, tested or experienced before or after consumption, and for which no physical evidence exists after consumption. Tourism suppliers' products are often described as intangible because:

- Tourists often make reservations and pay for tourism products before their departure from the generating regions; they are therefore unable to check or test destination-based suppliers' products before making the purchase decision. At the end of the trip they will have no evidence of it apart from souvenirs, photographs and memories.
- The benefits that the tourism product provides are experiential and not physical. For example leisure tourists might seek relaxing, indulgent or challenging experiences, while business tourists may seek professional, efficient or prestigious experiences. These experiences require the use of a tangible physical infrastructure such as transport, accommodation and attractions in destinations, but these are used as a means to achieve more experiential benefits.

Intangibility creates challenges for tourism suppliers. They need to understand the benefits sought from their products by tourists but are impeded from researching consumer needs by the distance between generating and destination regions. In addition, any language or cultural differences create difficulties in communicating with potential tourists while language, distance and currency differences create practical difficulties in processing reservations and payments. This was particularly challenging before the emergence of the Internet and created a role for businesses based in the generating region who sold suppliers' capacity on their behalf. These businesses are known as 'intermediaries' and we discuss them in detail in Chapter 6.

The snapshot on p. 106 identified franchises as one solution for intangibility. Franchises and soft brands (marketing consortia) are not exclusive to the hotel sector: franchising is common in the airline industry, for example British Airways franchises its brand to Comair in South Africa and SUN-AIR in Scandinavia, while consortia have been created by visitor attractions as a way of improving marketing effectiveness. For instance London Shh... is a marketing alliance of small historic houses in central London, and South Bank London is a consortium of venues on the south bank of the River Thames.

INSEPARABILITY

'Inseparability' describes products that are, to some extent, produced and consumed simultaneously. This requires the consumer's direct involvement with the suppliers' employees in interactions known as 'service encounters'. The quality of the service encounter is affected by the input of both the consumer and the service provider and therefore the interpersonal skills of the suppliers' employees are particularly important.

In tourism, service encounters often occur at different stages of the purchase and consumption experience and often involve interactions with several employees in different roles. For example, a tourist may reserve and pay for a hotel online, receive the confirmation by email, phone the reservations team with a particular enquiry, and on arrival be welcomed and checked-in by the front office, encounter housekeeping staff in corridors or in the room, and be served breakfast by food and beverage staff. Tourism suppliers must monitor and manage the quality of each service encounter to ensure consistency in the customer's experience (Grönroos, 2007).

PERISHABILITY

'Perishability' means that the life of an individual unit of available capacity is limited to a specific deadline and that once that deadline is reached the product ceases to be available for sale. All tourism suppliers' products are perishable; individual units of capacity (e.g. a hotel room, admission to an attraction or a seat on a transport departure) cannot be stored indefinitely until a consumer makes a decision to purchase it; if it is not sold by a certain time, then the opportunity to sell it disappears. Capacity that is approaching the end of its life without being sold is known as 'distressed inventory' or 'distressed stock'.

Middleton et al. suggest that perishability is a logical result of inseparability and that 'service production is fixed in time and space' (2009: 48). They interpret service production as a 'capacity to produce' rather than a volume of products. If demand is lower than the capacity to produce, spare capacity remains unsold or unused. Conversely, if demand is higher than the capacity to produce, extra capacity cannot usually be added. Perishability creates challenges for suppliers in matching capacity and demand; demand can be forecast based on previous experience and knowledge of the market and the external environment, but these forecasts are unlikely to be exact. It is therefore crucial that effective ways to sell as much available capacity as possible are found, and that prices are set to ensure that optimum yield is earned. We explain a common approach to this on p. 128.

HETEROGENEITY

'Heterogeneity' means that each consumer's experience of a supplier or a service is unique to that consumer. As a result of inseparability, tourism suppliers are unable to guarantee that each tourist's experience of their product will be the same. Heterogeneity therefore creates quality control and service quality management challenges for tourism suppliers – maintaining a consistent quality in all service encounters and ensuring that all consumers' experience of the same company is considered to be at least satisfactory or better. Employees providing services to consumers therefore have a crucial role in delivering customer satisfaction. We explore this issue further in Chapter 11.

In addition to service characteristics, tourism suppliers are also affected by demand variations, complementarity, and high fixed-to-variable costs (Middleton et al., 2009).

DEMAND VARIATIONS

'Demand variations' mean that the level of sold capacity will vary significantly on dates throughout the year or times throughout the day; that is, the demand for a product is not consistently the same. Most tourism suppliers experience significant demand variations on a seasonal, daily or hourly basis. Middleton et al. (2009) point out that for some tourism suppliers seasonality creates 90–100 per cent filled capacity for some weeks or months of the year, but less than 30 per cent filled capacity for the remainder of the year. Indeed many tourism suppliers choose to close down during their low season.

These demand variations, together with perishability, create pressure on suppliers to earn enough revenue during periods of peak demand to compensate for the lower revenue when demand falls. Many tourism suppliers respond to this challenge through the use of creative pricing to smooth demand (Hoffman et al., 2009), which we discuss later in this chapter.

COMPLEMENTARITY OF SUPPLIERS

'Complementarity' means that there is an inter-relationship or an inter-connectedness between suppliers; decisions made by suppliers in one sector may affect the demand for suppliers in other sectors (Middleton et al., 2009). For example, the decision by a transport operator to terminate a route into a destination will affect the accommodation and attractions sector there, while the range and quality of attractions in a destination will affect the demand for accommodation and transport suppliers too. Therefore tourism suppliers in one destination must depend on each other, even though they may operate completely independently of each other.

This complementarity creates a need for cross-sectoral cooperation and collaboration to ensure that decisions are made that will benefit tourism within the destination as a whole; in particular decisions about product design and quality and the messages about the destination that are communicated to consumers. This collaboration is often led by a department of the local government, a local, regional or national tourism organisation, or by a partnership of representatives from each tourism sector within a destination (Middleton et al., 2009). This issue is explored in detail in Chapter 10.

HIGH RATIO OF FIXED-TO-VARIABLE COSTS

Tourism suppliers are characterised by the nature of their fixed and variable costs. Fixed costs are costs that must be paid regardless of the volume of units sold; for example an accommodation property must pay the costs of loans, wages, equipment, advertising and energy regardless of its occupancy rates. The price charged for each occupied room contributes to these fixed costs. Variable costs are only incurred when a unit of capacity is sold; for example in our fictional hotel below, the additional energy, water, laundry and housekeeping costs incurred whilst a room is occupied, and the cost of breakfast.

Most tourism suppliers are characterised by high fixed costs and low variable costs. This is important because it creates opportunities to use flexible approaches to pricing, and potentially to sell each unit of capacity at different prices. The potential to do this, combined with variations in demand and the problem of perishability discussed earlier, allows tourism suppliers to stimulate sales for distressed inventory by selling a proportion of their capacity at lower prices. Figure 5.3 simplifies the concept of fixed and variable costs and their relationship to price and profit in a fictional two-room hotel.

Figure 5.3 illustrates the flexibility that tourism suppliers have in pricing their products. Very large companies use sophisticated software to calculate the impact of price on profit and to determine the most profitable prices to charge, in a process known as 'revenue management'.

Pricing opportunities for a two-room property. The published price is £200 and total fixed costs are £120 per night.								
50% occupancy			**100% occupancy**			**100% occupancy**		
	Room 1	Room 2		Room 1	Room 2		Room 1	Room 2
Room revenue	200	0	Room revenue	200	54	Room revenue	200	100
Fixed cost	60	60	Fixed cost	60	60	Fixed cost	60	60
Variable cost	20	0	Variable cost	20	20	Variable cost	20	20
Contribution (room rate-variable cost)	180	0	Contribution (room rate-variable cost)	180	34	Contribution (room rate-variable cost)	180	80
Profit	120	−60	Profit	120	−26	Profit	120	20
Total profit: £60			Total profit: £94			Total profit: £140		

FIGURE 5.3   Variable pricing in a hotel

Revenue management is used widely in the hotel, transport, venue and cruising sectors to manage demand profitably. Revenue management forecasts sales, calculates the required yield or RevPAR, and determines the price to charge for each unit of capacity. The aim of the method is to manage demand through pricing in order to maximise revenue (Kimes, 2000).

Revenue management manages demand for, and supply of, a supplier's capacity by monitoring availability and sales and adapting prices continually, based on the forecasted load factor or occupancy rate and the required level of contribution to fixed costs required by each unit. When demand is high, some consumers will be prepared to pay a much higher price for the limited number of seats/rooms that are available, and the tourism supplier will sell to these customers at the highest possible price. Effective marketing ensures that customers who would pay the higher prices are unable to purchase the product at the lower prices. We discuss this in more detail in Chapter 11.

The characteristics described above create challenges for tourism suppliers in effectively communicating with consumers in order to sell optimal levels of their capacity at the highest prices, before it perishes. Fyall and Garrod (2005) suggest that as a result of IT advances and globalisation, business organisations have the opportunity to overcome these challenges by collaborating with other businesses who were formerly regarded as adversaries: 'This trend is particularly apparent in the tourism industry, where the fragmented, multi-sectoral and independent nature of tourism provides a powerful catalytic focus for inter-organisational co-ordination and collective decision-making' (2005: 3).

We have already discussed examples of collaboration between hotels in the form of franchising and consortia. The snapshot below describes another common form of collaboration: the alliance.

SNAPSHOT 5.4

Star Alliance

Star Alliance was founded in 1997 as an innovative strategic partnership between five airlines: Air Canada, Lufthansa, Scandinavian Airlines, THAI and United. It was the first, and is the largest, airline alliance.

Star Alliance now has 28 member airlines. Star Alliance members include: Air China, Air New Zealand, ANA, Asiana, Austrian, Egypt Air, Ethiopian, Eva Air, LOT Polish Airlines, Singapore Airlines, South African Airways, TAP Portugal,. Each airline retains its own brand and service style but by working together gains benefits including:

- reducing costs by sharing facilities at airports – lounges, baggage facilities, check-in desks
- generating revenue through access to global markets – sharing flights through code sharing (where one airline operates the flight but partners sell it using their own airline codes)
- coordinating flights for smooth connections between carriers
- integrated frequent flyer programmes, allowing passengers to earn points across all member airlines.

The combined power of Star Alliance includes a fleet of 4,600+ aircraft, 18,500 daily flights to 1,330 airports in 192 countries, serving 640 million passengers a year.

Source: Star Alliance 2017

In addition to the characteristics discussed above, ownership is an important factor in the supply of tourism.

OWNERSHIP OF TOURISM SUPPLIERS

The supply of tourism is provided by a range of types and sizes of organisation. In this section we consider ownership in the context of the private, public and voluntary sectors, and explain how the main characteristics of each affect tourism suppliers.

The term 'private sector' or 'commercial sector' describes firms which are owned by individuals or groups of individuals and provide products and services that are purchased by consumers. Profits from their operation are retained by their owners. The survival of private sector firms depends on their profitability and often their growth. The private sector plays a major role in tourism but there is great diversity in the size of firms (Buckley, 1994). Firms are described as large, medium, small or micro and are usually defined by employee numbers, annual turnover and the annual balance sheet; definitions of each do vary between countries. The EU definition of SMEs, established in 2005, is outlined in Table 5.6.

In the EU, large companies are defined as firms that employ more than 250 employees, with an annual turnover of over €50 million. Large companies usually benefit from access to finance and expertise and therefore are better equipped to overcome the challenges created by intangibility, inseparability, perishability and heterogeneity, and to grow and compete effectively.

TABLE 5.6   EU definitions of SMEs

Enterprise category	Headcount	Annual turnover	Annual balance sheet total
Medium sized	< 250	≤ €50 million	≤ €43 million
Small	< 50	≤ €10 million	≤ €10 million
Micro	< 10	≤ €2 million	≤ €2 million

Source: European Commission (2005) © European Communities, 2005.

Throughout this chapter we have identified the major suppliers in each tourism sector and have shown that there are many high-profile multinational tourism suppliers with a portfolio of globally recognised brands, particularly in the hotel, airline, cruise and theme park industries. However, tourism supply is actually dominated by small and medium-sized businesses, and micro-businesses, known collectively as SMEs.

The domination of tourism by SMEs is very important because these face different challenges to those experienced by large companies. For instance SMEs often:

- have limited access to financial resources; Haven-Tang and Jones (2005) suggest that tourism entrepreneurs often use personal and family savings as their main source of capital.

- lack marketing and management expertise; Middleton et al. (2009) suggest that managers of visitor attractions with fewer than 100,000 visitors a year lack formal management and marketing training, and are likely to be knowledgeable enthusiasts who focus on daily operations rather than on strategic growth.

- lack long-term business ownership experience; Haven-Tang and Jones (2005) found that many SME business owners entered the tourism industry as a lifestyle choice to escape from what they perceived as the rat race, to semi-retire or to supplement a lifestyle in a more desirable location: their business goals may not prioritise growth.

These characteristics will often restrict an SME's ability to overcome the challenges created by the nature of services and of tourism that we discussed earlier. In addition, SMEs may face difficulties in competing with multinational suppliers which have expanded into destinations worldwide and enjoy a range of operating advantages such as professional management, access to international investment and lower costs through economies of scale and integration.

The potential skills gap in SMEs suggests a need for additional support for SMEs through training provision, marketing research to identify and understand potential markets, and promotional activities to reach consumers effectively. This support is usually provided by the public sector.

The term 'public sector' describes state intervention in the supply of products and services. Public sector provision exists through ownership of shares in a commercially operated enterprise, through local government and other statutory agencies financed by public funding, and through state enterprises. In tourism the public sector has a major role; for example 55.63 per cent of Singapore Airlines is owned by Temasek Holdings, a state enterprise (Singapore Airlines, 2017); the French railway SNCF is wholly owned by the French state (SNCF Group, 2017); national museums in the UK are state owned and funded (DCMS, 2016a); while in China, CITS (China International Travel Service) is a large state-owned tourism group that promotes China as a destination to inbound markets and operates tours within China (CITS Group Corporation, 2017).

The public sector assumes responsibility for the provision of public goods and services in a variety of circumstances because:

- the benefits are shared by the whole population, for example well-maintained road networks, access to international transport routes, or collections of national importance in museums and art galleries.

- the private sector is unable to provide such goods or services profitably or in sufficient quantity, for example perhaps because tourists use a resource free of charge or because demand is low but the economic benefits to the whole community are great (i.e. the state-owned Paradores de Turismo hotel chain in Spain operates 94 hotels in historic properties in rural regions where tourism and other economic activities are low).

- the private sector is reluctant to invest due to the risk of failure, the amount of capital required and the slow return on investment, for example airport, resort, venue and attraction construction in new destinations where demand has not yet been established.

The level of public sector provision of tourism products and services is a reflection of government ideology. Many European states have experienced a process of privatisation since the 1980s whereby state-owned activities and assets were sold to the private sector and became commercial entities; for instance, in the UK British Airways and the British Airports Authority were privatised in 1987.

The term 'voluntary sector' or 'third sector' refers to organisations that are independent and self-governing and comprise people who have joined together voluntarily to take action for the benefit of the community. A voluntary organisation may employ paid staff or volunteers, but must be established other than for financial gain. In tourism many attractions are provided by the voluntary sector, particularly museums and heritage attractions. The National Trust in the UK purchases and manages historic buildings by using charitable donations and membership fees and charging admission fees to the public.

SUMMARY

Tourism supply is complex and fragmented. It consists of a variety of sectors which can be sub-divided into individual industries and within which a diverse range of ownership types, objectives and resources exist. The private, public and voluntary sectors operate alongside each other and the state has a clear role in providing elements of tourism supply, particularly where the private sector cannot see profitability.

It is clear, however, that individual tourism suppliers are but one element of a whole tourist experience of a destination and that their inter-reliance creates a need for them to be coordinated and to collaborate. Suppliers that lack the skills or resources to operate, manage or market themselves effectively require additional support from an external source in order to ensure that tourism in the destination is not compromised. In addition, there is a growing trend for alliances and collaborations between operators within the same sector to avoid a duplication of effort, achieve marketing power and economies, and reduce costs in order to compete more effectively with operators outside their alliance.

SELF-TEST QUESTIONS

1. Consider the place in which you live as a tourism destination. Which elements of tourism supply exist there?

2. Describe the characteristics of this supply with reference to ownership, demand variations and complementarity.

3. Consider the extent to which the public sector plays a role in supplying the tourism product in your home town.

FURTHER READING

Dallen, J., Victor, T. and Teye, B. (2009) *Tourism and the Lodging Sector*. London: Taylor & Francis.

Fyall, A., Garrod, B., Leask, A. and Wanhill, S. (2008) *Managing Visitor Attractions*. Oxford: Butterworth-Heinemann.

Gross, S. and Klemmer, L. (2014) *Introduction to Tourism Transport*. Wallingford: CABI.

USEFUL WEBSITES

Cruiselines International Association (CLIA): www.cruising.org/

International Civil Aviation Organisation (ICAO): www.icao.int/Pages/default.aspx

International Council of Museums (ICOM): http://icom.museum/

International Live Events Association (ILEA): www.ileahub.com/ilea-landing

Marriott International: www.marriott.com/marriott-brands.mi

Merlin Entertainments: www.merlinentertainments.biz/

Routesonline: www.routesonline.com/

Six Flags: http://investors.sixflags.com/investor-overview/six-flags-at-a-glance

Skift: Skift.com

Travelmole: travelmole.com

Travel Trade Gazette Media: www.ttgmedia.com/

Walt Disney Parks and Resorts: https://aboutdisneyparks.com/

6

INTERMEDIARIES IN THE TOURISM SYSTEM

'... it's fairly unanimous that nearly every hotelier wishes he or she would have more direct bookings versus bookings made through an online travel agency.'

D. Ting, 2017c

LEARNING OUTCOMES

After reading this chapter you will understand:

- the types and roles of travel intermediaries
- the constraints under which travel intermediaries operate
- how intermediaries are affected by changes in the external operating environment.

Trivago advertising campaign, London, summer 2017

Source: Clare Inkson

INTRODUCTION

In Chapter 2 we discussed the distance between generating and receiving regions that is inherent in tourism. Since tourists often reserve and pay for travel products some time in advance of consuming them, this geographical distance creates challenges for travel suppliers in destinations to promote and sell their capacity. Where there are language or currency differences between suppliers and the potential consumers of their product, these difficulties may be exacerbated.

This challenge creates opportunities for companies acting as intermediaries between suppliers and consumers: facilitating the process for tourists of buying travel products, and for suppliers of selling them. **Travel intermediaries** are mainly composed of agencies, operators and wholesalers, and are usually, although not always, based in the generating region. Some large travel companies consist of more than one of these types of intermediary. Travel intermediaries may serve the leisure market, the corporate market or both, and are known collectively as 'the travel trade'.

Travel intermediary: A company acting between two separate parties in the distribution of travel products, e.g. between the consumer and supplier

The travel trade has experienced great upheaval since the end of the twentieth century as a result of regulatory changes, new technologies that have shifted travel distribution from offline to online, and the emergence of more experienced, independent and confident tourists in some generating regions who seek more flexible travel experiences that are tailored closely to their individual needs. Travel intermediary businesses have had to adapt quickly to these changes and as a result the sector is very dynamic and in a state of constant development. The emergence of OTAs, plus P2P platforms that act as intermediaries between private owners and tourists, has added new dimensions to the travel intermediary sector. We discussed these trends in Chapter 1.

In this chapter we identify each type of intermediary, its role in the tourism system and its main operating features. We consider how the travel trade is regulated, and common structural features of intermediary businesses.

TYPES OF INTERMEDIARY IN THE TOURISM SYSTEM

There are three main types of intermediary in the tourism system: agencies, operators and wholesalers (Buhalis, 2001). Each of these is defined in detail in Table 6.1.

Intermediaries do not usually directly produce any individual elements of the travel experience, and usually they don't own the capacity that they sell, but they play an extremely important role in the distribution of travel products produced by other companies and organisations. That is, they sell travel products – transport, accommodation, amenities and attractions – on behalf of suppliers, creating a link between suppliers in destinations and the potential consumers of their products in generating regions.

In practice the distinction between wholesalers, operators and agencies is not always clear because there has been some blurring of their activities in recent years. For example, some intermediaries may act as both an agency and an operator because they use two different models to purchase suppliers' capacity. Legally though, the distinction between types of intermediary is important because the financial risk, contractual responsibilities to tourists, liabilities and regulatory controls will differ depending on the nature of the contract between intermediary and supplier.

TABLE 6.1   Intermediaries in the tourism system

Wholesalers	Operators	Agencies
Wholesalers buy capacity from one type of supplier (e.g. hotels, airlines or attractions) and sell the capacity on in its original form to other intermediaries or direct to the consumer. Wholesalers of air seats are known as 'brokers' or 'consolidators'. Wholesalers of hotels are sometimes known as 'bed banks'.	Operators buy capacity from accommodation, transport and attraction suppliers and combine them together to create an inclusive tour, or package, which is sold at one price. The customer does not know the price of each component of the package. Operators may create holidays, short breaks or day trips for the leisure market, or organise meetings, incentive trips, conferences and exhibitions for the MICE market.	Agencies represent suppliers and process sales on their behalf, usually through computerised reservations systems (CRS) or global distribution systems (GDS). In some generating regions, agencies will often specialise in either the leisure or the business travel market. Some online accommodation sellers, such as Airbnb and Booking.com, act as agents and earn commission or a fee on each sale.

Source: Buhalis (2001)

Intermediaries negotiate contracts with individual suppliers specifying dates, capacity and rates. Rates given to intermediaries may be:

Commissionable rates: The supplier determines the price at which capacity will be sold and pays an agreed percentage of the sale price to the intermediary. In this case the tourist's contract is with the supplier, known legally as 'the principal', who is responsible for the fulfilment of the contract (Renshaw, 1992).

Net rates: Suppliers give rates that are discounted compared to their published rates and the intermediary adds their own mark up. Legally, the supplier's contract is with the intermediary who then creates another contract with customers at the time of booking. In this case responsibility for the fulfilment of obligations, and provision of the supplier's capacity, lies with the intermediary. This is the standard approach used by wholesalers and operators, although agencies in some generating regions negotiate net rates too (Beaver, 2002).

Inclusive tour rates (ITX): net rates given to intermediaries who must use the capacity to create a package (Beaver, 2002). Usually contracts will specify that the selling price of the package cannot be lower than the supplier's published rate. ITX rates are usually negotiated by operators when they contract capacity from a transport supplier. Again, the legal obligation is with the intermediary for the fulfilment of the contract and supply of the product.

The actual net or ITX rates negotiated reflect the financial value of the intermediary to the supplier. This may be measured in the volume of bookings that the intermediary makes or the type of consumer that the operator brings to the supplier. Some intermediaries have significant power and are able to negotiate very low rates because of the value they can offer to the supplier; this is particularly the case with OTAs and the hotel industry, where OTAs dominate online search results and even global hotel brands struggle to draw customers to their own websites.

THE ROLE OF INTERMEDIARIES IN THE TOURISM SYSTEM

Intermediaries offer a number of benefits to suppliers and to tourists, and consequently in major generating regions, a complex network of travel intermediaries has developed. These networks may serve the leisure or the business travel market, or both.

Figure 6.1 illustrates the network of intermediaries traditionally used to distribute tourism capacity from supplier to consumer. The figure shows that suppliers of travel products have four options for distributing their capacity to customers. These are a combination of direct or indirect (sometimes called mediated) distribution. Each option is known as a 'channel of distribution'. Suppliers may use one or more of these channels and intermediaries themselves may also use another channel of distribution to reach their customers.

Benefits of Intermediaries for Suppliers

Yale (1995) and Buhalis (2001) identify a number of benefits that intermediaries offer to suppliers based in destination regions:

Sales volume: by selling large quantities of their capacity either on the same date, or on different dates over a season or during the whole year.

Market access: by reaching certain types of consumers that the supplier may be unlikely to reach easily alone.

Market knowledge: by understanding the detailed requirements of consumers in a particular generating region, the prices they are likely to pay, and the most effective ways of communicating with them.

Reduced marketing costs: by incurring the cost of researching markets in generating regions and promoting to consumers.

Simplified sales process: by processing reservations, payments and ticketing on behalf of suppliers.

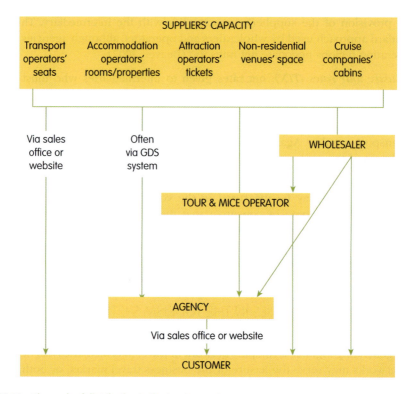

FIGURE 6.1   Channels of distribution in the tourism system

Disposal of distressed stock: by selling some capacity that would otherwise remain unsold.

Complaint handling: by mediating between supplier and consumer and attempting to resolve disputes.

Intermediaries contract capacity with suppliers in different forms:

Allocation: The reservation of a specific number of rooms, seats or tickets, for specific dates. If the intermediary is unable to sell all of the allocation by a specified deadline, known as the release date, the unsold element is released back to the supplier to sell through other channels (Gale, 2006). Operators and wholesalers usually contract capacity on this basis.

On request: Intermediaries negotiate prices with a supplier for irregular bookings that cannot be predicted at the time of contracting – also known as 'ad hoc bookings'. No reservations are made until the intermediary receives an enquiry from a customer (Yale, 1995), but if there is no availability then capacity must be sought from an alternative supplier. This form of contract is used by wholesalers, operators and agencies.

Guarantee: the reservation of confirmed capacity for which the intermediary must pay, regardless of whether or not they have sold it (Yale, 1995). Guaranteed contracts are effective in negotiating very low rates from suppliers, but carry a significant financial risk for the intermediary.

In addition to the advantages that intermediaries offer to suppliers, they also provide benefits to tourists who purchase travel services through them.

Benefits of Intermediaries for Tourists

Pender (2001) and Buhalis (2001) identify the benefits to tourists of buying travel products through intermediaries:

- Easier access to information about destinations and the suppliers within them.

- Advice and guidance about the most appropriate travel products to buy.

- The ability to make reservations in their own language and currency in the generating region.

- Possibly obtaining lower prices than if they booked with the supplier directly.

- In some generating regions, for instance the EU, financial protection for customers' payments to agencies and operators in the event of the intermediary's insolvency.

- Advice and assistance during the trip for customers of operators, and travel management companies.

In theory, the growth of online and mobile technologies has created opportunities for suppliers to cut out intermediaries and promote and sell to customers direct: this is known as disintermediation (Pender, 2001). The relative ease with which consumers and suppliers can reach each other through the Internet, plus the increasing demand for travel experiences that are tailor-made to the needs of the consumer, were viewed as a very clear threat to the long-term future of intermediaries (Law, 2009). We return to this point later in the chapter.

We now consider each type of intermediary in more detail.

WHOLESALERS

Wholesalers have played an important role in tourism for many decades. Until recently, however, they were a hidden intermediary in the tourism system because they provided a business-to-business (B2B) service: they sold suppliers' capacity to agencies and/or operators rather than to the consumer.

The impact of internet technology, together with increased demand from some consumer segments for greater flexibility and independence in their travel experience, has created new opportunities for the travel wholesale sector: they can now target the consumer direct via the Internet, and offer enhanced services to agencies allowing them to tailor-make travel packages to the needs of individual customers.

Wholesalers usually specialise in a particular type of product (e.g. airline seats, hotel rooms or attraction tickets) and are able to negotiate lower rates from suppliers than many travel agencies or operators as a result of the volume of capacity they contract. They then sell the capacity on in the same form to operators, agencies or direct to the customer (Pender, 2001). The original B2B function of wholesalers exempted them from the consumer protection regulation that affected operators and agencies; this has considerable implications for consumers now that wholesalers often sell direct. We discuss this issue in more detail later in the chapter.

OPERATORS

Operators combine tourist products into packages and sell them as pre-arranged inclusive tours (ITs) at one price (Pender, 2001). Usually the package consists of transport and accommodation but could be accommodation and an attraction, or transport and an attraction, or all three. The key point is that the package is sold at one price and the consumer is unaware of the cost of each element.

The operator sector can be subdivided into:

Tour operators: Based in the generating region these create holiday, touring or recreational ITs for leisure tourists. These ITs may be mass produced or tailor-made. Mass-produced ITs are programmes of hundreds or thousands of identical trips that are sold 'off the shelf' and appeal to a very broad market. Tailor-made ITs are arranged specifically to meet the individual requirements of each customer and are usually more expensive. Poon (1993) describes mass-produced ITs as 'old tourism' that stimulated the expansion of mass tourism demand during the 1960s and 1970s in northern Europe.

MICE operators: Also known as 'conference' or 'event' organisers, are usually based in the generating region and arrange meetings, conferences, incentive trips or exhibitions for companies and organisations. Usually these are tailor-made to the clients' individual requirements.

Incoming or inbound operators: Also known as 'destination management companies' or 'ground handlers', these are based in the destination and provide local expertise and organise local transport and accommodation for tour or MICE operators or travel agencies from different generating regions (Pender, 2001). Buhalis (2001) suggests that the incoming operator sector is the least-known in tourism and one that is often forgotten by researchers, but they actually play a vital role in some destinations as the link between local suppliers and operators in generating regions.

Although tour operators, MICE operators and inbound operators create products for very distinct markets, they share the same function: they create a link between suppliers and some or all of their potential customers, as well as facilitate the organisation, purchase and operation of the travel experience for their customers.

The practical organisation and operation of an IT requires similar processes regardless of whether the operator is a tour, MICE or incoming operator. The organisation of ITs can be extremely complex, requiring careful planning, often well in advance of the departure date.

THE PLANNING PROCESS

The process of research, negotiating with and contracting the suppliers, pricing the trip, and marketing and selling it, often starts at least one year before departure, particularly for large tour operators whose customer base is made up of hundreds of thousands, or millions, of customers a year (Pender, 2001). MICE operators organising a major conference or incentive trip for hundreds or thousands of delegates, and tour operators planning a programme of continuous departures to a range of destinations throughout a season, may start their planning several years in advance.

Operators with small programmes with limited departures are often able to organise ITs and launch them for sale more quickly (Pender, 2001). The snapshot below describes a single incentive travel trip.

SNAPSHOT 6.1

Sample Planning Process for an Incentive Travel Trip

An incentive trip activity

Source: © Executive Group Travel

The planning process for a single incentive trip often begins more than one year in advance. Executive Group Travel, based in Boston, USA, specialises in incentive travel for corporate groups of between 30 and 325 delegates. The company's planning consists of five steps:

1. **16 months in advance: Design the Brief**: learning about the company and its culture and the objectives to be achieved. Research destinations and activities, develop and present proposals.

2. **14 months in advance: Negotiations with Suppliers:** Negotiate capacity and rates with hotels and airline and reserve capacity. Book local transfers and activities.

3. **9–11 months in advance: Communications and Promotions about the Trip:** Design and set up a branded micro website for the trip and begin raising awareness of it among potential delegates using competitions and personalised email campaigns.

(Continued)

4. **2 weeks to 1 month in advance: Finalise the Trip Details:** confirm final details with the client's planning committee. Send rooming lists to hotels, issue tickets, vouchers and itineraries. Brief guides and tour managers.

5. **1 week after trip:** Conduct a survey to collect feedback from delegates. Report back to the client.

Source: Executive Group Travel (2014)

This snapshot shows the time lag between the negotiation of rates with suppliers and payments being made by customers. The long time period between setting up and pricing the programme and its operation leaves operators vulnerable to many factors beyond their control which may have a serious effect on their projected profit margins: in particular, exchange rate fluctuations, increases in fuel prices or a sudden collapse in demand for a destination because of political unrest, disease outbreak, natural disaster, or crime or terrorist attacks targeting tourists.

Surcharges: The addition of extra costs to the customer, after the original selling price has been agreed

An operator's ability to add **surcharges** to a sale in the event of cost increases is usually governed by consumer protection legislation of the state or country where the sale is made. EU legislation limits operators to a 10 per cent surcharge, of which the first 2 per cent of the package price must be absorbed by the company, and prevents them from adding surcharges within 30 days of departure (ABTA, 2015a). Many operators guarantee no surcharges as a way of competing more effectively. Operators are therefore vulnerable to exchange rate fluctuations or rises in fuel prices (Pender, 2001). To reduce risk, operators may purchase currency strategically using **forward contracts** or **stop loss contracts** (Laws, 1997); however, the cost of these financial tools may prohibit small operators, who require relatively small amounts of foreign currency, from using them. Small operators are therefore less able to alleviate the risks of contracting in one currency and selling in another.

Forward contract: Future purchases of a currency can be ordered at current rates by payment of a deposit

Stop loss contract: Specifies the maximum rate at which a currency should be bought

CHARTERING TRANSPORT

Operators often reduce the cost of the transport element of an IT by chartering transport. Any mode of transport can potentially be chartered, such as a train and a cruise boat or ship, but this is most commonly used in the coach and air sectors.

If an operator requires a large number of seats on a single departure, series of departures or a tour, it is often cheaper to hire the required mode of transport for their own use, as a whole charter, rather than buy a number of seats on a scheduled service. In the coach and air sectors, many transport suppliers will specialise in charters and only sell their services through intermediaries, mostly operators. For this reason, many chartered transport suppliers are relatively unknown to the public. For example, many coach companies will hire their coaches and drivers to operators for transfers or for tours, and charter airlines will operate on routes and timetables determined by an operator. The operator negotiates a rate for the charter and is responsible for filling all of the seats. The growth of luxury leisure travel has increased demand for private air charters.

Laws (1997: 177) identifies a range of charter agreements:

Ad hoc charter: A one-off contract to operate one leg of a journey, a round trip or a tour. Used by tour and MICE operators.

Series charter: Regular departures operating specific routes within a certain time period, but the coach, ship or aircraft is also chartered to other operators during that time period. Mainly used by tour operators.

Time charter: Exclusive use of the coach, ship or aircraft for the whole of a specified period, often a whole season. Mainly used by tour operators.

Part charter: The departure is shared between two or more organisers – this is most common with charter flights. Mainly used by tour operators.

Whole charter: All the seats on one departure are contracted to one operator. Used by tour and MICE operators.

Block charter: Operators contract a number of seats on a scheduled departure at ITX rates that must be combined with other travel products to create an inclusive tour. Common in the airline industry but also used on trains and ferries. Used by tour and MICE operators.

Operators select the most appropriate type of charter based on sales forecasts and costs.

PROFITABILITY OF OPERATORS

Operators work in a very competitive environment and often the basis for such competition will be price. MICE and niche tour operators are less susceptible to price competition because reputation and quality are a priority for their customers whose budgets are usually higher. Operators that organise mass-produced ITs and compete for the same customer markets will often feature the same destinations, and sometimes even the same accommodation and transport suppliers; the only distinction between their ITs is often the selling price. This leads to pressure to reduce costs in order to reduce prices and often results in a precarious profit margin (Pender, 2001). Consider slim profits per passenger with the risk of currency fluctuations and fuel price increases discussed above, plus the restriction on surcharging imposed in the EU, and this narrow margin could be quickly depleted, leaving the operator just breaking even, or possibly suffering a loss. Terrorist attacks targeting tourists in North Africa, Turkey and in several European cities, along with wars and tensions in the Middle and the Far East have, at the time of writing, severely affected operators who specialise in these destinations, adding further financial risk. If the operator fails to sell all of its capacity and has contracted on a guaranteed basis, this risk is heightened.

In addition, seasonal revenue patterns create further financial challenges (Yale, 1995). If an operator's product has an identifiable peak season, for example summer sun, or only operates during certain months of the year, for example a winter sports operator, there will be specific times of year when revenue is highest – when customers pay the balance for their trip, usually eight weeks before departure – and other times when little or no revenue is earned, thereby putting pressure on cash-flow.

Such a precarious financial environment creates financial instability in the tour operator sector and there are not infrequent financial collapses as a result. For instance in January 2017, All Leisure Holidays, a UK-based cruise holiday specialist which owned the Swan Hellenic and Voyages of Discovery cruise brands, ceased trading overnight, leaving 400 British tourists overseas, and cancelling 13,000 future bookings. Under EU/UK legislation all customers are protected; those overseas were repatriated at no extra cost, and customers for future cruises were refunded in full (BBC Newsbeat, 2017).

AGENCIES

The agency sector has experienced huge upheavals since the last decade of the twentieth century. Traditionally agencies provided points of sale in the generating region for suppliers of tourist capacity, known as 'principals', and they earned a commission on each sale (Laws, 2001; Pender, 2001). Agencies accessed suppliers' inventory to check availability and prices, make reservations, and issue documents using GDSs such as Amadeus, Sabre, Galileo, and Worldspan. The Internet now enables customers to research availability and prices, make reservations and issue travel documents themselves, and consequently the agency sector has had to adapt to a new business environment.

Agency businesses bear relatively little financial risk as they do not purchase stock and have no contractual responsibility for the capacity they sell at commissionable rates. In practice, agencies have a duty of care to their customers and have responsibilities to their principals (Beaver, 2002), but the contract resulting from the sale is between the principal and the consumer.

Until the 1980s the agency sector was relatively stable: most agencies represented the same principals and were usually paid the same rates of commission by all principals operating in the same sector. For example, airline commission rates were commonly 9 per cent and tour operators and hotels paid 10 per cent. Travel agencies were unable to reduce the prices quoted by principals and consumers could buy the same product at the same price from most travel agencies.

Over-ride commissions: An increase in commission rate when a sales target is reached, e.g. from 10 per cent to 12.5 per cent

Changes to legislation in some generating regions, and revised agency agreements with some suppliers, relaxed the business environment in the 1980s and 1990s, allowing travel agencies greater flexibility to compete with each other. Airline deregulation in the USA in the late 1970s and 1980s forced changes to the traditionally inflexible relationship between airlines and travel agencies and greater freedom was given to airlines in the sale of their seats; in the USA, airlines could in theory sell tickets in the USA through banks, hotels and retail chains (Dilts and Prough, 1991; Hodgson, 1987) and airlines there began reducing commission rates or paying a flat fee to travel agencies (Beaver, 2002). In 2002 in the USA, commission payments by airlines to travel agencies were eliminated (Amadeus, 2007). A similar pattern followed in Europe where several airlines reduced commission from 9 per cent to 7 per cent between 1997 and 1999, with further decreases since 2001; several airlines now pay a zero rate or 1 per cent commission to travel agencies in Europe (Amadeus, 2007). Suppliers in other industries such as hotel, theme park and car rental also began to negotiate more flexibility into their relationship with travel agencies, selecting travel agencies strategically rather than selling through them all, and incentivising them through **over-ride commissions** (Renshaw, 1992).

Agencies responded to this by becoming more selective about the principals they represented (Renshaw, 1992; Yale, 1995). The volume of an agency's sales with one principal had a direct effect on the commission rates earned and therefore the profit-ability of the travel agency and its ability to compete. Agencies with more than one outlet and thus larger volumes of customers could benefit from higher commission levels if they directed sales towards specific principals. Some agencies began to charge fees to their customers to compensate for reduced commission rates. This has been particularly common in agencies specialising in business travel.

In theory, one agency can serve the leisure and business travel markets because fre-quently the suppliers used, with the exception of operators, are the same. However, in mature markets a distinction between leisure and business travel agencies has developed since the 1980s, as a result of more selective distribution by principals and the divergence of the needs of business and leisure travellers (Pender, 2001).

Demand for seats on scheduled full-service airlines is generally higher from business tourists, and the IATA requirement that travel agencies selling seats on IATA-member scheduled airlines must have an IATA licence was regarded as an ineffective investment by agencies who mainly sold package holidays. Agencies began to specialise in serving either leisure or business travellers (Mayhew, 1987) and although some do still serve both markets, specialisation is common. Leisure-travel agencies focus on selling suppliers' capacity to leisure tourists, while business-travel agencies focus on the business tourist market. We now consider each of these in detail.

BUSINESS-TRAVEL AGENCIES

Business-travel agencies specialise in selling tourism suppliers' capacity to corpo-rations and organisations, for their employees who travel as part of their work. Business-travel agencies are also known as 'corporate' travel agencies and because of changes in the way they work, the term travel management company (TMC) is often used (Beaver, 2002).

TMCs are not usually visible to the public as they do not require a public location, but need to be accessible to the companies and organisations they target. Consequently, they are located in business districts, often in office premises, and may even establish an office within the premises of a corporate customer that generates a large volume of business for them; this situation is known as an 'implant' (Pender, 2001). Increasingly, they offer their services online as well as, or instead of, a physical location.

The reduction in commission rates paid by suppliers to agencies that we discussed on p. 144 has forced TMCs to adopt a new business model. To replace the reduction in commission revenue, TMCs charge fees to their customers – either transaction fees on each booking or management fees for a period of time specified in the contract. To justify the fees, TMCs offer greater value to their customers than simply reserving travel products and issuing documents. Consequently TMCs provide comprehensive travel management services; they still process the purchase of capacity but also offer additional value by advising on and managing their clients' business travel policies, organising meetings and business events, and reducing their clients' expenditure on business travel through strategic purchasing (Davidson, 2001).

There are a number of very powerful global TMC providers, for example Carlson Wagonlit Travel, American Express Global Business Travel and UNIGLOBE Travel International, who have strong purchasing and marketing power. The snapshot below describes American Express Global Business Travel.

SNAPSHOT 6.2

American Express Global Business Travel (AMEX GBT)

GLOBAL BUSINESS TRAVEL

AMEX GBT logo

Source: Image courtesy of American Express GBT

American Express Global Business Travel provides travel management services to companies and organisations:

- Corporate travel services include reservations of transport and accommodation plus emergency support to business travellers. In addition, AMEX GBT advises companies on their business travel policy, monitors purchasing compliance, and tracks and reports expenses to ensure an optimum return on business travel investment for the client company.

- Meetings program management – 1000+ meeting professionals design and deliver corporate meetings and events including conferences, product launches, training and team-building experiences. Services provided include sourcing suppliers, event planning and management, group travel reservations, communications about the event and attendee management, plus analysis and reporting of the impact of the event.

AMEX GBT offers their business travel clients access to their negotiated rates and technology innovations that have been achieved through their purchasing power. They have a presence in 120 countries worldwide.

Source: American Express Travel Related Services Company Inc. (2017)

TMCs are able to clearly demonstrate the value they offer to their customers. In the leisure travel agency sector, this value is harder to demonstrate.

LEISURE-TRAVEL AGENCIES

The growth in internet use by consumers has made the role of the conventional physical leisure-travel agency unclear (Law, 2009). Consumers are now able to research, reserve and pay for travel products direct from suppliers via the Internet or mobile apps, as well as print their own travel documents. The value offered by leisure-travel agencies has diminished since consumers have been able to fulfil their functions themselves.

Changes to leisure travel agencies' operating environment – a reduction in commission rates, competition from suppliers targeting consumers direct through the Internet – have forced the leisure-travel agency sector to innovate in order to survive. At times the future of the sector has been considered to be very bleak and there is evidence that the number of agencies in mature generating regions is declining, although this is partly due to the shift from offline to online agencies and the increasing dominance of OTAs which we discuss later in this chapter.

Some leisure travel agencies charge transaction fees to their customers, although this varies between countries; in the UK specialist leisure travel agencies that serve niche markets may charge a service fee, but in general the practice is not yet being used widely.

The process of disintermediation, discussed at the beginning of this chapter, has created a more flexible method of organising leisure travel, called 'dynamic packaging'.

Dynamic Packaging

Dynamic packaging is the process whereby an inclusive tour is constructed without the use of an operator, specifically to the individual requirements of the consumer. For leisure-travel agencies, the ability to dynamically package has created important new opportunities.

Dynamic packaging allows an agency to tailor-make an inclusive tour for a customer by buying individual components of the travel experience at net rates, either direct from the supplier or from wholesalers, thus adding on their own mark-up and selling the package at one price. This responds to the falling demand for a 'one size fits all' approach to inclusive tours by offering flexibility to the customer. It also responds to the reduction in commission payments that some suppliers are pursuing and provides agencies with the opportunity to increase their revenue. Dynamic packaging may alter the consumers' legal relationship with agencies, creating the contractual and regulatory liabilities that operators are subject to.

While the growth of internet and mobile technologies was considered to be a threat to the leisure-travel agency sector, it has actually created opportunities for agencies as well, and in generating regions where internet penetration is high agencies must also develop e-distribution to remain competitive (Buhalis and Kaldis, 2008). Agencies with websites are able to increase their market penetration by reaching customers in geographic regions that are far beyond the catchment of the traditional physical agency outlet (Law et al., 2004). In generating regions with a high penetration of internet access, agencies have their own websites and many no longer have a physical sales location.

The late twentieth century saw the emergence of a new type of agency – the online travel agency (OTA). These agencies have no physical sales outlets and often have a global customer base that targets markets in all of the main generating regions in the world. OTAs have gained enormous power in travel distribution by investing heavily in search engine optimisation and sponsored search results; the hotel industry in particular has experienced increases in the cost of sales because a substantial portion of guests book through OTAs rather than direct, and the hotel must pay a commission to the OTA. Hotel brands are now taking steps to encourage guests to book direct by offering incentives through their own loyalty programmes.

The case study below describes two of the largest OTAs.

CASE STUDY 6.1

OTAs – The Priceline Group and Expedia Inc.

Since the late 1990s, travel distribution has seen a considerable shift from offline to online channels. Many entrepreneurs who were quick to recognise the potential of new technologies have since become major travel intermediaries.

priceline.com was originally set up in 1997 as a travel auction site where consumers offered a price and traders chose whether or not to accept it. In 1999 the company was offered for public sale and valued at US$12.9 billion. Since 2004, The Priceline Group has acquired several online travel retail sites: Booking.com (2005), agoda.com (2007), TravelJigsaw (now rentalcars.com; 2010), KAYAK (2013), OpenTable (2014), Rocketmiles (2015). In addition it acquired reservation-management technology companies that provide revenue and marketing solutions to hotels or restaurants that sell via Booking.com or OpenTable: PriceMatch and AS Digital (2015). The Priceline Group operates six brands, employs 18,500 staff and operates in 224 countries. In 2016 it handled US$68.1 billion in gross bookings (The Priceline Grou,p 2017).

Expedia Inc. logo

Source: Expedia

Expedia was set up in 1996 as a division of Microsoft and since then has been acquired by other, larger companies, and has itself acquired several online travel companies. In 2005 it was spun-off by its then owner, IAC, to become an independent publicly traded company, Expedia, Inc. Its acquisitions of travel retail sites since then include: CarRentals.com (2008), Venere.com (2008), Via Travel (2012), Trivago (2013), Auto Escape Group SAS and Wotif Group (2014), Orbitz Worldwide, Travelocity, and HomeAway (2015). In 2010 it acquired Mobiata, a mobile travel app specialist company. Expedia Inc. operates eight brands, employs 14,000+ staff, has offices in over 30 countries, and in 2016 earned US$81 billion in revenue.

Both companies earn revenue via three business models:

Agency model: Suppliers determine the selling price for their available inventory and display it on the OTA's website(s). The customer makes a booking and details of the booking are made available to the supplier. On arrival the customer pays the supplier direct, and the supplier then pays the OTA the agreed rate of commission on the booking. Commission rates are typically between 10–30 per cent (Xotels, n.d.).

Merchant model: Suppliers negotiate a net rate with the OTA, who then adds their own mark up and determines the selling price. Capacity may be dynamically packaged with other travel components (e.g. flight, hotel or car rental). The customer pays the OTA at the time of booking, and the OTA pays the supplier at a time agreed in the contract.

Advertising model: Travel and non-travel advertisers display content on the OTA's websites to gain access to the OTA's viewers, and then pay the OTA for click throughs. The OTA's metasearch sites, KAYAK (Priceline) and Trivago (Expedia), earn referral fees from other travel companies when a customer clicks through from the OTA site to the advertiser's website.

Reflective Questions

1. Look at the websites of each Priceline and Expedia brand. Can you find examples of wholesalers, operators and agencies within their family of companies?

2. Using Figure 6.1, draw channel of distribution diagrams for Expedia and Priceline. What do you notice about the structure of each company?

3. What might the impacts of this structure be on consumers and suppliers?

Some forms of travel intermediary are subject to complex regulations that govern their operations.

REGULATION OF INTERMEDIARIES

In some generating regions, particularly within the EU, intermediaries are closely regulated: their business practices, the accuracy of the information they provide to consumers, and their liability to consumers are stipulated either through self-regulation or government legislation.

SELF-REGULATION

'Self-regulation' is the voluntary adoption of regulation and is usually implemented through membership of a trade association that stipulates minimum standards of operation for all of its members.

Self-regulation through trade associations is common in the travel agency sector (e.g. ABTA in the UK, ASTA in the USA, AFTA in Australia, and TAANZ in New Zealand) and in the tour operator sector (e.g. AITO in the UK, and USTOA in the USA). Regulations establish a code of conduct for members, set standards of training and qualifications for staff, and monitor the financial performance of trade association members. Membership of an association often acts as a mark of quality for its members, providing reassurance to customers about the security of their payments or the reliability of the company.

Some suppliers require travel agencies to be licensed by their own trade association, for example travel agencies that sell scheduled airline seats require an International Air Transport Association (IATA) licence, which is granted after inspection of the financial performance of an agency and stipulates the minimum levels of qualification and staff required in order to hold a licence. IATA's Passenger Sales Agency Agreement (PSA) defines the minimum requirements that agencies and airlines must adhere to in their transactions (IATA, 2017).

LEGISLATION

Travel intermediaries are subject to the same laws as non-travel businesses, for example the consumer protection legislation that enforces consumer rights and the responsibilities of manufacturers, retailers and consumers. In some generating regions, laws specifically regulating travel intermediaries have been introduced. For instance in some US states, travel agencies require state registration in order to trade (State of California Department of Justice, 2017) and since 1993 operators selling ITs within the EU have been subject to very strict legislation governing their business practices as Snapshot 6.3 describes.

The main consumer protection elements of regulation of intermediaries relate to:

- the security of customers' payments
- the accuracy and clarity of information provided to customers
- for operators selling to customers in the EU, the safety of the tourist during the trip.

Each of these will now be discussed.

Security of Customers' Payments

Customers booking through intermediaries pay in advance of departure – the reservation is secured by payment of a deposit when the reservation is made and the balance is usually paid six to eight weeks before departure. Intermediaries may not be required to pay suppliers until after the customer has consumed the product. If the intermediary business collapses whilst holding these payments, customers who have not yet travelled will lose their reservations with no refund, and customers who are travelling at the time of the company's collapse will be stranded in the destination with no transport home and probably no accommodation. Suppliers in destinations will also not be paid. When this happens, consumer confidence in travel intermediaries is adversely affected and suppliers in destinations may be less willing to work with intermediaries from the same generating region.

In order to prevent this, some trade associations require operators and agencies to guarantee the security of their customers' payments; in the event of financial failure, all monies paid by customers will be refunded and customers who are in the destination will complete their trip and be transported back as originally planned if possible.

Bond: A promise from an organisation, a bank or an insurance company to refund payments if a company collapses

Often financial assurance is provided through a **bond** which is administered by a trade association, for example the United States Tour Operators Association's (USTOA) $1 million Traveler's Assistance Programme which requires all members to post a bond or letter of credit of $1 million as security to refund customers in the event of insolvency (USTOA, 2017). Travel agencies that are members of ABTA in the UK must have a bond (ABTA, 2015b).

Operators within all EU member states are required by law to provide financial protection to their customers, the implementation of which may vary between EU countries. In the UK, all packaged tours that include flights must be bonded with the Civil Aviation Authority (CAA) through the Air Tour Operator's Licence scheme (ATOL), to which all ATOL holders contribute a fee per passenger. In the event of a company failure, the CAA arranges repatriation and refunds (CAA, 2015). Purchasers of packaged tours that do not include flights can be protected through a bond operated by a trade association, such as the Association of Independent Tour Operators (AITO), through an insurance policy, or through the holding of all monies paid to the operator in a trust account such as the Travel Trust Association (TTA).

Wholesalers are not generally required to be licensed by a government agency, nor to provide financial guarantees for their customers' payments in the event of insolvency, because traditionally they have provided a B2B service. However, the development of online sales of wholesalers' products direct to the consumer, or to travel agents who dynamically package them together with transport on behalf of the consumer, is beginning to reveal the vulnerability of wholesalers' consumers. Snapshot 6.3 describes updated EU legislation to protect consumers of dynamically packaged travel.

Accuracy and Clarity of Information

Until the emergence of the Internet, intermediaries' customers made their decision to purchase a travel product from the information provided by the intermediary. The customer could not verify this information until their arrival at the destination.

Tour operators' customers were particularly vulnerable because their purchase decision was usually based on brochures provided by the tour operators themselves. These brochures depicted destinations and suppliers with photographs and elaborated on these using descriptions. The brochure was a sales tool and some less scrupulous operators exaggerated, misrepresented or withheld some facts in order to sell their holidays (Horner and Swarbrooke, 2004). For example, the fact that a hotel was located on a very busy road may have been omitted, or the photograph may have inaccurately implied that all rooms had balconies or sea views. In extreme cases in the 1960s and 1970s, customers arrived at destinations to find that the building of their hotel was incomplete and they had to be accommodated elsewhere (Delaney-Smith, 1987).

Scrupulous operators could be the victims of poor business practices by suppliers: over-bookings were not unusual and last-minute changes to the product (e.g. flight times or the closure of facilities at a hotel) would undermine operators' ability to provide the experience that customers expected. As a result, the tour operator sector gained a reputation for being unreliable and untrustworthy.

Some trade associations, for example ABTA in the UK and the Council of Australian Tour Operators (CATO), fought against this by implementing and enforcing codes of conduct for their members and setting higher standards of clarity, accuracy and reliability. As a result, a tour operator's membership of such an association became a mark of quality that provided customers with assurance about the packaged trip they were purchasing.

In the EU, legislation to ensure accuracy was included in the 1992 Package Travel Regulations (described in Snapshot 6.3) and set comprehensive laws about descriptions, notifications of any changes and contractual terms relating to surcharges, cancellation and compensation for changes (Pender, 2001).

The Safety of Tourists During their Trip

Regulation for the safety of intermediaries' customers is also applied in some generating regions.

Safety is an important issue because intermediaries select suppliers in destination areas on behalf of their customers. These suppliers are governed by the legislation of their own national governments in terms of health and safety, for example of hygiene standards in kitchens, fire protection in hotels, or the licensing of coach drivers. However, these local standards may be lower than the level that tourists are accustomed to in their home regions. In addition, local inspection processes to ensure compliance may not be as rigorous as would be necessary in some regions. Therefore, consumers may be at risk if a supplier selected for them by an intermediary does not comply with health and safety legislation, or if the local standard is inadequate. This has important implications for operators in particular because they have a legal responsibility for the fulfilment of the contract.

Many operators ensure that the suppliers they contract comply with acceptable standards by conducting their own health and safety audits when contracting. In the EU this is particularly important for operators because European regulations since 1992 hold the operator legally responsible for the safety of their customers; if a customer is injured or killed as a result of the negligence of a supplier, the operator acting as intermediary is liable to prosecution (Yale, 1995).

The snapshot below describes the EU legislation.

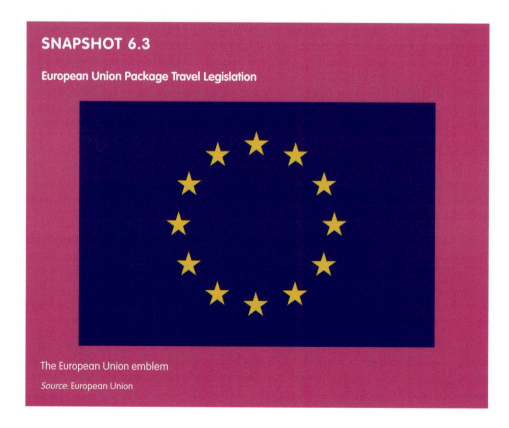

SNAPSHOT 6.3

European Union Package Travel Legislation

The European Union emblem

Source: European Union

In November 2015 the EU adopted a new Package Travel Directive (2015/2302/EU) to become law in all member states on 1 July 2018. The new legislation extends the original 1990 EU Package Travel Directive from tour operators to include more recent forms of combined travel that have emerged in the digital age.

A package is a booking that involves two or more travel elements, for example a flight and a hotel, or a hotel and car hire. Any booking for a single item, for example a hotel-only booking, is not covered by the legislation.

The legislation requires the provider of the package to guarantee that if the seller or any of its suppliers cease to trade, the customer will receive a refund, an alternative holiday or repatriation to the region of departure.

The new legislation defines package travel as one of three types of travel combinations:

Pre-arranged packages: Ready-made holidays purchased from a tour operator.

Customised packages: A selection of elements for the same trip purchased from a single business online or offline, for example an agency or an operator. This includes dynamically-packaged trips.

Linked travel arrangements: A looser combination of elements that are booked through linked websites within 24 hours of each other, for example an airline's website and a link to a hotel booking agency.

The legislation also requires types one and two to adhere to specific obligations, clarity and accuracy of information, and correct fulfillment of the contract.

Source: European Commission (2015a)

INCREASING CONCENTRATION IN THE TRAVEL INTERMEDIARIES SECTOR

The discussion of each type of travel intermediary highlights the significance of buying power in negotiations with suppliers. Buying power allows more efficient production which can be translated into lower, and therefore more competitive, prices or greater profit margins. In addition, the low profit margins and precarious profitability of some intermediaries mean that their survival depends on massive volume of sales. Therefore market power is a key motive in the growth strategies of travel intermediaries. OTAs establish market power through the volume of traffic that they drive to their websites, and the range of brands that they own. Case Study 6.1 shows how The Priceline Group and Expedia Inc. consist of several different brands that offer complementary travel services and/or target a range of market segments. This is a typical structure amongst travel intermediaries. As a result the offline and online travel distribution sector has been dominated by a small number of very powerful companies that are vertically and horizontally integrated and are forging expansion into emerging generating regions in Asia and South America.

We will now consider integration in the context of all intermediaries.

TRAVEL INTERMEDIARY INTEGRATION

'Integration' is a form of strategic growth that is prevalent in the tourism system and in particular among the intermediaries sector (Pender, 2001). Integration is the creation of formal links between companies and provides three broad advantages to companies – security, efficiency and monopoly. Integration can be achieved in two ways: horizontally and vertically; Snapshot 6.4 describes the vertical and horizontal structure of Airbnb.

Horizontal Integration

Horizontal integration occurs when a company expands through an acquisition or merger with another company at the same stage of the same industry. Horizontal integration occurs within all types of travel intermediary, on a domestic or international basis, for example two agency companies, two wholesalers or two operators uniting under the same ownership.

Horizontal integration provides a number of advantages that can allow companies to compete more effectively:

- Economies of scale – the combined companies reduce costs per sale through rationalising business functions such as reservations, human resources (HR) or marketing, or closing down duplicate sites (Yale, 1995). Their increased size may enhance their bargaining power with suppliers (Renshaw, 1992).

- The opportunity to move into complementary products for which growth in demand is intensifying. The acquisition of an existing successful company achieves benefits more quickly than setting up a new one (Pender, 2001).

- A rapid increase in market share by buying into an existing market. Large intermediaries in mature markets are expanding their geographical spread by acquiring small intermediaries in emerging markets.

SNAPSHOT 6.4

Airbnb

Airbnb is a platform offering P2P home-shares by connecting home owners in destinations with tourists seeking accommodation. Established in 2008, it now offers over three million property listings worldwide and has booked over 160 million guests. It charges the host 3 per cent commission on each booking (Airbnb, 2017).

Airbnb aspires to offer a range of tourism-related services (Airbnb, 2017) and since 2011 has expanded into new products and markets:

- Airbnb for Business specialises in 'Business Travel Ready' accommodation for companies. Travel managers can book, track and report business travel activity via the 'Airbnb for Work' dashboard. In 2016, American Express Travel and Carlson Wagonlit Travel began selling Airbnb, and Delta Airlines and Qantas entered a partnership with Airbnb to enable their loyalty scheme members to earn points on Airbnb bookings (Airbnb, 2017).

- A number of technology and travel acquisitions since 2011 including Crashpadder (2012) Vamo (21015), Trip4real (2016) and Luxury Retreats (2017) (Schaal, 2017).

Airbnb property, Majorca

Source: Claudia Dolezal

- Two new products launched in December 2016:

    i.   Trips – tour and activities offered by locals, 20 per cent commission charged

    ii. Places – recommendations for restaurants, events and meet ups (Ting, 2016b)

- Future plans include car rentals, restaurant reservations and grocery delivery through its Airbnb app (Ting, 2016b).

- Speculation, in late 2016, that Airbnb would soon offer flight reservations (Schaal, 2016).

Vertical Integration

'Vertical integration' refers to the merging of companies that operate at different levels of the stages of production in the same sector, for example a retailer and a manufacturer. Figure 6.1 at the beginning of this chapter, showing the traditional channels of distribution in the tourism system, would demonstrate vertical integration if one company owned subsidiaries that operated within separate channels. For example if an airline, a wholesaler, an operator and an agency, or any two of these, were owned by the same parent company, the company would be described as vertically integrated, and known as a travel organiser or travel group. For example TUI Travel PLC and Thomas Cook Group comprise their own airlines, hotels, operator and agency companies.

Vertical integration can be described as forward or backward (Pender, 2001). Forward, or downstream, integration occurs when the original company integrates with a company that operates at a later stage of production, for example an airline integrating with a tour operator, or a tour operator integrating with a travel agency.

Backward, or upstream, integration occurs when the original company integrates with another company that operates at an earlier stage of production, for example an agency with an operator, or an operator with an airline.

Sometimes operators integrate forward with agencies, followed by a backward integration with charter airlines, and sometimes hotel companies and cruise lines. In the leisure-travel market, vertically integrated travel intermediaries are very powerful because of their size. Many destinations, particularly in coastal regions such as the Mediterranean, rely heavily on the two main leisure travel intermediaries in Europe – Thomas Cook and TUI Travel – as a source for their tourists.

Vertical integration is very common in the travel industry due to the competitive advantages that it creates, identified by Pender (2001) as:

- Forward integration that provides a secure source of buyers for all or part of the company's capacity, and may reduce the cost of those sales through the reduced marketing effort required, which may in turn impact on pricing.

- Backward integration that secures the supply of a product, perhaps at a more attractive price than competitors would be able to purchase it for, and controls competitors' access to the product.

- Both of these forms of integration provide control over supply and pricing, and provide the opportunity of maintaining a consistent quality of product and standard of service throughout most of the customer's travel experience.

- Vertical integration provides a competitive advantage over rivals who are not vertically integrated, possibly pushing them out of the market and creating barriers to entry for new entrants.

Online distributors, in the form of search engines, target the independent market and offer reduced distribution costs compared to traditional channels of distribution.

TRAVEL AGGREGATOR SITES

Travel aggregator sites, also known as 'travel metasearch' sites, are internet search engines that collect data from travel suppliers and intermediaries' websites and display the best prices for a requested availability.

Transportation, accommodation, attractions, wholesalers and OTAs may allow some or all of these search engines access to their computerised inventory. When a customer clicks through from the aggregator site to a supplier's or intermediary's website to make a booking, the search engine receives a fee. Some travel aggregators specialise in one form of supply, for instance flights or hotels, while others offer a full range of travel supply.

The largest travel aggregator sites include Google Flights, Google Hotel Planner, KAYAK, Momondo, Skyscanner and Trivago.

Travel aggregators are not agencies, wholesalers or operators and for this reason do not fit easily into the traditional channels of distribution. They create a promotional channel which potentially can be used by other intermediaries and suppliers to advertise on.

SUMMARY

The travel intermediary sector is a volatile and at times unstable part of the tourism system that experiences frequent change. The ability to compete effectively in mature markets often depends on the expansion of individual companies and the eventual domination of a market by a small number of very powerful companies.

The development of online and mobile technology has had a major impact on the intermediaries sector, not least because it has enabled suppliers to reach some consumers directly and cut out intermediaries. However, through dynamic packaging, the agency and wholesale sectors have been able to defend their positions.

Although the role of intermediaries has changed, there will always be a role in the tourism system for them. Some markets will never purchase travel products direct from suppliers, some types of travel product are too complex for individuals to arrange independently, and large intermediaries will continue to offer suppliers' capacity at prices below that which individuals can purchase directly. While the travel intermediary sector will continue to evolve in response to external influences, and there will be shifts in the structure of the sector as a whole, intermediaries will continue to fulfil a vital function in the tourism system.

SELF-TEST QUESTIONS

1. Consider your most recent trip. Which channels of distribution did you use to make the bookings? Why did – or didn't – you use an intermediary?

2. Why are OTAs so popular? What benefits do they offer the consumer?

3. Look at the website of either TUI Travel PLC or Thomas Cook Group (listed below). Which types of intermediary does the business consist of? Can you find one example of a wholesaler, tour operator, MICE operator, TMC and leisure travel agency?

FURTHER READING

Dredge, D. and Gyimothy, S. (eds) (2017) *Collaborative Economy and Tourism: Perspectives, Politics, Policies and Prospects (Tourism on the Edge)*. Cham: Springer International.

Holland, J. and Leslie, D. (2017) *Tour Operators and Operations: Development, Management and Responsibility*. Wallingford: CABI.

Strauss, M. (2011) *Value Creation in Travel Distribution*. lulu.com.

USEFUL WEBSITES

Airbnb: www.airbnb.co.uk/about/about-us

American Association of Travel Agents (ASTA): www.asta.org/

Association of British Travel Agents (ABTA): https://abta.com/

European Tour Operators Association (ETOA): www.etoa.org/

Expedia, Inc: www.expediainc.com/expedia-brands/

Priceline Group: www.pricelinegroup.com/

Skift.com: https://skift.com/

Thomas Cook Group: www.thomascookgroup.com/

Travelmole: www.travelmole.com/

TTG Media: www.ttgmedia.com/

TUI Group: www.tuigroup.com/en-en/about-us/about-tui-group

United States Tour Operator Association (USTOA): www.ustoa.com/

PART III
IMPACTS OF TOURISM

CONTENTS

7

THE ECONOMIC IMPACTS OF TOURISM

'It has become a cliché to state that tourism is the world's largest industry. Does the claim really matter? Perhaps it was made simply to attract the attention of the politicians and those who fund the research.'

C. Ryan, 2002: 148

LEARNING OUTCOMES

After reading this chapter you will understand:

- the economic benefits tourism development can bring to a destination, but also the disadvantages that tourism development may bring
- two ways used to measure the economic impacts of tourism: the multiplier effect and Tourism Satellite Accounts
- the value of tourism as an economic regeneration tool for urban and rural areas
- the basic principles that can help a destination optimise the economic benefits of tourism.

Shop display in Marmaris, Turkey

Source: Lynn Minnaert

INTRODUCTION

In Chapter 2 we saw that tourism arises as a consequence of the physical movement of individuals from the generating region to the destination region to engage in tourist activities. This physical flow of tourists into a destination is usually accompanied by flows of their money too; money that is earned in the generating region, but spent in the destination on products that would be unlikely to exist without tourism, such as commercial accommodation, attractions and conference facilities, and also on products that primarily serve the local community, for instance shops, restaurants and local transport.

The injection of tourists' spending into the local economy has great economic potential and for this reason tourism is viewed by national, regional and local governments as a sector with the potential to stimulate or revive economic growth. The potential economic impacts of tourism are often the main motive for the planned development of destinations by the state, but many destinations have developed in response to entrepreneurial opportunities created by visits by venturers or explorer type tourists who require accommodation and catering services during their stay.

In this chapter we consider how tourism may benefit the destination economy and the reasons why these benefits may not be fully realised. We discuss how the economic impacts of tourism are measured and end the chapter by considering how economic impacts can be managed to ensure that the benefits for the host community are optimised.

TYPES OF ECONOMIC IMPACT

Before we consider how tourism affects a destination economy, it is useful to understand how these impacts are described by economists. The economic effects of any sector on an economy can be direct, indirect or induced:

Direct economic impacts: This refers to the impacts that are generated directly via tourism expenditure. Tourist income directly generates income and jobs in hotels, attractions, tour companies and travel agencies. Much of the passenger transport in airlines is tourism-related – be it for leisure or business purposes. Tourists' expenditure may also generate direct economic impacts in places that are not strictly part of the tourism industries, such as health spas, clothing stores, cinemas and internet cafés.

Indirect economic impacts: This refers to instances where tourist expenditure indirectly augments the local economy, via purchases made by the businesses that cater for tourists. If a hotel, for example, buys in foodstuffs from a local producer or wholesaler, it will increase its order if business is going well: either because there are more tourists or because the tourists are spending more. Similarly, if a local retail store attracts more customers because of tourism, it may need to hire extra staff. In both cases businesses that are not within the tourism sector are benefitting from tourism indirectly.

Induced economic impacts: This refers to the economic impacts that are the result of expenditure by residents of the region, who have been directly or indirectly affected by tourist expenditure. This type of economic impact is the least visible of the three: it refers to the general economic situation of the region. If through tourism many residents of a region are better off (because of income that is generated directly or indirectly), they are likely to spend more and make many local businesses flourish. They may in turn hire more staff or pay more taxes. The idea is therefore that because the region is generally better off due to tourism this affects almost everybody, even people who do not benefit directly or indirectly from tourism income.

Vanhove (2005) classifies the economic impacts of tourism into six types (see Table 7.1). We will now consider each of these and how their impact may be positive or negative.

INCOME GENERATION

The economic significance of the tourism sector can be clearly demonstrated by the level of income or revenue it generates. In 2016 international tourism generated

TABLE 7.1 Economic impacts of tourism

Income generation	The income that is generated via tourism activities, where it is generated, and how it is distributed.
Employment generation	The number of jobs that are generated via tourism activities, the type and quality of the jobs, and the type of employees that work in them.
Tax revenue generation	The revenue that the government makes via taxation of tourist activities, and the products and services that are taxed.
Balance of payments	A record of the financial transactions between one country and the rest of the world.
Improvement of the economic structure of a destination region	The development of different linkages between tourism and other sectors in the economy of the destination.
Encouragement of entrepreneurial activity	The extent to which tourism encourages entrepreneurs in the host community to start or expand their business.

US$1,260 billion, which equalled 10 per cent of the world's GDP (UNWTO, 2017c: 3). This statistic only includes the revenue generated from international tourism; domestic tourism revenues are often less frequently or accurately recorded, but are in many countries very significant. As a worldwide export category, tourism ranks third after fuels and chemicals, and ahead of food and automotive products.

Eurostat, the EU's statistical office, offers statistics on both domestic and international tourism expenditures. In 2015, EU residents spent an estimated €408 billion on tourism trips. Of this, they spent 46 per cent on trips in their country of residence (domestic tourism) and 54 per cent on trips abroad (outbound tourism). For each tourism trip, Europeans spent on average €348. Broken down by destination, they spent €212 on average on a domestic trip and €751 on an outbound trip. Accommodation took up 36 per cent of tourism expenditure, while transport accounted for 32 per cent and miscellaneous other costs for 32 per cent. German and French tourists were the biggest spenders overall.

Tourism Australia calculated that international tourists spent almost AU$40 billion in the country in the first half of 2017. Domestic tourists spent an even larger amount: AU$42 billion (Tourism Australia, 2017c). In the USA, the travel and tourism industries contributed nearly US$1.6 trillion to the US economy in 2015, or 2.6 per cent of its GDP.

EMPLOYMENT GENERATION

As tourism plays an increasingly important role in the economy of many countries, its role as a creator of jobs is becoming widely apparent. Tourism is often seen as particularly suitable to tackle unemployment and underemployment by policy makers because:

- it is a growing sector in many destination regions

- it is varied and resilient

- it is labour-intensive

- it provides many jobs with low entry possibilities – many tourism jobs are relatively low-skilled, and employees do not need extensive training or experience. These jobs are especially suitable for individuals who may face challenges or discrimination in the labour market, such as unemployed young people, the long-term unemployed, the less-skilled, ethnic minority groups and, to some degree, women (re-entering the labour market) (OECD, 2008b: 127).

Worldwide, the tourism sector was estimated to directly and indirectly generate 292 million global jobs in 2016. By 2027, travel and tourism is expected to support more than 380 million jobs globally, which equates to 1 in 9 of all jobs in the world, and the sector is expected to contribute around 23 per cent of total global net job creation over the next decade. However, the proportion of total employment supplied by tourism is often very high in island economies: in Aruba in 2016, 91.2 per cent of the population was directly or indirectly employed in the tourism sector (WTTC, 2017a). In comparison, VisitBritain reported that in 2013, the tourism industry generated approximately over 3.1 million jobs: 1.75 million of those were direct tourism jobs, while 1.35 million were indirect tourism jobs. The combined direct and indirect employment of tourism represented about 9.6 per cent of the UK's overall employment (Deloitte and Oxford Economics, 2013: 1). Even though tourism can be used to increase overall employment and reduce the number of people on unemployment

Gross Domestic Product (GDP): A term used to indicate the overall economic performance of a country; takes into account consumption, investments, government spending, exports and imports

benefits, not all tourism labour achieves this. Critical labour shortages in the peak season are often filled by immigrant seasonal workers. Such workers may be hired to fill poorly paid, insecure and unpleasant jobs. Sometimes they are employed illegally. Immigrant seasonal workers, and also casual or student workers, can be used by employers to keep their costs down (OECD, 2008b: 131). This sort of employment has little impact on the overall employment levels in a destination.

The impact of tourism on employment can be measured by counting the number of individuals employed, or the number of jobs generated. The two figures can be different, as several people can be employed in a part-time capacity to fill one job. The structure of tourism in a destination creates problems in measuring employment because it is a heterogeneous sector, with a wide variety of types and sizes of businesses. Some jobs are *directly* generated by tourism (by businesses selling products and services directly to tourists, e.g. travel agents and cruise operators), whereas other jobs are *indirectly* created (with the suppliers of tourism businesses, e.g. food producers, wine merchants or printers of promotional material). Therefore it can be very difficult to get an overview of all the jobs directly and indirectly linked to tourism. An added difficulty here is that tourism incorporates many sub-sectors: accommodation, food and beverage, transport, retail and insurance, to name but a few.

To overcome the fact that direct and indirect tourism jobs cannot be easily counted, tourism employment is often measured by translating expenditure or consumption into a number of jobs using a labour coefficient or ratio. This means that the total expenditure of tourists is divided by a figure that is calculated to represent how many direct jobs this expenditure would normally generate. The result of this calculation is an approximate number of *full-time equivalent* jobs. The ratio can then be used to predict how many extra jobs an increase in tourism expenditure would create. It can also be used as the basis of an estimate of indirect employment (OECD, 2008b: 137). It is important to note here that by using a ratio of tourist expenditure one can only estimate the number of jobs in the sector: although this process will lead to a rigorous estimate, it is important to remember that it is an estimate nonetheless.

TAX REVENUE GENERATION

Tourism can be a source of income for the government via taxes. A tax, as opposed to a user charge, is an involuntary payment to the government that does not entitle the payer to receive a direct benefit or equivalent value in return (Mak, 2004: 149). Taxes related to tourism can be levied on tourism businesses, or directly on tourists. The UNWTO has identified 40 different types of these taxes. Examples of tourism businesses and products that can be taxed are airports and airlines, hotels, accommodation, food and beverages, and gambling facilities. Although most taxes are payable by residents of a country and tourists alike, some are specifically targeted at tourists. A common example is entry/exit charges and visa fees. Accommodation taxes, such as a 'bed tax', or taxes on car rentals, are also mainly aimed at tourists (Gooroochurn and Sinclair, 2005). The practice of getting non-residents to pay tax is called 'tax exporting' (Mak, 2004: 149).

Taxation aims to create revenue, which may correct market failure. The term 'market failure' refers to a situation where markets provide either too little or too many of the specific goods and services we desire (Mak, 2004: 153). Tourists, for example, use a range of public goods that they do not pay for: they use roads, pavements, parks and beaches; their rubbish and waste needs to be collected; they expect certain security measures to be in place at free events, and require the provision of signage, parking facilities and information about the destination. While tourists generate costs for the destination economy, the local population pays for them via taxation: it is clear that here the market system is 'failing' to divide these costs fairly. This is why taxes targeting tourists can be seen as a justified way to recuperate these costs. Moreover, tourists tend to have no voting power in the local area. Local politicians can thus easily target them for taxation without losing local support. Local tourism businesses, however, may be against taxing tourists, as this may affect the destination's ability to compete with other destinations.

Statistics Canada publishes a detailed report on the portion of government revenue that is directly attributable to tourism. In 2015, this figure amounted to CAN$24.7 billion. Domestic tourism spending accounted for 77.4 per cent of this revenue, with the remainder coming from tourism exports. Taxes play an important role in the generation of this tourism revenue. The biggest source of revenue was found to be taxes on products (or final sales) – in most countries this is referred to as Value Added Tax or VAT. These taxes accounted for CAN$14.2 billion for the federal government (Statistics Canada, 2017a).

BALANCE OF PAYMENTS

A country's balance of payments is 'a systematic record of all transactions between residents of one country and the rest of the world' (Begg et al., 1994: 513). In this record money coming into the country is entered as 'credits', whereas money leaving the country is entered as 'debits'. A balance of payments record can be compiled specifically for tourism: in this case, the money foreign tourists spend in a country will be compared to the money residents of that country spend on holidays abroad. In some countries, the tourism balance of payments will be positive because inbound tourists' expenditure is greater than that of outbound tourists. Often developing countries whose residents have low propensities (see Chapter 3) to travel internationally and where inbound tourism for leisure or business is well established will have a surplus on their tourism balance of payments – burgeoning tourism industries such as those of Kenya and the Gambia are examples here. This is called a 'surplus'. Other countries can have a negative tourism balance of payments: their residents spend more abroad than inbound tourism earns. Developed economies whose residents have a high propensity to travel internationally, for example Japan, are likely to be in this position. This is called a 'deficit'. The following case study identifies the countries with the highest surplus or deficit on their tourism balance of payments.

CASE STUDY 7.1

International Tourism Balance of Payments

UNWTO figures show the tourism balance of payments for a number of important tourism-generating and tourism-receiving countries. Figure 7.1, with figures from 2012, shows the countries that have a significant surplus: in other words, they receive more revenue from tourism than the money their residents spend on holidays abroad. These are usually

FIGURE 7.1 International tourism balance of payments by country, US$

Source: VisitBritain (2012)

popular 'sun and sea' tourism destinations (e.g. Spain and Turkey). Countries that have strong domestic tourism industries (USA, France, Italy, Spain) benefit in terms of the tourism balance of payments: if a resident of a country takes a domestic holiday, the money

(Continued)

spent does not leave the economy, and thus does not cause a deficit. Germany, the UK, Russia and Japan recorded the largest deficits in 2012. Countries with deficits are usually Northern and Western European countries, as well as developed economies in Asia and the Middle East.

VisitBritain researched the Tourism Balance of Payment for the UK and recorded a significant increase in the deficit after 1998. The main reasons for this were growth in demand for outbound tourism fuelled by a booming economy and a more affluent population, on the demand side, and cheaper flights provided by low-cost airlines, on the supply side, so more people had the opportunity to travel internationally, with a whole range of new destinations to explore. In the 1970s the UK had a temporary surplus in its balance of payments, as shown in Figure 7.2. This was due to worsened economic conditions in the UK, rising unemployment, restricted access to credit and a restriction in the amount of sterling that could be taken outside the UK, resulting in fewer people travelling and a weaker pound (VisitBritain, 2012).

FIGURE 7.2   The UK's international tourism balance of payments

Source: VisitBritain/Office for National Statistics (2012).

The UK's tourism deficit continues to grow: in 2016, UK residents spent £43.8 billion on visits abroad in 2016, whereas overseas residents spent £22.5 billion on visits to the UK (Office for National Statistics, 2017b). Figure 7.3 shows the countries where the UK has the biggest deficits.

For some countries, the amount of money their residents spent in the UK was slightly higher than the money British residents spend there – for these countries, the UK is showing a surplus. Please note, however, that the scale of Figure 7.4 is much smaller than the scale of Figure 7.3: this highlights that UK surpluses in these countries are much smaller than the deficits with the popular destinations in Figure 7.3. As such the overall tourism balance of payments for the UK is clearly negative, even though for a few countries surpluses are noted.

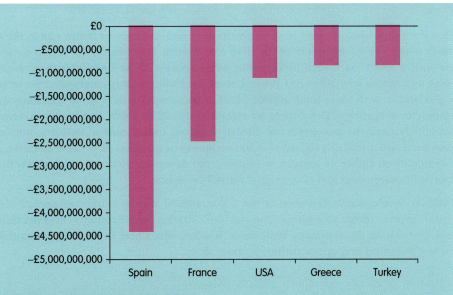

FIGURE 7.3   UK tourism balance: deficits

Source: VisitBritain/Office for National Statistics (2012).

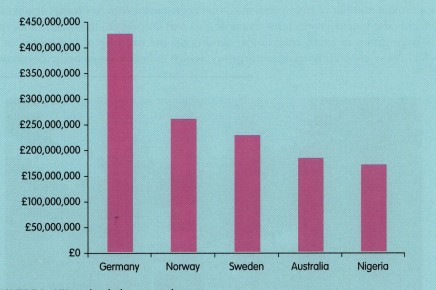

FIGURE 7.4   UK tourism balance: surpluses

Source: VisitBritain/Office for National Statistics (2012).

Reflective Questions

1. What characterises the countries that show the biggest balance of payments surpluses in tourism? What characterises the countries with the biggest deficits?

2. What can destinations do to reduce the balance of payments deficits in tourism?

IMPROVEMENT OF THE ECONOMIC STRUCTURE OF A REGION

This economic impact refers to the contribution one industry or sector can make to other sectors in the economy of the host community. Tourism can be seen as a sector with a lot of 'backward linkages' to other sectors in the destination's economy (Wall and Mathieson, 2006: 84). A local hotel, for example, may establish close working relations with local food and drink suppliers, entertainers, tradespersons and employment agencies. Developing tourism in a destination can thus bring economic benefits not only to those who are directly involved in the tourism industry, but can also have wider indirect impacts on the economy of a region. It is often because of this perceived ability of tourism to improve the economic structure of a region that tourism is supported and encouraged via public policy.

Tourism development, however, is not a guaranteed way to bring widespread economic improvements to regions. The sections 'Tourism and Economic Regeneration' and 'Optimising the Economic Benefits of Tourism' elsewhere in this chapter explain these challenges and opportunities in more detail.

ENCOURAGEMENT OF ENTREPRENEURIAL ACTIVITY

The tourism sector in many destinations is characterised by a dual structure: the tourist product is supplied by either large national or multi-national companies, or by small and medium-sized enterprises or microbusinesses. On the one hand, there are a limited number of large companies that organise tourism to various destinations or supply the tourist product, for example TUI and Disney. On the other hand, there is a large group of small companies, making up the majority of businesses in the sector. These are mainly micro-enterprises, which deliver tourism at the destination.

A shop along a tourist road in Mali

Source: Lynn Minnaert

The large companies are mainly in charge of the organisation, information and transport, whereas small companies are directed towards welcoming tourists, hospitality and leisure (Ecorys, 2009: 20).

The smaller companies in the tourism sector are mostly characterised by self-employment and small family firms (Boer et al., 1997; OECD, 2008a). This is often due to the fact that many tourism businesses do not require large amounts of investment to set up: a food and beverage outlet, bed and breakfast or souvenir shop has a relatively low entry level, which makes it an attractive business to start up as an independent entrepreneur. In developing countries, tourists may be a particularly attractive market for producers of foodstuffs, handicrafts and souvenirs – or for tourism services such as those of tour guides, taxi drivers and entertainers. Pro-poor tourism is a form of tourism that is particularly aimed at bringing the economic and social benefits of tourism to poor communities in the destination via enterprise and entrepreneurship (for a fuller exploration of pro-poor tourism, see Chapter 8).

The presence of multinational businesses can make working as an independent entrepreneur rather difficult: this is particularly true for all-inclusive resorts whose guests tend to stay on the property and only consume the products and services offered there. Amalia Cabezas has researched the experiences of independent guides in the Dominican Republic and found that local entrepreneurs were at times displaced by foreign-owned businesses:

> The agents of these corporations are talking bad about us, about assaults, assassinations, and such things. We are walking guides; we provide a service. My friends and I speak different languages. Why is it that all the hotels and the travel agencies and the stores in the resorts have to use foreigners to work there? Why, if I speak German, I can defend myself in Italian, I am excellent in English? I can sell anything in German. It is something that I do not understand. I used to sell horseback riding tours; now all those are owned by Germans. They are displacing us in our own country. (2008: 30)

DISADVANTAGES

Although the development of tourism can bring a range of economic benefits to a region, not all the economic impacts are always positive. Tourism development is also associated with a number of economic disadvantages – the most prominent disadvantages are reviewed here.

Costs

While tourism may be able to bring money into the economy, there are also certain costs to the local community associated with it. These are usually paid by public money, which in turn is often reliant on taxes paid by the local community. These costs can be divided into three categories: direct, indirect and opportunity costs.

> *Direct costs* are costs that are directly linked to the provision of tourism products or services. A museum, for example, that is run by the local government needs to be staffed, cleaned, marketed and maintained. Most destinations have a tourist office or tourism information centre; again, this is mostly funded by

public money, although in many destinations tourism suppliers may contribute voluntarily through membership. The reasoning is that the provision of these goods and services stimulates the local economy, resulting in higher consumption by tourists and increases in employment. As stated in the previous section, some of these costs can be recouped via taxation on tourist activities.

Indirect costs are costs that are not directly linked to the provision of tourism goods and services, but that rise when the volume of tourists in the destination rises. Waste collection is an example: this service is not there purely for the tourists, but will be more intensively used when there are large numbers of tourists around. Another example is policing costs: staging events may require the police to be at hand to guarantee the safe running of the event, which may result in the need to pay overtime or extra staff.

Opportunity costs are costs of the opportunities that are lost because of the development of tourism. Instead of investing in a tourist information centre, for example, the destination could invest in a job centre that helps unemployed people find employment. If this option or opportunity had been chosen, the costs to the local community could have been reduced, as fewer unemployment benefits may have needed to be paid. If the savings made by the job centre would have been higher than the income from tourism, then those surplus savings can be seen as an opportunity cost. The concept of opportunity costs is particularly useful when thinking about encouraging tourism in developing countries, as a vehicle for economic advancement. Policy makers need to weigh up the projected costs and benefits of developing tourism up against the projected costs and benefits of other industries (e.g. agriculture, manufacturing etc.).

Inflation

Inflation can be described as a rise in the general level of prices or a fall in the purchasing power of money (Tribe, 2005: 272). Tourism can cause inflation because it can make the demand for a certain product or service go up sharply where it may be in limited supply. A typical example would be tourists buying holiday homes in a foreign destination. Because the demand for homes goes up the prices will generally rise, unless the supply of homes keeps up. As the prices for homes go up, it may be difficult for local people to buy a home, as they may be priced out of the market by foreign tourists who may be more affluent or come from countries with a stronger currency. This type of inflation, caused by an economy that is growing so rapidly that supply cannot follow demand, is called 'demand-pull inflation' (Tribe, 2005).

Over-dependence

Although tourism has been shown to potentially bring a range of economic benefits to a region, over-dependence on tourism can make the area more economically vulnerable. A decrease in demand for the destination, a new competitor or an economic downturn in the source markets can all cause impacts on revenues and employment – and if tourism is the only major economy in the destination, then there are few other options to make up for the losses.

SNAPSHOT 7.1

Tourism in Egypt

Egypt, with its ancient pyramids and temples, beautiful beaches and stunning coral reefs, was long a top destination for international tourism. After a small drop in tourist arrivals in 2008, linked to the economic downturn, tourism in the country was on a steady upward trajectory, reaching over 14 million arrivals in 2010 (World Bank, 2017). In 2011, however, a popular uprising erupted – violent clashes between security forces and protesters resulted in the deaths of hundreds of people. The period of political instability that followed, as well as the downing of a Metrojet flight to Russia by ISIL in 2015, caused tourists to seek alternative destinations. As a result, Egypt's Central Agency for Public Mobilisation and Statistics (CAPMAS) reported only 4.8 million international arrivals in 2016.

A decline in arrivals of this magnitude has extensive economic and social consequences, particularly in a country that has been heavily dependent on tourism in the past. Prior to January 2011, tourism was Egypt's second-largest source of foreign currency and a significant source of employment. In 2010, the sector brought in US$12.5 billion in revenue, and employed 2.5 million Egyptians – over 10 per cent of the workforce. CAPMAS reported that in 2016, almost 30 per cent of the population was living below the poverty line. The devalued currency has led to inflation, resulting in families spending an ever greater proportion of their income on food. As tourists are staying away, foreign investment in tourism infrastructure (which can lead to job creation) has also declined. With little investment to diversify its economy, Egypt will remain dependent on a rebound of tourism for its economic recovery.

Sharm El Sheikh

Source: Roger Louis

Seasonality

Many destinations do not have the same influx of tourists all through the year: they are busy during the peak season and may then be rather deserted during the low season. Seasonality can have various negative economic impacts on destinations, listed by Baum and Lundtorp (2001: 2) as:

- A short business operating season with major periods of closure or a reduced level of operation.
- The consequent need to generate a full year's revenue within a short operating season while servicing fixed costs over a 12-month period.
- Under-utilisation of capital assets which are inflexible, and, generally, do not have obvious alternative uses.
- The consequent problem of attracting inward investment in tourism.
- Problems in maintaining the supply chain on the basis of a short operating season.
- Problems in ensuring sustained support from transport providers such as airlines and shipping companies, who are reluctant to maintain their commitment to and invest in highly seasonal operations.
- Short-term employment rather than sustainable long-term jobs, creating high levels of either off-season unemployment or temporary outward migration.
- Problems of maintaining service and product quality standards in the absence of permanent, long-term employees.

The supply chain: Made up of the business processes that get a product from the producer to the consumer

Increased Propensity to Imports

The economic benefits of tourism can be diminished strongly if the destination becomes more dependent on imports because of tourism development. If a luxury hotel, for example, builds a resort hotel in a developing country, many of the luxury goods the tourists desire and expect may not be available locally. In this case they will need to be imported from other regions, which causes the economic benefits of tourism to 'leak' out of the destination. This may cause a situation whereby the destination bears the disadvantages of tourism development (in terms of resource use, congestion and pollution) whereas the local population enjoys few of the economic benefits that are caused by tourism.

MEASURING ECONOMIC IMPACTS

This section will discuss two methods that can be used for measuring the economic impacts of tourism: the multiplier effect and Tourism Satellite Accounts (TSA). These are not the only two methods that can be used for this purpose: for a more in-depth review of measuring tools, see Vanhove (2005: 193–199).

MULTIPLIER EFFECT

Vanhove (2005) states that the multiplier concept is based on the idea that different sectors in the economy are interdependent. This would mean that tourism does not stand on its own in the economy: a hotel, for example, needs to source foodstuffs from the agricultural industry, a tourist attraction may need a website and therefore make use of the telecommunications industry, or a travel agency may take out loans and other products in the financial industry. The income that is created through tourism is thus dissipated (or multiplied) throughout the local economy via many of its sectors. The same idea can be applied to employment: a strong tourism industry creates jobs in the area, and as the employees of the tourism industry become financially better off, they may start using more services in the local area, thus creating jobs in other sectors and industries. In this section we will take the income multiplier as an example. At its most basic level, this multiplier can be seen as the sum of 'direct, indirect and induced income generation' (Vanhove, 2005).

The concept of the multiplier is based on the work of the economist John Maynard Keynes, who saw the economic wealth of a region (also called GRP or Gross Regional Product) as determined by injections (money coming in) and leakages (money flowing out) (Ioannides, 2003). The equation for calculating GRP is:

$$GRP = C + I + G + E - M$$

The following sections describe the meaning of the different components of the formula.

C = Consumption

'Consumption' stands for the money that is spent by consumers on goods and services (direct consumption) and by the producers of these goods and services (indirect consumption). For example: when consumers (in this case, tourists) spend money on tourism goods and services, this leads to direct income generation; when money is spent within the region to produce tourism goods and services, this leads to indirect income generation (see above).

Levels of consumption vary between different purposes of tourism and different types of tourist; for instance, leisure tourists usually use their own financial resources, whereas business tourists are funded by their employer. Business tourists tend to spend more than leisure tourists: 'As a rule of thumb, the ratio of daily expenditure by business travellers to that of leisure visitors is generally situated somewhere between 2:1 and 3:1. In other words, business visitors spend on average two to three times more per day than leisure visitors' (Rogers, T., 2013: 14).

The sum of all consumption related to a trip is called 'gross' consumption. Gross consumption also includes expenditure in the home environment before travelling (e.g. buying suntan lotion or new clothes before the holiday, or booking travel via an agent at home who earns commission on the trip) or after returning (e.g. getting your photos developed). The money that is spent at the destination is called 'net' consumption: to calculate net consumption, the consumption at home is thus deducted from the gross consumption (Mihalič, 2002). To calculate GRP, it is the *net* consumption that is of importance, as expenditure at home does not impact on the economy of the destination.

I = Investment

Tourism development can attract investment from individuals or businesses who consider tourism as a way to make a profitable return. Investors can be local, or can come from outside the region. Small destinations that attract large numbers of tourists are particularly prone to attracting outside investment. The risk with outside investors is that the profits may leak out of the region, thus reducing the multiplier effect (see M = Imports/leakages).

Investment incentives:
Government
schemes that are
aimed to encourage
the interest of
private investors in
certain sectors or
projects

Destinations in early stages of development, for example in developing countries, usu-ally need substantial financial investments to develop accommodation, infrastructure and attractions. Staff training may also be needed (Wall and Mathieson, 2006). This type of investment is often long-term and risky: not only is there no guarantee that the destination will be successful, the tourism industry is also heavily reliant on the general state of the economy and can be very seasonal. Private investors are usually not keen to tie up large sums of capital in investments that will only yield profits in the longer term. This is why the public sector may provide certain **incentives** (such as subsidies, tax concessions or low-cost loans) to encourage private investment (see also: G = Government spending).

G = Government Spending

National, regional and local governments can decide to spend money on developing tourism in a region. This is often seen as an investment, in the hope that tourism will generate substantial income or employment opportunities or economic restructuring. Public investments in tourism usually take one of the following forms:

Incentives to attract new suppliers: As discussed in the section above, tourism investments can be risky and public bodies may provide incentives to stimulate investment from private suppliers. Tax concessions, for example, are schemes whereby the government (temporarily or permanently) reduces taxes on certain business activities so that they become financially worthwhile. The government may also make available loans with low interest rates, or put in place a grants scheme whereby businesses can apply for money for tourism projects.

Promotion: Governments may stimulate demand by investing in destination pro-motion and branding. Tourism promotion campaigns are often largely (or even completely) publicly funded. The services of tourist information centres, tourist offices and convention bureaus can all be seen as ways to stimulate demand for and promote the destination.

Planning and regulation: The public sector plays an important role in the plan-ning and regulation of tourism (see Chapter 13 for a fuller discussion of this subject). The public sector covers the costs of providing this role.

Infrastructure: The government may invest in tourism-related infrastructure such as airports, roads, attractions, the maintenance of historic buildings and green spaces, museums, attractions, convention centres and festival halls.

E = Exports

Inbound tourism is an export because it involves the flow of money into the national economy from outside. This may seem like a paradox: after all, tourists are coming to visit the destination, and goods and services are thus not physically shipped (or exported) to them in their home country. International tourism, however, causes foreign consumers to buy a local product with foreign money; as such, this can be seen as an export, even though the tourist travels to consume the goods and services in the destination.

For many developing countries, generating foreign currency is particularly vital to pay for those goods and services that they import. Tourism can be an important

Departures board

Source: Lynn Minnaert

generator of foreign currency. In Japan in the 1980s, tourism was used to redress the international balance between imports and exports in the opposite direction: the country incurred an extreme trade surplus, which meant that it exported many more goods than it imported (mainly due to the popularity of the cars and technological products that were produced in the country). To offset this surplus, it sponsored the Ten Million Programme – it encouraged 10 million Japanese citizens to travel abroad by 1990 (Milner et al., 2000).

M = Imports/leakages

In tourism economics, 'leakage' is the part of national income that is not spent on domestically produced goods or services (Aramberri, 2005: 145). The term refers to tourists and tourism businesses buying imported goods and services, and the repatriation of profits by foreign owners (Mowforth and Munt, 2008). If tourists or tourism businesses buy imported goods, the indirect income generation of tourism is not achieved locally. If a hotel in Trinidad, for example, serves its guests asparagus imported from Peru, rather than vegetables that are grown locally such as ochroes or patchoi, then it is the farmer in Peru who indirectly benefits and not the local producer. Money that could have been multiplied within the region is thus instead 'leaked' out of it. Similarly, if the hotel in Trinidad is owned by a foreign corporation, then the profits of the hotel may leak out of the destination.

Leakage can already start before a tourist reaches the destination (Holden, 2008). If the holiday is booked by foreign intermediaries, such as tour operators and travel agents, then a share of the revenue leaks out of the destination here. If a tourist uses a foreign airline, that share is increased even further. This may mean that the main portion of the tourist's expenditure never reaches the destination.

The level of leakage in a destination is not always static and may change over time. When the destination is in the early stages of development, for example, it may be reliant on short-term imports of goods and services that are not available locally. As the destination develops, there may be more entrepreneurial activity and those goods and services may become available at the local level. Certain tourism products (e.g. high-end, luxury tourism) may require more foreign imports, but in some cases this may result in higher profits – in some cases, a higher level of leakage may thus cause a higher level of income because the profit margins are higher (Benavides, 2002).

TOURISM SATELLITE ACCOUNTS

TSAs are a set of tables, which, taken together, enable the user to understand the true economic significance of tourism within a nation, a region or a specific destination (UNWTO, 2008b). In other words, TSAs describe the structure of a nation's tourism activity and measure its economic size and contributions (Mak, 2004).

The method originated in the 1990s because many organisations and tourism scientists felt that the sector was underestimated (Vanhove, 2005). This underestimation was mainly due to the fact that different countries estimated the economic impacts of tourism using various definitions and methodologies – this made valid comparisons between nations impossible. Using TSAs, the direct contribution of tourism to the economy can be measured on a more consistent basis with more traditional industries such as manufacturing, agriculture and the retail trade (Tribe, 2005: 260).

TSAs are constructed on the basis of a number of tourism surveys and statistics. When fully built a TSA can have up to 10 separate but often inter-related tables as shown below (Office for National Statistics, 2013):

Table 1: Inbound tourism expenditure (equivalent to an export)

Table 2: Domestic tourism expenditure (one element of overall domestic consumption)

Table 3: Outbound tourism expenditure (equivalent to an import)

Table 4: Domestic 'tourism final consumption' (based on Tables 1 and 2)

Table 5: Production of tourism commodities (services and products of tourist and non-tourist industries)

Table 6: Domestic supply and consumption by product (a key TSA table, based on Tables 4 and 5)

Table 7: Employment and labour use

Table 8: Tourism fixed capital formation (equivalent to 'investment')

Table 9: Tourism collective consumption

Table 10: Non-monetary tourism indicators (e.g. the total number of inbound or domestic visits).

Collecting these different tables can be expensive and time-consuming, and can usually only be achieved via multi-agency cooperation. No single organisation can develop a functioning TSA in isolation, nor can a TSA be constructed without the input of considerable resources in terms of finance, time and expense. This is why, although the UNWTO has been calling for a uniform and comprehensive measurement methodology for the economic impacts of tourism since 1983, the first comprehensive TSA was only developed in Canada in 1994 (Frechtling, 1999).

The main benefit of TSAs is the measurement of the economic impacts of tourism that is comparable across countries, consistent over time, and compatible with the standard measures of a national economy (UNWTO, 2008b). TSAs allow a country to ascertain:

- tourism's contribution to its gross domestic product
- tourism's role in final consumption
- tourism's part in capital investment
- the productivity of the tourism supply sector
- the tourism's impact on its transactions with the rest of the world
- the tourism sector's net output relative to the output of other industries
- tourism-related employment
- tourism-generated tax and other government revenue
- how the above are changing over time. (Frechtling, 1999: 167)

Final consumption: Goods and services used by households

Capital investment: Money invested to buy a capital asset, such as real estate or machinery – usually longer-term investment

Output: Amount of work, goods or services produced

In 2000, the United Nations Statistics Division (UNSD), the Statistical Office of the European Communities (Eurostat), the Organisation for Economic Co-operation and Development (OECD) and the World Tourism Organization (WTO) developed a common conceptual framework for the design of TSAs. In 2008, this framework was updated. The framework includes international recommendations which should increase consistency and comparability across nations.

SNAPSHOT 7.2

Australia's TSA 2015–2016

Figure 7.5 shows the different elements that make up the Tourism Satellite Account for Australia. Starting at the top, we see that tourism consumption is divided between the consumption of international tourists and the consumption of domestic tourists. Domestic tourism consumption is almost three times larger than inbound tourism.

The total tourism consumption is then equalled by the total supply of products at purchasers' prices. This just means that the money tourists, businesses and government clients have spent on tourism products is equal to the money tourism suppliers have received when they sold their tourism products – the money spent and the money received is the same money, after all. The model then divides these receipts into tourism products and the taxes levied on these tourism products. In the discussion of the multiplier effect, it was

(Continued)

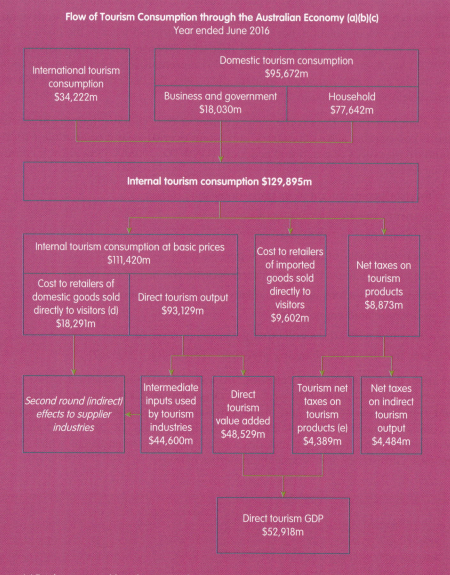

Flow of Tourism Consumption through the Australian Economy (a)(b)(c)
Year ended June 2016

International tourism consumption $34,222m

Domestic tourism consumption $95,672m

Business and government $18,030m

Household $77,642m

Internal tourism consumption $129,895m

Internal tourism consumption at basic prices $111,420m

Cost to retailers of domestic goods sold directly to visitors (d) $18,291m

Direct tourism output $93,129m

Cost to retailers of imported goods sold directly to visitors $9,602m

Net taxes on tourism products $8,873m

Second round (indirect) effects to supplier industries

Intermediate inputs used by tourism industries $44,600m

Direct tourism value added $48,529m

Tourism net taxes on tourism products (e) $4,389m

Net taxes on indirect tourism output $4,484m

Direct tourism GDP $52,918m

(a) Totals may not add up due to rounding.
(b) Tourism consumption is measured in purchasers' prices unless otherwise specified. Other monetary aggregates are measured in basic prices.
(c) All figures in this diagram are in current price terms.
(d) Includes wholesales and transport margins supplied domestically.
(e) In the case of goods, this will only include the net taxes attributable to retail trade activities.

FIGURE 7.5   Australia's Tourism Satellite Account

Source: Tourism Australia (2017a).

shown that imports can be seen as leakage: this is why the model differentiates between the imported goods tourists have bought and the contribution of Australian products and services to the economy: the tourism output.

To produce tourism goods and services, Australian businesses have used goods and services supplied by other businesses or other industries – this is indirect revenue. To calculate the direct revenue generation of the tourism sector (and only the tourism sector), the intermediate (indirect) outputs are then deducted from the total output: this then results in the value tourism adds to the total economy, in terms of outputs at basic prices. Combining this number with the tax revenue that is generated through tourism results in a figure that reflects the total contribution of tourism to GDP.

TOURISM AND ECONOMIC REGENERATION IN URBAN AND RURAL AREAS

This section will discuss tourism as a tool for economic regeneration in two types of destinations: urban and rural areas. For each type of destination, the macro-economic circumstances that have encouraged tourism development will be reviewed. The advantages and disadvantages of tourism development will also be considered for both cases.

URBAN AREAS – DEINDUSTRIALISATION

Law (1996, 2003) states that cities may be attractive to tourists because they can be seen as 'multi-purpose centres' with a wide range of attractions and amenities. Cities tend to have museums, hotels, entertainment facilities such as cinemas and nightlife, and cultural attractions such as theatres and museums, and sometimes they also have a political importance for the nation or the region (parliament buildings and royal palaces). Cities are often well-connected via transport links as well. There is thus a clear case for developing tourism in cities.

For some cities, however, tourism has become more than just an economic product worth exploring and selling – it has in some cases become a central part of economic regeneration. This has particularly been the case for many former industrial cities that have lost much of their industrial income and employment during the deindustrialisation period. Deindustrialisation can be defined as 'the decline in the importance of manufacturing' (Worthington and Britton, 2006: 278) in some regions. This decline was particularly notable in cities in the Western world in the 1970s and 1980s because of a range of factors such as increased international competition (with countries where wages were lower, so that production units were moved to these countries), a lack of skilled workers, and a lack of investment in research and development. The snapshot below describes how tourism was used as a tool to regenerate the economy of Detroit, a city in the 'rust belt' of the USA.

Tourism development in cities can have several advantages. It can contribute to economic diversification, which is particularly important for cities that used to rely on manufacturing and warehousing in the past. Cities also have a product that is interesting to tourists because they are multi-purpose centres. In large cities tourists may blend in well with the local population, as the facilities there will be better equipped to deal with large numbers of people than, for example, those in small coastal resorts.

This is not to say tourism development has no disadvantages. Tourism, for example, is a fickle industry: in many destinations it is highly seasonal and often dependent on the general economic situation. Leakages and the reliance on low-paid, low-skilled labour are also aspects that make tourism less attractive. Finally, a disadvantage can be the increased competition between cities, so that an investment in tourism is less likely to pay off. Page and Hall (2003) refer to the phenomenon of 'serial reproduction' in cities whereby all cities are starting to look the same, with, for example, a shopping mall, a redeveloped waterfront and a flagship cultural attraction.

SNAPSHOT 7.3

Tourism and Regeneration in Detroit

Detroit is the largest city in the state of Michigan, and became a center of the automotive industry in the early 20th century through Henry Ford, who founded the Ford Motor Company. Ford introduced the assembly line and mass production, and the influx of workers resulted in Detroit becoming the largest city in the USA by 1920. The city continued to grow in the post-war period, and its population peaked at 1.8 million in 1950. In the 1970s, however, as fuel prices rose, consumers started preferring smaller, more efficient foreign

Detroit

Source: Arthur Griem

cars, causing spiraling unemployment in the auto industry. Crime and urban decay became widespread in the downtown area, and the population steadily declined – in 2014, the city had 680,000 inhabitants.

Because of this decrease in population, thousands of industrial buildings and homes sit empty. With a smaller population, the city receives less income from taxes – this means that providing municipal services, such as waste disposal and emergency care, is harder to do within the widespread city limits (Detroit is larger than Boston, San Francisco and Manhattan combined). In 2013, Detroit became the largest US city to file for bankruptcy (Detroit Historical Society, 2017).

In recent years, however, there are signs that Detroit's fate is changing again. Developers are attracted by the city's rock-bottom real estate prices, and have started heavily investing in the downtown area. The riverfront area has been transformed, with a 5.5 mile walking and biking path along the water. Tech start-ups, artists and small manufacturers flock to the city because of cheaper rents. Tourism is also starting to thrive: in 2017, Visit Detroit used the slogan 'America's Great Comeback City'. The Detroit Institute of Art and The Henry Ford museum complex are major attractions. In 2015, Richard Branson visited the city to celebrate the launch of a new daily route from London Heathrow to Detroit. In the same year, the Cobo Convention Center also completed major renovation works, attracting large conferences. Around 15 million people visited Detroit in 2015, although most were from the surrounding region (Kiley, 2016).

RURAL AREAS – THE DECLINE OF AGRICULTURE

Rural areas have many attractions for tourists: visitors may look for a peaceful and quiet way of life, enjoy the fresh air and the scenery or engage in outdoor activities. Rural tourism has seen strong growth over the past 20 years. One of the reasons for this is that tourists have started to look for an alternative to the typical, overcrowded sun-sea-sand holiday (Lane, 2005). This increased demand has gone hand in hand with a decline in the agricultural industries in many Western nations, and a subsequent need for economic diversification. Page and Getz (1997: 18) state that:

> With changes in the economic structures of rural areas, as agricultural employment declined in the post-war period, rural planning has adopted a more positive strategy towards rural tourism as a form of employment generation to off-set out-migration and a declining population base, and to sustain thresholds for service provision.

Tourism can thus be used to diversify the economy. Intensely farmed or prosperous areas with a diverse rural economy may be less in need of (and less suitable for) tourism development. However, tourism can be a suitable economic regeneration strategy for economically marginal areas which depend on traditional, small-scale agrarian industries (Frochot, 2005) and suffer from out-migration, an ageing population and poverty.

Apart from economic diversification, tourism development in rural areas can have a number of added benefits. Rural tourism is characterised by a large number of private **SMEs** and microbusinesses that are locally owned and therefore reduce leakages (e.g. accommodation providers, restaurants, attractions and facilities). Through the

SMEs: Small to medium-sized enterprises

creation of jobs, tourism may encourage employment and stop outward migration in the area. Tourism can also valorise conservation (Lane, 2005: 13): revenue from certain tourism products, for example taxes or entry fees to national parks, can be used to maintain the natural environment.

Frochot (2005), however, highlights that tourism in rural areas is not necessarily a magic solution for economic regeneration. As discussed above in relation to urban tourism, tourism is a fickle and seasonal industry and one typified by low-waged, low-skilled labour and leakages. Moreover, rural tourism takes place in a fragile natural environment. This not only has environmental but also commercial implications: the tourist is looking for an unspoilt environment and tourism can be an urbanising influence (Lane, 2005). Limited transport networks mean that tourists must often rely on private cars, and alternatively there is a need to supply public transport for tourists. Due to the large number of SMEs in the sector, it may be hard to coordinate an effective strategy to ensure environmental sustainability (Hall et al., 2005). Finally, the costs for development and operations are often higher in rural areas, so obtaining finance may be difficult. A range of public grants and assistance programmes is often put in place to help rural communities diversify their economy through tourism (Page and Getz, 1997).

SNAPSHOT 7.4

Lavaux Vineyard Terraces
An example of a rural area that has diversified its economy through tourism is the Lavaux area in Switzerland, stretching for about 30km along the northern shore of Lake Geneva. Vineyards cover the terraced mountain slopes that run down to the lakeshore, providing

Lavaux Vineyard Terraces

Source: Lynn Minnaert

a peaceful and picturesque region for hiking and cycling. There are a few small villages and in the tourist season there is now a tourist train that provides tours with wine tasting sessions. The area is careful to avoid the negative impacts of tourism like congestion and environmental damage: strict land use laws on a local and regional level are in place to protect the environmental assets of the area. Moreover, the local tourism authority adopts a 'low volume – high value' approach to tourism development. François Margot, president of Montreux-Vevey Tourism, explains: 'We can't welcome hundreds of thousands of additional tourists. The structures do not allow it. Our communication is targeting quality tourism – individuals or small groups' (Bradley, 2009). Planning laws prohibit the construction of further hotel accommodation in the area, which means that a rapid growth rate is impossible. The aim is to attract high spending visitors by offering a quality experience. Margot adds: 'The most important thing is that we respect the people who live in the region. It's not going to be a kind of prostitution of the region, it cannot be a zoo, and people just coming through like Disneyland' (Bradley, 2009).

Sources: Bradley (2009); UNESCO (2017c)

OPTIMISING THE ECONOMIC BENEFITS OF TOURISM

The previous section highlighted some of the challenges for destinations that want to use tourism as a way to regenerate or diversify economically. The seasonal nature of tourism, the fact that it is often income-elastic, the reliance on low-skilled and low-paid labour, and the possibility of leakages are just a few of these challenges. This section will review three strategies that aim to optimise the economic benefits of tourism for the destination.

REDUCING LEAKAGES – INCREASING LOCAL LINKAGES

One of the reasons why tourism may not fulfil its potential as a tool for economic regeneration is the fact that foreign imports of goods and/or labour may result in income leaking from the area. To counter these leakages, the tourism sector has been encouraged by the UNWTO to develop greater linkages: in other words, to build relationships for sourcing goods and labour locally.

Linkages are central to the tourism sector in general: tourism intersects with a number of other industries to provide the goods and services tourists need on holiday. Industries such as transport, retail, catering, agriculture and arts and crafts, for example, can benefit from linkages with tourism. The key to avoiding leakages is to make sure that these linkages are formed at the destination level. One example could be to encourage hotels to serve local, seasonal ingredients in their menus, bought from local suppliers, rather than importing foreign foodstuffs, and to employ local residents.

There are two types of linkages: backward and forward (Kweka et al., 2003). Backward linkages are the linkages between tourism businesses and their suppliers. A local attraction, for example a museum, can have backward linkages with printing companies for the production of the museum maps, with catering companies that provide products for the café, and with the merchandising company that supplies the items in the gift shop. Forward linkages are linkages between the tourism business and business in other sectors that will benefit if tourism volumes increase. A local shopping centre with clothing and gift retailers, for example, may generally benefit if there are more tourists in the area.

To increase the benefits of tourism, it is important to foster backward linkages that are local and can reduce leakage. Local Chambers of Commerce may be well-placed to encourage these links. Not only may the use of local suppliers come with economic benefits for the area, it can also be an environmental policy as transport emissions may be reduced.

EQUITABLE DISTRIBUTION OF INCOME

As already indicated with regard to the social impacts of tourism, it is elementary that the local community can participate in and influence tourism planning and development, so that the costs and benefits of tourism are evenly distributed. In too many destinations the economic benefits of tourism are allocated to a happy few, whereas a great number of local people have to bear the costs in terms of congestion, environmental and cultural degradation, or inflation.

Encouraging local businesses to trade with tourists or tourism businesses in the area is one way of achieving a wider distribution of the economic benefits of tourism. Tourism is an industry that is largely characterised by a high number of small businesses with low start-up capital – locals may, for example, start selling arts and crafts in a small shop, or start up a surf or dance school. Godfrey and Clarke (2000) suggest that if local suppliers are available, they should be given the chance to renegotiate their prices so that they can become more competitive. This can apply to suppliers on all levels, from financial services providers to construction contractors. Government policies can encourage equitable distribution and several tourism charities could also encourage local entrepreneurship and provide training sessions for local populations.

BETTER EMPLOYMENT OPPORTUNITIES

One of the important economic benefits tourism can bring is access to employment opportunities. In many cases, though, employment in tourism is low-paid and low-skilled, part-time or seasonal, and with unsocial hours. The more high-skilled jobs in tourism may go to foreign employees, particularly in developing countries. By training local people and giving them opportunities to progress in their jobs, tourism employment can bring much greater value to local populations.

Tourism can also be used as a way of accessing employment. In New York City, Ladders for Leaders is a nationally recognized programme that offers high school and college students the opportunity to participate in paid professional summer internships with leading corporations, non-profit organisations and government agencies. The programme is an initiative of the NYC Department of Youth and Community Development (DYCD, 2017). Tourism and hospitality is one of the five sectors featured in this programme that aims to provide young New Yorkers with the practical skills and work experience they need to start their careers. The programme fosters local talent and helps young adults enter the challenging NYC job market.

SUMMARY

This chapter has highlighted the many economic benefits tourism can bring to destinations and also the disadvantages that go hand in hand with tourism development. Evaluating tourism's economic impacts is dependent on how well we can calculate these impacts and two different methods have been reviewed here: the multiplier effect and Tourism Satellite Accounts. Tourism was then assessed as a tool for economic regeneration – an idea that was applied to both urban and rural environments. Again, this emphasised that tourism was not a magic solution to all the economic difficulties that destinations faced: it had to be planned and coordinated carefully if the benefits from tourism development were to outweigh the costs. Three basic strategies for optimising the economic benefits of tourism concluded the chapter.

SELF-TEST QUESTIONS

1. Tourism can bring a range of economic benefits to destinations. Why is it that in some destinations, though, these benefits do not seem to reach the local population? Do you know of initiatives that work towards a more equitable distribution of the economic benefits of tourism?

2. What can rural/urban destinations with few famous or popular attractions do to attract tourists? Are there other ways in which they can regenerate?

3. What are the strengths and weaknesses of multipliers and TSAs to calculate the economic impacts of tourism?

FURTHER READING

Dwyer, L., Forsyth, P. and Dwyer, W. (2010) *Tourism Economics and Policy.* Bristol: Channel View Publications.

Vanhove, N. (2005) *The Economics of Tourism Destinations.* Oxford: Elsevier.

Wall, G. and Mathieson, A. (2006) *Tourism: Change, Impacts and Opportunities.* Harlow: Pearson Education.

USEFUL WEBSITES

swissinfo.ch: www.swissinfo.ch

Tourism Australia: www.tourism.australia.com

UN World Tourism Organization: www.unwto.org

8

THE SOCIAL AND CULTURAL IMPACTS OF TOURISM

'Should we have stayed at home and thought of here? Where should we be today? Is it right to be watching strangers in a play in this strangest of theatres?'

E. Bishop, 1968: 32

LEARNING OUTCOMES

After reading this chapter you will understand:

- the different socio-cultural impacts tourism can have, both positive and negative, on the destination and the tourists themselves

- the factors that influence how destinations, and the individual members of the host community, are affected by the socio-cultural impacts of tourism

- the underlying views and theories that influence how one sees the role and responsibilities of the tourism industry and the tourist with regard to socio-cultural impacts

- a range of strategies that can be used to manage the socio-cultural impacts of tourism on destinations.

Worshippers burn incense for good fortune, Lantau Island, Hong Kong

Source: Lynn Minnaert

INTRODUCTION

Of the three main types of impact, the socio-cultural consequences of tourism are the least obvious and hardest to measure. While the economic impacts of tourism are often the main objective of tourism development in destinations, and its environmental impacts are often visible, the impacts of tourism on the host community and culture emerge more slowly, affect each destination and individuals within it in different ways, and are difficult to isolate from other causes.

Although the social and cultural impacts of tourism are often discussed together, there are certain differences between the two. Social impacts usually refer to interpersonal relations, social conduct, crime, safety, religion, language and health. Cultural impacts usually refer to material and non-material forms of culture (e.g. heritage and religious buildings, artefacts, rituals) and processes of cultural change (Wall and Mathieson, 2006). A body of literature regarding the socio-cultural impacts of tourism has developed since the 1970s, with key scholars such as Cohen, Mathieson and Wall, Piznam, Pearce and Moscardo.

Like all impacts, tourism's social and cultural impacts may be positive or negative. Major claims have been made for tourism as a force for peace and greater understanding between communities, but the experience of tourism in host communities in many destinations shows that, in reality, tourism can be a force for rapid and undesirable social change.

In this chapter we identify the potential positive and negative social and cultural impacts that are linked to tourism development and consider the factors that determine the extent of these impacts. We conclude the chapter by discussing how the social and cultural impacts can be managed effectively to ensure that tourism development adheres to the principles of sustainability.

THE SOCIO-CULTURAL IMPACTS OF TOURISM ON HOST COMMUNITIES

Tourism can be seen as a form of meeting: between people from different places, between cultures and between lifestyles. In tourism the nature and quality of personal contact between tourists and the host community form an important part of the tourists' experience of a destination and many destinations promote the friendliness of the community as an attraction. For example:

'Tajikistan: Feel the friendship'

'Amazing Thailand: It begins with the people'

'The Gambia: The smiling coast of Africa'

'Taiwan wears a smile'

These slogans imply that the host community is welcoming to tourists and supportive of tourism development, and that the encounters between tourists and members of the host community will be positive. Tourism can bring people together, foster friendships and enable contacts between people from all around the world. However, in many cases, the contacts between hosts and tourists are superficial and formalised. For example, tourists who do not venture outside of the 'tourist bubble' may only encounter the local community in their role of employees or in commercial transactions. The duration of a tourist's visit may limit the opportunity to have close contact with members of the host community, and the opportunity to communicate may be restricted by language or cultural barriers. These factors can limit deep, meaningful contacts between hosts and tourists. The contact that the two groups have can lead to social and cultural impacts on both sides, which can be positive as well as negative.

POSITIVE IMPACTS

Potential positive socio-cultural impacts of tourism for host communities include:

- A better understanding between cultures.
- Revival of culture.
- Improved standard of living.

BETTER UNDERSTANDING BETWEEN CULTURES

The UNWTO names the 'contribution of tourism to the mutual understanding and respect between peoples and societies' as the first article in its Global Code of Ethics (UNWTO, n.d.). Tourism can be seen as a chance to understand unfamiliar people, places and cultures. From this can grow a deeper understanding, tolerance and respect for different religious, and moral and philosophical beliefs. This, however, is only possible if the different stakeholders in tourism are accepting and appreciative of these differences and needs to be supported by tourists' sensitivity to the cultural and social norms of the destination.

A better understanding between cultures can potentially lead to the breaking down of negative stereotypes. Mark Twain, the nineteenth-century American author, said: 'Travel is fatal to prejudice, bigotry, and narrow-mindedness, and many of our people need it sorely on these accounts. Broad, wholesome, charitable views of men and things cannot be acquired by vegetating in one little corner of the earth all one's lifetime' (Twain, 1869: 129). By increasing the cultural awareness between hosts and visitors, tourism can contribute to reducing stereotypes and prejudices about nationalities, religions and cultures. Prejudices are often inaccurate and tend to emphasise the negative attributes, whereas the positive attributes are ignored. They may lead to discrimination or rude and hostile behaviour (Reisinger, 2009).

Tourism has not only been claimed to encourage a better understanding between cultures, it has also been described as a force for peace. The link between tourism and peace dates back to the 1980s. The year 1986 was the UN Year of Peace, an initiative that followed several severe instances of terrorism around the world, many of which were aimed at tourism. Many scholars have since argued that tourism can achieve an attitudinal change in tourists and promote cross-cultural understanding (Higgins-Desbiolles, 2006a). In 2016, the World Travel and Tourism Council (WTTC) published a report in collaboration with the Institute of Economics and Peace, highlighting that countries with a more sustainable and open tourism sector tend to be more peaceful. Tourism can help support peace by 'putting pressure on governments to cease fighting or establish harmonious relationships between citizens in order to attract tourists. This is particularly important if tourism is an important sector for the economy' (WTTC, 2016: 2). Examples provided in the report include Rwanda, where efforts to clear land mines were in part driven by increasing gorilla tourism, and Kashmir, where cross-border tourism is a significant factor in reducing friction between India and Pakistan in the disputed territory.

REVIVAL OF CULTURE

The admiration of tourists for local culture, arts, traditions or customs can increase the cultural pride of the local community and revive aspects of this culture that might have been declining. Certain art forms or traditions, for example, can be mainly kept alive by an older generation: the positive attention of tourists can encourage young people in the host community to become actively involved as well.

SNAPSHOT 8.1

Tourism in Nunavut, Arctic Canada

Nunavut, or 'Our Land' in Inuktitut, is the Northernmost territory of Canada. It encompasses over 2 million km² and has a population of 35,944 residents (2016 census), approximately 85 per cent of whom are Inuit. Tourism development in this remote region is relatively recent, but arrivals show an upward trend, particularly in cruise tourism (Insignia, 2015). The region is known for its pristine natural beauty, but is beset by economic difficulties,

(Continued)

such as low educational achievement and high levels of unemployment: 20 per cent of Inuit residents were unemployed in 2016 (Nunavut Bureau of Statistics, n.d.).

While the natural environment is a large part of Nunavut's appeal, Inuit culture and arts are also top attractions. Tourism Nunavut claims that the destination has more artists per capita than any other region in the world. While Inuit art tends to be most famous for its carvings in stone, ivory, antler and bone, print making, weaving and clothing are also art forms commonly practised (Nunavut Tourism, 2017). Tourists on organised tours tend to visit craft studios and tours, and participate in native culture exhibitions including traditional ceremonies, throat singing, Arctic games and a drum dance (Okrant and Larsen, 2016).

Proponents of tourism in Nunavut highlight that these cultural expressions, even if they are staged for tourists, can be of importance to younger generations in Nunavut, and give them an opportunity to learn more about their own culture. As Nunavut has the youngest population in Canada – in 2016, with a median age of 27.7 (Statistics Canada, 2017b) – this may be a particular benefit of tourism in the region: the preservation of their culture is in their hands. However, Okrant and Larsen (2016) raise concerns about the limited planning that has accompanied the expansion in the region, which may lead to commodification of the Inuit's culture.

IMPROVED STANDARD OF LIVING

Tourism development often requires infrastructural improvements that improve the host community's standard of living if the resources that tourists use are shared with them. These improvements include: better accessibility through the provision of new roads, new services or new transit routes; the provision of new amenities and attractions that may also be used or enjoyed by the host community, for example cultural, sport or entertainment events, or the construction of facilities for cultural, sport or leisure activities; the redevelopment or improvement of neglected buildings and areas; and the improved provision of water and electricity supplies.

Tourism development may also bring new employment opportunities to the destination for the local population – these are discussed in more depth in Chapter 7. Finally, tourism development can support the conservation and enhancement of the local environment, thus improving the quality of life of the local residents (see Chapter 9).

Although tourism can thus be linked to a range of socio-cultural benefits, it is not always a positive socio-cultural force. We will now review the potential negative socio-cultural impacts of tourism for host communities.

SNAPSHOT 8.2

Tourism and standard of living in Guizhou, China

Guizhou province is located in southwest China, and is characterised by its tranquil mountains and traditional rural villages. Until fairly recently, it was rarely visited: until 2000, Guizhou attracted less than 300,000 overseas tourists (Donaldson, 2007). However, this changed with the opening of superhighways spanning nearly 3,200 miles of the province, connecting remote villages with progressive cities like Guiyang, the capital.

The expressways are engineering marvels that compete with the spectacular scenery, traversing hundreds of long tunnels and towering bridges (including the world's highest). In 2014, the trip across the province from Guangzhou to Guiyang was cut from 20 hours to 5 hours. Thanks to the new roads, tourism in Guizhou grew by 50 per cent in 2016, much of it due to domestic visitors (Leatherman, 2017).

What is interesting about tourism development in Guizhou, however, is not just how fast tourism developed, but where it developed. Historically, Guizhou's most popular sites, including nationally sponsored tourist sites, ethnic minority villages and other popular sites, are primarily located in rural areas designated as poor counties, helping spread the economic benefits of tourism directly to poor rural residents (Donaldson, 2007: 341). While Guizhou remains one of China's poorest provinces, and faces problems that tourism alone cannot fix, household incomes in tourism villages grew sharply: in these villages, tourism enabled residents to improve their standard of living. A study showed that compared to tourism development in other Chinese provinces like Yunnan, the benefits of Guizhou's tourism were more evenly spread, reaching more poor areas and reducing poverty to a much greater extent, despite the relative lack of economic growth (Donaldson, 2007: 345).

NEGATIVE IMPACTS

Potential negative socio-cultural impacts of tourism for host communities include:

- conflict of interests
- pressure on limited resources
- resentment
- loss of cultural pride
- staged authenticity
- demonstration effect
- commodification – trinketisation – Cocacolonisation
- displacement
- crime and prostitution
- begging by children and child labour.

CONFLICTS OF INTEREST

Relations between tourists and the host community are not always problem-free. Tourists may see the destination as a place of rest, relaxation and enjoyable activities, but for many locals it is a place of work and this can cause tensions between the two groups. Tourists enjoying a beach holiday may complain about noise created by fishermen when they bring in their catch in the early morning, or may be deterred by a new farm building erected in a rural landscape. The conflict here is that many of the things tourists enjoy in a destination, such as the beach, the sea, the landscape or the view, are not actually owned by tourism suppliers. (Private beaches and gardens are notable exceptions here.) This implies that the tourist sector has little control over these resources and has to compete for them with other industries. Often the economic importance of the industry to the local community is therefore a key factor. Especially when these resources are limited, this can cause conflict and negative social impacts. It is usually the task of governmental bodies in charge of tourism planning to address these conflicts of interest (Gunn and Var, 2002).

In 2017, around 2,000 people staged an 'occupation' of the Rambla, Barcelona's famous boulevard, to protest against the city's continuous growth in visitor numbers. Around 18 million tourists visited Barcelona in 2016 – the city has a population of only 1.6 million (Statista, 2017). Tourism makes up about 12 per cent of Barcelona's economy — up from less than 2 per cent before the 1992 Olympic Games. But tourism revenue is not shared equitably, and not all residents see its benefits. Short-term rental accommodations and hotels are driving up rents and displacing businesses. Overcrowding, and some tourists' rowdy behaviour, also lead to resentment and resistance from the local population. After the protest, Barcelona City Council took action and implemented a new law, limiting the number of beds available and prohibiting new hotels in certain city zones. The new law is expected to take effect in 2019, and other cities, like Venice, have expressed an interest in exploring similar options. The Barcelona Hotel Association and the Council of Trade, Service and Tourism, however, have argued that the new law will do little to stem the flow of day visitors, who cause significant overcrowding and tend to contribute less to the local economy (*The Local*, 2017).

PRESSURE ON LIMITED RESOURCES

Tourists put extra pressure on local resources such as public transport, parking facilities, waste collection and hospitals, particularly during periods of peak demand. In large cities these extra pressures are often more easily dealt with than in small coastal or rural destinations or historic towns where local residents may experience delays and inconvenience when going about their daily activities.

In developing countries, where resources may be scarce, the pressure from tourism can be very significant. A common example is the development of golf tourism in climates with limited rainfall. Golf courses in these places require constant irrigation to keep the fairways and greens up to standard. It is estimated that an 18-hole golf course can consume more than 2.3 million litres of water per day. This means that an average golf course in a tropical country such as Thailand uses as much water as 60,000 rural villagers (UNEP, 2008). Luxury resorts and swimming pools also put great pressure on the water supply. Tourism Concern (2012) highlights that in Goa, India, tourism has proliferated in an unregulated way, which has made access to water dependent on the ability to pay, not human need. Hotels and resorts have either attached large pipes to the main supply, or have dug boreholes: both practices reduce the availability of (piped and ground) water for local communities.

RESENTMENT

The negative social impacts of tourism can cause a feeling of resentment against the tourist within the host community. The Irridex model, discussed later in this chapter (p. 207), illustrates how resentment can build up, especially when the economic impacts do not benefit the host community directly. Where it is felt that the benefits brought by tourism do not outweigh the social costs, the local community may become frustrated and dissatisfied with tourism and express this in their relations with the tourists. In areas that are dependent on tourism and where the economy relies on the income derived from it, negative attitudes of the host community towards tourists can undermine the quality of the tourists' experience and the success of the destination. This resentment can also be increased by possible racial tensions if the tourists and the host population are from different racial backgrounds.

Resentment within the local community can also be caused by the behaviour of the tourist, which can be seen as inappropriate or in breach of local customs and traditions. In Zanzibar, for example, an island in the Indian Ocean off the Tanzanian coast, the cultural values of predominantly Western tourists do not always match the predominantly Islamic and Swahili culture of the island. The consumption of alcohol in public, for example, and the tourists who stroll around the town in shorts and bikini tops, can cause offence to the people of the local community and put a strain on relations between hosts and tourists. Even though many tour operators advise tourists to cover up and respect local customs not all tourists follow these guidelines, which can then lead to discontent within the host community. This is the case, for example, in Muscat, Oman – a destination that has recently started promoting itself for tourism. Compared to nearby Dubai, Muscat is more traditional, with most men wearing white dishdashas and women black veils. In the hotels, bikinis, shorts and T-shirts are accepted, but when going into the town, tourists are advised to wear respectful clothing and cover their legs and shoulders (Sultanate of Oman Ministry of Tourism, 2017).

LOSS OF CULTURAL PRIDE

It has already been highlighted that tourism can increase local cultural pride, but tourism can also have the reverse effect and cause a feeling of inferiority in the host population. This is often the case when there is a big difference between the financial power of the tourist and the host community. Local residents may feel that they are objectified in front of the camera and that their culture is overly commercialised (Cole, 2008). A contributing factor to this loss of cultural pride may be that the local population does not feel a part of tourism development and does not share in the benefits it brings: tourism development may be in the hands of foreign investors or large corporations, or the policy makers may not have consulted the locals in their decision making. To encourage a feeling of ownership and pride trough tourism development, community participation should be a key element of socially sustainable development.

STAGED AUTHENTICITY

Many tourists are attracted by what is called the **authenticity** of other cultures: they want to see and experience events, customs, traditions and other aspects of culture that they perceive as genuine, real and meaningful. Often these events, customs and traditions will be different from what the tourist is used to at home. Cultures in less developed countries may be seen as more 'primitive' and 'pure' and representing certain values that the tourist might feel are lost in the home society.

Authenticity: In tourism, aspects of culture and the tourist experience (such as cuisine, festivals, housing, artifacts) are said to be **authentic** when they are considered to be traditional, original, unique, and intrinsically linked to the culture that is visited

When tourism is developed, however, culture becomes a selling point for many destinations. This means aspects of culture might be commercialised and lose their true meaning: for example events that used to take place annually may be *performed* weekly for the benefit of the tourist; or local delicacies that are only cooked at certain times of the year may be made available all year around. In many cases the tourist still experiences the core of an authentic aspect of culture, but it may have been adapted to some extent so that it becomes more easily 'consumable'.

The staged authenticity of many Polynesian cultural experiences is also referred to as 'the Bali syndrome'. In these mature tourist destinations, resorts have developed that protect the tourist from unpleasant encounters with beggars and street sellers, and instead offer an enclave that is seen as pure and unspoilt. In those enclaves, tourists typically experience artificial cultural experiences and stylised representations of local people, which do not necessarily match reality. Rosenbaum and Wong (2008) argue that, in reality, contemporary locals in Polynesia are quite similar to people in Western urbanised areas. The cultural experience that is sold in the tourist enclaves does not always respond to actual culture, but rather to tourists' romanticised expectations of that culture. The tourism sector responds to this by providing a cultural product that itself is a form of staged authenticity.

Another example is the Paduang tribe in Northern Thailand: this tribe is famous for its tradition of beautifying women by elongating their necks. This is achieved through adding brass rings to a girl's neck from the age of 5, pressing down the collarbone and ribs, and pushing up the chin. This traditional custom is now mainly practised for commercial reasons: each girl who decides to wear the rings is paid by the tourist boat operators (Keyte, 2016).

Authenticity is an issue not only for intangible aspects of culture such as cultural customs and norms, but also for tangible aspects of culture. The development of cultural sites, such as heritage sites, for tourism needs to balance commercial interests with the conservation of the authenticity of the site, and those two objectives

The Taj Mahal, India

Source: Sandra Charrasse

may be in conflict with each other. Over-commercialisation may reduce the authenticity of the visitor experience. In 2009, a plan was proposed to develop the Taj Mahal site in India with a Ferris wheel, a suspension bridge and cable cars. This plan met with a lot of opposition, as many were concerned that the original significance and meaning of the site would be lost. The Taj Mahal was built by the grieving Mughal emperor Shah Jahan in memory of his wife, Mumtaz, who had died in childbirth. Its white marble minarets, dome, jewel-inlaid mosaics and classical Persian garden took thousands of craftsmen from 1632 to 1652 to complete. It is protected from surrounding development by a 500-metre conservation zone. The development of the tourist park was proposed at a distance of 800 metres from the site. In 2008 about 3 million people visited the Taj Mahal, but officials hoped to increase the figure by linking it to neighbouring historic buildings and adding the Agra Eye – a Ferris wheel modelled on the London Eye. Cable cars between the Taj Mahal and other attractions were expected to increase tourist spending at each. Conservationists and other activists, however, strongly opposed the plans, arguing that the development would not be in keeping with the ambience of the attraction (Kerr, 2009).

DEMONSTRATION EFFECT

Originally this was a term used in sociology and economics when describing the effects on behaviour from observing other people's actions. In tourism, it is used to refer to the copying of tourists' behaviours, dress codes or preferences by the host community. An example could be that younger generations stop wearing traditional dress and adopt the clothing style of visitors.

In contemporary society, the power of tourism as a medium for the demonstration effect must not be overestimated. Television and the Internet are now much more likely to contribute to the changing tastes and behaviours of host populations than tourists alone. Only a few destinations and host communities (e.g. primitive tribes) mainly have contact with the wider world via tourism – now that technology is more common and widespread, tourism is only likely to be a contributing factor, if that, to the demonstration effect. Even tribes that do not tend to have contact with tourists can still be exposed to different cultures via TV researchers and film crews. The BBC programme *Tribe*, for example, focused on some of the most isolated peoples in the world. The presenter of the programme, Bruce Parry, lived with each tribe and explored their cultural traditions and way of life. Even though great care was taken not to cause any negative socio-cultural effects on the participating tribes, they were still exposed to technological equipment, cultural habits and artefacts they were not accustomed to.

COMMODIFICATION – TRINKETISATON – COCACOLONISATION

'Commodification' means that a value, a cultural aspect or an artefact is turned into a commodity: in other words, that it is commercialised. This can cause changes or mutations in those values or cultural aspects and may lead to staged authenticity (see p. 196). Another consequence of commodification may be standardisation: this means that everything becomes consumable and thus similar and familiar. A clear example of standardisation can be seen in popular souvenirs: in many tourist destinations the same souvenirs are sold and only the name of the destination differs. Think of T-shirts with 'My girlfriend went to … and all I got was this lousy T-shirt', or black bags with the name of the destination printed on them in colourful letters.

'Trinketisation' is a term that refers to the commercialisation and trivialisation of culture. Cultural motives and traditions are still recognisable, but they are no longer linked to their history and meaning. Artefacts and crafts that are supposed to be the expression of a destination's rich cultural heritage may, for example, be mass-produced and sold as mere trinkets. Fake native American dream catchers may have been produced in a factory in India, and the Murano glass a tourist brings home from a trip to Venice might have been made in China.

The commodification and trinketisation of culture can also be linked to a process of 'Cocacolonisation' (also referred to as 'McDonaldisation' or 'Disneyfication'). In the field of tourism, these terms refer to the spreading of Western cultures and values throughout the world: just as these brands are present everywhere, so are Western cultural values increasing their influence worldwide. These values often represent (over-)consumption and the free market, materialistic wants, homogeneity and a distancing from nature and the natural environment. 'Disneyfication' additionally refers to the sanitising of environments into clean and safe places, removing all risk, until these places feel like a Disney theme park. Although safety and cleanliness are no doubt positive attributes for a destination, the term is used negatively to refer to the modification of what is authentic and complex into easily understandable and consumable chunks.

Commodification – Britain

Source: Lynn Minnaert

Commodification – Istanbul

Source: Lynn Minnaert

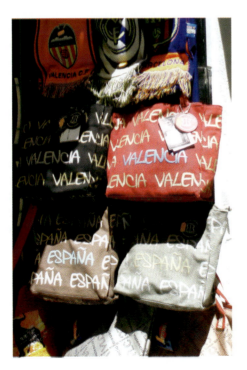

Commodification – Valencia

Source: Lynn Minnaert

DISPLACEMENT

'Displacement' means that local residents, because of the development of tourism, are forced to move away from their homes. This may be because they have been evicted, to make way for a hotel complex for example. Another reason could be that because of the influx of tourists, property and land prices have gone up, so that local residents can no longer afford to buy or rent in the area. They might be priced out of the market by developers, or by tourists from wealthier areas looking to buy a second home.

In some cases, this may mean the local residents lose not only their homes, but also their livelihoods. Tourism Concern, a charity that fights exploitation through tourism, raises awareness of the displacement of tribes in Eastern Africa. Several tribes in Kenya and Tanzania, for example, were evicted from their homes to make way for game reserves for tourists. They received no compensation and in many places had to move with large amounts of cattle and livestock. Because the cattle are no longer allowed to graze in the new wildlife reserves, this impacts on the livelihood of the tribal community. According to Tourism Concern, 'this is a pattern that has been repeated throughout East Africa. National parks and wildlife are being conserved at the expense of the people who have lived there and been guardians of the land and the wildlife for centuries, and who understand the bush in much more detail than Western wildlife 'experts' and have a low-impact, sustainable lifestyle' (Tourism Concern, 2017).

CRIME AND PROSTITUTION

Tourism development can lead to an increase in crime in the destination community. Tourist-related crimes include theft, robberies and assaults on tourists: although these affect the tourist rather than the host directly, it can lead to an increased sense of a lack of safety within the host community. Members of the host community may also be victims of crime. Sports events, for example, are sometimes linked to an increase in crime, and football matches are sometimes blighted by hooliganism, violence and vandalism (Barker, 2004).

Although prostitution is not solely linked to tourism, in many destinations the problem gets worse as tourism increases. In some destinations, this may include child prostitution. This is mostly the case when there is a big financial divide between the tourist and the host community, and when the fact of being in another country gives the sex tourist a feeling of being 'untouchable'. ECPAT International is a global charity that aims to protect children from sexual exploitation. Although child prostitution is mainly linked to the tourism industries of Asian (e.g. Thailand) and Latin-American countries (e.g. Costa Rica), this negative impact of tourism is now becoming noticeable in growing tourism destinations in Africa and even Europe (e.g. Estonia and the Czech Republic) (ECPAT, 2016).

BEGGING BY CHILDREN AND CHILD LABOUR

Tourism opportunities can divert children from education by encouraging them to sell souvenirs, provide street entertainment or beg for money rather than going to school. Begging by children is common in tourism destinations in developing countries – in some cases for money, in others for sweets, pens and other small items. In several countries, such as Morocco and Mexico, giving money to begging children is often frowned upon because it is seen to encourage a culture of dependence on hand-outs.

Tourism can also encourage child labour. Many children are not officially employed by the tourism industry but are working in the so-called 'open air economy': they derive an income from the recreational spending of the tourists. Children can earn money as street sellers, car attendants or shoe-shine boys and girls. Tourists may be more generous when they pay for their services, perhaps because it is easier for young children to win sympathy and compassion (Andriotis, 2016). Children may also be involved in prostitution and the sex industry: see above.

A child vendor in Peru

Source: Sonia Rosiers

SNAPSHOT 8.3

'Orphan tourism': Are You Really Helping?
One of the fastest growing segments of the tourism industry – and one that affects children both positively and negatively – is 'voluntourism'. Some of the most popular volunteer activities involve children, for example working at an orphanage or teaching them English. However, voluntourism is the subject of a heated debate. One concern is that international

(Continued)

volunteers might replace local staff or disrupt the regular work of local staff, thus hindering the sustainability and quality of the work. Another is that voluntourism makes the community dependent on receiving volunteers.

Specific concerns have, moreover, been raised with regard to volunteer tourism involving children. The fact that volunteering opportunities generate income both for the mediating agency that arranges the trip and for the project at the destination, may constitute a threat to children. In both Cambodia and South Africa, this was particularly true for volunteer placements at orphanages, where children in some cases were not orphans but children from poor families unable to provide for them. Some parents are lured into signing adoption agreements, making it very hard to reunite with the child as the family's circumstances improve. Furthermore, sending inexperienced volunteers to look after children who may have attachment disorders for a short period of time may not be in the best interests of the child, even if it might be a 'life-changing' experience for the volunteer. As voluntourism tends to focus on developing countries with a lack of regulation, tourists should do careful research into the experiences on offer so that children are not harmed in the process (Schyst Resande & Fair Trade Center, 2013).

SOCIO-CULTURAL IMPACTS ON TOURISTS

Tourism can have profound impacts on the host communities and destinations, but travelling can also have impacts on the tourists themselves. After all, if tourism does not do the tourist any good, why do so many people travel and love to travel? Tourists may decide to travel for different reasons (see Tourist Motivations, Chapter 4), and the types of holidays they take may be very different; still, we can distinguish some general impacts on tourists. Positive impacts mostly have to do with a sense of psychological and physiological well-being, negative impacts with feelings of anxiety and disturbance.

POSITIVE IMPACTS

Many tourists will decide to go on holiday because of the positive effects of travelling on their well-being. A holiday is something we may look forward to all year, save up for and plan carefully; it can also be a source of happy memories that are treasured long after our return. Hazel (2004) discusses common positive impacts of holidays on tourists:

Rest and renewal: Holidays provide a break from routine and an escape from the daily surroundings and activities that may seem stressful or just rather boring. On holiday the tourist has a chance to relax, to take a break from it all. This allows tourists to rediscover themselves and what is most important in life (recreation is after all linked to the word re-create). On holiday, the tourist has a chance to recharge their batteries and return to the daily routine refreshed and motivated.

Mental and physical health: Rest and renewal can also be important at a mental level. Holidays have been linked to improvements in health – mainly mental health and mental strength. There is also isolated evidence that holidays can reduce the risk of stress-related illnesses such as heart disease.

Social interaction – strengthening relationships: Holidays can provide opportunities to meet new people, be it fellow tourists or people from the host community. This can increase the tourist's social support network and contribute to higher confidence levels. The tourist can also gain a better understanding of peoples and cultures he or she was not familiar with before, which may increase intercultural understanding and counteract incorrect negative stereotypes (see p. 191). Tourism can also mean spending quality time with loved ones – a partner, friends or family. Being away from the home environment and the stresses and routines it represents often encourages tourists to purposely make time for each other.

Broadening experiences: On holiday, tourists not only get the opportunity to visit a place they might not have been to before, they can also easily engage in activities that are new to them. Trying out windsurfing on holiday or picking up a few words of Italian may, for example, lead to the development of a new hobby or a new skill. The tourist may also be more inclined to try a different cuisine or take an interest in a new art form whilst on holiday. Back home, these new interests and skills may lead to increased well-being and confidence.

Developing independence: Travelling, especially for young people, can also increase independence. On holiday, tourists may be faced with new situations or unexpected problems that need to be dealt with: luggage may get lost, or the dishes on a menu will be written in a language the tourist does not understand. Dealing with these requires a certain level of independence and confidence. When a young person travels alone, he or she may develop new skills by having to be independent in a new environment.

While these benefits may seem obvious, not all cultures value the positive impacts of tourism and time off equally. One example is the USA: while the majority of employers in the USA offer paid leave (for more detail, please see Snapshot 3.2), millions of vacation days go unused each year. In 2015, American workers reported taking off just 16.2 days, almost a full week less compared to the pre-2000 average. Because of this 'work martyr' syndrome, the USA was dubbed the 'no vacation nation'. In response, the US Travel Association launched 'Project: Time Off', an initiative aimed at encouraging American workers to take a break and travel. Their research showed that taking time off is linked to better relationships, improved mental and physical health, and more positive attitudes towards work. It also showed that, beyond the personal and professional benefits, the reluctance to take days off also had economic consequences: had Americans used their vacation time, it would have resulted in $223 billion in spending for the US economy, and 1.6 million jobs (Project: Time Off, 2017).

NEGATIVE IMPACTS

Tourism can also have negative socio-cultural impacts on tourists. Certain holiday situations can lead to tension, stress and anxiety instead of relaxation and well-being:

Terrorism: Tourists, because of their high visibility and their capacity to attract large amounts of worldwide media attention, can be prime targets for terrorism. Examples of destinations that have experienced terrorist attacks specifically targeting tourists are Paris, Istanbul, Berlin, Nice and London (see also Chapter 13). Tourists that have a close experience of these attacks may experience high levels

Psychogenic:
Resulting from an
emotional conflict

of anxiety and tension in their daily lives after their return from holiday. Bongar et al. (2007: 6) explain just how extensive the psychological effect of terrorism can be, even for persons who were not affected by an incident directly. He states that military psychologists have long known that fear, stress and exhaustion do much more damage than guns and bullets. For example, in 1995, a chemical attack in the Tokyo subway killed 12 people, but more than 4,000 non-affected individuals went to hospital afterwards with **psychogenic** symptoms. The long-term effect of this increased stress can be linked to lower activity rates, depression and suicide.

Crime against tourists: Several elements of the tourist destination may result in increased levels of crime. If there is a large discrepancy between the wealth and lifestyle of the tourist and the local population, for example, tourists may run an increased risk of having their belongings stolen via pick-pocketing or burglary of their holiday home. Some tourist destinations are famous for their nightlife and clubs, which may lead to an increase in alcohol-related violence during the tourist season. Tourists may also not be aware of more dangerous areas in a destination, or perhaps take more risks on holiday, and so put themselves in a more vulnerable position. Experiencing or witnessing a crime on holiday may lead to fear and anxiety, even after a tourist has returned home, and thus counter the positive impacts of the holiday.

Scams: Scams are schemes that are aimed at conning tourists out of their money. They are influenced to hand over cash voluntarily, only to find out later that they have been duped. Because many tourists are unfamiliar with the destination and its customs, they are prime targets for scams. They may, for example, be asked to hand over their passport by a fake police officer, who will subsequently disappear with it. Another famous scam is the fake holiday club, which mainly targets older tourists in the Canary Islands. The tourists are offered a scratch card, and by scratching off three equal symbols they win a luxury holiday. To get this holiday, they are asked to sit through a lengthy sales presentation, where they are offered membership to an exclusive holiday club with exclusive offers at bargain prices. After paying the expensive membership fee, they find they have only bought access to an online booking service, offering no better deals than the average travel agent. The UK National Trading Standards eCrime Team has launched a campaign to warn British tourists not to sign the contracts offered in this scam (National Trading Standards, n.d.).

FACTORS GOVERNING THE EXTENT OF SOCIO-CULTURAL IMPACTS ON HOST COMMUNITIES

It has been established that tourism can have a range of positive and negative socio-cultural impacts on destinations. Not all of these impacts are present in all destinations, and in some the overall balance will be positive whilst in others the balance will be negative. A range of destination characteristics can be distinguished that determine the extent to which positive and negative socio-economic impacts of tourism will develop. Inskeep (1991) suggests that these mainly depend on the magnitude of the differences between the hosts and the tourists in terms of:

- basic value and logic systems
- religious beliefs
- traditions

- customs
- lifestyles
- behavioural patterns
- dress codes
- sense of time budgeting
- attitudes towards strangers.

Faulkner and Tideswell (1997) developed an alternative model and divided the factors that would determine the extent of socio-cultural impacts of tourism on destinations into two groups. On the one hand there are factors that apply to the *host community as a whole*, as an homogeneous group. But destinations are made up of individuals and within communities different groups might experience tourism in different ways. This means that on the other hand there are factors that apply to some *individual members of the host community*, but not to others.

CHARACTERISTICS OF DESTINATIONS

Whereas Inskeep (1991) focuses mainly on the differences between the hosts and the tourists in his model, Faulkner and Tideswell (1997) have extended this to include a range of characteristics of the host destination. These characteristics are the stage of development of the destination, the tourist type it attracts, the pace of development, the dominance of tourism, the relationships between hosts and guests, the ratio of tourists to residents, and the level of seasonality.

STAGE OF DEVELOPMENT

The intensity of certain socio-cultural impacts can be linked to the stage of development of the destination. The tourist area life cycle model (the TALC; see Chapter 10) is a representation of how resorts may develop: starting with low visitation and limited tourism development, the destination becomes more and more established until it reaches a peak in tourist numbers, after which it either declines or rejuvenates via further investment.

Many of the negative socio-cultural impacts, such as commodification of culture, staged authenticity and displacement, will only appear when tourist numbers and the level of development have become significant. In the earliest stages of development, the number of tourists, their impacts and their visibility may be low. In further stages of development these negative impacts may become ever clearer, and it is important that the host community is protected from them via effective policy and destination management.

TOURIST TYPE

The type and level of socio-cultural impacts of tourism on destinations are often linked to the type of visitor to those destinations. Here the Faulkner and Tideswell (1997) model is similar to Inskeep's (1991) model as it examines the magnitude of the cultural differences between the host community and tourists, and how far tourists are willing to adapt to the host culture. The type of tourist the destination attracts is therefore important from the perspective of these cultural similarities/differences.

A range of tourist typologies exists (see Chapter 4). A typology that is helpful to esti-mate the level of socio-cultural impacts of tourism on host communities addresses such questions as: are the visitors very different from the host population in terms of wealth, race, religion, or cultural background? Are the visitors adapting to the culture of the destination, or do they want that culture to adapt to them? Valene Smith's (1977) model specifically focused on the socio-cultural impacts of different tourist groups to the destination. For every tourist type, the model links the number and visibility of the tourists to their willingness to adapt to the local culture. The further down the model, the more pressing negative socio-cultural impacts may become, and the higher the need for effective policies and management (see Table 8.1).

TABLE 8.1   Tourist types

Tourist type	Visibility/pressure	Attitude towards local culture
Explorer	Very limited	Adapts fully
Elite	Rarely seen	Adapts fully
Off-beat	Uncommon but seen	Adapts well
Unusual	Occasional	Adapts somewhat
Incipient mass	Steady flow	Seeks familiar amenities
Mass	Continuous influx	Expects familiar amenities
Charter	Massive arrivals	Demands familiar amenities

Source: adapted from Smith (1977). Reprinted with permission of the University of Pennsylvania Press.

PACE OF DEVELOPMENT

The pace of development is another factor that influences the level of socio-cultural impacts. If tourism develops slowly and gradually, the local community is given the opportunity to develop policies and management strategies to deal with the socio-cultural impacts, maximising the positive impacts and minimising the nega-tive impacts. If the development of tourism is sudden and fast (e.g. if an investor is allowed to build a big hotel complex in a small and little-developed destination), it may be more difficult for the local community to consider effective ways to deal with the influx of visitors.

Dubai is a typical example of a tourist destination that has developed very rapidly. Dubai is one of the seven autonomous sheikhdoms in the United Arab Emirates. Since the 1990s it has started to develop tourism in response to fluctuating oil prices and revenues. Since then, it has become one of the fastest growing tourism destinations worldwide. The main markets are other Gulf States, Europe and Africa. From 2003, earnings from tourism have surpassed those from oil in most years. In 2020, Dubai will be hosting the World Exhibition: more developments, such as theme parks and museums, are fast developing in anticipation for this event. Even though rapid tourism development is undeniably linked to economic benefits, it has also caused a degen-eration of the urban environment and negative social impacts. The influx of tourists has caused congestion, pollution and noise. The futuristic new developments push emblems of traditional culture, such as the Persian wind towers, into the background (Henderson, 2006). Therefore the negative impacts in this case are inconvenience and Westernisation.

DOMINANCE OF TOURISM

Destinations can also experience different levels of socio-cultural impacts depending on the dominance of tourism as a source of income. If the area is economically largely dependent on tourism, it may become more difficult to slow down tourist development, even if it is seen to bring negative impacts to the local area.

The example of Dubai can again apply here: due to over-construction of accommodation, prices in many older hotels have recently fallen. The cruise terminal, built to attract stopover tourism, is under-utilised during the summer. By becoming more and more dependent on tourism instead of oil, the tourism industry is now of vital importance as a source of revenue and employment: this may mean that the need for economic benefit could override socio-cultural concerns in the future (Henderson, 2006).

HOST–TOURIST RELATIONS (IRRIDEX)

Doxey (1975) proposed a model to describe the different community reactions to tourism. He suggested that as tourism develops and the industry becomes bigger, the attitude of the local population is expected to become more negative (see Figure 8.1).

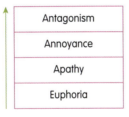

FIGURE 8.1   Doxey's Irridex Model

Source: Adapted from Doxey (1975)

Doxey suggested that when tourism first develops (in the earliest stages of the TALC), the host community is likely to welcome the positive impacts this has on the area, and the relationship between hosts and visitors will be positive (Euphoria). As the tourism industry becomes more established and the local population gets used to the visitors, this positive relationship may be transformed into a state of Apathy. If the tourist industry then develops even further and more negative impacts start to become clear, the local attitude towards visitors may turn into Annoyance, or in the most extreme cases Antagonism (e.g. violence against tourists).

Doxey's model applies most to destinations where the impacts of tourism are not managed. It can be seen as pessimistic because it seems to indicate that tourism development will necessarily lead to antagonism within the host community. Still, this does not have to be the case: with careful planning and management in the destination (see Chapters 12 and 13), it is possible to foster positive relationships between hosts and visitors.

THE RATIO OF TOURISTS TO RESIDENTS

This ratio refers to the number of tourists versus the number of local residents in a destination. In a large city like London, Tokyo or New York, this ratio is much lower than in a small seaside or island resort with a small population. If the ratio is high, it becomes more likely that the socio-cultural impacts of tourism on the destination will be more pronounced.

In 2015, Iceland had an overnight tourist ratio of 0.039: this meant that for every Icelandic resident, the country received 3.9 overnight tourists (Statistics Estonia, 2017). This is a relatively low number compared to Hawaii: here, the tourist ratio in 2015 was 0.062. This means that in 2015, the destination welcomed 6 tourists for every resident. Unless the tourists are carefully managed, the chance of negative impacts occurring is substantial.

SEASONALITY

If tourism in the destination has a distinct seasonal pattern such as, for example, in beach or ski resorts, the impacts on the community will be accentuated during peak periods. The destination may become congested, it may become more difficult for the local community to carry out daily tasks or worship, and feelings of resentment may grow.

Tourism in Spain is highly seasonal and geographically concentrated, which causes a particular set of social problems. The main season is from June to September, when tourism employment levels are high and a lot of the bed space is likely to be occupied (Hudman and Jackson, 2002). In response to this seasonality, the Spanish government supports a social tourism programme called IMSERSO: this programme allows older people to travel off-peak, via special grants, to destinations that would otherwise be under-visited. The programme provides holidaymakers with a grant of 30 per cent of the total cost of the holiday. This achieves the social aim of increasing the mobility of older people and supports out-of-season employment. Because this means that the government has to pay less unemployment benefit and receives income via taxes, the scheme has directly or indirectly generated more than 30,000 jobs in the tourist sector alone (Minnaert et al., 2010).

CHARACTERISTICS OF INDIVIDUAL HOST RESIDENTS

This section refers to the characteristics of individual members of the host population. These may influence how they perceive the socio-cultural impacts of tourism on the destination. The section highlights that even though some characteristics will apply to the destination as a whole, this does not mean that all members of a host community will have the same views of tourism development and its impacts. Ap (1992) has described this as an adaptation of the 'social exchange theory': he sees the relationships between hosts and tourists as a trade-off between positive and negative impacts, and how far an individual benefits or suffers from tourism development will determine his or her attitude towards tourism and tourists.

> *Involvement in tourism*: If persons in the host community are dependent on tourism for their livelihood – if they are employed in the tourism industry or if they operate a tourism business themselves – they are more likely to be more accepting of the negative socio-cultural impacts of tourism. For them the benefits of tourism often outweigh the costs, meaning the social exchange is positive.

Period of residence: Depending on the destination, the period of residence may be a positive or negative factor in determining the socio-cultural impacts of tourism on residents. If individuals move to the destination because they seek peace and tranquillity, the development of tourism there may seem rather threatening. However, if the tourism destination is rather developed already, new residents are often aware of the impacts of tourism before they move, so they may be more prepared to accept these than the residents who have lived there longer.

Residential proximity to tourist centre: This characteristic refers to how far from the tourist centre the resident lives his or her daily life. If the resident lives far away and has limited contact with tourists, he or she may experience fewer impacts of tourism development. Residents who live and/or work in the tourist centre and have frequent interactions with tourists are likely to experience the impacts of tourism more acutely.

Socio-economic characteristics: This characteristic is mainly applicable to tourism in developing countries, where the socio-economic gap between the visitors and the hosts can influence the relationships between the two groups. More educated and affluent groups in the destination may, for example, experience more positive contacts and impacts whereas more disadvantaged groups in the destination might mainly experience negative impacts.

UNDERLYING THEORIES

Cultures and societies are complex entities and tourism is just one factor that influences them. This is why tourism and its impacts do not operate independently from the ideas and ideologies that shape the rest of our social worlds. Tourism, as a relatively new industry, can be seen as an expression of ideas and theories that have influenced society for much longer – tourism researchers have thus frequently looked towards other disciplines such as history, sociology and ethics to frame the moral and philosophical aspects of the socio-cultural impacts of tourism. Sometimes this leads to opposing views of how tourism affects/should affect host communities and tourists – two examples are discussed here.

TOURISM AS AN 'INDUSTRY' VERSUS TOURISM AS A 'SOCIAL FORCE'

Higgins-Desbiolles (2006b) argues that since the 1960s, tourism has increasingly been seen as an 'industry', a phenomenon that is created and governed by the private sector and driven by profit. As such, tourism is industrialised, and just like many other industries it is normal that damage to the environment and culture will occur in its development. Tourism is seen as a discretionary activity: in other words, an activity we will choose to engage in if we are willing to pay the price for it. Tourism can therefore be seen as a commodity and in this sense it is no different from a car or a luxury handbag.

According to Higgins-Desbiolles (2006b), tourism can have other impacts than just income generation. Tourism can be seen as a way to gain human enrichment and education, and as a stimulus for a better understanding between cultures and a better society. Tourism can even be seen as a human right: the Universal Declaration of Human Rights (UN, n.d.) mentions the right to leave and return to one's own country

(Article 13.2) and the right to leisure and recreation (Article 24). In this paradigm, tourism is not private sector-led, but led by the public sector and community organisations. It emphasises the potential of tourism to bring a multitude of benefits to the tourist and the host community. It does not see tourism as a commodity, but rather as a social force with transformative capacities.

NEO-COLONIALISM VERSUS TOURISM AS A 'SACRED JOURNEY'

Tourism for some can be seen as a 'sacred journey', as a means to find oneself and make meaningful connections with places and people in other parts of the world. Researchers like MacCannell and Graburn link the origins of tourism to pilgrimages and argue that current forms of tourism are modern interpretations of these religious quests (Cohen, 1984). If tourism is seen this way, it should be able to bring positive impacts to both the tourist and the host community: the tourist gains a meaningful experience and visits the destination with respect, looking for a better way of life. The focus in this interpretation is on a search for meaning and truth, and the belief that these may be found in the destination culture.

It would seem that in some destinations, mostly in developing countries, this balance is not always retained. It often seems as if the tourists come to a destination and use and enjoy all that is good about it with little regard to the negative impacts of tourism: they then go again, leaving the destination to pick up the pieces. The power balance is often in favour of foreign developers and tourist dollars, forcing the local community into a subservient role. Tourism can also be considered a way to spread Western culture, consumption patterns and behaviours around the world: Western eating habits and products find their way around the globe via tourism. The globalisation of the tourism industry also plays a role here: the increased bargaining power of multinational tour operators means they can pressurise local providers to charge the lowest possible price. They may block-book a large amount of rooms to sell to their customer base, which gives them great power over the local accommodation provider. On the basis of this, tourism and the tourist industry have been compared to a form of neo-colonialism or imperialism: the focus is on the role of tourism in creating dependencies between tourism-generating, 'metropolitan' countries and tourism-receiving, 'peripheral' nations that replicate colonial or 'imperialist' forms of domination and structural underdevelopment. This was first argued by researchers such as Nash and Matthews (in Cohen, 1984) and is still prominent in tourism studies today.

An example of a destination where tourism could be seen as a neo-colonial force is Cyprus. The great majority of tourists travel to Cyprus on inclusive tour (package) arrangements: in 2013, for example, 58 per cent of international tourists travelled on a package tour, while 42 per cent of international tourists travelled independantly. Cyprus tourism is heavily reliant on three markets, the UK, Scandinavia and Germany, where large tour operators TUI and Thomas Cook have a market share of 50 per cent. Because of an over-supply of accommodations, these large tour operators can negotiate, or even dictate, high discounts with the majority of accommodations, leading to a downward pressure on the agreed prices (Karyopouli, 2016). Although there is no immediate cultural conflict between tourists and local residents, resentment can be the result of this type of development, as the local community is faced with the negative impacts of tourism whereas the bulk of the revenue goes to multinational companies.

MANAGING SOCIO-CULTURAL IMPACTS

Tourism development in a destination should aim to minimise the negative socio-cultural impacts of tourism and maximise the positive socio-cultural impacts – in other words, it should aim to be sustainable. Different stakeholders are involved in this process. The *public sector*, through planning and policy, often plays an important role. The public sector is not out to make a profit, and their responsibility is to represent the views of different groups in the destination. The *private sector*, for example accommodation providers, service providers and tour operators, can also have an influence over how impacts are managed. Although these businesses are profit-driven, there are ways for them to reduce their negative impacts. In areas where drinking water is scarce for example, hotels may decide to fill pools with sea water so as not to put an excessive strain on resources. The *host community* is another stakeholder. Already it has been discussed that a host community is not an homogeneous group (see p. 205) – some residents will experience more positive or negative impacts than others. The final stakeholder is the *tourist*, who influences the destination socio-culturally via his or her behaviour and consumption pattern.

SNAPSHOT 8.4

Travel+SocialGood

As this chapter has shown, managing the socio-cultural impacts of tourism so that they benefit the different stakeholder groups in tourism is a complex task. It requires creative and innovative collaborations between professionals in tourism, business, technology and policy. Travel+SocialGood, launched in the spring of 2013 in partnership with the UN Foundation's +SocialGood network, aims to build the travel industry of the future: one in which sustainable travel acts as the catalyst for a more equitable society. The organisation hosts a yearly summit, and has over 20 hubs around the world, which bring together thought leaders, entrepreneurs and travel professionals who are passionate about transforming their cities into capitals of sustainable travel. Hubs host events that are focused on education, advocacy and building a community. Through projects with local government, lecture series, community days and other unique endeavors, each hub engages with destination stakeholders to create a positive impact. Travel+SocialGood also has a media network: an alliance of journalists, content creators and social media influencers around the world, passionate about sustainable tourism in order to promote awareness and positive change within the industry (Travel+SocialGood, 2017).

VISITOR MANAGEMENT

Visitor management aims to minimise the negative impacts of tourism in three ways: controlling the number of visitors at a given place or time; modifying the way tourists behave; and adapting tourist resources to cope with visitor numbers (Mason, 2008).

Diversifying the product offer of a destination can be a first strategy to spread the numbers of tourists more evenly throughout the year, week or day. This could be achieved, for example, by promoting the destination in the off-peak season, by offering price promotions during these periods, or by staging events. Business events such as conventions, conferences, trade exhibitions and consumer fairs, for example, often run outside the leisure tourist season. By focusing on the segment of the business travel-ler, destinations may also avoid certain negative socio-cultural impacts of tourism. Seeing that business travellers often stay indoors for most of the day, they are less visible and less likely to cause congestion than leisure travellers, for example. Visitor numbers can also be regulated via pricing strategies and advance-booking systems. These ensure that the number of tourists does not exceed the attraction's or destina-tion's carrying capacity (see Chapters 9 and 12 for a full exploration of this concept).

A second visitor management strategy can be to modify the way tourists behave. This aim can be achieved in different ways. Education and information provision to the tourist is a first strategy: making visitors aware of their negative impacts makes it more likely that they change the behaviours that cause them. Positioning the destination to a different visitor type is another strategy: by replacing clubs and bars with more family-friendly facilities, for example, a destination can reduce the number of tourists who come to party and may cause a disturbance.

A third visitor management strategy could be to adapt tourism resources to minimise damage: certain areas of historic sites may be cordoned off, for example, or replicas may be provided to protect the original attraction. Wardens and guides may also be put in place to stop unruly behaviour.

For a full exploration of visitor management concepts and techniques, see Chapter 12.

PROTECTING CULTURE

It has been discussed here how tourism can have profound impacts on the culture of a destination: commodification, staged authenticity and the trinketisation of culture and its expressions are some examples. To counter these impacts, a range of strategies has been developed in many host communities to protect cultures from the negative impacts of tourism. Boissevain (1996) describes these strategies as covert resistance, hiding, fencing, organised protest and aggression.

Boissevain (1996) presents *covert resistance* as a first, uncoordinated defence against the negative impacts of tourism on culture. Covert resistance is not direct defiance or an organised form of protest, but rather a subtle but clear message to the tourist in the host community's behaviour. The local taxi driver might not challenge tourists directly, but may be sullen or rude towards them. The locals may gossip about or ridicule the tourists to express their feelings of discomfort or hostility.

Hiding is another strategy to protect culture and happens when certain aspects of a culture become 'insider only'. Religious or cultural events may, for example, be pur-posely held before the tourists arrive or after they leave. Tourists are not informed about these events and they may function as alternatives to other events that have been expropriated by tourists.

Fencing is a more explicit strategy to protect culture. It can literally refer to fencing off certain areas of the host community to stop tourists from accessing them: restricting access to (certain parts of) a religious building, for example, or not allowing them to disturb fisherman at work. Fencing can also be used in a figurative sense, referring to preventing certain behaviours by tourists. Tourists may, for example, be discouraged from taking pictures of residents.

Organised protest mostly occurs when the negative impacts of tourism have over-shadowed the positive impacts. This strategy may take the form of campaigns, demonstrations or boycotts. In extreme cases, the feelings of frustration and anger within the host community may even lead to *aggression* and violence.

COMMUNITY PARTICIPATION

A further principle in the management of socio-cultural impacts is community participation in tourism. The basic idea is that if the local community are more involved in the decision-making process, tourism development will be more adapted to their needs and circumstances. The participation of the local community can take different forms, depending on how many local residents participate, whether these participants are representative of the community as a whole, and how much weight their views carry when making decisions. The community may, for example, be asked for their views in a public consultation that informs decision making, or they may be involved in the complete tourism development process.

Although extensive community participation is a theoretical ideal for equitable tourism development, there are often practical problems in destinations to achieve this. Destinations are not homogeneous groups (see p. 205) and it is not always possible to reconcile the different interests of all the community members. In destinations in developing countries, it is also possible that not all community members will have the educational skills or the confidence to participate in tourism decision making. They may be unclear about the procedures and ways to have their say, or there may be a profound distrust between the community and the decision makers. The views of stakeholders with more financial power (such as the business community and local investors) might also carry more weight than the views of members in the community who live in poverty. In certain cases, it would therefore be more useful to include community members in the tourism development process in a practical way, rather than via consultations and negotiations, to build on the involvement of the local community and make further participation possible. The example of pro-poor tourism in Case Study 8.1 is one way to achieve this.

Stakeholder: A person, group or organisation that is affected by (has a direct 'stake' in) an organisation's actions

---

CASE STUDY 8.1

Pro-poor Tourism

The Pro-Poor Tourism partnership (http://propoortourism.org.uk/) defines pro-poor tourism as tourism that results in increased net benefits for poor people. It is not a specific tourism product, but rather an approach to tourism management that improves the socio-economic and socio-cultural quality of life for poor people in the host community. In other words, pro-poor tourism is not a new type of holiday, but rather a way of doing business differently. It is this focus on new business strategies that makes pro-poor tourism different from many other approaches: pro-poor tourism allocates a central role to business and trade, not public sector support and interventions by voluntary organisations, to bring positive impacts to poor communities in a destination.

Pro-poor tourism strategies have economic and socio-cultural aspects. The economic impacts mostly have to do with building linkages with local suppliers (see p. 186), such as

(Continued)

sourcing food and other products locally rather than relying on imports. Another important economic aspect is job creation for the local community: employing local staff, training them and paying them a fair salary. The increased income for the local community can lead to socio-cultural improvements such as a better infrastructure and quality of life. A socio-cultural aspect of pro-poor tourism can be the development of excursions and cultural attractions in the local area, increasing the local population's opportunities for finding pride in their culture and developing their own business. This can increase positive contacts between hosts and visitors, encourage capacity building within the poor population, and improve the balance between tourism and other forms of resource use.

Ashley et al. (2001) have compiled a report for the Overseas Development Institute with guidelines for the development of pro-poor practices in the Caribbean. Examples of these guidelines include:

- Pay smaller, local suppliers regularly. Hotels often pay for goods 30 to 90 days after these have been delivered, but small producers do not always have the working capital to wait that long for payment.

- Local producers often offer goods that can be used in hotels, but the quantity, quality and reliability of the supply are often inadequate. Consider working with smaller contracts and appointing a facilitator who can inform and work with the local suppliers.

- Develop and implement a policy which encourages openness and a lack of stigma towards HIV. Educate managers as well as staff about HIV/AIDS, safety in the workplace, and working with HIV+ colleagues.

- Integrate local interaction and local shopping into existing excursions. Visiting local craft markets or workshops can enhance tourists' experience and expenditure. Offer retail space to local craftspeople and advertising space to local taxis, excursions and guides.

- Find out about the goals local people have: these may be different from what tourism operators expect. In several pro-poor tourism projects local income has been welcome, but poor people also have non-financial priorities such as training, dignity, access to natural resources, access to infrastructure, and the ability to participate in decisions.

Reflective Questions

1. Think of a place you have visited or tourism in your own country. Can you think of any examples of measures that aim to include poorer groups in society in tourism?

2. Pro-poor tourism is aimed at bringing benefits to poorer groups in the host community. Can you think of any benefits pro-poor tourism brings to the private businesses who engage in it?

SUMMARY

This chapter has highlighted the socio-cultural impacts of tourism on destinations and host communities, some of which are positive (a better understanding between cultures, a greater appreciation of the own culture) and some of which are negative (commodification of culture, prostitution, Disneyfication). It has also explained the positive and negative socio-cultural impacts tourism can have on tourists: positive in terms of confidence, relaxation and relationships with others; negative in terms of anxiety due to violence or scams. The extent to which these impacts affect destinations can be linked to certain destination characteristics, such as how dominant tourism is, which type of tourists visit the destination, and the pace of development. Some members of the host community have also been shown to be more tolerant of these impacts than others, depending on, for example, their involvement in tourism or their proximity to the tourist centre.

The way we look at these impacts, and to what extent we see them as inherently linked to tourism, will depend on our underlying theory of tourism itself: is it an industry with unavoidable externalities? Or is it a social force, a sacred journey that affects both the tourist and the destination? The chapter has concluded by highlighting ways to manage the socio-cultural impacts of tourism, so that the positive impacts outweigh the negative impacts for both the destination and tourists.

SELF-TEST QUESTIONS

1. Think about the countries you have visited, or about the tourism sector in your own country. Which of the above socio-economic impacts of tourism on destinations have you noticed? Can you give examples of these?

2. When you travel, how does that affect you as a person? How long do the effects of a holiday last after you get back home?

3. Think of a destination you have visited. Do the positive socio-cultural impacts of tourism outweigh the negative socio-cultural impacts it brings?

FURTHER READING

Boissevain, J. (ed.) (1996) *Coping with Tourists: European Reactions to Mass Tourism.* Providence, NY: Berghahn Books.

Cole, S. and Morgan, N. (eds) (2010) *Tourism and Inequality: Problems and Prospects.* Wallingford: CABI.

Faulkner, B. and Tideswell, C. (1997) 'A framework for monitoring community impacts of tourism', *Journal of Sustainable Tourism*, 5(1): 3–28.

Moscardo, G. (ed.) (2004) *Building Community Capacity for Tourism Development.* Wallingford: CABI.

USEFUL WEBSITES

ECPAT International: www.ecpat.net

International Institute for Peace through Tourism: www.iipt.org

Office for Fair Trading – Safe from Scams: www.safefromscams.co.uk

Pro-Poor Tourism Partnership: http://propoortourism.org.uk/

UN World Tourism Organization Code of Ethics: http://ethics.unwto.org/content/global-code-ethics-tourism

9

THE ENVIRONMENTAL IMPACTS OF TOURISM

'Many tourists who visit such places become fascinated by, and protective of, reef fish, corals, nesting turtles, migrating cetaceans, whale sharks and so on. They will often actively support conservation initiatives; but they may also be the unwitting necrotic travelling agents of change.'

J. Mair, 2006: 1

LEARNING OUTCOMES

After reading this chapter you will understand:

- the potential environmental impacts of tourism, both positive and negative
- the role of environmental sustainability in new tourism forms, and the different characteristics of these tourism forms
- a number of key concepts and management tools for the environmental management of tourism.

Signage in Ulu Temburong National Park, Brunei

Source: Lynn Minnaert

INTRODUCTION

Tourism experiences are intrinsically linked to the environment they take place in: we often travel to experience places and environments that are different from the one we are familiar with. Many destinations are popular because of their natural assets: beaches, lakes, mountains, rolling countryside and empty plains are all examples of natural environments that can make a destination popular with tourists. At the same time, however, many of these environments are fragile, and by introducing tourists and their activities to them, we run the risk of damaging them. Tourism can also cause changes to the built environment, such as resort towns or parts of cities. This chapter reviews how tourism impacts on the environment it takes place in, and how these impacts can be managed.

This chapter also provides an overview of the different impacts tourism can have on the environment of a destination. Both positive and negative impacts are reviewed. The concept of sustainability is examined, and linked to new tourism forms such as eco-tourism, responsible tourism and agro-tourism. Finally, the chapter discusses how environmental impacts can be managed in the destination, by maximising the positive impacts and minimising the negative impacts. Key management concepts and tools to achieve this aim are presented.

ENVIRONMENTAL IMPACTS OF TOURISM ON A DESTINATION

The rapid growth of international tourism in the past 50 years or so has gone hand in hand with its ever more visual impact on the environment. Several once popular and beautiful resorts now seem to be typified by polluted beaches, an over-developed seafront and hordes of tourists who are not always respectful of their surroundings. This has led to an interest within tourism studies in how sustainable tourism is: although the concept of sustainable development has been around much longer, the debate about sustainable tourism is a phenomenon of the 1990s (Swarbrooke, 1999). This section will present the negative environmental impacts of tourism on the natural and the built environment, as well as on animal life. It will also highlight how tourists, via their behaviour, may exacerbate the negative environmental impacts of their holiday, although the extent of these impacts depends strongly on the scale of development in the destination, the environmental controls that are in place, and the visitor management techniques that are employed. Even though these negative impacts of tourism attract a lot of attention and are not to be minimised, tourism can also make positive contributions to the natural and built environment. The section will give examples of these positive environmental impacts of tourism.

NEGATIVE ENVIRONMENTAL IMPACTS OF TOURISM

Tourism can cause a wide variety of negative environmental impacts. These are most visible within destinations but may also occur within the generating region and along transit routes. This section will start by reviewing the negative environmental impacts of tourism on three aspects of the destination:

The natural environment and resources: Climate; water and soil pollution; waste/litter; over-use of resources.

Animal life: Habitats; animal behaviours; eco-systems; and the dangers of the souvenir trade.

The built environment: Over-development; pollution via building work; aesthetic pollution.

THE NATURAL ENVIRONMENT

Tourism, and most particularly mass tourism, is being increasingly acknowledged as a human activity that poses huge threats to the natural environment. Not only does tourism often develop in fragile natural environments, such as lakes, beaches and mountains, it is also reliant on transport via air, sea or road. Tourism is a contributor to climate change, and can cause damage to the natural environment via pollution, an increase in waste and an over-use of resources.

Climate change

The Earth's climate has changed throughout history. Just in the last 650,000 years there have been seven cycles of glacial advance and retreat, with the abrupt end of the last ice age about 7,000 years ago marking the beginning of the modern climate era – and of human civilization. Most of these climate changes are attributed to very small variations in Earth's orbit that change the amount of solar energy our planet receives. Current global warming, however, is different, as it is the result of human activity since the mid-20th century, and proceeding at a rate that is unprecedented over decades to millennia. Human activity, in particular the burning of fossil fuels, has increased the 'greenhouse effect': warming that results when the atmosphere traps heat radiating from Earth toward space (NASA, 2017).

The energy sector, with its oil, gas and coal producers, is the largest contributor to global warming (Heede, 2014). Road and air transportation, due to their dependence on fossil fuels, are also heavy polluters. Tourism, in turn, is dependent on transportation, and as a discretionary activity has been linked to climate change.

Exact figures for the impact of tourism on our climate are difficult to provide, as tourism has a broad nature and various components which all contribute to a different extent to climate change (CO_2, heating, air-conditioning, construction etc.). Despite these difficulties, the UNWTO (n.d.) estimates that tourism is responsible for about 5 per cent of global CO_2 emissions.

The transport sector, including air, car and rail, generates the largest proportion, with 75 per cent of all emissions. In terms of carbon emissions, air causes 54–75 per cent while coach and rail cause 13 per cent. Air travel is considered the main tourism contributor to global warming: it is responsible for 40 per cent of the total carbon emissions caused by this sector (UNWTO, n.d.).The accommodation sector accounts for approximately 20 per cent of emissions from tourism. This involves heating, air-conditioning and the maintenance of bars, restaurants, pools and so on. Clearly, this varies according to the location and size of the accommodation, as well as the type of establishments – hotels having greater energy consumption than pensions or camping sites.

Furthermore, activities such as museums, theme parks, events or shopping also contribute to certain amounts of emissions (approx. 3.5 per cent) (UNWTO, n.d.).

Air transport mainly contributes to air pollution through the emission of carbon dioxide (CO_2) and nitrous oxides (N_2O) that create global warming and ground-level pollution at airports. The contribution of aviation to carbon dioxide emissions is relatively low compared to other sectors: as a percentage of the global population, relatively few people can afford to fly; however, a transatlantic flight is estimated to add as much to a person's carbon footprint as one year of driving. However, the projected increase in demand globally suggests that aviation's contribution will increase. The International Air Transport Association (IATA) reports that in 2016, air capacity went up about 5 per cent globally, which means more airlines are flying more planes to more destinations. The 2017 Global Air Travel Outlook reports that average ticket prices are falling due to this increased competition, which will encourage more people to fly (ARC and Expedia, 2017). In 2016, the aviation industry transported 3.7 billion passengers, compared to just over 2 billion in 2006 (World Bank, 2017). Despite technological, regulatory and operating advances that reduce the emissions of individual flights, these have not neutralised the additional emissions caused by the increased volume of flights. In addition, it is widely believed that the climate change effects of aviation may be worse than those of other industries because of the altitude at which they occur, and the resulting cloud formation and condensation trails. Regulation is starting to develop to mitigate the impacts of air travel: since 2012, the EU requires all air carriers (both EU and non-EU) to offset CO_2 emissions from any flight within the European Economic Area (EEA). In 2016, the International Civil Aviation Organization (ICAO) finalised the details of a global offsetting initiative, which will first be implemented as a voluntary system from 2021–2026 and will be mandatory from 2027–2035 (ICAO, 2017).

Motorised road transport contributes to greenhouse gases and climate change through exhaust emissions, reduces air quality through the release into the atmosphere of fine particulates that cause respiratory illnesses, and creates congestion and environmental damage. Tourism by road increases these negative environmental impacts which within destinations affect the quality of life of local residents and visitors' experience of the destination. However, tourists who travel by coach, on public transport or private group tours reduce the number of equivalent tourists' cars on the road, and the National Household Survey (2009) suggests that the occupancy level of cars used for tourism purposes is often higher than when used for other purposes such as commuting. Greyhound Lines in the USA claim that one departure removes the equivalent of 34 cars from the road and achieves 184 passenger miles per gallon.

Rail transport is becoming increasingly acknowledged as a viable sustainable alternative to road and air transport. Rail is the most emissions-efficient major mode of transport, and electric trains powered by renewable energy can offer practically carbon-free journeys. Rail contributes less than 1.5 per cent of the EU transport sector's total CO_2 emissions even though it has over 8.5 per cent of total market share (CER, 2015).

Sea transport makes considerable contributions to air pollution, particularly because of the volume of shipping globally. According to the International Maritime Organization (IMO), international shipping emitted 2.2 per cent of global man-made emissions in 2012 (IMO, 2014), and this is expected to increase alongside global trade. It should be noted, though, that most sea transport is for freight rather than passengers; however, the growing popularity of cruise travel has led to the increasing importance of sea transport for tourism. Howitt et al. (2010) have calculated emissions for cruise ship

Passengers arrive at the start of their Princess cruise

Source: Lynn Minnaert

journeys to and from New Zealand, and report that the energy use per passenger night for the 'hotel' function of these cruise vessels was estimated to be 12 times larger than the value for a land-based hotel.

An additional moral issue is that transport does not only pollute the air in the tourism-generating areas – in other words the tourist's own geographic region – but also in the destination countries, some of which produce a lot less CO_2. Tourists who visit developing countries, for example, pollute the air by flying to the destination, thus causing air (and noise) pollution for people who cause a lot less pollution themselves. The same goes for countries that tourists tend to drive through on the way to their destination: many northern Europeans, for example, drive to southern Europe via the Benelux countries. In these countries, emissions due to tourism will thus be high, even though tourists do not bring many environmental, social or economic benefits to the local communities. In both cases, the tourists do not pay for the environmental damage they cause to these destination or transit regions.

Benelux: Belgium, the Netherlands and Luxemburg

Water Pollution

Tourism often takes place in areas close to water, such as seas or lakes. Still, it is usually not the activities of tourists in the water that have the biggest negative impacts. Pollution tends to be caused by inadequate facilities that are unable to cope with the large influx of tourists at peak times. Holden (2008) indicates that inadequate sewage systems may result in human waste being disposed directly into the sea. Rapid development in the past, to keep up with growing numbers of tourists, has sometimes left destinations with infrastructure that cannot cope with the demands that tourism places on it. Another form of water pollution results from the use of fertilisers and herbicides for hotel gardens and golf courses. These chemicals seep down to the ground water lying between 5 and 50 meters under the surface, and from there flow into rivers, lakes and seas.

The Mediterranean Sea is one of the most heavily polluted, semi-enclosed basins in the world. According to Greenpeace, thousands of tonnes of toxic waste are pumped directly into it – mainly by industry. Tourism is a contributing factor to this: the Mediterranean is one of the most popular tourism destinations in the world, and accounts for up to one-third of the global tourist arrivals. Overcrowding and inadequate facilities, often built at a distance from population centres and amenities, result in increased pollution in the peak months (Greenpeace International, 2006). In 2016, Princess cruises was fined a record $40 million for its deliberate pollution of the seas. Between 2005 and 2013, the *Caribbean Princess* cruise ship illegally used a bypass pipe to discharge oily waste directly into the sea, while disabling the monitoring equipment that is in place to prevent this practice. A single illegal discharge dumped 4,227 gallons of oil-contaminated waste about 20 miles off the coast of England on 26 August 2013. The oily bilge waste comes from a ship's engines and fuel systems. Instead of being dumped raw into the ocean it is supposed to be offloaded when a ship is in port and either burned in an incinerator or taken to a waste facility; however, the chief engineer responsible wanted to avoid the costs associated with this (US Department of Justice, 2016).

The Blue Flag programme is an internationally used quality label for beaches that guarantees good water quality, environmental education and information, environmental management, safety and other criteria. It is awarded by the independent charity Foundation for Environmental Education (FEE). In 2017, over 4,400 beaches and marinas were awarded Blue Flag status. Most of these were in Europe, but some were located in other parts of the world, for example Canada, New Zealand and South Africa (Blue Flag, n.d.).

SNAPSHOT 9.1

Surfers Against Sewage

Surfers Against Sewage is a not-for-profit organisation campaigning for clean, safe recreational waters, free from sewage effluents, toxic chemicals, marine litter and nuclear waste. Surfers and recreational water users who come into contact with sewage or other toxins may contract health problems, ranging from ear, nose and throat infections, eye and wound infections, and gastro-intestinal complaints such as diarrhoea and vomiting, to more serious illnesses such as bacillary dysentery, pneumonia, botulism, hepatitis A, meningitis and septicaemia. Research by the organisation showed that surfers were three times more likely to contract hepatitis A than the general public. Surfers Against Sewage highlight that popular British destinations such as Guernsey and Brighton discharge raw sewage in the sea, and campaign for greater awareness and regulation. The organisation also campaigns against marine litter and water pollution via the flushing or dumping of chemicals. The majority of these chemicals can be found in everyday household products such as shampoos, skin-care creams, washing detergents and paints. Some chemicals have been found to change the hormonal balance of wildlife: they are partly responsible for the feminisation of around one-third of the male fish population in Britain (Surfers Against Sewage, 2017).

Soil Pollution

Soil pollution, or 'soil contamination', refers to the presence of chemicals or other man-made substances that interfere with the natural soil environment. This type of pollution is often caused by underground storage tanks (e.g. containing fuel), the application of pesticides and the dumping of industrial waste. Although the tourism industry is not the biggest cause of soil pollution, certain of its activities can contribute to the problem. The use of pesticides on golf courses and hotel grounds is an example. Boniface and Cooper (2005) have also linked the use of artificial snow in ski resorts to soil pollution. Because ski seasons are becoming shorter and less reliable, ski cannons are increasingly used to top up the snow in these resorts. Not only do these snow cannons use a large amount of water, there are also chemicals in artificial snow that speed up the crystallisation process. Some resorts also infuse their artificial snow with salt to make the runs faster for skiers. These chemicals can then contaminate the soil in an already very fragile natural environment.

Waste/litter

Tourism, and in particular mass tourism, increases the destination's population size temporarily, and therefore the level of waste that is generated too. This can cause environmental problems if not properly managed. Some waste (such as food) can be classified as organic, whereas other forms (such as packaging) are inorganic. Litter can have various effects on a destination: in some cases, it will just make the environment unpleasant for tourists and the local community, for example if the beach is littered with bottles, papers and cigarette butts. Ultimately, there is no completely safe method of waste disposal, and the only way to truly avoid environmental harm from waste is to prevent its generation (Ceballos-Lascuráin, 1996).

One of the most famous effects of litter and waste caused by tourism is the widespread pollution in the Indian Himalayas. Mount Everest, the highest mountain in the world, is also referred to as 'the highest junkyard in the world'. Solid waste management is a problem, particularly along the trekking routes. During the tourist periods, food stalls pop up along these routes, selling their wares in disposable containers (Cole and Sinclair, 2002). Even though a large amount of the waste could technically be recycled, it needs to be transported to the main road and then to recycling centres, making this an intensive and costly enterprise. Since 2014, climbers have been provided with canvas bags to collect waste after scaling the peak, and are fined if they do not bring enough rubbish back. Sherpas are also contributing to the clean-up efforts, and are paid US$2 per kilo of trash (BBC Newsbeat, 2017).

Over-use of Natural Resources

When large numbers of tourists come to a destination with limited resources, increased competition for these resources may ensue. Energy resources, such as gas and electricity, and water reserves, may come under severe pressure. In destinations with limited water supplies, for example, the construction of large resorts with swimming pools may place disproportionately high demands on this resource.

In Cyprus, the tourism industry is placing a heavy burden on the scarce water reserves of the island. Because of limited rainfall, demand has outstripped supply for many years. The island has a number of desalination plants to supply drinking water, but these plants are energy-heavy and thus cause their own environmental impacts. In 2008, the situation became so drastic that tanker ships from Greece were sent to relieve the water shortage in the southern part of the island (BBC News, 2008). The tourism industry has been forced to adapt to the restrictions of water use, but these are less stringent than those placed on the local population.

Animal Life

Swimming with dolphins, riding elephants and petting tiger cubs are popular activities in many destinations, but unfortunately, interaction with humans is often detrimental to the animal's life. For example, the tiger cub that looks so adorable in the tourist's selfie was separated from its mother after only 2 or 3 weeks, and may be handled dozens of times a day, which may lead to stress and injury (World Animal Protection, 2016). Even in cases where the contact between animals and tourists is less direct, tourism development and tourist activities may affect the behaviour and habitat of animals. Tourism may also introduce foreign life forms and micro-organisms (such as viruses and bacteria) into their environment.

Animal Behaviours

Contact with tourists may alter the behaviour patterns and habits of animals, especially when that contact is frequent and intense. Orams (2002) classifies human contact with animals in the context of tourism in three broad categories: *captive* (in zoos, aquariums, aviaries and oceanariums), *semi-captive* (in wildlife parks or sea pens), or *wild* (in wildlife parks, along migration routes, and at breeding/feeding/drinking sites). Animals in the wild may seem to be least affected by tourists, but because seeing the animals is not as guaranteed in a wildlife park as in a zoo, the animals are sometimes fed by the tourists and guides in order to allow closer contact. This practice may affect the behaviour of the animal profoundly. The animal needs to spend less time hunting and foraging, which can result in increased breeding, higher population levels or a change in migration patterns – the animal may stay in one place throughout the year, rather than migrating to another place where usually food would have been more abundant. The danger is that the animal becomes dependent on these human hand-outs and does not develop or maintain the necessary skills to feed itself. Another risk is that the animal becomes habituated to human contact and even approaches humans where they would usually keep a safe distance. This may result in animals being hurt or killed. Finally, there are also reported cases whereby animals fed by people have become aggressive towards humans, as shown in the case study below.

CASE STUDY 9.1

Feeding by Tourists and its Impact on the Behaviour of Monkeys in Gambia and Gibraltar

Bijilo Forest Park is a small nature reserve in Gambia. It was opened in 1991 to preserve the area from deforestation and to provide a safe habitat for several species of wildlife, amongst which are the green monkeys. These monkeys, also called 'velvet monkeys', are medium-sized primates and were threatened by dogs and hunting. Now they are a key attraction for the country, featuring on marketing materials for the marketing campaign 'Gambia, the smiling coast of Africa'. The park receives about 2,000 visitors per year, most of whom stay in nearby hotels. The park, and with it the monkeys, was meant to be a place to enjoy the animals in their natural environment, but now seems to have become a victim of its own success. Although feeding the monkeys is officially forbidden, tourists can buy bags of groundnuts especially for this purpose. The monkeys have understood that rather than foraging for their own food, they can just sit along the path that leads from the hotels and wait for hand-outs. Tourist guides do not enforce the environmental rules and let tourists feed the animals. This practice has profoundly altered the behaviour of the monkeys: their travel range has become much smaller, and they are overfed and overweight, risking illness and diabetes. They have also become more aggressive, both amongst themselves and towards tourists (Starin, 2008).

The Gibraltar Upper Rock Nature Reserve is home to over 200 Barbary macaques. The macaques have free range throughout the reserve, and occasionally move into areas in the neighbouring urban zones. Interactions with humans have been a substantial factor in the daily lives of the Gibraltar macaques for several generations, and this has impacted on their social behaviour. Fuentes (2006) highlights how the presence of tourists affects breeding patterns, and may lead to physiologically stressful outcomes. The rise of tourists in Gibraltar, and their interest in the monkeys, has resulted in an explosion in their numbers. Although there are signs indicating that feeding the monkeys is forbidden, and that they may bite, taxi and coach drivers tend to encourage interactions by luring a monkey onto the shoulder or the head of a tourist for a picture. This behaviour culminated in 2008 with the Gibraltar government ordering a group of aggressive monkeys to be killed after 25 broke into hotel rooms and were found scavenging in bins in the town centre. The motivation behind the cull was that tourists and children were frightened and that the monkeys would damage the tourism sector. The killings resulted in protests from researchers and animal rights groups, who argued that the animals would have returned to the hills if tourists and locals had stopped feeding them.

Both stories show how tourism and tourist activities can profoundly impact the lives and behaviours of monkeys in certain tourism destinations, and in both cases the interactions with tourists have resulted in negative outcomes for the monkey population.

Reflective Questions

1. Which strategies could be adopted to minimise the negative impacts of tourism on these monkey populations?

2. Can you think of other examples where interactions with tourists have changed the behavioural patterns of animals?

Animal Habitats

Tourism and tourism activities can be a threat to animals when their habitats are cleared to make way for tourism infrastructure. Habitats may be destroyed during the construction of hotels, lodges, camping grounds, roads or attractions. Trees, shrubs and other elements that are vital to the lives of the animals may be removed during the construction process. Tourism facilities might also fragment the habitat of certain animals, and make it harder for some of them to access sources of food and water. The use of off-road vehicles may damage vegetation in the habitat. All these factors can severely impact on breeding and feeding habits (Higginbottom, 2004).

Certain types of sports tourism can be seen as particularly intrusive from this perspective because they are intrinsically linked with the natural environment they take place in. Water sports are an example – several of these (e.g. diving and snorkelling) take place in animal habitats, as viewing the animals is one of the attractions of engaging in the activity. Egypt's Red Sea coast, for example, is famous for diving and snorkelling, and attracts many thousands of visitors each year. Hunting and fishing are other examples.

Sports activities like these need to be carefully managed so that the activities of tourists do not endanger the animal habitats they have come to visit. Trophy hunting (tourists hunting for specific animals that are seen as trophies because of their body size, large tusks or skull length) is often presented as a source of income for conservation areas, but causes a set of problems. It is difficult, for example, to set reliable hunting quotas in areas where there are insufficient data about animal populations, and because of corruption the quotas that are set may be exceeded. In the developed world, there is also a growing ethical resistance against the idea of killing animals for sport (Lindsey et al., 2006).

Habitat: Ecological surroundings that are inhabited by an animal or plant species

SNAPSHOT 9.2

Diving Tourism and Coral Reefs

Coral reefs are an example of habitats that are under threat from tourism, mainly from water sports and diving tourism. Some destinations, like Australia, Egypt, Mexico and Belize, have developed thriving niches for diving tourism. Particularly in destinations like these, where there is intensive diving, the activity can lead to broken coral and sediment covering the reefs. Most of the damage is accidental and involves unintentionally touching, trampling and hitting corals with loose equipment. Divers are not the only problem: fishing and diving boats can also damage the coral when they drop anchor. In the USA, states like Florida, Washington and Hawaii have mooring buoys where boats can tie up, sparing the ocean floor from the repeated impact of anchors – but this isn't the standard in California for example, where the purple hydrocoral typical for the region is suffering severe damage. Purple hydrocoral grows extremely slowly, so any damage takes a very long time to repair (Wel, 2017). The damage affects not only the corals, but also the fish for which the reef is a vibrant habitat. Damage caused by divers and tourist boats to coral reefs may lead to higher fish mortality, or cause them to migrate to other reefs (Hasler and Ott, 2008).

Diving tourism in Egypt

Source: Roger Louis

Introduction of Foreign Life Systems

Most countries operate strict rules for tourists who want to export or import foodstuffs, seeds, bulbs, or live animals and plants. One of the reasons for this is that these can carry microbes, bacteria, viruses, pests and diseases that can deeply impact on the environment of the area they are introduced to. For example when tourists bring exotic flowers home, this may cause invasive micro-organisms that were once confined to a small area to spread around the world.

The introduction of new life forms is particularly dangerous in pristine and fragile environments, for example the Galapagos Islands. These islands were studied by Darwin, who found a wealth of endemic species there. Tourism activity in the islands has been steadily growing, and although care is taken not to disturb the environment unnecessarily, it is not without its problems. The Darwin Foundation has highlighted how tourist boats in the Galapagos introduced new insects, mainly moths, to the islands from countries such as Ecuador. The boats also transport insects from one island to another because the insects are attracted by the lights on them. In fragile ecosystems, the introduction of a new species with no natural predators can cause its numbers to grow rapidly, in time endangering or even replacing domestic species. A simple solution to the problem would be to equip the boats with lights in colours that are less attractive to the insects (Roque-Albelo et al., 2008).

Endemic: Native to a certain region, e.g. because of the isolated location of the Galapagos Islands, there are a great number of species here that cannot be found anywhere else

Souvenir Trade

The trade in certain souvenirs can pose a direct threat to animals in the destination. Ivory, exotic leathers and fur, animal teeth and claws, and foodstuffs such as shark fins can be offered to tourists, who may buy them because they are unaware of the environmental impacts of this, or because this adds to their value as a novelty item. Tourists may also be invited to eat endangered species in local restaurants, such as turtle eggs, shark's fin soup or iguana meat. Because the products are sold so openly, many tourists do not realise that they are driving up the demand for these products and so putting the environment in danger.

IFAW, the International Fund for Animal Welfare, runs the campaign 'Think Twice, Don't Buy Wildlife Souvenirs' to educate tourists about the environmental impacts of certain behaviours and activities. The campaign website offers an extensive list of souvenirs and foods to avoid whilst on holiday and gives tips on how to be a more responsible tourist (Hiel, 2012). There is also a link for travel agents and tour operators to support the campaign.

THE BUILT ENVIRONMENT

Tourism impacts not only on the natural environment, but also on the built environment. The development of tourism often requires extensive development of supporting facilities such as accommodation, attractions, roads and airports. In some destinations, the extensive and rapid development of these facilities has caused the built environment to deteriorate. This section will look at the effects of over-development and aesthetic pollution. It will also address the problem of sedimentation caused by construction activities and how this impacts on the destination.

Over-development

Most long-established tourism destinations have developed tourism facilities and infrastructure over time on a large scale, to cater for the large numbers of tourists that visit them. In many cases, faced with the strong economic benefits of mass tourism, this development has taken place in a rather unplanned fashion, resulting in long strips of poorly built hotels, cafés and shops that are not always in keeping with the local environment. Not only does this cause the built environment to look ugly (see Aesthetic Pollution below), it can also negatively affect the quality of life of the local community, for example through a lack of green space, a loss of local pride, and overcrowding and congestion.

In some destinations, action is being taken to remove inappropriate developments. The Spanish coast is one of the most over-developed tourist destinations in Europe and the coastline is largely built up. Even though there is a law that forbids buildings to be erected within 500 metres of the water, it is estimated that about 300,000 holiday homes have been built within this zone. The Spanish government has threatened several times to demolish these holiday homes, but so far only limited demolition has actually taken place. The effects on the natural and built environment can be far-reaching, as Charles Clover (2007) commented:

> I was driving down an obscure part of the coast of Almeria last year, one of the driest and so least developed parts of the Mediterranean coast, when I came across a hill in the middle of nowhere being consumed by bulldozers and cranes as if by maggots. White tourist homes with no connection to existing settlements were sprouting out of bare rock and scrub. [I drove] around the rows and rows of largely empty new tourist homes, the golf courses, shops and restaurants most with British names which are devouring the last hillsides around La Manga del Mar Menor.

Aesthetic Pollution

Tourism development can also lead to what Holden (2008) refers to as 'aesthetic pollution': a decline in the visual, aesthetic appeal of a destination. This can be particularly apparent in destinations that have developed rapidly for tourism, where hotels and infrastructure have been constructed without much planning and regulation, often resulting in over-developed and built-up environments. Many coastal resorts have also started looking very similar, with little sensitivity shown towards local cultures or building styles. Aesthetic pollution not only adversely affects the built environment for the local population, it also influences the overall popularity of the destination and the type of tourists it will attract. Uncontrolled growth and aesthetic pollution are often connected to the 'decline' stage in Butler's TALC model (see Chapter 10). An example of a destination that can be argued to be in this phase is Bugibba in Malta. The *Lonely Planet* guide for Malta and Gozo describes this destination as follows:

> The unattractive sprawl of Bugibba, on the eastern side of the bay, is the biggest tourist development in Malta. Bugibba is the heartland of the island's cheap-and-cheerful package holiday trade, and is absolutely mobbed in the summer. It is not the prettiest or most inspiring of places to end up on a holiday (and there are no sandy beaches) but at least it's cheap, especially in the low season when there are some real accommodation bargains and the swimming areas are not so crowded. (Bain and Wilson, 2004: 99)

Sediment and Destabilisation After Building Work

Construction activities such as dredging, digging and land clearing can cause large amounts of sediment to settle over the surrounding areas. This sediment can smother

A viewing point in Buggiba, Malta

Source: Lynn Minnaert

vegetation, or be washed away via runoff water from rainfall and pollute waterways and aquatic life. Hotels, runways, roads, and other tourism facilities are often constructed in naturally fragile areas such as beaches, mountains or around lakes, where sediment can threaten the natural environment. Burke and Maidens (2004) examined the health of coral reefs in the Caribbean, and noted that sediment and pollution from construction and agriculture threaten about one-third of them. Their study identified 20 per cent of coral reefs at high threat and about 15 per cent at medium threat. Sediment control measures, such as the installation of sediment fences, can reduce this potential damage.

The construction of new tourist facilities may also involve the removal of certain natural barriers against erosion, thus causing a destabilisation of the area. On beaches and in dune areas, for example, palm trees and dune grasses are key stabilising elements that stop beach erosion: in other words, they stop the sand from being washed or blown away. Seagrasses are crucial for the natural environment because their roots bind and consolidate the soil, but many hotels remove them because they are seen as unsightly, or dangerous for bathers. To provide an aesthetically pleasing environment for swimmers an increasing number of hotels are removing the seagrass bed, resulting not only in destabilisation but also generally in a less robust ecosystem that is more vulnerable to environmental change and extreme weather. In 2014, the US National Fish and Wildlife Foundation created the Puerto Rico Seagrass Fund in order to restore or re-establish vegetation buffers along coastal areas in this popular Caribbean destination. Beaches that suffer from erosion often need to be artificially replenished to maintain their tourism appeal.

POSITIVE IMPACTS

Although tourism, as described in the sections above, is often linked to negative environmental impacts, it can also have a number of positive impacts for the natural environment. Even though it is hard to argue that tourism makes the environment better per se, tourism can replace or prohibit activities that are even more damaging, such as mining, logging or heavy industries. The economic benefit from tourism can also be a stimulus for destinations to appreciate the local environment and enforce stronger environmental controls. Tourism can encourage the protection or enhancement of the environment in two ways: it can conserve and protect the natural environment on the one hand, and regenerate and enhance the built environment on the other hand.

Conservation/Protection of the Natural Environment

Although tourism, as explained in the previous paragraphs, can often be seen as a threat to the natural environment, it can also act as a driving force for conservation and protection. This is because, via tourism, leisure and recreation, the natural environment can become a source of income for the local community – this means that there is less need to replace the natural area with housing, industry or commercial uses. For many destinations, natural attractions like beaches, mountains, lakes and countryside are important elements of the tourism product. If these destinations want to experience the economic benefits from tourism, it is important that they take good care of this asset. Tourists who visit the area can also play a role in the awareness-building process, if they are being told about the fauna and flora in the area and the various threats that may affect their habitat.

SNAPSHOT 9.3

US National Park Service

The US National Park Service (NPS) is often presented as a global leader in responsible and sustainable tourism development in fragile natural areas. It is a bureau of the US Department of the Interior that manages the 417 parks of the NPS. Some of its most famous parks are Yellowstone, Yosemite and the Grand Canyon. Founded in 1916 by President Woodrow Wilson, the mission of the NPS 'is to conserve the scenery and the natural and historic objects and the wild life therein, and to provide for the enjoyment of the same in such manner and by such means as will leave them unimpaired for the enjoyment of future generations.' In 2015, the NPS received $2.8 billion in state funding; its contributions to the economy, however, are substantial. Annual visitor spending in communities within 60 miles of NPS sites supports more than 295,000 mostly local jobs and contributes about $32 billion to the US economy. In 2016, the National Parks attracted over 330 million visitors.

The NPS has implemented rigorous visitor management and conservation policies: in 2017, for example, the Green Parks Plan was introduced, which emphasises a holistic approach to sustainable operations (e.g. energy and water conservation, procurement and recycling, transportation). However, the enduring popularity of the parks also poses challenges. Increasing visitor numbers (including a growing percentage of overseas visitors) have led to more frequent instances of illegal camping, vandalism, theft of resources, wildlife harassment and other misbehavior from visitors (Interagency Visitor Use Management Council, n.d.).

Regeneration of the Built Environment

Tourism can be a driver for the protection and enhancement of not only the natural environment, but also the built environment. The term 'regeneration' refers to the revitalisation of run-down urban areas so that they become an attractive place to live, work and visit. Regeneration projects usually include impressive buildings, hotels, shopping malls, and entertainment and cultural facilities. In many former industrial cities, regeneration schemes became popular after the deindustrialisation of the Western economy: with many industries moving production to countries with a cheaper labour force, and the growth of the service economy, much of the industrial infrastructure was no longer needed. Tourism, leisure and recreation spending increased rapidly in modern society as the **disposable income** of many families grew. This resulted in a range of industrial buildings being transformed into museums and cultural attractions. In London, for example, a former power station along the river Thames has been transformed into a major cultural attraction: the Tate Modern museum of modern art. This is an example of how tourism development may create new uses for existing buildings and make an area more aesthetically pleasing via the removal of graffiti and the prevention of dereliction.

Disposable income: This is the income of a person after taxes and bills for necessities (food, rent/mortgage, utilities)

Regeneration can involve the conservation and restoration of heritage buildings, but is often associated with grand projects of modern architecture that become symbols or 'flagships' of the city. The Guggenheim museum in Bilbao, for example, is often used as an illustration of how flagship buildings can enhance the image of a city and increase visitor flows. Even though these developments are usually not purely aimed at tourists, their cost and scale can often transcend the needs of the local population. They often become tourist attractions, thus strengthening their symbolic function as showcases for cities.

Although regeneration projects can bring a range of benefits to the destination, some have also been linked to a number of negative environmental and social impacts. Certain urban regeneration projects have been criticised because of the 'placelessness' they can create: the regenerated area of one city, with its modern architecture, waterfront apartments and entertainment complexes, may look exactly like that of another city. There are sometimes few links between the culture of a place and the regenerated area, so that landscapes become increasingly 'global' (Smith, M., 2007). Regeneration can also lead to **gentrification** and displacement: as the area becomes more and more desirable as a place to live and work, the local residents who used to live there may be forced out of the area due to increased rents or housing costs.

Gentrification: The rebuilding of an area leading to an influx of more affluent people, often resulting in an increased living cost which may drive out the original residents

On the basis of these examples, it can be stated that tourism can have a variety of negative impacts on the natural environment. Mass tourism moves a large number of people to an often fragile natural environment, which may put pressure on resources, cause pollution, affect animal life, and cause detrimental changes to the built environment. There is a growing awareness of these negative environmental impacts of tourism and a mounting pressure on tourism to protect and enhance the natural and built environment. The remainder of this chapter will discuss the concept of environmental sustainability and examine how the environmental impacts of tourism can be managed so that the positive impacts are maximised and negative ones are minimised.

SNAPSHOT 9.4

The New York City High Line

A great example of regeneration in NYC is the High Line, an elevated railroad track constructed in 1929 that fell into disuse when the subway system was moved underground. Much of the line fell into disuse in the 1960s, and more was shut off in the 1980s. A short section remained, unused, until the turn of the century. In 1999, Manhattan residents and property owners began campaigning for the disused rail line to be converted for public use. The track was often too narrow to be redeveloped into buildings, but offered the opportunity to develop a much-needed green space in the city. While the southern section was demolished to make way for new apartments, the rest remained unused for 40 years while the surrounding neighborhoods of Chelsea and the Meatpacking District became sought-after locales. The regenerated High Line opened in 2009, and offers flower and art displays, food stalls, viewing points and a traffic-free walkway from Midtown to the Whitney Museum in the Meatpacking district (www.thehighline.org).

The High Line has been a big success with locals and tourists alike, and property prices nearby have soared. Since the High Line was unveiled, numerous cities in the US and elsewhere have talked of similar projects. Chicago, Philadelphia, Jersey City and St Louis have considered the same solution for their disused urban spaces, while Europe's capitals have enthusiastically discussed similar designs.

High Line

Source: Sandra Charrasse

ENVIRONMENTAL SUSTAINABILITY

In the face of a relentlessly growing tourism industry, and the growing awareness of its negative environmental impacts, the concept of sustainability has become central to the tourism debate. A fuller exploration of sustainability can be found in Chapter 1.

This section will briefly introduce environmental sustainability and discuss three recent approaches to tourism that aim to provide alternative and more environmentally sustainable tourism choices.

THE FOCUS ON THE ENVIRONMENT IN DEFINING SUSTAINABLE TOURISM

The term 'sustainability' is defined in Chapter 1 as 'the term chosen to bridge the gulf between development and environment' (Rogers et al., 2008). The concept has an economic, social and environmental component, but when it is applied to tourism, the environment has for a long time taken a central role in the debate. The term 'sustainable tourism' has come to represent and encompass a set of principles, policy prescriptions and management methods which chart a path for tourism development such that a destination area's environmental resource base (including natural, built and cultural features) is protected for future development (Lane, 1994). Hunter (1997, 2004) has long argued that this overemphasis on the environment in tourism needs to be rebalanced and that the tourism industry should take a more holistic view of sustainability.

Recently, a new emphasis on social sustainability can be noted within the tourism industry, with forms of tourism such as community-based tourism, **pro-poor tourism** (see page 253) and social tourism receiving increased attention from scholars and practitioners. This evolution, together with a continued focus on environmental issues, should move the tourism industry towards a more general implementation of the sustainability concept. The following forms of tourism may focus mainly on environmental conservation and protection, but each of these also includes economic and social elements.

Pro-poor tourism: Tourism in which the poor are key stakeholders, and that particularly aims to achieve net benefits for poor people in the host community, often by building partnerships between them and the private sector

RESPONSIBLE TOURISM

'Responsible tourism' is a term that does not tend to refer to a product in particular, but to a new attitude to tourism. This attitude sees tourism not as a mere product, that is consumed and then discarded, but as an activity with far-reaching consequences, for which all stakeholders are in part responsible. This means that the tourists are responsible for their behaviour at the destination; the tourism providers for their operations, sourcing policies and developments; the local communities for their involvement in tourism; and the governments for planning and regulating tourism in a responsible fashion. Responsible tourism, just as with the concept of sustainability, has an environmental, social and economic element.

Although 'responsible tourism' is thus an umbrella term for different forms of tourism, the environmental aspect plays an important role. Leslie (2012) points out that tourism is by nature often an unsustainable form of consumption, and that mass tourism in particular often destroys the natural beauty it is in search of. In contrast, responsible tourism tends to favour small-scale, slow, steady development. This should go hand in hand with tourist education so that they are more aware of the impacts of their activities. Even though these are laudable objectives, concerns have been raised for many years about how realistic this objective is. Wheeler (1991), for example, highlighted over 25 years ago that small-scale and paced development may be more responsible, but how will this speed of development keep up with the ever increasing volume of tourists? At that time, international arrivals amounted to fewer than half a billion tourists – in 2016, that number has grown to over 1.2 billion (World Bank, 2017). Educating all these tourists so that they behave in a more responsible way is also a mammoth task. There is also the question of whether raised awareness will automatically lead to a change in behaviour by tourists. Many will have a certain understanding of the environmental impacts of tourism, but this does not always mean they will be willing to change their habits or behaviour. Despite these challenges, awareness of responsible tourism is growing, and many destinations are actively encouraging visitors to be mindful of their behaviours when they travel. In 2017, for example, the Icelandic Tourist Board invited tourists to take a pledge to travel responsibly when visiting the country. 'The Icelandic Pledge' is an online agreement tourists can sign, in which they promise to respect the natural environment while travelling in Iceland. On signing they get a certificate they can share on social media with the hashtag #IcelandicPledge. The initiative responds to a steep increase in the number of international visitors to Iceland: arrivals grew from fewer than half a million in 2010 to almost 1.3 million in 2015 (Icelandic Tourist Board, 2017).

ECO-TOURISM

Fennell (2015) highlights that there is no single definition for eco-tourism – a range of definitions and approaches exists. He identified a range of characteristics that typify eco-tourism initiatives: these tend to be centred on nature-based attractions, but, as opposed to other nature-based tourism forms, there is usually an educational element involved in the experience. This educational element can be intensive or rather light, but learning about the environment is usually one of the motivations for tourists to participate in eco-tourism. The eco-tourism project should also make a credible attempt to be environmentally sustainable. It should be low-impact, and benefit local communities.

One of the key benefits of eco-tourism is that it presents a revenue stream that can be used to fund conservation activities. Eco-tourism can also encourage the tourist to adopt a more environmentally friendly attitude in general. Finally, if the local community is involved in providing the eco-tourism experience, they may take on the role of environmental advocates and stewards (Weaver, 2006: 202). On the flipside of eco-tourism development is the fact that tourism – even eco-tourism – increases the likelihood of negative environmental impacts on the destination's environment. It may increase pollution, change the behaviour of animals, and put pressure on limited resources. This has resulted in eco-tourism sometimes being criticised as being a mere marketing ploy, also referred to as 'greenwashing' (Holden, 2008) – indeed Wheeller (1991) goes even further and points to eco-tourists as an inherent part of the problem. He says eco-tourists add to the environmental damage of tourism by constantly looking for the new, the exotic, the unspoilt and the vulnerable. By their very presence in a vulnerable natural environment, they risk causing the most irreversible damage.

AGRO-TOURISM

Agro-tourism is sometimes confused with rural tourism, but the two are inherently different. 'Rural tourism' is the more general term and refers to tourism activities that take place in rural areas. 'Agro-tourism' refers to a specific set of activities organised by farmers for tourists: the tourist stays on the farm and engages in everyday working activities. This form of tourism is firmly based in the customs and culture of the area and tends to involve close contact between hosts and visitors. The customers for this type of tourism, who usually travel with their families, tend to be educated and of predominantly urban origin. They avoid mass tourism and tend to be environmentally conscious (Lopez and Garcia, 2006).

Israel was an important destination for agro-tourism in the 1960s and 1970s, when many young people travelled to the country to volunteer in kibbutzim, or communal farms. Each kibbutz was run by a community of families who aimed to be self-sufficient. Tourists who visited the kibbutz helped with the farm work and learnt about the traditions, language, history and customs of the residents. A traditional kibbutz experience like this still exists, but increasingly kibbutzim are inviting tourists to stay as guests and not volunteers. Although ecology and the working of the farm usually still takes a central place, the guest can also engage in leisure activities such as relaxing by the pool, going on hiking tours or playing sports (Raz, 2013).

MANAGING ENVIRONMENTAL IMPACTS

Because of the new emphasis on the need for environmental sustainability within the tourism sector, the purely economic view of tourism is increasingly being left behind in favour of a more realistic view that also takes the environmental costs of the industry into account. The management of negative environmental impacts therefore becomes central. Part of this will be achieved via efficient visitor management (discussed in more detail in Chapter 12). This section will specifically look at managing environmental impacts and will examine three key steps in achieving this: determining carrying capacity, policy and planning, and the role of partnerships.

Managing environmental impacts

Source: Lynn Minnaert

CARRYING CAPACITY

'Carrying capacity' can be defined as the maximum pressures a tourism destination, attraction or resource can be subjected to before irreversible damage is inflicted. Carrying capacity can be interpreted in different ways: socially, economically and environmentally. On an environmental level, it can refer to the maximum number of people that can visit or make use of a natural area before it is damaged irreversibly, or it can refer to the maximum level of development (in terms of constructing buildings, roads and other infrastructure) before the same effect ensues (Coccossis and Mexa, 2004).

Although carrying capacity is a widely used concept in tourism studies, scholars are increasingly agreeing that a fixed, quantitative view of it is not useful: in other words, the notion that there is a fixed ceiling, a threshold number of visitors which tourism should not exceed, has been largely discredited (Holden, 2008: 190). Instead, a more flexible view of the concept is now often adopted: carrying capacity assessments today usually allow for a gradual increase in visitation, whilst management strategies are implemented to make this possible in a sustainable way. However, it needs to be emphasised here that this more flexible approach may not be suitable for highly fragile natural environments or destinations where there are no resources available to allow for environmental management strategies (Weaver, 2006).

Limits of Acceptable Change

An alternative to the concept of carrying capacity is 'limits of acceptable change' (LAC). Where carrying capacity is focused on keeping the destination the same and not causing irreversible change, this model projects which changes would be desirable or acceptable, considering the potential of the area for tourism. LAC does not view the environmental needs of the destination as separate entities, but links them with social and economic factors: some level of environmental change may be accepted if there are significant social and economic benefits. In practice, the system adopts a set of indicators (e.g. pollution levels, tourist satisfaction, employment etc.) that are regularly monitored to see if the environmental, social and economic aims of the project are being achieved (Holden, 2008).

Within environmental management, determining the carrying capacity or the limits of acceptable change should be the first task. Together with environmental impact assessments, these can form the basis of effective environmental management via policy, planning and partnerships. The complexity and expense of managing this process has led to it mainly being implemented in destinations in developed countries.

Environmental Impact Assessments

Environmental impact assessments (EIAs) systematically examine the potential future environmental impacts of development on the destination. Where carrying capacity assessments are carried out for existing facilities and attractions, an EIA is often (but not always) conducted ahead of new developments – the positive and negative impacts on the local environment are predicted and evaluated. Although there is no set structure for how an EIA should be conducted, this usually includes five stages:

- Identifying the impact.
- Predicting/measuring the impact.
- Interpreting the significance of the impact.
- Displaying the results of the assessment.
- Developing appropriate monitoring schemes. (Holden, 2008: 192)

Conducting an EIA is an intensive process that includes the participation of, and consultation with, the different stakeholders in the development – as such it is a time-consuming and expensive exercise. Nevertheless, because of the growing emphasis governments place on reducing the negative environmental impacts of tourism, it has now become a part of the legal requirements for new developments in many countries. EIAs are mostly used in the planning stage, where they play a role in identifying environmentally unsound proposals, or in supporting planners in making amendments to proposals to make them more environmentally friendly. Despite their benefits as a planning tool, EIAs have also been criticised: because of their cost, they are difficult to enforce in developing countries.

POLICY AND PLANNING

The public sector can play an important role in minimising negative environmental impacts via effective policy and planning. (The role of policy is discussed in more detail in Chapter 13.) These strategies can usually be divided into two main groups: land use strategies (how the space is used and which new developments are allowed) and visitor management strategies. Visitor management strategies are explained in more detail in Chapter 12. This section will focus more specifically on land use strategies such as zoning and development standards. Apart from policy and planning, the public sector also has a range of practical management tools at its disposal, such as legislation and taxation. These will be discussed later in this chapter.

The negative environmental impacts of tourism tend to increase as tourism develops in the destination. 'Land use planning' refers to the actions and decisions governments take with regard to how the land is used, which types of uses are allowed, and which guidelines for development are set. A good way to control the negative environmental impacts of the tourism industry is to regulate where and how it is developed in the first place. 'Zoning' is a tool for land use planners: the term refers to regulating land use by dividing the area into zones with specific uses. The guiding principles of zoning are usually to conserve environmental features and to not mix uses that are incompatible. A nightlife area, for example, would not necessarily be compatible with residential developments built very close by. Similar activities may be clustered, the access to certain areas may be restricted, and undesirable buildings may be relocated to alternative areas (Jafari, 2003). To achieve a sustainable balance of tourism use and natural conservation on beaches, for example, specific zones may be allocated for boating and water sports. Jet skis and recreational boating could lead to foreshore erosion and water and air pollution (Lück, 2008). Planners can reduce the pressure on the natural resources by providing an alternative space for the water sports activities – this is referred to as 'space zoning'. On top of this, the activity may be only allowed at certain times of the day – this is referred to as 'time zoning' (Hall and Page, 2002). It needs to be noted here that environmental concerns may not be the only reason for establishing different zones: a separate zone for water sports might also improve the safety and enjoyment of both the sports users and recreational users of the beach.

'Development standards' are another tool that governments and local communities can use in land-use planning. These are conditions and restrictions that are set for different aspects of new developments. Weaver (2006) gives the following examples:

Density controls: The number of accommodation units that are allowed per hectare or square kilometre. These apply not only to residential developments, but also to hotels.

Height restrictions: Although high buildings are not necessarily environmentally unsustainable, they can cause aesthetic pollution in areas where they are inappropriate, such as rural areas.

Site coverage: The amount of space that is covered by buildings, compared to the level of open space.

Setbacks: The amount of space that needs to be maintained around landscape features. An example here is the mandatory distance between a tourism development and the beach.

Building standards: These can relate to energy efficiency, waste management and building materials.

Landscaping: The conservation of open spaces, trees and native plants.

Noise regulations: Restrictions on the levels of noise that are allowed and the times during which they are allowed. Theme parks, airports and nightclubs may be affected by these regulations.

PARTNERSHIPS AND COLLABORATIONS

The provision of tourism depends on a range of different stakeholders, for example transport providers, accommodation facilities, public sector planners and attractions. All of these stakeholders potentially have an impact on the environment, and there is a growing consensus that to achieve environmental sustainability all of these stakeholders need to work collectively. Partnerships or collaborations are often cross-sector initiatives, including representatives from the public and private sector, and from the local community:

This is not to say that sustainable tourism development cannot result from partnerships within one sector. Examples from the tourism field abound, such as recent initiatives by hotel and restaurant associations to promote environmental responsibility through recycling and other eco-efficiency measures. However, the negotiation, mutually determined goals and actions, and monitoring resulting from cross-sector partnerships make it more likely that these initiatives will result in sustainable outcomes. (Selin, 1999: 261)

Bramwell and Lane (2000) highlight a number of benefits of partnerships and collaborations. The involvement of a wide range of stakeholders gives a better overview of the problems under discussion, improves democratic decision making, and may increase the likelihood of a successful implementation. A more creative solution may be found by working together. By pooling their resources, the different stakeholders in the partnership may also put these to more effective use. Nevertheless, there are also a number of potential problems. It is important that a wide range of stakeholders take part in the collaboration or partnership for it to be effective. There is also the risk that the collaboration is mere window-dressing, because the more powerful stakeholders do not take the views of other stakeholders into account. The process can also be costly and time-consuming.

MANAGEMENT TOOLS

Environmental management strategies can be executed via two approaches: these are also called 'hard' and 'soft' measures (see also Chapter 13). Kuo (2002) summarises the differences between the two approaches as follows. Hard measures aim to regulate tourist activities in a destination: they can take the form of access restrictions, rules and regulations, zoning and patrolling. These measures are firm and binding, and not voluntary. Soft measures aim to educate and influence the visitor and can take the form of information provision, recommendations and declarations, and marketing. Soft measures are moral rather than legal and cannot be easily enforced. The following sections will discuss examples of both hard and soft measures that are used in environmental management. Legislation, taxation and the idea of carbon credits are introduced as hard measures, whereas labelling schemes and codes of conduct are introduced as soft schemes.

LEGISLATION AND REGULATIONS

Tourism businesses, like other businesses, are required to comply with environmental legislation and regulations. In most countries, legislation exists regarding air quality, noise levels, land contamination, planning and land use, vehicle emissions, and waste management. So far the industry has largely relied on self-regulation and soft measures (such as recommendations, codes of ethics and eco-labels), but due to the size and rapid growth of the industry perhaps more hard legislation is necessary. Unsurprisingly, the tourism industry generally fears the restrictive effect these laws could have. Holden (2003: 105) comments that increased litigation and more extensive environmental legislation, including the requirement for more detailed EIAs, would be likely to restrict tourism development and increase the likelihood of a denial of access to nature areas for tourism. Subsequently, there would seemingly be little direct benefit or incentive for the majority of tourism stakeholders, including government, industry and local communities.

TAXATION

Environmental taxation puts into practice the 'polluter pays' principle: the person who causes the environmental damage is also the person who needs to pay to rectify that damage. Taxes can be levied on tourism businesses or directly on tourists. Both methods may be implemented either through the general tax system of the economy or through specific plans. The UNWTO has identified 40 different types of taxes applied to the tourism industry in both developed and developing countries (Gooroochurn and Sinclair, 2005: 479). Of these 41 forms of taxation, three are environmental: eco-tax, levies on CO_2 emissions and landfill tax. Economists have long argued that taxes and charges can achieve the same goals as regulation and in a shorter time (Mak, 2004).

The levy of environmental tourist taxes is a popular notion, but so far the implementation of these taxes has proved to be problematic. A tourism tax was introduced in the Balearic Islands (Mallorca, Minorca, Ibiza and Formentera), but was soon dropped. The Balearic Islands, and Mallorca and Ibiza in particular, are well-established mass tourism destinations, but also ones that are characterised by poor planning and overdevelopment. Tourism here is highly seasonal and the high visitor numbers in the peak season lead to pollution and water shortages. The eco-tax was introduced in 2002, after heavy political resistance, and was charged via accommodation providers. The tourist paid an average of €1 per day – the cost ranged from €0.25 to €2 depending on the accommodation classification. The proceeds were used to support green marketing, clean up beaches, encourage energy-saving projects in hotels, and contribute to the acquisition of areas of natural beauty in the countryside and the revitalisation of agriculture (Boniface and Cooper, 2005). Even though the tax raised almost €25 million in its first year, it was dropped in 2003 as soon as a new government was elected.

The most common form of environmental tourist tax is probably levies on transport. Aviation in particular has been targeted due to its high level of carbon emissions compared to other transport modes. For example, Air Passenger Duty (APD) is a tax imposed by the UK government on all passengers flying out of the country. The tax depends on the distance to the destination (destinations that are further away are taxed more) and on the class of travel (economy travellers pay less than those in premium classes). Air Passenger Duty was introduced in 1994 to pay for the environmental costs of air travel, but also because airlines do not pay tax on fuel for international flights – the sector is seen as undertaxed. The airline industry, as well as the WTTC, have lobbied heavily against this tax, which they say threatens growth and employment in the sector. Proponents of the tax, however, argue that as air travel is a discretionary activity only enjoyed by parts of the population, air passengers should bear some of the financial responsibility for the environmental impacts of flying.

CARBON CREDITS/CARBON TRADING

Carbon credits and carbon trading are concepts that play a role in the creation of an international carbon market: this market-based system is proposed as a potentially effective way to reduce carbon emissions. In theory, the mechanism is simple. Participating nations agree to reduce their carbon emissions to a certain level. Nations that struggle to meet their emissions targets can buy carbon credits from other nations, which either have no emissions target (e.g. developing nations) or have reduced their emissions below their agreed target. Like any tradable commodity, the price of carbon credits is largely determined by supply and demand (Laurance, 2007: 20).

In practice, implementing carbon trading on a global level has proven more problematic. The 1997 Kyoto Protocol encouraged trading schemes on a national and international level, and some commentators even called for trading schemes between individuals (also called 'personal carbon trading'). This would involve allocating every individual a number of tradable energy units per year (Egger, 2007). An individual who takes a large number of flights per year, for example, would have to pay for extra credits, or try to reduce their carbon credits somewhere else, by using public transport or using less energy. These individual carbon trading initiatives have had limited success; however, the EU has operated an Emissions Trading System (ETS) since 2005.

The 2015 **Paris Climate Accord** takes a different approach from the Kyoto Protocol. Rather than binding emission limits for each country, the new climate agreement requires all parties to set their own emission targets. The goal is to keep a global temperature rise this century well below 2 degrees Celsius above pre-industrial levels. The agreement does not provide a concrete mechanism for carbon trading on a global level, however, but reaffirms the role of carbon markets in achieving its climate goals (United Nations Framework Convention on Climate Change, 2017).

Paris Climate Accord: An environmental treaty aimed at combating climate change and helping countries adapt to its effects

LABELLING/AUDITING SCHEMES

Eco-labels can be awarded to tourism providers and destinations. A range of eco-labels exists, targeting different aspects of the tourism industry: beaches, hotels, camping sites, marinas and events. Font and Buckley (2001) describe the role of eco-labels as threefold:

For the consumer: To guide consumers in choosing more environmentally friendly product choices.

For the suppliers: To market and promote the environmental efforts of companies and destinations, to incentivise them to improve their economic performance, and to support and guide their efforts.

For the government: To provide a voluntary instrument that encourages environmental sustainability, which can complement legislation.

Most labels are funded by the public or the voluntary sector. This funding is needed to pay for the development of the label, to manage the verification process, and to hire staff to do the administration. Most labels cannot fund these activities via membership fees alone.

These labels are often presented as a way to standardise and validate the green claims companies make: as consumers are becoming more environmentally aware, it is often said that 'green sells' – still, many companies are accused of greenwashing, so that consumers do not always know which claims to believe. The labels can help tourists to make an informed choice. This can only happen if a label is credible: because many labels exist, the interest and knowledge of the public about them can be rather low – in the worst case, it may even put customers off. At present, there is no label that is globally recognised and subscribed to, although there are some that have gained popularity on a more local level. The Nature and Ecotourism Accreditation Programme (NEAP) in Australia, for example, is a dominant label for tour operators. Europe has the largest number of eco-labels, most of which are small-scale and apply to the accommodation sector. Eco-labels are also appearing in the developing world: Kenya, for example, has its own eco-rating scheme, which awards accommodation providers with a bronze, silver or gold rating. The Smart Voyager scheme also certifies eco-friendly cruise ships in the Galapagos Islands.

Developing one global eco-label for tourism may be beneficial in terms of credibility, but is hard to achieve in practice. It would be difficult to ensure, for example, that the verification process would be carried out to equal specifications in different countries, and misuse may be likely. The tourism sector consists of complex and varied industries: it would be hard to develop one eco-label that could certify a ski chalet, a beach and a marina at the same time. It may be more realistic to aim towards a range of eco-labels that could be used on a wide geographical scale by their product category.

Greenwashing: Companies are said to 'greenwash' when they make green claims to improve their image but do not make profound changes to the way they operate

CODES OF CONDUCT/CODES OF ETHICS

Weaver (2006) describes codes of conduct (also called 'codes of ethics') as a set of guidelines that aim to influence the attitudes and behaviour of those claiming adherence to these. Such codes are voluntary: people or businesses can choose to sign up to them, but there are no legal penalties for not adhering to them. They can be useful awareness-building tools and are quick and easy to implement as opposed to hard legislation. From this perspective they offer many advantages for the tourism industry, but there are also disadvantages: because they are not binding, it is easy for a tourism business to sign up to a code of ethics and not significantly change their business behaviour. As with any form of self-regulation, the success of the code is dependent on how serious the business decides to be in implementing it. Mowforth and Munt (2003) highlight that most codes of conduct are not even monitored by independent bodies and can be seen as covert marketing exercises. Codes of ethics can also be rather general and focus on environmental principles, rather than providing real help and support mechanisms that are also economically sustainable.

A wide range of different codes of conduct is in use, some of which focus particularly on tourists or communities involved in tourism, whereas others target tourism businesses. For tourists and the local community, codes of conduct will usually promote a responsible use of resources, showing respect for wildlife and local cultures, reducing waste, and using local products and suppliers. For tourism businesses, they tend to focus on the same issues, in addition to the use of environmental auditing and business practices.

An increasing number of eco-tourism tour operators have developed their own code of conduct that is sent out to clients before their holiday. These may provide a form of 'moral suasion' (Weaver, 2006: 114) for the tourist: even though these codes are not legally binding, on a group holiday there is a form of social control, and not following the code could result in disapproval from fellow travellers and a loss of face. Many of these codes include practical guidelines instead of focusing on more general environmental principles. Asia Adventures, a private tour operator in Cambodia, sends its travellers a code of conduct before departure that includes (amongst other advice) the following environmental guidelines:

1. Consider what you pack in your suitcase before leaving home. Waste disposal systems in many developing countries are ill equipped to deal with the increased pressures that tourism brings, and a few simple measures can make an enormous difference to the effect you have on your destination. Where possible remove the wrapping of packaged goods before you leave, e.g. unwrap soaps and take bottles/ tubes out of boxes. Please take more harmful waste, such as batteries, back home with you where they may be disposed of or recycled more responsibly.

2. Consider bringing a refillable water bottle with you as these can often be refilled hygienically from large water containers in hotels and certain attractions – this limits the amount of plastic bottled water you would use.

3. Try to reduce other plastic use, for example when shopping use your own bag to carry purchases, and refrain from having straws with your drinks.

4. On our tours we have a 'zero litter' policy – 'carry in, carry out' – so please do not drop litter. As well as being unsightly, bottles, cans, plastic, cigarette butts, etc. can be deadly to wild animals.

5. Remember that in many places water is a very precious commodity and should not be wasted, so use a minimum both in your accommodation and whenever possible throughout your trip, e.g. turn off the tap when brushing your teeth, take a shower rather than a bath.

6. In addition where toilet facilities exist, however unsavoury, they should be used. Where they do not, always bury your waste and make sure it is never near (at least 30m away from) a water source (Asia Adventures, 2017).

SUMMARY

This chapter has provided an overview of the environmental impacts of tourism. Many of these are negative: tourism may increase pollution, disturb animal life and habitats, and have a detrimental effect on the built environment. The activities and behaviours of tourists may add to the environmental cost of tourism. Nevertheless, tourism can also have positive impacts, by increasing protection and conservation or encouraging regeneration. The concept of environmental sustainability has been discussed and linked to a number of new tourism forms that have this concept at their core. A number of guiding principles of environmental management were reviewed and a set of management tools discussed.

In brief, it can be said that the development of mass tourism has tended to take the natural environment, on which it is often very dependent, for granted. Tourism operators and tourists themselves nowadays often show a greater awareness of these impacts, and positive signs of change can be noted. However, with the industry growing at a relentless pace, much still needs to be done before it can pride itself on being environmentally sustainable.

SELF-TEST QUESTIONS

1. The environmental problems caused by tourism are often highlighted in the media and there are groups who discourage regular foreign travel. How do you think this has impacted on tourist behaviour? Has it affected the travel choices you make?

2. This chapter has discussed hard and soft measures to reduce the negative environmental impacts of tourism. Which do you think are most effective and why?

3. Regeneration schemes have been accused of leading to placelessness and an homogenisation of the built environment. Do you feel this is true in the case of The High Line? Would this be a place you would be inclined to visit?

FURTHER READING

Ballatyne, R. and Packer, J. (2013) *International Handbook on Eco-Tourism*. Cheltenham: Edward Elgar.

Holden, A. (2008) *Environment and Tourism*. London and New York: Routledge.

Smith, M. (2007) *Tourism, Culture and Regeneration*. Wallingford: CABI.

Weaver, D. (2006) *Sustainable Tourism*. Oxford: Elsevier Butterworth-Heinemann.

USEFUL WEBSITES

Blue Flag: www.blueflag.org

The Darwin Foundation: www.darwinfoundationorg

Greenpeace: www.greenpeace.org

The International Fund for Animal Welfare: www.ifaw.org

Responsible Tourism Awards: www.responsibletourismawards.com

Secretariat of the Antarctic Treaty: www.ats.aq

Surfers Against Sewage: www.sas.org.uk

The Travel Foundation: www.thetravelfoundation.org.uk

PART IV
TOURISM MANAGEMENT AND MARKETING

CONTENTS

10

DESTINATION DEVELOPMENT AND MANAGEMENT

'Destination areas carry with them the potential seeds of their own destruction, as they allow themselves to become more commercialised and lose their qualities which originally attracted tourists.'

S. C. Plog, 1972: 8

LEARNING OUTCOMES

After reading this chapter you will understand:

- the principles of key destination development models
- the links between destination development and the impacts of tourism
- the role of destination management
- the importance of collaboration between the public and private sectors in managing destinations.

Backpackers crossing from Sihanoukville to Koh Rong, Cambodia

Source: Eric Ryan

INTRODUCTION

In Chapter 2 we discussed Leiper's (1979) tourism system and the relationship between generating and destination regions. Destinations are of particular interest in tourism studies because they provide most of the individual components of tourists' travel experiences, and because the majority of the impacts of tourism are concentrated there. Most importantly, tourist destinations are usually also places with a resident community, other industries, and natural or built resources that may be vulnerable to over-use.

Tourism is a dynamic activity that creates economic, social and environmental changes in destinations. Since the emergence of mass tourism in the twentieth century, many places have experienced rapid, dramatic and frequently undesirable change as a result of tourism development. Plog's quote at the beginning of this chapter suggests that the damage caused by tourism may even destroy a destination's tourism potential.

In this chapter we consider how places become destinations, how they may change over time, and how intervention is necessary to ensure the long-term success of tourism for the benefit of the host community, economy and environment. The chapter is divided into two main parts. In the first part we examine a range of theories and models of destination development, and in the second part we consider how destinations are managed.

DESTINATION DEVELOPMENT

Tourism destinations are frequently described as dynamic and evolving because of the way they change in response to changes in tourism demand; for example as demand increases, the destination may grow physically through the development of accommodation properties, new attractions, transport links and the services that support tourism in the destination. If demand decreases over the long term, suppliers may reduce investment in their businesses or may withdraw from the destination entirely.

Plog's quote at the beginning of this chapter, written in 1972, suggests a typical pattern of development in destinations that creates irreversible and often undesirable change as a result of tourism. The term 'overtourism' was first used in 2012 to describe destinations 'where hosts or guests, locals or visitors, feel that there are too many visitors and that the quality of life in the area or the quality of the experience has deteriorated unacceptably' (Responsible Tourism Partnership, 2017). The term 'overtourism' is now widely used by the media in relation to destinations such as Venice, Barcelona, Berlin, New York City and London.

Concern about how destinations change and evolve in response to tourism is not a twenty-first century issue though. Evidence from 1860 in the UK and 1883 in the USA reveals concerns about undesirable physical tourism growth in summer resorts and coastal towns (Butler, 2006c). However, research into the process of tourism-led change in destinations was limited until the 1970s, despite some analysis by geographers of how destinations develop, how their tourist markets change, and the dynamics of change, published between 1930s and 1950s, which laid the foundations for future research into destination development (Barrett, 1958; Gilbert, 1939, 1954; House, 1954; Ogilvie, 1933; Pimlott, 1947; Wolfe, 1952).

In the 1960s and 1970s, research into the dynamics of destination development progressed with studies of flows of tourists (Williams and Zelinsky, 1970; Yokeno, 1968), identification of a pattern of tourism development in destinations (Christaller, 1963), the link between changes in tourist markets and changes in destinations (Plog, 1972), how hosts' attitudes to tourism change as destinations develop (Doxey, 1975), identification of a destination development cycle (Noronha, 1977) and evidence of a destination's rebirth through the addition of new attractions (Stansfield, 1978). Thurot's 1973 study identified changes in the socio-economic profile of tourists over time in Caribbean destinations, and, in 1977, Miossec developed a framework of destination growth describing phases to changes in tourist behaviour and attitudes of decision makers and host populations as destinations develop.

Drawing on evidence from these earlier studies, in 1980 Butler published a conceptual model that has become the best known and most widely cited theory about the dynamics of destination development: the Tourist Area Life Cycle, known as the TALC, which we discuss in detail later.

It is difficult to generalise about how destinations develop because the transformative effect of tourism is influenced by many factors that are internal and external to the destination. Pearce (1989) refers to these factors as the 'contextual characteristics of tourism development'.

THE CONTEXTUAL CHARACTERISTICS OF TOURISM DEVELOPMENT IN A DESTINATION

Pearce (1989) identifies four main contextual characteristics that affect how destinations develop:

Physical: The physical context includes location, climate and landscape. Location affects physical accessibility and influences the potential generating regions for a destination. Landscape and climate may be attractions for tourists, and therefore influence the type of tourism that develops. For example, a mountainous region with reliable snow conditions suggests potential for winter sports tourism. The potential physical development and growth of a destination is determined by its topography and the vulnerability of its landscape and ecosystem, particularly in fragile environments such as coastlines and alpine regions. In some destinations, the potential environmental impacts of new development have often determined its acceptability to decision makers and host communities.

Social/cultural: The social context refers to local culture and heritage that may be a tourist attraction, and also to the host society's characteristics such as education, demographics, class, attitudes and political influence. The extent of participation of the local community in the planning process will influence the type, scale and timing of destination development, facilitate or limit the involvement of multinational corporations, and subsequently influence the impacts of tourism on the destination.

Political: The political context refers to the ideology of the ruling national or local government, the decision-making process, and the level of public sector involvement in destination development. Political ideology will influence the government's attitude to regulation, commercial ownership and free-market principles, and the right of host communities to influence the development process. For example, governments that deregulate their airline industry directly influence tourism demand because of the resulting fall in fares to some destinations, and subsequent increase in arrivals (see Chapter 5 for a more detailed discussion of deregulation). Legislation limiting foreign investment or ownership influences the involvement by multinational corporations in the provision of attractions and amenities such as hotel companies and theme parks, affecting the scale and type of tourism that develops and the image of the destination. The extent to which host communities are active in the decision-making process will affect the scale, design and timing of new tourism development, and perhaps prevent it or fundamentally change proposals where there is significant opposition to plans. In 2017, anti-tourism protests by some residents in Barcelona, San Sebastian, Mallorca and Venice were organised to influence decisions about the future development and management of tourism in those destinations.

Economic: The economic context refers to the economic system (e.g. free-market, planned or mixed economy), the availability locally of capital and the willingness to invest it in tourism, land prices, land ownership patterns and the potential of other sectors of the economy. The level of economic development domestically, and therefore the wealth of the domestic market, will determine the potential of domestic markets or the dependence on inbound tourists.

As these contextual characteristics vary from one destination to another, even amongst destinations within the same geographic region, a number of different processes of tourism development have taken place.

PROCESSES OF DESTINATION DEVELOPMENT

There are several models of destination development providing an analytical framework against which a destination's experience can be evaluated. Models may be useful to destination managers by suggesting the likely effects of policy changes, or to guide decisions on the best value opportunities (Howie, 2003). Many destination development models were based on research into particular types of destination, for example coastal, ski or urban tourist destinations, but often they share common elements (Pearce, 1989):

- The nature of developers and the resources being used.
- The sequence of development.
- Spatial changes to the destination.

We have selected the best known models to consider.

BARBAZA'S SPONTANEOUS AND PLANNED TYPOLOGIES

Barbaza (1970, in Pearce, 1989) identified three types of coastal destination development: spontaneous; planned and localised; and planned and extensive.

Spontaneous Tourism Development

Spontaneous tourism development occurs when demand precedes supply, and the construction of facilities for tourists occurs before planning measures can be introduced, resulting in spatial reorganisation that may be undesirable, and often, degradation of the environment. In some destinations, for example in Cannes and Nice, tourism development of villas for the wealthy occurred in the eighteenth and nineteenth centuries, before the introduction of planning laws, and subsequent new demand after 1945 led to a massive unplanned **ribbon development** of tourism on land between urban centres, resulting in hundreds of kilometres of urbanisation of the Mediterranean coastline. Similar spontaneous development occurred along the Spanish Mediterranean coastline. It could be suggested that, in the twenty-first century, the supply in some destinations of short-term sharing economy lets that contravene planning or housing regulation is also an example of spontaneous tourism development that can encourage the unplanned spread of tourism into residential areas of a destination.

Ribbon development: Continuous construction along a road or a coastline

Planned and Localised Development

Planned and localised destination development occurs when tourism development is led by a carefully planned and researched decision-making process that investigates markets and impacts, and the resulting destinations are concentrated in specific locations, with a limited effect on existing urban centres. Barbaza (1970, in Pearce, 1989) identified this development process in resorts along the Black Sea coastline in Romania and Bulgaria during the socialist era, where tourist complexes with 15,000–25,000 beds were rapidly built. The process was facilitated by economic and political contextual characteristics that included collective ownership of the land and state financing of development. A more recent example is Saudi Arabia's Red Sea Project, announced in August 2017. The project will create coastal tourism on the western coastline between Umluj and Al Wajh in a development comprising luxury resorts on 50 islands and an airport in a region where there is little existing physical development (BBC, 2017b).

Planned and Extensive Development

Planned and extensive development occurs when planned tourism development involves a spatial reorganisation of the whole area, with the development of new resort complexes and the expansion of existing urban centres and the infrastructural links between them. Barbaza (1970, in Pearce, 1989) identified this form of development on France's southwest Mediterranean coast, Languedoc-Roussillon, where rapid and massive development occurred in the 1960s, led by the state but financed by private sector investment. Existing coastal villages were expanded to accommodate tourists, new purpose-built tourism complexes were constructed and transport infrastructure was upgraded to create faster connections to the cities in the region such as Perpignan and Montpellier.

PEARCE'S INTEGRATED AND CATALYTIC DEVELOPMENT

Pearce (1978) identified two broad types of tourism development based on studies into the development of ski destinations in the European Alps.

Integrated Development

Integrated tourism development occurs when the impetus for development, and its subsequent management, comes from a single developer, excluding involvement by any other participants. For example, a ski or golf resort, marina development, time-share resort or resort hotels complex, where the recreational, accommodation, catering, entertainment and retail amenities are owned and managed (although perhaps not operated) by one developer. This requires extensive financial and technical resources which are usually derived from companies based outside the destination or from foreign investors; occasionally the state may finance such developments wholly or through joint ventures with the commercial sector. Opportunities for the local community are limited to employment at the construction and operational stages, and government agencies may finance infrastructure projects such as road and utility provision. The snapshot below describes a major provider of integrated resort destinations.

SNAPSHOT 10.1

Vail Resorts, Inc.

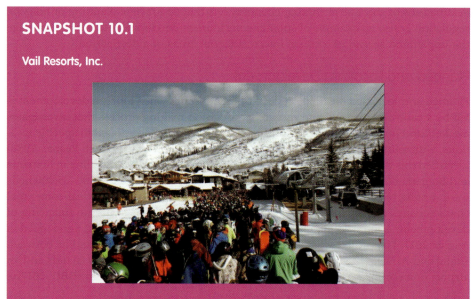

Vail ski resort, 2014

Source: SkiNEwhere (Own work) [CC BY-SA 4.0 http://creativecommons.org/licenses/by-sa/4.0)], via Wikimedia Commons

Vail Resorts, Inc. is a property development company that specialises in mountain tourism resorts. It operates under three divisions:

Mountain The company owns and operates 10 mountain resorts and three urban ski areas including some of the best-known and most visited in the USA: Vail, Beaver Creek, Breckenridge, Keystone, Park City, Heavenly, Northstar, Kirkwood, Wilmot

Mountain, Afton Alps and Mt Brighton in the USA; Whistler Blackcomb in Canada; and Perisher in Australia. The company owns and operates the ski lifts, ski and snowboard schools, and more than 230 retail and rental outlets.

Vail Resorts Hospitality (VRH): Owns and/or manages hotels, condominiums and private second-home residences in and around its US resorts, manages the rental of the second homes, and also operates road shuttle services from airports to resorts. Its luxury brand, RockResorts, manages hotels throughout the US and Caribbean. VRH also operates three destination resorts in Grand Teton National Park.

Vail Resorts Development Company (VRDC): Owns, constructs, buys and sells real estate around its resorts to develop accommodation capacity.

The company employs more than 26,000 staff and is a publicly held company listed on the New York Stock Exchange.

Source: Vail Resorts, Inc. (2017)

Pearce (1989) suggests that integrated development and management offer several advantages for the single developer:

- Balanced development through capacity consistencies, for example bed and ski lift capacities are matched.

- Quality consistencies through control of all elements of the visitor's experience of the destination.

- Financial synergies – the return on investment can be achieved more rapidly through the provision of more profitable amenities such as accommodation, as well as the basic amenities like ski lifts.

Integrated developments create a functional, concentrated and localised destination where all amenities and attractions are close together, but this often occurs in isolated areas away from existing residential and economic communities. This isolation may incur higher development costs but these can be offset by the provision of high-standard facilities targeted at higher-spending tourists. Pearce (1989) suggests that the relative isolation of an integrated destination development may enhance its image and allow premium prices to be charged. In the Middle East several tourism destinations have been, or are being, constructed as integrated resorts (i.e. in Dubai, Oman and Saudi Arabia) while the Las Vegas Sands Corporation develops and operates integrated resorts in urban centres worldwide that contain luxury hotels, a casino, retail facilities, dining and entertainment, and MICE facilities.

Catalytic Development

'Catalytic tourism development' describes development that is initiated or dominated by one developer but allows complementary development by other participants. Pearce (1989) identified three stages in catalytic development:

1. Conditions for 'take off' are provided by a single developer through the provision of specific amenities in a destination. For instance an airport, ski lifts, a golf course, marina moorings, a theme park, or large-scale accommodation units such as a large hotel or villa and apartment complexes, in accordance with the local government's development policy.

2. Demand for these stimulates opportunities for other participants to provide complementary amenities such as catering (restaurants, cafés and bars), entertainment (nightclubs, casinos, theatres), retail (shopping), recreational (golf, water parks, excursions and tours, guides and instructors, equipment hire) and accommodation facilities.

3. Further expansion and success depends on the initial and secondary developers satisfying demand, so that new investors are attracted. To avoid excessive expansion, planning regulations should be in place to control growth.

Catalytic tourism developments usually occur in areas with an existing residential and economic community. The involvement of several participants in the provision of tourism amenities and attractions creates a more diverse destination, but also creates challenges in coordinating quality, prices and promotion. Several cities have supported the development of a landmark attraction to act as a catalyst to transform their tourism economies or regenerate a part of the city that has fallen into neglect. For instance, London's riverside South Bank has been completely regenerated as a result of the opening of the London Eye in 1999 and the conversion of a power station into the Tate Modern art gallery in 2000; visitor numbers grew from 3 million a year in 2000 to around 25 million in 2013 (South Bank Bid, 2017).

The distinction between integrated and catalytic destination development is an important one because of their influence on the impacts of tourism in a destination. Catalytic development creates potential for the local community to participate in the tourism economy through ownership of amenities (in theory at least – limited availability of capital or the poverty of the host population may constrain this). Integrated development offers many advantages for a single investor but limits local community participation in the tourism economy to employment, and often requires external funding, with the subsequent leakage of profits to the investor's source region. This issue is discussed in detail in Chapter 7.

Destination Regions

The term 'destination regions' refers to areas of a country that contain several destinations that have developed separately over time. Miossec studied the development of tourism regions in the 1970s when understanding of the impacts of international tourism was beginning to emerge. His research investigated how regions change over time and space; he found that destination regions tend to develop over five phases, each of which demonstrates distinct changes in the number of destinations within the region, transport links to and within the region, tourist behaviour or knowledge of the region, and the attitudes of decision makers and the host community within the region (Miossec, 1977):

Phase 0: The region has few or no transport links, is not known by tourists, and therefore has no tourism development. The host community regards potential tourism development either very positively or very negatively.

Phase 1: Development of a pioneer destination, either by accidental discovery by explorer-type tourists (see Chapter 4 for a detailed discussion of types of tourists) or as planned tourism development policy. Transport links to and within the region begin to develop, along with growing awareness of the region by tourists, as a result of word-of-mouth promotion by tourists or active promotion by suppliers of the destination itself. At this stage the host community will observe to assess the impact of the pioneer resort.

Phase 2: The multiplication of **identikit destinations** with more infrastructural developments creating transport links between resorts. Visitor numbers increase as tourists become aware of the range of the tourism destinations in the region, and the introduction of policy and infrastructure to service the destinations.

Phase 3: Host community attitudes to tourism change. They accept, reject or call for planning controls to limit or direct further development. Where tourism is accepted, tourism development and growth continues across the region; where control is demanded, further tourism growth is confined to specific destinations. Destinations in the region compete for tourists and some restructuring results in each destination targeting specific tourist markets. The region as a whole has a well-known tourism image but the original tourist types no longer visit.

Phase 4: Specialisation continues with distinct tourist attractions and types in each destination, and each destination is served by a network of transport links across the region.

Pearce (1989) identifies several regions that have developed in line with Miossec's model. In the late 1980s, Provence, in France's Mediterranean south, showed evidence of an advanced stage of Phase 4, with a coastline saturated with tourism development, an integrated network of road, rail and air transport links, and the strong influence or even domination of the regional economy by tourism. Individual destinations appealed to specific types of tourists, attracted by the type of accommodation and related amenities in each. Pearce (1989) suggests that by the late 1980s, Languedoc-Roussillon in southwest France, and the Costa Brava, Costa Blanca and Costa del Sol in Spain, were at an earlier stage of development but were showing growth patterns in terms of transport and destinations that mirrored Miossec's model.

Miossec's model is useful because it describes a number of factors that influence destination development, and shows how these may change over time and in response to further physical development. In particular, he identifies the role of transport in stimulating demand, and the link between transportation and the growth of destinations (Prideaux, 2000). Many academics (Brenner and Aguilar, 2002; Davidson and Maitland, 1997; Pearce, 1989) suggest that Miossec fails to identify the context of tourism development: that is, who invests in building resorts, who owns the amenities within them, and the purpose of the investment and how this may affect each stage.

The snapshot below illustrates some of the destination development concepts that we have already discussed in relation to the Sultanate of Oman.

> **Identikit destinations:** A term used to describe destinations that are so similar that they are almost indistinguishable from each other

SNAPSHOT 10.2

Destination Development in Oman

The Sultanate of Oman, on the Arabian Peninsula, has great tourism potential with almost 2,000 miles of coastline, nature reserves, mountains, caves, deserts, beaches, lagoons and canyons. It offers cultural and heritage attractions including four UNESCO World Heritage Sites (UNESCO World Heritage Centre, 2017b).

(Continued)

Beach Resort, Oman

Source: Image courtesy of Kurban Tours, Oman, and Travel To Marketing

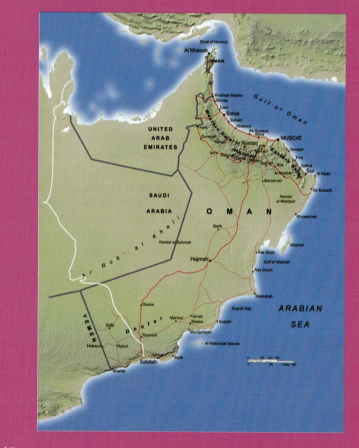

Map of Oman

Source: Image courtesy of Oman Ministry of Tourism

Tourism is a key element of Oman's economic diversification strategy, Vision 2020. The government has invested heavily in road, rail and airport development in key locations, and in joint ventures to construct tourism facilities. By 2010, 229 hotels and 11,037 rooms were available, mostly in the capital, Muscat (UNWTO (n.d.), cited in Mintel, 2012).

Oman's 2040 Tourism Strategy (The Consulate General of the Sultanate of Oman, 2017) forecasts 11.7 million tourists by 2040 and plans massive destination development: 80,000 more rooms – 33,000 in hotels, 29,000 in vacation homes and 17,000 in integrated tourism complexes (ITCs). The strategy identifies 14 clusters of tourist infrastructure around the country including:

Mina Sultan Qaboos Waterfront: Six hotels, shopping mall, recreation facilities, port services for cruise ships and yachts, retail units, business and residential zones.

Jebel Sifah: Six hotels (1,062 rooms), 950 residential units, golf course, 85-berth marina, commercial centres, entertainment facilities (Orascom (2017a).

Hawana Salalah: Luxury villas, apartments, 7 hotels (1,800 rooms), 2 golf courses, 2 marinas, commercial centers, 171-berth superyacht marina, waterpark restaurants, water activities, cultural and retail outlets (Orascom 2017b).

Butler's Tourist Area Life Cycle (TALC)

'... the TALC is one of the most cited and contentious areas of tourism knowledge ... [it] has gone on to become one of the best known theories of destination growth and change within the field of tourism studies.'

C. M. Hall, 2006: xv

The TALC demonstrates the process of change in destinations as the volume of tourist arrivals increases. The TALC suggests that destinations evolve through a number of stages, depicted in the model as a life cycle that starts with the 'birth' of tourism in a destination and ends with its decline, leading to 'death', or, if action is taken to prevent this, the resurrection of tourism, usually in another form. The TALC is presented in Figure 10.1.

The TALC is a hypothetical model, derived from Butler's research and experience of British and northern European coastal and mountain tourist destinations, during the period that Mediterranean resorts were developing as competitor destinations. Butler was interested in flows of tourist demand (i.e. volumes and patterns of visitation) and the implications for destinations when flows expand or decrease or when their characteristics change. The model doesn't specify a time period or numbers of tourists, as these vary for each destination.

There are six stages to the lifecycle. Each stage is characterised by:

- different volumes of tourist arrivals
- different capacity levels and types of accommodation and other amenities
- different levels of involvement in tourism by the host population
- different types of tourists.

As tourist arrivals increase and the destination moves through the life-cycle stages, greater stress is put on the environmental, infrastructural and social carrying capacities, reducing the quality of the tourists' experience and increasing the resentment of the host community. These issues are discussed in detail in Chapters 7, 8 and 9.

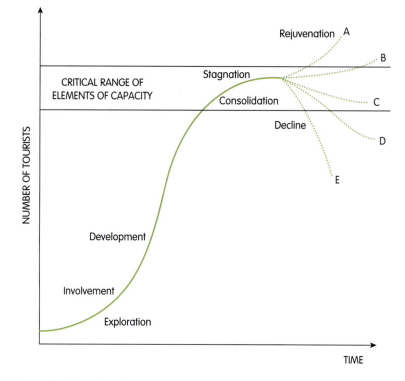

FIGURE 10.1   Butler's hypothetical evolution of a tourist area

Source: Reprinted from Butler (2006a: 5). Reproduced with permission from the Canadian Association of Geographers ©

Tourists who were attracted to the destination during one stage find the changes taking place undesirable and no longer visit, seeking alternative destinations that they consider to be unspoilt by tourism. These tourists are replaced by other tourist types. The characteristics of each stage are as follows:

- *Exploration*: Small numbers of independent tourists (Plog's allocentrics or Cohen's explorer types: see Chapter 4) who use local facilities and have close contact with the host population. Irregular visitor patterns are seen throughout the year. The physical appearance of the destination is unchanged by tourism. The economic and social life of the host community remains relatively unaffected by tourism. At the time of Butler's research, parts of the Canadian Arctic and Latin America showed evidence of the exploration stage.

- *Involvement*: The host community begins providing facilities primarily or exclusively for tourists, with close contact between the host community and tourists, especially those directly involved in tourism. An identifiable tourist season begins to emerge, to which suppliers and their employees adjust. Advertising is undertaken to stimulate demand in specific generating regions. Organisation by tour operators or travel agencies of some elements of the tourists' visits increases. Pressures increase on government and other agencies to provide or improve particular services, for example transport infrastructure, water or electricity supply, or refuse collection and beach maintenance. Butler identified this stage in some small, less developed Caribbean and Pacific islands, and more remote areas in North America and western Europe.

- *Development*: Attracts tourists from specific generating regions. Local involvement and control decrease as external organisations invest in larger and more modern facilities, particularly accommodation. Natural and cultural attractions are supplemented by man-made attractions, for example water parks, nightlife entertainment or shopping centres. The destination's physical appearance changes noticeably, which may not be welcomed by the host community. Planning decisions and the provision of facilities may become more remote from the destination, passing to regional or national governments, and tourist volumes during peak season may equal or exceed the host population. As this stage progresses, more labour is imported, and the type of tourist attracted reflects Plog's mid-centrics and Cohen's institutionalised or Smith's incipient mass type. Butler identified this stage in parts of Mexico, the developed Pacific Islands, and the North and West coasts of Africa.

- *Consolidation*: The growth in tourist arrivals slows, but total visitor numbers now exceed the destination's resident population. Much of the local economy is dependent on tourism, and marketing and advertising are used to lengthen the season and attract tourists from other generating regions. The supply of many amenities is provided by national or international chains, but expansion of the destination stops and a distinct tourist district can be identified. Older facilities may be perceived as outdated and undesirable and therefore attract the lowest-spending tourists. Tourist domination is opposed by parts of the host community, particularly those not involved directly in the industry and whose own activities may be restricted by tourism. Butler identified this stage in areas of the Caribbean and on the northern Mediterranean coast.

- *Stagnation*: Visitor numbers stop growing and capacity levels are reached or exceeded, creating social, environmental and economic costs. The destination is well known but no longer fashionable as new destinations develop and the destination now attracts Cohen's organised mass tourist and Plog's psychocentrics (see Chapter 4). Suppliers struggle to maintain high occupancy rates, using pricing and advertising to maintain demand. The destination's original attractions are probably less important than the man-made attractions that complement them. New tourist developments are on the peripheries of the original tourist district and ownership of the original facilities changes frequently. This stage was identified in 1980 in the resorts of Spain's Costa Brava and the cottage resorts of Ontario. At this stage action can be taken to rejuvenate the destination, or it can be left to enter the decline stage.

- *Decline*: Visitor numbers decrease and the length of stay decreases as day-trips and short-breaks replace holidaymakers. The supply of tourist facilities shrinks as properties are converted for other uses, such as residential homes for the elderly or children, or for housing, jeopardising the viability of the remaining tourism plant. Local involvement in tourism increases as facilities can be purchased at lower prices, but if facilities are not updated or more attractive destinations are available, ultimately the destination 'may lose its tourist function completely' (Pearce, 1989). In 1980, Butler identified this stage in the older resort areas in northern Europe, and in Miami Beach (Curve D in Figure 10.1). Curve E represents a catastrophic event such as war, long-term political instability or disease, from which a recovery in demand is very difficult to achieve (Butler, 1980).

There are several examples of destinations that have declined in line with the TALC, but the economic and social consequences of this in destinations are now regarded as morally unacceptable. Sustainable destinations need to be proactive in anticipating changes in demand, in understanding the needs and expectations of the host community and tourist markets, and in monitoring the environmental, socio-cultural and economic 'health' of destinations, and intervening where necessary to avoid the decline stage being reached (Howie, 2003).

The TALC also identifies a potential rejuvenation stage that restores tourism demand to a destination. If action is taken, usually through the collaboration of the local public and commercial sectors working in partnership, tourism demand may be restored. This often requires 'a complete change in the attractions on which tourism is based' (Butler, 2006a: 8).

Successful rejuvenation can be achieved in three ways:

- Continued growth and expansion beyond capacity limits (Curve A), through adding a new attraction and drawing greater volumes of tourists; in 1980, Butler identified this stage in Atlantic City in the USA, where casinos were developed to restore tourism demand by attracting a new visitor market.

- Continued growth at a slower rate (Curve B) through the modification of resources and capacity levels, for example in Aviemore in Scotland and some spa towns in Europe, where the reduction in demand from traditional summer tourists was compensated for by the promotion of the destinations for winter sports and the addition of the necessary amenities.

- A reduction in capacity levels and decrease in tourist numbers (Curve C), attracting new tourist types (Butler, 2006a: 7).

In destinations where rejuvenation has been successful in restoring tourism demand the cycle begins again and Butler acknowledges that, over time, the destination will again lose its competitiveness, potentially leading to a decline or further rejuvenation.

Butler (1980) acknowledged that the shape of the TALC curve would differ for each destination depending on the context of development – the speed of development, the rate of increase in transport accessibility, types of amenities, government policies, and the number of competitor destinations. The exploration stage may be particularly long if there is local opposition, capacity constraints in access or accommodation, or a lack of external investment. Some destinations demonstrate the stages of the TALC more explicitly than others; Butler described Cancun in Mexico as an 'instant resort' that started the cycle at the development stage, virtually omitting the exploration and involvement stages, and suggested that in developing countries this was often the pattern of destination development (Noronha, 1976: 27). Resort destinations in developed countries, for example in western Europe, the northern Mediterranean, northeast USA and parts of Florida, show evidence of having moved through all stages of the TALC.

Publication of Butler's TALC in 1980 attracted much attention from tourism academics and since then it has been scrutinised, evaluated, criticised and adapted by numerous researchers. By 1990, 15 research studies had been published that assessed the TALC's applicability, with a further 33 during the 1990s (Lagiewski, 2006). Modifications to the model have been suggested, for example using length of stay rather than tourist numbers, amending the characteristics of each stage, adding on more stages, or applying it to distinct products in a destination (Legiewski, 2006).

The TALC is widely regarded as a useful descriptive tool to understand how destinations have changed and how decline is likely to occur in the absence of appropriate intervention (Howie, 2003). Importantly, the TALC reflects common destination development scenarios that occurred in destinations before the 1980s, where destination development was frequently led by entrepreneurs in destinations without an appropriate planning and policy framework. Its relevance to more complex destinations with several economic sectors that compete for resources, such as cities and towns, is less clear (Howie, 2003).

Since the 1980s, understanding of the role of the public sector, and of multi-sector partnership organisations, in planning and managing destination development has increased considerably and the evolution of destinations through the TALC to the decline phase is no longer inevitable.

MANAGING DEMAND FOR DESTINATIONS

Until the turn of the century, it was accepted practice in many destinations that the responsibility for attracting and serving tourists lay with the commercial sector: individual suppliers of attractions and amenities in the destination, transport operators to the destination or intermediaries in generating regions (Ritchie and Crouch, 2003). Many of the models of destination development referred to earlier in this chapter were based on observation of destinations with limited or no active management which became victims of commercial responses to changes in demand from their tourist markets.

Reliance on the commercial sector creates several challenges for destinations:

- Some tourism SMEs and microbusinesses may have difficulties in researching and meeting the expectations of tourists, which affects the ability of a destination to consistently provide satisfying experiences through all its components.

- Tension between the financial objectives of individual suppliers and the interests of the host community, economy or environment may create local opposition to tourism, resistance to new development, or perhaps detrimentally affect the relationship between the host population and tourists.

- Individual operators may withdraw from a destination if demand begins to decline, for example hotels may close down or be converted to apartments or residential care, transport operators may close down routes or tour operators may stop operating to a destination, thereby compromising the destination's tourism sector's ability to survive.

The fragmented nature of destinations, their vulnerability to long-term changes in demand, the need of host populations for a tourism sector that meets their economic, social and environmental needs, and the tourists' need of destination experiences that provide consistent product and service quality have each created a need for effective management of destinations.

While the type and volume of tourists to a destination will change over the long term as a destination grows and changes, many destinations will also experience regular fluctuations as a result of seasonality.

SEASONALITY

'Seasonality' refers to the cyclical changes in demand for a destination over the course of a year, or 'the temporal concentration of tourism' (Pearce, 1989: 123).

In destinations this is reflected by the creation of peak periods, when demand is at its highest, and off-peak periods, when it is at its lowest. The intervening period is known as the 'shoulder season'. Some destinations effectively shut down in their off-peak season, with accommodation and other amenities closing for a number of months.

Destinations whose attractions depend on climate and weather conditions (e.g. heat, sunlight hours, low rainfall, snow, wind or wave conditions) develop identifiable patterns of demand, where tourist arrivals are high at certain times of year but significantly lower at other times, creating surplus capacity and an under-utilisation of attractions, amenities and transport. The length of the high season influences the economic impact of tourism on a destination and the investment potential it offers; longer seasons enable a greater utilisation of tourism infrastructure and higher returns on the capital invested (Pearce, 1989).

In addition to climatic influences, seasonality is also caused by patterns of leisure time in the generating regions (i.e. institutional holiday periods such as school or religious holidays or business shut-downs), creating a surge in demand for tourism from particular tourist markets. The snapshot below illustrates seasonality in the Caribbean.

SNAPSHOT 10.3

Seasonality in the Caribbean
Seasonality presents a challenge to many Caribbean destinations. Figures 10.2 and 10.3 show how demand for the region varies significantly throughout the year.

FIGURE 10.2   Monthly Tourist Arrivals 2009–2013

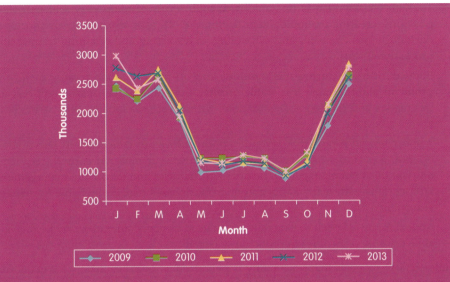

FIGURE 10.3   Monthly Cruise Passenger Arrivals 2009–2013

Source: Reproduced with permission of Caribbean Tourism Organisation

Traditionally the region was perceived as a 'winter' destination for North Americans escaping harsh winters. Its tropical climate and miles of coastline and beaches lent the region to leisure tourism, particularly sun, sea and sand tourism. The pattern of demand above seems to reflect the attractiveness of the climate (Kulic, 2004).

Attempts by Caribbean destinations to reduce seasonality include developing attractions that are less influenced by climate, for example MICE, cultural and heritage, and adventure tourism. Many now offer leisure events such as as music, sport, and culinary festivals (Carribean Tourism Organisation, 2014).

Howard and Jackman (2014) investigated seasonal trends in Barbados and discovered key variations by each generating region. For example Canadians visit mostly during the 'winter' season, while July is the peak month for US visitors, although the 'winter' is also important. The UK market visits throughout the year but demand is lowest in June and September, and demand from other Caribbean nations peaks in the 'summer' months. These patterns suggest that factors within each generating region, and the activities available in the Caribbean, are influential (Howard and Jackman, 2014).

While seasonality is more pronounced in destinations with outdoor attractions, other types of destination also experience seasonal fluctuations in demand. Urban destinations that attract business tourism in the form of meetings, conferences and exhibitions usually experience reduced demand during traditional holiday periods and at the weekend.

Seasonality is considered to be a problem because:

- Peak tourist volumes can create environmental and social pressure through congestion, overcrowding and higher prices. Acute seasonality can exacerbate the negative social and environmental impacts of tourism. This is discussed in detail in Chapter 7.

- Tourism employment is unstable with high levels of temporary and part-time positions, creating unemployment during the off-peak season, labour shortages during the peak season, and difficulties in attracting and retaining trained and professional staff.

- Reduced income during the shoulder and off-peak seasons creates cash-flow problems and therefore less stable profitability and a higher investment risk for businesses and investors. Destinations with severe seasonality may struggle to attract investors.

- A short season means that revenue opportunities are concentrated into a short operating period when income for the whole year must be earned, requiring tourism business managers to be adept at financial and marketing management. Destinations with many SMEs and microbusinesses may be less able to manage seasonality.

- Appeal in the off-peak season may be reduced as many amenities may be unavailable, creating difficulties in reducing seasonality.

Butler (2001) suggests that seasonality is perceived as negative mainly for economic reasons, but that in some destinations the host community regards seasonality positively because it gives time for rest, recuperation, social bonding and environmental recovery after a period of intense tourist arrivals.

One of the greatest challenges for destinations is to reduce fluctuations in demand by balancing demand and supply. This can be achieved in a number of ways:

- Using pricing to encourage some tourists to visit at a different time, thereby redistributing some demand from the peak period to the shoulder periods. Pricing strategy is determined by individual suppliers and is outside the control of destination marketing or management organisations.

- Extending the high or shoulder seasons through the development of additional attractions, for example some destinations host annual events in order to attract visitors in the shoulder or low season, or develop all-weather attractions that are not affected by climate. Snapshot 10.3 shows how this approach was applied in the Caribbean.

- Attracting new markets through the provision or promotion of particular activities, for example ski destinations that promote their summer lakes and mountains attractions to outdoor-adventure markets such as mountain bikers, hikers and bird watchers.

Pricing decisions are made by individual operators, while the development of new attractions or promotion to new tourist markets usually requires the involvement of public sector agencies. Public sector management is discussed in detail in Chapter 13. In order to ensure that decisions that affect the whole destination are coordinated and consistent, there is a need for leadership and direction of the destination through destination management.

DESTINATION MANAGEMENT

We have seen from the previous discussion that the conditions in which tourism destinations exist are often unstable and unpredictable. These conditions create particular challenges in ensuring the long-term success of destinations.

Gilbert (1984) conducted research into destination success and found that in order to compete effectively destinations needed to differentiate themselves from other destinations. His 'differentiation strategy' placed destinations on a continuum between two points – commodity and status – and suggested that the more unique a destination's products were, the greater the willingness of tourists to pay a higher price for them (see Figure 10.4).

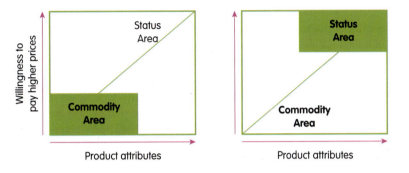

FIGURE 10.4 Gilbert's differentiation strategy

Source: Reprinted from Gilbert (1990) with permission from Emerald Group Publishing.

According to Gilbert's model, commodity destinations offer standardised attractions that are available in many other destinations. They attract price-sensitive markets that will visit if the destination's products are among the cheapest, but are easily substitutable if the other destinations offer the same benefits at a cheaper price. Demand for commodity destinations is therefore highly price elastic (see Chapter 3). Suppliers in commodity destinations often seek to reduce costs wherever possible in order to achieve competitive prices and consequently risk reducing the quality of the tourists' experience of the destination, damaging the destination's image and creating obstacles to its success. Commodity destinations would be considered 'old tourism' using Poon's (1993) approach that we discussed in Chapter 2.

Gilbert suggests that the long-term success of a destination depends on it developing unique, high-quality product attributes, for which some tourists are prepared to pay more, and because of their positive experiences will return to the destination in later visits or recommend it to others. This uniqueness may be a particular attraction that is not available elsewhere, although few destinations are endowed with such advantages. Alternatively, the differentiation may be achieved through higher-quality resources, for example well-maintained beaches, the hospitality of the local community, the service skills of tourism employees, the range of shopping facilities, or the event programme. Destinations should strive to be a status area in order to attract higher spending, loyal tourists, and increase the economic benefits of tourism.

Ritchie and Crouch investigated the features of a destination, and the pressures on it, that will affect its ability to sustain success and compete with other destinations:

> [W]hat makes a tourism destination truly competitive is its ability to increase tourism expenditure, to increasingly attract visitors while providing them with satisfying, memorable experiences, and to do so in a profitable way, while enhancing the well-being of destination residents and preserving the natural capital of the destination for future generations. (2003: 2)

The quote identifies some important points:

- Each destination competes with some other destinations for the same tourist markets; indeed Kotler et al. (1993) refer to 'place wars', suggesting that destinations must adopt a marketing approach in order to compete more effectively. This requires the production of a range of high-quality attractions and amenities that will meet the needs of desired markets and the promotion of a distinct image that draws together various disparate elements of the destination.

- The quality of the tourists' experience of all elements of a destination is a crucial part of a destination's success, requiring coordination and collaboration between the components to ensure consistent standards and quality.

- Tourism must make a positive contribution to the host community and environment, as well as to the host economy. Fundamentally, tourism in a destination must be guided by the principles of sustainability: that is, its resources must be carefully managed to avoid their degradation. In this approach, evaluation of the likely impacts of new developments and activities is required along with careful management of the tourism resources. Sustainability replaces the traditional focus on the volume of tourist arrivals with an emphasis on the value that particular tourists bring to a destination. Therefore the type of tourists, the benefits they seek, their activities and the impacts of these on the environment, host community and economy, and the volume and pattern of their spending locally, become more important determinants of planning and management decisions.

Ritchie and Crouch's quote illustrates the multiple indicators of a destination's success – preservation of resources, high levels of tourist satisfaction, resident well-being, the profitability of local tourism suppliers, and increased tourist expenditure in the destination. In reality, however, individual stakeholders do not always view these equally and may prioritise some over others. In destinations where stakeholders are not all working towards the same goals, it is less likely that the destination will be able to compete effectively and sustain success.

Destinations therefore face a number of challenges: to create cohesion amongst all stakeholders, to balance their diverse priorities, to develop a single image from fragmented resources, and to ensure consistent high-quality experiences for tourists throughout their visit. How destinations achieve this in practice is a relatively recent area of research in tourism. Traditionally, the public sector has taken a leadership and coordinating role in destinations, although recent research suggests that partnerships between the public and private sector may be more effective. The public sector's role in tourism development and management is discussed further in Chapter 13.

WHAT IS DESTINATION MANAGEMENT?

'Destination management' refers to the activities, programmes and processes that are implemented across all of the tourism industries in a destination to create supportive and enabling conditions that will achieve policy goals and the destination's long-term success (Keyser, 2002).

Ritchie and Crouch (2003: 183) describe destination management as 'the key to maintaining a sustainable competitive advantage', and its role has become more significant as the number of destinations has increased and the competitive environment in which they operate has intensified.

Research into destination management is relatively recent and its contribution to a destination's long-term success is being increasingly recognised (Howie, 2003). Until the late 1990s, destination management was widely interpreted to mean either promotion or planning, and while these roles are still important, destination management is actually much broader.

The role of destination management includes:

- Coordinating the fragmented supply that together provides the tourists' experience in a destination, for example local transport, hospitality and attractions providers, the local government whose decisions affect the destination's tourism resources, and the local community, to create a single cohesive vision and voice for tourism.

- Providing information about the destination to prospective and actual tourists and to provide information about markets and trends to destination stakeholders.

- Developing and maintaining high-quality resources for tourism and an effective image to promote the destination.

- Liaising with agencies inside the destination, for example trade associations, chambers of commerce and local government departments and regulatory bodies, or with agencies outside the destination such as regional or national tourist organisations or funding sources.

- Leading the tourism sector and being its advocate to the local community and local government (Gartrell, 1994).

While individual activities to fulfil these roles are often implemented by a number of organisations or by separate departments within the local government, many destinations have recognised the value of a separate single body to lead and coordinate these activities to ensure that tourism policy goals are being achieved. Ritchie and Crouch (2003) suggest that leadership and coordination of a destination is achieved most successfully by a destination management organisation (DMO) made up of commercial and public sector partners that represent local tourism.

DESTINATION MANAGEMENT ORGANISATIONS

There is no widely accepted definition of the structure or activities of a DMO. Until relatively recently, a DMO was understood to mean a destination 'marketing' organisation and was usually considered to be either the tourism unit of a local government or a local tourism trade membership organisation that collectively represented the interests of the local tourism industry, often known as a 'convention and visitor bureau' (CVB). Often CVBs also received some public funding. The primary role of these organisations was the provision of information to promote the destination.

DMOs are now increasingly interpreted as autonomous partnership organisations whose membership represents public and private sector tourism interests in the destination. Public/private partnership organisations are considered to provide a number of advantages:

- The sharing of stakeholders' knowledge, expertise, capital and other resources to collectively strengthen the destination's ability to compete effectively (Kotler et al., 1993).

- Efficient use of resources through collective activities that stakeholders would be unable to achieve independently, or at a lower cost than could be attained individually, for example promotional, training and networking activities.

- Participation by all sectors in strategic decision making about the destination's future.

- A sense of ownership of tourism policies and strategies across all of the tourism industries in a destination, leading to 'empowerment, equity, operational advantages and an enhanced tourism product' (Bramwell and Lane, 2000: 2).

The case study below describes destination management in a small coastal destination in the south of England.

CASE STUDY 10.1

Destination Management Bournemouth, England

BOURNEMOUTH BEACH

Source: Clare Inkson

Bournemouth has been a successful coastal destination since the early nineteenth century. Located on the south coast of England, it offers seven miles of sandy beach, many parks and gardens, a variety of free festivals and events staged in public spaces, indoor attractions, and a busy programme of conferences, exhibitions and shows held in its conference centre, hotels and theatres. The resort offers around 13,000 beds in hotels and guesthouses. Bournemouth attracts over 6 million visitors a year, including the MICE market for conferences and exhibitions, educational tourists to its English Language Schools, and leisure tourists to its beach (National Coastal Tourism Academy, n.d.).

Bournemouth's tourism offer is regularly refreshed and the destination often innovates with first-to-market products. For instance, the first artificial surf reef in the northern hemisphere (2009), the UK's first beach wedding 'chapel' (2012), the world's first pier-to-shore zip wire (2014) and the UK's first Coastal Activity Park (2014). Ownership and management of Bournemouth's tourism supply is fragmented across many public and private sector organisations. Bournemouth Borough Council manages the beaches, owns hundreds of beach huts and owns Bournemouth International Centre – the destination's conference centre. It is also responsible for marketing the destination through its tourism unit, Bournemouth Tourism.

The private sector provides and operates built attractions, transportation links and accommodation in hotels, guesthouses and self-catering units.

In 2006, Bournemouth introduced an innovative new destination management structure, Bournemouth Tourism Management Board (BTMB). The board consisted of representatives of public and private sector organisations from the destination, for example the local hotel, transport and attraction associations, the local government and the local Chamber of Commerce. Further innovation was introduced in October 2017 with the revision of this structure to incorporate the management body of the neighbouring destination, Poole (BPTMB). The two destinations will collaborate and work in partnership on the future development, marketing and management of the two destinations. The new board's structure is illustrated in Figure 10.5.

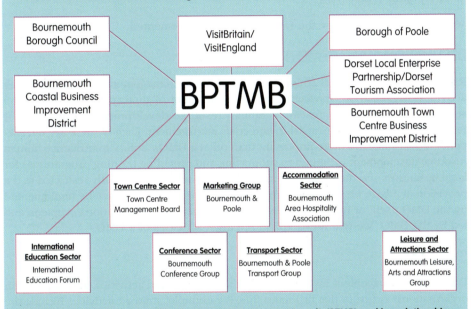

FIGURE 10.5   Bournemouth and Poole Tourism Management Board's (BTMB) working relationships

Source: Courtesy of Bournemouth and Poole Tourism Management Board

Each tourism supplier sector is represented by a delegate from its local trade association, while the public sector is represented by officers from both local authorities and town centre management. Experts from the national tourism organisations, VisitEngland and VisitBritain, are also on the board.

BPTMB is a steering group that develops the tourism strategy and creates a single voice for tourism in the area. It oversees the tourism strategy's implementation and monitors the effectiveness and value of marketing activities. Each year it sets priorities to be achieved collectively through the activities of one of more of its sector members, relating for example to the development of events and marketing activities.

Source: Bournemouth Tourism (2010, 2017)

Reflective Questions

1.   How does a single leadership organisation benefit a destination?

2.   Why do you think that industry support for a DMO is important?

Regular and clear communication with stakeholders, strong and dynamic leadership, political astuteness and a balanced representation of stakeholders are highlighted as key determinants in a DMO's success (Dredge, 2006). The importance of balanced public/private partnerships in DMOs is now becoming apparent.

Dredge (2006) suggests that the DMO is the leading tourism body in a destination, supported by other formal and informal networks that span the public and private sector, for example BPTMB is a partnership between the public and commercial sectors at local and national level. Each member may also be part of another formal or informal network, for example a chamber of commerce or a trade association. Dredge suggests that the linkages between a DMO and local government 'represent one of the most important and influential networks shaping the development of the industry at a local level' (2006: 270).

We will now consider how the DMO's roles are implemented.

DESTINATION MANAGEMENT ACTIVITIES

Ritchie and Crouch (2003) suggest that destination management involves nine key activities: organisation, marketing, the enhancement of quality of experience and service, information and research, human resource development, finance, visitor management, resource stewardship and crisis management. Each of these are interdependent and some are more important than others; DMOs' ability to influence human resource development is limited to supporting and providing training programmes for local businesses and their employees, while its financial role is usually restricted to the provision of advice on sources of funding. These nine activities may be implemented by the DMO itself, or be the responsibility of its member organisations overseen and led by the DMO. We will now explain the main activities of a DMO.

Organisation

Destination management involves strategic and operational activities, and requires an organisational structure that facilitates this. For example, strategic activities include the development of a strategic vision for the destination, a long-term strategy to achieve the vision, and short-term plans of activities to progress through the strategy, while operational activities may include training provision for local businesses and their employees, quality enhancement and promotional activities.

There is no prescribed structure for destination management as it should be customised to the needs of local businesses and the nature of each destination in accordance with the destination's tourism policy. Tourism policy is discussed in detail in Chapter 13. The Bournemouth case study describes the structure of its first DMO and the innovative joint DMO with its neighbouring destination, Poole.

The proportion of commercial/public sector financing often influences the focus of the DMO. For example where public funding dominates, the DMO's focus is more likely to centre on public service and community well-being, while domination by commercial sector funding will centre on the return on investment, cost controls and accountability (Ritchie and Crouch, 2003).

The relationship between the DMO and its members, and the stakeholders that its members represent, will affect its credibility with industry and therefore its viability.

Howie (2003) suggests that a DMO's authority largely depends on its ability to influence and persuade stakeholders, therefore clear and regular communication of the DMO's activities and performance is very important.

Marketing

Marketing and promotion is traditionally considered to be the most important DMO activity (Bornhorst et al., 2010) and this is often implemented through the operation of information services to tourists before their visit through advertising, printed materials and a website, personal sales at exhibitions and events, and public relations (PR) through press releases and familiarisation trips (or 'fam trips') for the media and intermediaries. Marketing continues within the destination via visitor information centres or screens, and increasingly through apps which visitors download onto their smartphones. Using geo-referenced data, the app can promote offers and make recommendations to tourists when they are in the vicinity, for example of an attraction or point of interest.

Marketing activities are directed by the objectives of the tourism strategy, for example to increase the value of each tourist's visit or reduce seasonality. However, DMOs are unable to control all aspects of marketing in the destination because individual suppliers are likely to engage in their own independent marketing activities (Fyall and Garrod, 2005). This is particularly the case with large commercial suppliers, for example national or international hotel or attraction brands, who may market themselves unilaterally and perhaps not support local trade associations or the DMO.

The marketing role of DMOs has become more powerful since the development of e-tourism platforms in the form of destination management systems (DMS). DMS allow a customer-centred approach by tailoring information to the needs of the enquirer through dynamic mapping, itinerary planners and product descriptions that are designed for particular segments. DMS also present the destination with a single consistent image to reinforce the brand image, and this is particularly beneficial to small independent suppliers who would be unable to achieve the same promotional opportunities on their own. DMS allow information to be distributed through different channels depending on the stage of booking, for example on the website at the enquiry stage or on touch screen information kiosks or on hotel TV in the destination during the consumption stage. DMS also provide availability searches and booking and secure payment functions.

DMS aid marketing research through tracking website visitors, monitoring enquiries and reservations and analysing data on bookings, customer profiles, availability and response to promotional campaigns, to allow the DMO to monitor the effectiveness of their activities.

In addition, 'smart' destinations harness a range of integrated technologies to collect real-time anonymised data about visitors within the destination, and then use these data to make recommendations based on the visitor's location within the destination. For example the Canary Island, El Hierro, was the first island destination to offer free WiFi. Beacons were placed around the island at points of interest and tourists were encouraged to share their information and images with their networks on social media. In addition, they could connect easily to the Tourist Information Office's own site and download an app to provide itineraries and information about, and access points to, attractions (Turespana, 2013).

Enhancing the Quality of Service or Experience

Much of the tourists' experience of a destination is beyond the direct control of the DMO. However, the importance of consistent quality of service and of standards across the whole of a tourist's experience of a destination has been increasingly recognised (Ritchie and Crouch, 2003).

DMOs can influence the quality of tourists' experience of a destination in a variety of ways:

- by including quality enhancement as a strategic objective in the destination's tourism strategy with targets for improved tourist satisfaction levels and monitoring the effectiveness of activities designed to improve quality
- by providing training for service providers to tackle particular issues, for example language or service skills
- by restricting promotional opportunities to suppliers that have been inspected and registered by an approved body
- by influencing tourists' expectations of a destination through the descriptions used in promotional materials.

The term 'smart destinations' is used to describe places that use the IOT and big data to learn about people's movements and take action to improve the experience. For example, the city of Barcelona has used big data and the IOT to manage flows of people around the city. Sensors placed around the destination track the mobile app Smart Destination, which visitors and residents download to their smartphone. The app provides real-time information and offers to the user, but also gathers valuable data about how people move around the city, the routes they use to access key sites and how long they spend there. These data can then be used to reduce or prevent congestion in real time by suggesting alternative routes or alternative sites to visit. Additionally, the data can be used to inform transport provision and marketing activities to encourage visits at other times or to alternative sites. The user should benefit from an enhanced experience in the city while destination authorities gather extensive data about visitor behaviour (Bismart, 2017).

Visitor Services and Management

Visitor services are a cornerstone of a DMO's role. The provision of information before and during the tourist's visit via a tourist information centre or website and provision of reservations services for accommodation and activities, and the organisation of guided tours, are common examples of visitor services.

Visitor services are in a position to influence visitor behaviour in the destination through the information they provide, for example by dispersing tourists more widely throughout the destination via the promotion of particular attractions or activities, or to increase their length of stay by promoting a number of activities. Visitor management is discussed in detail in Chapter 12.

Resource Stewardship

'Resource stewardship' refers to the management of the impacts of tourism to ensure that the physical and human resources for tourism in a destination do not deteriorate.

Often DMOs do not have direct responsibility for this as the owner of the resource is ultimately responsible. Where the public sector owns or manages a tourism resource, for example a beach, it will be responsible for its operational management.

Stewardship may include visitor management techniques implemented by a department of the local government or by individual site operators, for example zoning a beach for different activities or signposting to direct tourists along a particular route to an attraction. Some destinations use environmental certification and awards, which may be coordinated by the DMO. The Blue Flag award is a global eco-certification for beaches and a mark of quality of the cleanliness and management of the beach.

Crisis Management

Destination management occasionally involves steering the destination through the aftermath of a crisis. As the link between the public and private sector, the DMO is well placed to disseminate information to the trade and media, present a single voice to the media, and anticipate marketing activities to manage changes in demand as a result of the crisis. Young and Montgomery (1998, in Ritchie and Crouch, 2003: 223) developed a crisis plan for a Convention and Visitor Bureau that identified four key elements: physical emergency procedures (chain of command, formation of a safety team, communication procedure); internal communications with employees and public officials; external communications with the media, travel trade, members and consumers; and local assistance (helping with recovery, communications with local suppliers, information provision to tourists). The role of the public sector in crisis management is explored in detail in Chapter 13.

Destination management activities are diverse and may be carried out by different organisations overseen by the DMO – as in the case in Bournemouth. The DMO is the centre of the network of diverse tourism suppliers in the destination, creating a framework for communication between suppliers and the DMO through their industry representative. However, a growing form of tourism supply that bypasses any local management or marketing activities is creating serious challenges in some destinations. The snapshot below describes how the sharing economy can disrupt tourism supply.

SNAPSHOT 10.4

The Sharing Economy and Tourism Supply in Destinations

The sharing economy has disrupted conventional accommodation supply in many destinations. Unregulated short-term property lets to tourists add unplanned bed capacity, pressurise housing stock, and sometimes avoid contributions to destination marketing costs and business and tourist taxes.

Destinations have responded to the sharing economy in different ways:

Facilitating it by easing regulations: In 2015 London residents were given permission to let their properties for 90 days maximum per year without requiring planning permission. In Lisbon, rent controls are being phased out, and there is no limit on the number of short-term lets for a single property (Almeida, 2016).

(Continued)

Graffiti in Barcelona

Source: Alf Ryan

Regulating it by introducing controls: In New York, whole apartments cannot legally be let for less than 30 days. In San Francisco all hosts must be registered with the city council and obtain a business licence. In Amsterdam, short-term lets are limited to a maximum of four guests and a 60-night total limit per year; hosts must pay income and tourist taxes (Ting, 2016a).

Actively reducing it: Berlin has banned short-term lets and Barcelona stopped issuing short-term letting permits in 2014. In San Francisco, authorities are seeking to fine sharing platforms for displaying unregistered hosts (Ting, 2016a).

SUMMARY

Destinations are complex entities whose long-term success is determined by a number of contextual internal and external influences. Plog's quote at the beginning of this chapter suggested a cycle of commercialisation and decline that is common to many destinations, and many of the theories and models of destination development identify how destinations expand and change over time.

What is clear from the models is that unless preventative action is taken, some destinations change so much, or don't respond sufficiently to changes in demand, that their tourism sector is damaged irreversibly.

While there are several examples of destinations whose pattern of growth have mirrored the cycle of development and decline, it is now clear that sustainable tourism involves proactive management of the destination as a single entity.

Destination management involves a range of activities that may be implemented by a number of organisations but are guided by a single vision and a tourism strategy with clear objectives that synergises the complex tourism supply and balances the needs of all interests. Successful destination management requires a close collaboration between the various sectors that comprise tourism in a destination, their combined involvement in its strategic development, and the maintenance of a close working relationship. In practice this is not easy to achieve. Research into effective destination management is increasing and many destinations are introducing innovative management partnerships with cross-sectoral representation and shared goals.

SELF-TEST QUESTIONS

1. Consider a destination or a region that you have visited as a tourist – is there any evidence of its development through different stages?

2. As a tourist there, which destination management activities were you aware of?

3. How could you identify whether your visit was in the high, low or shoulder season?

FURTHER READING

Journal of Destination Marketing and Management, Oxford: Elsevier.

Morrison, A. (2013) *Marketing and Managing Tourism Destinations*. London: Routledge.

Wang, Y. and Pizam, A. (eds) (2011) *Destination Marketing and Management: Theories and Applications*. Wallingford: CABI.

USEFUL WEBSITES

Association of Town and City Management: www.atcm.org/

Blue Flag: www.blueflag.global/

Destinations International: https://destinationsinternational.org/

Green Flag Award: www.greenflagaward.org.uk/

Purple Flag: www.atcm.org/programmes/purple_flag/WelcometoPurpleFlag

Tourism Management Institute: www.tmi.org.uk/

11

TOURISM MARKETING

'Today marketing isn't simply a business function: it's a philosophy, a way of thinking, and a way of structuring your business and your mind.'

P. Kotler et al., 2017: 27

LEARNING OUTCOMES

After reading this chapter you will understand:

- what marketing is and the challenges of marketing tourism services
- common methods for segmenting tourism consumers
- how the marketing mix is applied in tourism
- how online and mobile technologies are used in tourism marketing.

Advert for Costa Rica on the London underground

Source: Clare Inkson

INTRODUCTION

Marketing is a complex, dynamic, creative and innovative process that seeks to influence consumer behaviour. Advertising is a highly visible part of this process but marketing consists of other important activities too.

The core principle of marketing is that companies and organisations achieve their objectives most successfully by focusing on satisfying customers' needs more effectively than competitors do. In order to do this, information must be collected about:

- consumers' motivations, needs, expectations and the way they purchase products
- which groups of consumers should be targeted as potential customers
- how products and services should be designed and how they can be made available for sale to consumers
- which prices to charge
- the best way of communicating with consumers and the most effective messages to provide
- how to keep customers loyal.

In addition, effective marketing considers the wider external environment as well; that is any changes to political, economic, social, technological and legal conditions, plus activities by competitors that may create opportunities or threats and how these will influence demand for the product. Marketing therefore involves a continual process of research in order to gather evidence on which to make decisions, and research to monitor the effectiveness of those decisions in order to inform future decision making.

Marketing became widely recognised as a management function and academic discipline in the 1960s, and since then our understanding of the principles of marketing theory and practice has evolved considerably. Research into marketing service products, of which tourism is one example, did not develop until the late 1970s and therefore a wider understanding of effective tourism marketing was late to emerge. Since the final decades of the twentieth century, competition between destinations, and between suppliers in the same destination, for the same visitor markets has intensified, and individual attraction, accommodation and transport operators, as well as destinations themselves, have had to adopt a marketing approach in order to sustain their success (Middleton et al., 2009).

Marketing is now approached by tourism academics and practitioners as a disciplined business function and has also been adopted by non-commercial tourism organisations such as museums, art galleries, natural attractions, state-funded transport operators and destination organisations in order to achieve the objectives on which their funding is dependent.

Tourism marketing has changed rapidly since the 1990s as a result of dramatic transformations in the operating environment. Globalisation and liberalisation in some sectors, particularly air transport, have intensified competition, new tourism markets have emerged as a result of economic and political developments in Brazil, Russia, India and China, and new digital technologies have revolutionised the way many consumers research and purchase tourism products and services.

This chapter is intended to introduce you to key principles of tourism marketing; at the end of the chapter we direct you to specialised tourism marketing texts that develop and expand on the topic further.

TOURISM MARKETING

Tourism industries are part of the service sector, for which a particular approach to marketing is necessary.

Services marketing theory evolved in the late 1970s and early 1980s with research by Shostack (1977), Grönroos (1978), Zeithaml (1981) and Lovelock (1983), whom Hoffman et al. (2009: 25) refer to as 'services marketing pioneers' because they proposed that services could not be marketed in the same way as goods.

According to Berry (1980, in Hoffman et al., 2009: 6), goods are 'objects, devices or things, whereas services can be defined as deeds, efforts or performances'. In reality, the distinction between goods and services is not always clear, as the production and sale of objects, devices or things often requires some service elements, for example during the sales process or in after-sales support, while the production and sale of a service like hospitality also requires physical objects as part of the customer's experience.

It is useful to consider the distinction between goods and services in the context of ownership: with goods, the customer owns something physical after the purchase, whereas with a service, there is not always any physical evidence after the service has been performed. For example, a holiday or a business trip requires the temporary use of physical products such as transport, accommodation and attractions, but at the end of the trip, none of these products are owned by the consumer.

Services are distinct from goods because they are characterised by intangibility, heterogeneity, perishability and inseparability. Each of these characteristics is discussed in detail in Chapter 5, so in this section we will consider how they affect tourism marketing.

Intangibility creates difficulties in communicating the benefits of a tourism service to potential consumers and increases the consumer's perceived risk of purchase because they cannot inspect products or services before reserving, travelling to, and often paying for, the product. For instance, tourist accommodation may be booked and paid for in advance, but the customer does not know for sure that the purchasing decision is the right one for them until they arrive. Tourism marketers need to find ways of assuring potential consumers that the product matches their needs and expectations.

The physical distance between tourism service providers in destinations and their potential consumers in generating regions magnifies this challenge by making it harder to research consumer markets and communicate with them. This is particularly true for SMEs and microbusinesses whose financial resources and level of knowledge and expertise in marketing are likely to be limited, and who may therefore require support from an external body in researching markets and communicating with potential customers. This support role is often provided by a destination marketing organisation, or is achieved through membership of a consortia or becoming a franchisee; we discuss these approaches in Chapter 5.

Inseparability creates variations between customers in their experience of a **service encounter** because of the consumer's involvement in its production. This causes difficulties in creating consistency in all consumers' experience of a service and highlights the importance of the individuals providing the service in managing the quality of customers' experience (McCabe, 2008).

Service encounter: Interaction between the customer and the service provider, sometimes called 'the moment of truth'

Inseparability does, however, create some marketing advantages because it provides opportunities to gather feedback from customers about the quality of their experience, either formally through surveys or interviews or informally during any stage of the purchase and consumption process. In addition, inseparability facilitates customisation of the product to the individual needs of each customer, for example through offering upgrades or additional products and services or allowing customers to select elements of the product, for instance the location of their seat on a flight or the preferred location of rooms in a hotel.

Perishability creates marketing challenges because of the difficulties in matching supply with demand and ensuring an adequate level of revenue for each unit of capacity before it expires. It is therefore crucial that effective ways to optimise revenue are found. Perishability is exacerbated in tourism by demand variations on a seasonal, daily or hourly basis that create pressures on suppliers to earn enough revenue during periods of peak demand to compensate for lower revenues when that demand falls. Tourism marketers use a range of techniques to manage demand and to 'smooth' it by reducing peaks and troughs. The high ratio of fixed to variable costs (see Chapter 5) that is characteristic of tourism services creates opportunities for marketers to use pricing as a tool to smooth demand by selling the same product at different prices depending on the consumer's price sensitivity. Effective marketing ensures that customers who would be prepared to pay higher prices are unable to purchase at lower prices.

Heterogeneity creates quality control and service quality management challenges for tourism marketers because of the difficulty in replicating the same experience for all customers and maintaining a consistent quality in all service encounters, either within the same company with different members of staff or across a number of suppliers within the same destination.

Wilson et al. (2016) stress the link between services marketing and making promises to customers. The ability of a company to deliver the promises made in their advertising during the service performance and service encounters is often the responsibility of individual employees. This crucial role of people in services adds an increased dimension to the services marketing process. This dimension is illustrated by the strategic framework known as the 'services marketing triangle'.

THE SERVICES MARKETING TRIANGLE

The services marketing triangle identifies three types of marketing: external, internal and interactive, as Figure 11.1 illustrates.

FIGURE 11.1   The services marketing triangle

Source: Adapted from Grönroos (2015: 58). Republished with permission of John Wiley and Sons, Inc.

External marketing: Involves the activities that communicate the promise to customers, such as the design of the product, promotional messages, the channels through which capacity will be sold and the prices charged, and is often the responsibility of a marketing department.

Interactive marketing: This is the process, or systems, by which services are produced and delivered when the customer is consuming them, and involves customer interaction with the organisation's resources, often staff. Grönroos (2015) proposes that interactive marketing involves all employees and the resources by which the physical product, technology and internal systems support the customer-focused service delivery. Therefore interactive marketing involves the whole company and not just the marketing department.

Internal marketing: This is the process by which the company provides systems and resources to equip all employees with the skills, equipment, technology, knowledge and attitudes necessary to enable the company to keep its promises to customers. The services marketing triangle suggests that the relationship between a company and its employees has a direct impact on the quality of the service product and the customers' perception of the company. Ultimately, in order to satisfy customers, employees themselves must be satisfied. Internal marketing is the process undertaken by an employer to develop good relationships with and between employees throughout an organisation.

Contemporary approaches to marketing recognise the contribution of external, interactive and internal marketing to customer satisfaction; indeed, the term 'customer journey' is often used to describe a service transaction because it often involves several steps, and many tourism companies claim that their employees are their main asset. The marketing mix, which we discuss later, has been adapted for services to reflect this. Before we discuss the marketing mix, we consider tourism customers in more detail, and in particular how the total tourism customer market can be broken down to identify groups of customers with common characteristics.

SEGMENTING THE TOURISM MARKET

The customer is at the heart of marketing because the marketing strategy and activities are intended to influence customer behaviour, for the benefit of the company or organisation. In order to plan and design marketing activities, the marketer must first identify exactly who their potential customers are and what they want.

In tourism, the whole consumer market consists of hundreds of millions of consumers in generating regions around the world, with varying needs, expectations, budgets and buying behaviours. Clearly, tourism suppliers and destinations cannot seek to attract them all as customers, so they need to divide the total market into those sections, or segments, which are most likely to desire and consume their products, and which will enable the company to achieve its strategic objectives.

Each segment will be defined by specific characteristics that are shared by the consumers within that segment. Once a segment is identified as a potential source of customers, it is known as a 'target market'. All marketing activities are then directed towards the target market, or markets, if more than one is identified. Kotler et al. (2017) identify segmentation as the identification of measurable criteria to segment the market, detailed profiling of each segment, and a careful assessment of its profitability. After the most desirable segments have been selected, the marketer must decide on the position it would like to be perceived by in the target market relative to its competitors, for example as the best quality, most luxurious, best value, largest, cheapest, most reliable and so on. Then appropriate marketing mix activities are designed to communicate relevant messages to the target market most effectively.

Market segmentation enables the design and implementation of focused marketing activities to influence and manage the consumer behaviour of each target market and is therefore a key part of the marketing process. However, identifying these segments is a complex activity.

Kotler et al. (2017) identify four main criteria by which tourism suppliers can segment their markets: geographic, demographic, psychographic and behavioural.

There is no single correct approach to market segmentation: each criterion varies in complexity and the resources required to gather data about it, and some are more useful than others. Marketers use their judgment to select the segmentation criteria to use. As a result, some criteria are more widely used than others, and tourism marketers often use several of these criteria simultaneously.

Kotler et al. (2017) stress that effective segmentation requires each segment to be:

Measurable: Its size and purchasing power must be measurable in order to monitor the effectiveness of marketing activities.

Substantial: The revenue generated from each segment will exceed the cost of targeting it, in line with financial objectives.

Actionable: It must be possible to develop effective campaigns and activities to influence the segment.

Accessible: The extent to which data about the segment can be gathered, and the needs of the segment can be met.

In addition, Middleton et al. (2009) stress that long-term sustainability of the segment is also crucial – that it will it endure into the future.

We now consider each of the four broad criteria that may be used to identify target markets.

GEOGRAPHIC CRITERIA

Geographic segmentation focuses on consumers within a specified national, regional or local geographic region; previously in the book we have called these 'generating regions', while the travel industry often refers to them as 'market regions'. National tourism organisations often use geographic segmentation as a primary step in their segmentation process to identify key generating regions to target. For example Tourism New Zealand focuses on 11 market regions: Australia, China, India, Japan, Canada, Germany, USA, UK, South-east Asia, South Korea, and Brazil/Argentina (Tourism New Zealand, 2017).

DEMOGRAPHIC CRITERIA

Demographic criteria identify market segments on the basis of one or more of the following: age, generation, sex, occupation, income, life cycle stage, education, religion and ethnicity (Kotler et al., 2017). 'Life cycle' refers to the stage of life of individuals – infancy, childhood, adolescence, single, couple, parenthood, empty nesters – because the needs and requirements from a tourism experience are significantly different at each stage. The generation into which we are born is now often used to segment markets too: for instance 'Generation Z' describes consumers born since 2000; 'Millenials', those born between 1980 and 2000; 'Generation X', those born between 1965–1979; and 'Baby Boomers' those born between 1946–64 (Kotler et al., 2017); broadly speaking, there are significant differences between each generation in terms of access to leisure time, property and pension wealth, and the use of technology, social media and smart phones.

Demographic information about consumers is relatively straightforward to find through consumer surveys. Often individual tourism companies and organisations will collect such data about their customers during the reservation and registration process. Tourism destination organisations research demographic profiles of tourism consumers from different generating regions, and commercial market research companies conduct regular surveys to gather profiles of tourists.

This form of segmentation facilitates a broad understanding of consumers' needs and levels of disposable income, but by itself does not provide sufficient information for a marketing campaign. It is particularly useful in refining segmentation when combined with other methods.

PSYCHOGRAPHIC CRITERIA

Psychographic segmentation uses social class, lifestyle and personality to identify a market (Kotler et al., 2017). Psychographic characteristics reveal consumers' attitudes, opinions and the psychological dimensions of their consumer behaviour, and help companies to understand the core benefits sought by consumers from tourism experiences. For example, in 2010 VisitBritain conducted research into luxury markets from India, Russia and Brazil; findings showed that high net-worth individuals feel successful and want to be perceived as successful by others, are concerned with status and prestige, and seek indulgence from their holidays. Crucially they are prepared to pay very high prices for luxury tourism experiences. This knowledge helped VisitBritain to implement a campaign for these markets by selecting appropriate products and services to promote and design messages to communicate the allure of Great Britain as a luxury destination (VisitBritain, 2010).

The collection of psychographic data is complex and expensive but is now facilitated by software that analyses responses to carefully designed research and identifies groups with common characteristics and consumer behaviour patterns. This helps marketers understand how to position their organisation in relation to competitors, which messages to include in communications, the services' design and appearance and the development of their brand. This method of segmentation is usually combined with segmentation by purpose and life cycle. Snapshot 11.1 illustrates this.

BEHAVIOURAL SEGMENTATION

Behavioural segmentation targets consumers based on their knowledge of and use of a product, purpose of purchase and benefits sought, and how they purchase and consume it. For example the purpose of travel, the lead-in time of the purchase, frequency of consumption, level of brand loyalty, expenditure per head, use of intermediaries, level of booking flexibility required, party size and composition, and sources of information used to plan the trip.

These characteristics are relatively easy to research; they can be identified through market research surveys of samples of customers as well as via database and website analysis that tracks customer behaviour. Several of the consumer behaviour characteristics are collected by companies as part of the reservations process and are therefore relatively easy to acquire.

Some segmentation criteria are easier or cheaper to research than others. It's now common for tourism businesses and organisations to use multiple segmentation criteria because this helps to define focused and clear target markets for which more effective marketing strategies and activities can be designed. Databases of consumer markets can be purchased by marketers; geodemographic databases are an interesting example.

Geodemographic databases combine geographic segmentation with demographic and behavioural criteria by integrating data from the census with consumer data and postcodes to identify the consumer characteristics of each household in specific countries. These households are then classified using a range of characteristics such as family structure, age, life cycle, income, attitudes and preferences, and those with common characteristics are clustered together into segments. For example Experian Mosaic UK is a database of 25.2 million UK households that are clustered into 66 types on the basis of over 450 variables. These data can be purchased by marketers to identify specific households for email, mobile, telemarketing, TV and video on demand, outdoor advertising, digital display and direct mail campaigns, and for location planning and design (Experian, 2017).

In Chapter 1 we explained the term 'big data'. It refers to the collection and analysis of consumers' online behaviour to predict how individuals will behave online and then to tailor offers specifically for that user. For example, O'Neil (2017) describes how she designed an algorithm for Expedia to distinguish between window shoppers and serious buyers on their website and then present results from which Expedia would earn revenue: window shoppers would see comparison adverts for competitor sites from which Expedia would earn a click-through fee, while serious buyers would be shown offers tailored to their requests.

Our online behaviour is tracked and monitored constantly in order to identify the best time to target us with offers and information, and the best prices to offer us. In addition, our internet protocol (IP) addresses can be combined with geodemographic data to tailor offers specifically to our own households; for instance Sky AdSmart combines Experian Mosaic geodemographic data with our IP address to target separate advertising to different households watching the same TV programme (Sky Media, 2017). Mobile targeting using geolocation technology allows messages and offers to be pushed to consumers via apps on GPS-enabled smartphones when the consumer is in physical proximity to the supplier. This is of particular interest to destination-based suppliers.

National and multinational tourism companies with large marketing budgets have a distinct marketing advantage over SMEs and microbusinesses. Tourism destination organisations often fill this gap in marketing intelligence by conducting research and identifying relevant market segments; this information is then made available to all suppliers within their destination.

The snapshot below describes accommodation products designed for different market segments by a division of the TUI Group.

SNAPSHOT 11.1

The TUI Group

The TUI Group is an integrated European travel company with over 20 million customers annually. Its portfolio of businesses includes outbound tour operators, agencies and leading online portals, 6 airlines, 300+ hotels, 16 cruise ships and many incoming agencies in destinations worldwide. TUI's hotel division includes several hotel brands designed to appeal to specific market segments using a range of segmentation criteria:

TUI Blue logo

Source: TUI UK and Ireland

Tui Blue offers 'authentic holiday encounters' for the lifestyle segment, including singles, couples and families. Property designs reflect the regional architecture, menus offer local cuisine, and cutting-edge technology allows guests to check-in, connect to in-room speakers and book activities using smart phones.

ROBINSON logo

Source: TUI UK and Ireland

ROBINSON Club targets premium segments offering 'time for feelings' to singles, couples and families in extensive properties that offer local architecture, modern facilities and international cuisine. The atmosphere is open and relaxed with a focus on 'shared moments' with group sports and entertainment programmes, and events featuring experts and celebrities.

TUI SENSIMAR logo

Source: TUI UK and Ireland

SENSIMAR targets adults, travelling without children, who appreciate tranquility, style and personal service. With an emphasis on relaxation, no organised activities or entertainment is provided and restaurants offer a mix of local and international cuisine.

Source: TUI Group (2017). Images courtesy of TUI UK and Ireland

The snapshot above shows the link between the segmentation of consumer markets using multiple criteria and the design of products to meet their needs. Product design is one of a range of activities in a process known as 'the marketing mix'.

THE MARKETING MIX

'The marketing mix' is a blend of actions taken by marketers to manage and manipulate demand for their products and services. Traditionally this mix has consisted of four variables – product, price, place and promotion – originally described by McCarthy in 1960 as the '4Ps framework' (McCarthy, 1981, in Middleton et al., 2009: 138). This framework has been adopted widely by marketing academics and practitioners and has since been extended to seven or sometimes eight Ps to reflect services marketing activities (Chartered Institute of Marketing, 2009).

Holloway (2004: 52) describes the marketing mix as 'one of the most important in marketing – indeed, it can be called the core of all marketing planning'. The way marketing managers adapt and blend the variables develops in response to marketing research into the external environment, the actions of competitors, the needs of the target market, and levels of customer satisfaction. These variables are the only elements that marketing managers can control directly, and the mix is used to create and communicate a **competitive advantage** to, and manage demand from, the target market segments. Control over the marketing mix involves a regular or continuous process of adjustment of the mix in response to research findings.

Competitive advantage: Factors that give a product, a service or a company superiority over its rivals

In the following section we discuss the marketing mix in relation to the services marketing triangle, beginning with external marketing.

External marketing involves the marketing mix variables that make promises to potential customers – product, price, place and promotion.

PRODUCT

Product forms the foundation of the marketing mix, because decisions about the other 'Ps' will depend on the design and operation of the product. For example, the prices that can be charged, the messages used to promote it to the target market, or the skills of the people required to produce it. Holloway (2004: 129) suggests that if the product does not match the needs and wants of the target market, then decisions about the remaining Ps are immaterial: 'if the product is not what the market wants, no amount of price adjustment, dependable delivery or brilliant promotion will encourage consumers to buy it – or at least, not more than once'.

The challenge with the tourist product is defining what it is that the consumer is actually purchasing.

We explained earlier that consumers seek particular benefits from their tourism experiences. These benefits aren't tangible products that can be purchased or consumed, but are actually the outcome of the experiences provided through the temporary ownership of physical products; that is, transport, accommodation and attractions.

In order to explore the link between product and benefits, Grönroos (1978, cited in Kotler et al., 2017: 255) deconstructed service products into four main product components: core, facilitating, supporting and augmented.

The core product: This element of the product is intangible and relates to the benefits that the customer is seeking. For business tourists this may be speed, punctuality, efficient service, comfort and a professional environment, while leisure tourists may seek relaxation, an escape from stress, stronger relationships, a physical challenge, cultural enrichment or fun. Marketing managers must identify the benefits sought from their target markets, develop a product that provides these, communicate this to the target market more effectively than their competitors, and monitor their success in satisfying them.

The facilitating product: This part of the product is physical and is essential in order for the service to take place. For example, a seat on a plane or a room in a hotel. This is also sometimes known as the 'formal' or 'tangible' product. In the tourism sector there is often great similarity in the facilitating product of suppliers competing for the same target market. For instance, airlines operating flights between the same two cities do not vary significantly in the facilitating product they offer, nor do two hotels of the same standard in the same destination. Marketing managers must ensure that the quality of the facilitating product matches the expectations of its target market, but must also find a way to make their own formal products stand out or differentiate themselves from those of their competitors. This differentiation is achieved through the final two product elements.

The supporting product: This part of the product offers non-essential extras that add value to the facilitating product. This part of the product is key to providing a superior value and positioning the product compared to that of competitors because it enables differentiation. The supporting product can be implemented relatively easily and may consist of tangible or intangible elements at any stage of the delivery process. For example accommodation providers may support their facilitating product by providing locally-sourced food, designer bathroom products or luxury bedding, and transport operators may support theirs by offering improved entertainment, onboard technology or catering. Some supporting products may justify higher prices and some may be copied by competitors. Supporting products can often be customised to the needs of individual consumers; for example hotels may support their facilitating product for families by offering adjoining rooms, cots, baby listening devices and children's meals. In some cases, a supporting product may transition into a facilitating product for some consumers; that is, it becomes essential to their purchase decision, for example the availability of WiFi in a hotel.

The augmented product: The augmented product relates to how the core, facilitating and supporting products are received by customers. Kotler et al. (2017) identify augmented products as the atmosphere within the place of consumption, accessibility in terms of opening hours and knowledge of staff, customer interactions with service delivery technology, with employees and with each other. These all affect the customers' perception of the quality of the service. Note that many marketing academics refer to these environmental elements as part of the extended marketing mix, separate from product (Hudson and Hudson, 2017). We discuss these in detail later in this chapter.

Snapshot 11.1 showed how TUI's different hotel brands augment their offer to tailor it to the needs of specific segments. Branding is a common method of developing an image and identity for a service product.

Branding

'Branding' is the process of developing, communicating and maintaining a particular identity and image for a supplier, as perceived by the consumer (Pike, 2008). A 'brand' is the image of a company, organisation or destination from the consumer's perspective, who then mentally positions it in relation to its competitors. This image is reinforced through the messages that are communicated about it, and by the consumer's experience of it during the consumption process. Branding has been widely used in goods marketing since the middle of the twentieth century, but it was only during the 1980s that its importance for service marketing was widely recognised (Grönroos, 2015).

Branding involves the blending of tangible and intangible qualities, symbolised by a trademark, which creates and communicates specific value in the minds of the target market, and may allow a higher price to be charged. The target market perceives the brand as superior to competitors', and if their experience of the product or service confirms this, the market remains loyal to it through repeat purchases. Successful branding helps to overcome the challenges of distance from markets and intangibility that is inherent in tourism services.

The services marketing triangle requires branding to be applied to external, interactive and internal marketing. As tourism usually involves prolonged service delivery processes, for example over several hours on a flight, days in a hotel or weeks on an inclusive tour, it is vital that the added values of the brand are integrated into every service encounter.

Kotler et al. (2017) identify a number of advantages that branding offers to tourism service providers:

- It creates a distinct identity for a supplier or a destination, which helps it to stand out from its competitors.

- It reduces intangibility and the perceived risk for the consumer by creating familiarity and signalling quality and reliability.

- It facilitates market segmentation by attracting some and putting off other market segments.

- The perceived additional value of the product provides some protection from price wars with competitors, and may reduce recovery time after a crisis.

- It may clarify employees' and destination stakeholders' understanding of consumers' expectations, and create greater consistency in service encounters.

- It may encourage customer loyalty, particularly where one supplier provides its product in several locations, for example a hotel chain, an airline, or a tour operator.

Successful branding requires detailed research and costly investment in the development and implementation of a brand identity and image. However, while there are several examples of successful and high-profile branding in tourism (e.g. Disney, Virgin and Singapore Airlines), in tourism, branding is not restricted to large suppliers with significant financial resources; through franchises and marketing consortia (which we explain in detail in Chapter 5), SMEs can also exploit the advantages of branding by adopting the brand of a third party, for example Marriott or Holiday Inn.

The concept of branding destinations is relatively new in tourism marketing: it was first included in tourism literature in the late 1990s (Pike, 2008) and is now increasingly used as a tool to communicate the value offered by a destination and to differentiate it from its competitors. A further exploration of destination branding can be found in Chapter 13.

PRICE

Price is the only element in the marketing mix that directly affects a company or organisation's revenue; all the others represent costs. Price therefore plays a crucial role in determining profitability for commercial enterprises. For public and not-for-profit organisations, price may be used to achieve societal benefits – perhaps through charging high prices to restrict demand to protect or conserve a fragile environment, for example historic or religious sites that introduce high entrance fees to deter some visitors; alternatively, low prices or even free access may be offered to encourage use of the resource by all social groups, for example entrances to museums and galleries whose function is to conserve their resources for the benefit and education of the public (in the UK, entry to national museums is free to encourage access by all).

Pricing in tourism is a complex activity for a number of reasons:

- Detailed information about potential consumers and their willingness to pay is not easily available, although the recent development of big data has facilitated the ability of software to predict how an individual may respond to certain prices.

- Prices charged by one supplier will be influenced by its competitors' own pricing decisions.

- There may be a long lead-in time between setting prices and selling the product.

- Demand from international markets may be increased or reduced by exchange rate fluctuations.

- The high fixed to variable cost ratio (see Chapter 5) creates opportunities to sell capacity at different prices to different market segments. This is known as 'price discrimination' and is widely used in the tourism sector.

- Pricing is often used as a tool to manipulate demand and smooth seasonal, daily or hourly variations in that demand by charging higher prices for capacity at peak times and lower prices at off-peak times. Demand with low-price elasticity will pay the higher prices, whereas demand with high price-elasticity will be shifted to periods where prices are lower. Price elasticity is explained in Chapter 3.

- Price has a significant role in achieving a competitive advantage in markets with a high elasticity of demand and often results in price-cutting and price wars.

Tourism service providers often use price as a tool to manage demand and many, for example budget hotels in the same destination and low-cost airlines operating the same routes, compete on the basis of price. Pricing decisions can be made using one of a range of approaches, as the list below, adapted from Hudson and Hudson (2017), describes:

Cost-plus pricing: The addition of a fixed percentage mark-up on costs. Does not account for competitors' prices or levels of demand.

Value-based pricing: Prices are based on the target market's perceived value of the product. Different segments may perceive different values. Continual monitoring of market perception and satisfaction is required, plus competitors' actions.

Competition-based pricing: Prices are set to match competitors' prices.

Differential (or demand-based) pricing: Different prices are charged depending on the consumer's willingness to pay. Requires constant monitoring of demand and amendment of prices. Usually prices will vary according to how far in advance and where reservations are made, and the degree of necessity of the purchase. This approach may be combined with discriminatory pricing.

Price skimming: A strategy used for some new, innovative products. Charging the highest possible price until demand falls, then reducing the price to attract the next segment and so on.

Penetration pricing: A strategy used for some new products or by some new suppliers to undercut competitors' prices in order to gain market share. However, competitors may copy prices and low prices may affect perceptions of quality.

Portfolio pricing: Pricing products in the same range differently by including different features, for example a hotel with standard, executive and deluxe rooms and suites.

Prestige (or premium) pricing: Maintaining high prices to reflect the exclusivity of the product, for example for apartments on Etihad Airways flights or rooms in the 7-star Burj Al Arab luxury hotel in Dubai.

Discriminatory pricing: Charging different prices to customers who will consume the same product at the same time, for instance passengers on the same flight in the same class or staying in the same room type in the same hotel on the same dates. Sophisticated software is used to calculate the highest price that should be charged at the time of booking in order to optimise the yield – in a process known as 'yield management'. We explain yield management in Chapter 5. The lowest prices may only cover the variable cost of the product plus a profit margin, but not the fixed costs; it assumes that fixed costs are met by charging higher prices to other customers. Marketers must ensure that consumers who would be prepared to pay higher prices are unable to purchase at the lower price. This is achieved through adding conditions to the lowest-priced sales such as advance purchase, minimum length of stay, 100 per cent cancellation fees and high amendment charges.

Price bundling: Combining products at a lower price, for example book Friday and Saturday night in a hotel, get Sunday free or free travel insurance with the sale of a package holiday.

Discount (promotional) pricing: Short-term measures to stimulate demand through price reductions, special offers, early booking discounts. Used to shift excess capacity, improve cash-flow or undermine competitors. Online travel discounters such as lastminute.com and Secret Escapes specialise in the distribution of distressed stock through discounted rates.

Sometimes the service provider doesn't have full control over pricing decisions: 'rate parity' has become a controversial issue. Rate parity is a clause in a contract between a hotel and an OTA to guarantee that the lowest rate for a room on the hotel's own website is also available to those OTAs entering into an agreement with the hotel; no official discounting on the rate by either party is allowed. Since 2010, several national competition authorities have investigated such rate parity clauses and some national laws in European countries have been reviewed or amended to restrict them. In 2015 Expedia and Booking.com removed clauses from contracts with European hotels that prevented the hotels from offering lower rates to other OTAs or to other sales channels, but retained the guarantee that the hotel itself would not offer lower rates on its own website. The European Competition Network (ECN) (2017) continues to monitor the impact of these changes.

PLACE

'Place' refers to the types of point of sale at which the product is purchased. In tourism this is particularly important because the point of sale of the product is often not the same as the point of consumption. For example, in the case of transport, accommodation or a major attraction, the purchase is often made some time in advance of consumption, often while the buyer is still in the generating region, and sometimes many months, or even years, in advance.

In tourism, the term 'place' can be confusing, so to avoid confusion, in tourism marketing the 'place' element of the marketing mix is more commonly called 'distribution'. Different types of points of sale are known as 'distribution channels'. Distribution channels can be direct or indirect, as illustrated in Table 11.1.

TABLE 11.1 Tourism distribution channels

Direct – the point of sale is provided by the supplier	Indirect – the point of sale is provided by intermediaries
A ticket office on the site of a visitor attraction or transport operator	Wholesalers who sell the product on to the trade or to the consumer
An airline sales office A hotel reservations department, in the hotel or through a reservations office	Tour and MICE operators who add other elements to the product to create a package or inclusive tour, selling via agencies or direct to the consumer
Online booking via the supplier's own website	Online or offline agencies and TMCs who are paid a commission for each sale.
	(Each of these types of intermediary is explained in detail in Chapter 6.)

Some suppliers may use only one channel of distribution while others, particularly large companies that target a range of market segments, may use multiple channels. The perishability of the tourism product creates a need to secure as many sales in advance of the time of consumption as possible; this in turn requires selection of the most effective distribution channels and reservations systems to manage and control sales.

Choice of Distribution Channel

The choice of distribution channel is flexible; suppliers can use one channel alone or several types simultaneously. Hudson and Hudson (2017) stress that the choice of channel is complex because suppliers must obtain market coverage at the lowest cost, and, if choosing indirect channels, the image of the intermediaries chosen should be compatible with the service provider's own image. We explain intermediaries in detail in Chapter 6.

Direct distribution, particularly when the physical, cultural or language distances between suppliers and consumers are large, can be complex and costly, and represent fixed costs paid in advance, increasing the financial risk of direct distribution. For example to sell direct, suppliers will need to invest in marketing communication campaigns to reach their target markets, may have to invest heavily in search engine optimisation, employ a sales team and provide a website with reservations capability. Suppliers that are franchises or members of a soft brand benefit from the communications activities of the brand; for example in 2015, the five largest hotel brands spent around US$5.3 billion on marketing (Ting, 2016c). Even so, these brands are engaged in a struggle with OTAs to capture sales; they offer incentives such as free WiFi and loyalty club points to those who book via the brand's website, but still OTAs retain channel power; in 2015, an estimated US$5.7 billion was spent by Priceline.com and Expedia on search advertising (Ting, 2016c).

Indirect distribution, through OTAs or other channels, requires less marketing effort than direct sales, and represents a variable cost that will only be paid if the distributor sells a unit of capacity. However, indirect distribution can also be costly: agencies usually charge a commission of 10–15 per cent, and operators and wholesalers will normally need a reduction on published prices of about 30 per cent. Table 11.2 lists the advantages and disadvantages of direct and indirect distribution.

TABLE 11.2   The advantages and disadvantages for suppliers of direct and indirect distribution

Advantages of direct distribution	Advantages of using intermediaries
Control over information provided about the product.	Much of the cost of promotion is borne by the intermediary.
Control over type of customer attracted.	Payment of commission to agencies, or discounted rates to wholesalers and operators, represent a variable cost – these are only incurred if a sale is made by the intermediary.
Gather detailed information about potential and actual consumers.	
Potential closer match between benefits sought by customer and their satisfaction by the producer.	Easier access to distant markets using the market knowledge of intermediary.
Disadvantages of direct distribution	**Disadvantages of using intermediaries**
Cost of market research.	Limited control over information provided about the product.
Investment required in facilities to process the sale – development and maintenance of a website, recruitment of more staff in reservations department, establishment of sales outlets in generating region or in the destination.	Limited control over type of customer attracted.
	Limited control over commitment of intermediary to prioritise supplier's product over competitor's.
	No control of service standards in intermediary.
Investment in promotion to guide potential customers to the direct points of sales.	Unable to gather detailed information about potential consumers, and limited knowledge of actual consumers.
These investments represent a fixed cost – they must be paid whether or not a sale is made.	Potential mismatch between benefits sought by the customer and their satisfaction by the supplier.
	Rate parity clauses in contracts with OTAs.

PROMOTION

This element of the marketing mix is more commonly referred to as 'marketing communications', in order to embrace the range of methods used to communicate messages to target markets. Marketing communications have a key role in overcoming the intangible and distant nature of tourism services and in conveying the value that the product or company offers. There are a number of methods available to communicate the benefits of a particular supplier or destination. Often a supplier will blend a number of methods, known as the communications mix, specifically for each target market.

Internet and mobile technologies have transformed the communication channels used by consumers, and suppliers and intermediaries have had to respond accordingly by providing websites, developing their social media presence on Twitter, Instagram, YouTube, Snapchat and Facebook, by responding to reviews left on Tripadvisor and other review sites, and by providing mobile apps. We will now explain the main communications methods and their applications in tourism. Methods of communicating include: word of mouth, advertising, public relations (PR), personal selling. Each of these will now be discussed.

Word-of-mouth or Customer-to-customer Communications

Word-of-mouth (WOM) or customer-to-customer (C2C) communication is the discussion of a company or organisation between people who appear to have no personal interest in promoting them. The intangibility of tourism services makes C2C communication particularly useful to consumers because it reduces the intangibility of the product and the perceived risk of purchasing it by providing first-hand accounts of the experience. However, the inseparability and heterogeneity features of tourism services create particular challenges for tourism suppliers because of the difficulties in ensuring consistency of quality across all consumers. Positive WOM is, of course, free good publicity, but negative WOM can be very damaging.

Internet and mobile technologies have revolutionised WOM communications and increased their importance in the communications mix by providing opportunities for C2C communication. C2C is available online through:

- Social networking sites such as Facebook, Snapchat, Twitter and Instagram.

- Online communities of individuals with shared interests who communicate via wikis, chat rooms, message boards and forums, for example fodors.com/community/; www.lonelyplanet.com/thorntree/

- Blogs – online diaries or video diaries produced by individuals and available for invited users to view. Bloggers with a large following are known as digital influencers; many tourism suppliers and destinations invite influencers to experience their product and service and then blog about it.

- Customer reviews where consumers share their experiences of a supplier, with reviews, photographs and information, for example tripadvisor.com; personal references from providers and users on sharing economy platforms.

- Information sharing sites such as YouTube and Instagram where content can be posted for worldwide audiences to view.

C2C communication is particularly important in the sharing economy where trust is fundamental to exchanges between providers and users. The snapshot below describes how sharing economy platforms develop a sense of trust between their communities.

SNAPSHOT 11.2

Trust and the Sharing Economy

Sharing economy platforms allow strangers to exchange goods or services. Trust between these strangers is fundamental, particularly in tourism when tourists visit or stay in the homes of home owners, borrow their cars or share journeys, or meet up for tours or other experiences.

In many destinations, the rapid rise of platforms such as Airbnb, CouchSurfing, BlaBlaCar and EatWith has preceded regulation, and the platforms themselves facilitate an atmosphere of trust by:

- verifying identities of individuals before they can register on a platform
- offering insurance protection to protect providers' property
- requiring providers and users to upload a detailed profiles about themselves
- encouraging providers and users to communicate via the platform rather than directly
- publishing feedback and references from providers and users about each other
- providing safety tips
- publishing policies on conduct, privacy, content and writing references
- providing a support team to whom negative experiences can be reported
- developing a strong brand identity.

Source: Stephany (2015)

Advertising

Advertising is the paid-for promotion of products to large audiences (Hudson and Hudson, 2017) and includes print adverts in newspapers and magazines, broadcast advertising on television, cinema and radio, outdoor advertising on transport and billboard, and online advertising on search engines, aggregator sites, social media and on the websites of other companies and organisations.

The key point about advertising is that it must be positioned in places where the target market is most likely to see or hear it. For example, a cruise line that sells through agencies may advertise in travel trade media, while operators organising clubbing holidays for young adults may advertise in magazines, on radio stations, on TV programmes whose audience is predominantly made up of that market or on social media. Online advertising matches advertisers to specific individuals using data held by social media sites or by the tracking of our online behaviour through cookies that are placed on our computers.

Pay-per-click (PPC) and pay-per-acquisition (PPA) are online advertising-pricing models where the advertiser only pays when the viewer takes action – either by clicking through to the advertiser's website (PPC) or by clicking through and making a purchase (PPA). Adverts are displayed using pop-ups and banners and appear to viewers who have been calculated to be part of the advertiser's target market. For instance, accommodation wholesalers and car hire companies may advertise on airline websites and hotels may advertise on search engine results pages when their destination's name is searched. Ski-holiday operators might advertise on the websites of ski equipment and clothing brands. Many social media websites and online community websites, wikis, reviews and blogs allow targeted PPC and PPA adverts based on the profile of users. For instance, tour operators specialising in activity holidays may advertise on community websites and blog pages for surfing, sailing or diving enthusiasts.

PPC and PPA advertising are important, particularly for tourism SMEs, for a number of reasons:

- Payment is required only when a potential customer clicks through to the website or makes a purchase, compared to traditional media advertising where payment is made regardless of the number of people who may see it, or the number of people who then make a purchase.

- Expenditure is controlled through setting a budget, allowing a quota of advert displays based on the financial resources of the company.

- Action is immediate because the advert is displayed when the potential customer is actively seeking information, rather than requiring them to remember the advert and take action at another time.

- The customer can be tracked from enquiry to purchase, which provides valuable information about consumer behaviour and allows for retargeting at a later date by redisplaying adverts to prompt action.

- Advertising is targeted more accurately at potential consumers who are seeking related information.

Search engine optimisation (SEO) is the process by which a company's listing on search engine results' pages is manipulated. When an internet user searches for information using a search engine such as Google or Yahoo, they type in keywords; if those keywords match the content of a website, that website will be listed. The greater the match, the higher up the list the website will appear. Website design and content is therefore crucial in manipulating the website's position on search engine results pages. Specialist agencies offer SEO services and also handle PPC and PPA advertising spend. Note though that large companies invest heavily in search advertising to ensure that their own website appears high up on the search results, pushing organic search results further down the page, or even off the first page.

Public Relations

> The aim of marketing PR is to obtain favourable publicity for an organisation and its products in the media. (Middleton et al., 2009: 306)

'Public relations' (PR) is the acquisition of media coverage that is not directly paid for. PR activities include press releases, press conferences, feature stories in travel magazines or supplements, familiarisation (fam) trips for journalists and intermediaries, event sponsorship, celebrity visits, product placement in films or TV programmes, and maintaining an image library for the media to use (Hudson and Hudson, 2017).

A major advantage of PR, particularly in tourism, is that the information is usually perceived to be coming from an impartial third party and therefore has greater credibility than advertising (Middleton et al., 2009). However, there is some risk here as the business, organisation or destination has no control over what is actually shown or said.

PR is a communication method widely used by national or regional tourism organisations to influence perceptions of their destination and to bring small suppliers and potential customers together. Familiarisation trips to destinations are organised by tourism organisations for carefully selected journalists who will then write a feature story about the trip, or for trade intermediaries in order to inspire them to sell the destination. For example each year, Tourism Australia invites up to 1,000 print, broadcast and online media representatives, and digital influencers, from over 20 countries to visit Australia on a tailor-made itinerary to inspire a story (Tourism Australia, 2017b).

PR is a crucial tool in the event of a crisis involving tourists or destinations, to manage the negative publicity generated by the media. Through a carefully managed relationship with the press, using press releases published on the website, press conferences and media site visits, it is possible to influence the way a crisis is portrayed by the media and its subsequent impact on the image of the destination or supplier, as well as on future demand.

Personal Selling

'Personal selling' is the use of personalised communication with potential consumers to establish and maintain relationships, gather marketing intelligence, provide sales support and generate sales (Hudson and Hudson, 2017).

Personal selling is important in tourism as it helps to reduce the intangibility of the product, but can be costly for suppliers because they are located some distance away from their potential consumers. Tourism destination organisations play an important role in creating opportunities for suppliers to use personal selling as a communications tool with intermediaries. In tourism personal selling is implemented through:

- Exhibiting at a trade or consumer travel exhibition, for example ITB in Berlin or World Travel Market in Cape Town, London and São Paulo. Tourism destination organisations sell space on their stands to small companies who would otherwise be unable to exhibit, while large companies have their own stands.

- Employing sales managers or account managers to liaise with travel trade intermediaries or corporate customers and maintain a relationship with them.

- Workshops organised by tourism destination organisations for producers and trade intermediaries to meet face to face, either at the destination or in the generating region.

- Telephone or face-to-face contact with customers via sales offices or sales desks.

- Chatbots are in their infancy at the time of writing. They are computerised sales assistants that support an online enquiry by asking questions of the viewer and presenting offers or providing general travel advice that match the viewers' needs. KAYAK and Skyscanner offer customer service interactions using chatbots via Faceboook Messenger.

Tourism suppliers have a range of communication options available to them. The choice of method, and its content, should be determined by knowledge of the methods that reach the target market most effectively. In addition, the success of each method used should be carefully measured to inform any future decisions about marketing communications.

In reality, often the choice of method and the ability to measure its effectiveness are constrained by cost considerations. Large companies that invest huge sums in advertising will employ specialist agencies to design campaigns, test proposed messages using focus groups, and use marketing research agencies to measure the effectiveness of campaigns through surveys or big data. Smaller companies, public sector and not-for-profit suppliers are usually unable to approach their marketing communications in the same way, but they benefit from the communications mix used by tourism destination organisations to promote the destination in which they are located. Where communication budgets are limited, marketers must be creative and innovative in using the communications mix to attract the attention of their target markets. The case study below describes a communications campaign mix implemented by Tourisme Montréal.

CASE STUDY 11.1

Tourisme Montréal

MTL Moments, Montreal

Source: Image courtesy of Tourisme Montréal – Aline Vinel

(Continued)

Tourisme Montréal leads the tourism sector in developing the city's tourism offer and positioning Montréal as a destination for leisure and business travel. In 2017, the city celebrated its 375th anniversary and a year-long programme of 175 celebratory events and festivities was organised. Tourisme Montréal captured this as the basis for its innovative 'Sorry Toronto!' campaign.

The campaign's objectives included:

- positioning Montréal as a must-see destination in 2017

- increasing intent to visit Montréal – motivate overnight stays in 2017's Q1 and Q2 (i.e. autumn and winter seasons)

- building Montréal's reputation and image internationally.

The campaign's communications focused on outdoor advertising and online activities using the message 'Come join the party!'. The campaign was structured into several phases including:

Phase 1: Targeted potential visitors in Toronto aged 18–49. In December 2016, a banner emblazoned with 'Sorry Toronto!' was flown across the city to attract interest in Montréal, and posters were displayed around the city. Montréal ambassadors visited Toronto to personally apologise to individual residents for the noise that the celebrations will create, and invited some residents to 'Come join the party!' with free flights to Montréal. Footage of the interactions was filmed and uploaded to YouTube (Tourisme Montréal, 2016). A similar campaign was repeated in New York.

Phase 2: Launched in January 2017, with a series of fun videos recorded by actor and native Montréaler William Shatner, apologising for the noise of the party and showcasing specific attractions with the message 'Come join the party!' (Tourisme Montréal, 2016). Each phase was supported by online resources to engage locals and potential and actual visitors:

- A dedicated website detailing the events programme (http://joinmontreal375. tourisme-montreal.org/).

- #mtlmoments was set up and used for social media campaigns on Facebook, Twitter, Pinterest, LinkedIn and Google+ to encourage Montreal locals and visitors to post and share messages and images about their experience of the city.

The campaign's results included:

- Phase 1: 2 million complete and over 5 million incomplete views of the 'Sorry Toronto' video, extensive press coverage and conversations on social media.

- Phase 2: 15 million complete and 29 million incomplete views of the William Shatner video (against an objective of 8 million complete views).

Source: Tourisme Montréal (2017)

Reflective Questions

1. List the communications activities used in Tourism Montréal's campaign.

2. What advantages did this blend of communications offer that could not have been achieved through traditional print, radio and TV advertising alone?

The case study above demonstrates two very important marketing approaches that have evolved in response to online communication channels:

Content marketing is the creation and sharing of stories digitally via videos, blogs and social media posts that are designed to stimulate interest rather than explicitly promote. Effective content marketing captures attention and is shared by the viewer with their own networks. It encourages interaction with the brand to create a two-way conversation and develop relationships. The importance of content marketing is demonstrated by Marriott International: in 2015, Marriott International launched its first content marketing centre, called M Live Studio, which creates real-time content and engages with travellers via conversations on social media. There are now M Live Studios in Asia-Pacific, the Caribbean, Latin America and Europe. The studios enable personalised interactions with guests or other travellers; it also tracks and monitors online and social conversations, global trends, marketing campaigns and brand reputation across social platforms (Marriott International, 2016).

Integrated marketing communications (IMC) is the transmission of clear, consistent and engaging messages across a range of communications channels. The case study demonstrates how a range of communication channels can be blended to convey the same tone and message. IMC should be the objective of all campaigns that use more than one communications channel to ensure that a consistent message is conveyed (Kotler et al., 2017), although sometimes this is not achieved and communications via different channels may contradict each other.

INTERACTIVE AND INTERNAL MARKETING – THE EXTENDED MARKETING MIX FOR SERVICES

The 4Ps framework discussed above is applicable to both goods and services. However, the distinct characteristics of services and the services marketing triangle create a need for more variables. In addition to the 4Ps, Booms and Bitner (1981) added three more marketing mix variables that are used in services marketing: people, processes and physical evidence.

Goeldner et al. (2000, in Fyall and Garrod, 2005) proposed that partnership be added to the extended marketing mix for tourism because of the growing importance of collaboration between suppliers, although this has not yet been incorporated into the marketing mix. In Chapter 5, a partnership between airlines is described in Snapshot 5.4.

We now consider people, processes and physical evidence.

People

The characteristics of inseparability and heterogeneity and the services marketing triangle demonstrate the importance of the role of people in the delivery and consumption of the tourism experience. Usually this marketing mix variable is interpreted as employees who interact with customers. However, from the tourist's perspective, there are two other groups of people that influence the quality of their experience: other customers consuming the product at the same time, and the local community with whom the customer may come into considerable contact.

Employees

Grönroos (2015) highlights the importance of employees' attitude, commitment and performance in the service process. Frontline employees have direct contact with customers and their behaviour, appearance and service skills will affect the customer's perception of the company or organisation. They also interact with customers in situations that can sometimes be stressful, for example at peak times with long queues, in the event of a delay or technical problem, or when customers are dissatisfied and complaining. The personalities of employees, their motivations and attitudes to their work, the level of support provided to them by other colleagues, management and technology, and the recompense provided to them will ultimately influence the quality of service they provide.

The services marketing triangle suggests that there is a direct link between employee satisfaction and customer satisfaction. Therefore the recruitment and training processes that a company or organisation implements, the benefits and support provided, and the way in which employees are managed, will influence the quality of service experienced by the customer, at all stages of the service delivery. Internal marketing is used to manage the relationship between employer and employee. The snapshot below describes how the 'people' variable is managed in a hotel company.

SNAPSHOT 11.3

Talent Management in the Hotel Sector

Logos for the Meliã group of hotels

Source: Image courtesy of Meliã Hotels International

'Talent management' is a term used widely in the hotel sector to emphasise the role of employees as the firm's most important asset, the source of competitive advantage and the key to business success.

Meliã Hotels International (2017) states that 'promoting a people management model that facilitates the achievement of strategic objectives and boosts the professional growth of our employees is a priority for the company.'

Meliã's talent management consists of three principles:

Recruitment and selection: Matching candidates' attitudes, personality and values to the company's own internal culture of flexibility, motivation, commitment and enthusiasm. Internal promotion is prioritised to demonstrate a long-term commitment to existing employees.

Training and development: Recognising employees' potential by preparing them for more senior positions through development and training programmes.

Commitment to employees: Fostering an environment of collaboration through internal marketing: measuring and reporting levels of staff satisfaction; facilitating communication within the company, and staff knowledge, through an internal website; offering discounts at Meliã hotels and partners' products.

Source: Meliã Hotels International (2017)

Other Customers Consuming the Experience at the Same Time

Other customers consuming the product at the same time have the potential to enhance or reduce the quality of each customer's experience of the tourism product.

Kotler et al. (2017) stress the importance of effective market segmentation in achieving compatibility between customers. This should ensure that all customers within the target market seek the same benefits and share some characteristics. This in turn will facilitate the selection of customers whose behaviour and attitudes are compatible and will contribute towards their harmonious integration during their consumption of the product.

However, when more than one segment is targeted, the potential for conflict between them can be high if the benefits sought are different. Marketing managers must ensure, through the design and operation of the product and its processes, that incompatible segments do not interact. This emphasises the importance of layout and design in facilitating the separation of segments with different needs. For example Disney Cruise Line designs areas on its ships such as pools, lounges, restaurants and entertainment that are dedicated for adults-only, and its private Bahamian island, Castaway Cay, offers a family beach and activities, and a beach exclusively for adults (Disney Cruise Line, 2017).

The Local Community

The third group of people that tourists will interact with during their tourism experience is the host community. Often, the nature of this interaction will be commercial; that is, a situation where the tourist is being served by a member of the local community, perhaps in a shop or restaurant. Less frequently, the interaction may be non-commercial, where the tourist shares facilities with local people, engages in conversation with them or seeks assistance from them. Contemporary definitions of tourism marketing include the host community as stakeholders who should benefit from the marketing process, but the attitude of the local community to tourism can also positively or negatively affect the tourism consumer's experience and perception of the destination. Destination marketing organisations can affect this through involving local communities in decision making and educating them about the value of tourism to the community. The Jamaican Tourist Board has a Tourism Awareness Unit that runs campaigns to raise awareness among the local community of the value of tourism to Jamaica and its role in conveying the destination's advertised warmth and hospitality (Tourism Action Club, 2017).

Physical Evidence

'Physical evidence' relates to the tangible cues provided in the location where consumption of the service occurs and where the organisation and the firm interact. Bitner (1992, cited in Hoffman et al., 2009: 371) describes this environment as the 'servicescape' and as a crucial element in services marketing because its design influences customer expectations before a purchase, their satisfaction during the service, and also influences customer and employee behaviour and actions during service encounters (Hudson and Hudson, 2017). It is useful to think of the servicescape as a stage upon which the service is performed and consumed – it is visible to customers and easily evaluated.

Zeithaml et al. (2013) identified three environmental dimensions that constitute the servicescape. Although they are presented separately, Zeithaml et al. stress that people respond to their environment holistically in a 'holistic pattern of independent stimuli' (2013: 296):

Ambient conditions: These are the environmental conditions that affect our five senses, and influence our emotional well-being, attitudes and behaviours, consciously or unconsciously. For example the style and volume of background music, air temperature, scent and visual appeal such as lighting, colours and orderliness. Decisions about ambient conditions influence how comfortable customers feel in a space and therefore should be designed carefully to the preferences of the target market.

Spatial layout and functionality: This includes the layout of the space, the design and arrangement of furniture, desks and equipment, and how these facilitate the performance and consumption of the service. For example modern budget hotels often design the lobby area to enable employees to fulfil several functions seamlessly by creating a continuous counter that connects the front desk with information, luggage services and the bar, behind which staff can move between roles. Queuing systems for rides in theme parks are designed to reduce anxiety about waiting time by revealing only sections of the line at one time.

Signs, symbols and artefacts: These visual guides lead the customer through the service process to reduce anxiety, confusion and conflict. For example giving directions, reminding of acceptable behaviours such as no photography, no smoking and informing about the service system such as 'wait here', 'take a number', 'items to remove from hand luggage during airport security' and so on.

Hudson and Hudson (2017) added a fourth dimension based on recent research by several researchers:

Staff and customer behaviour and image: Social aspects of the servicescape influence customers' perception of employees' competence, credibility and commitment to customer satisfaction; for example through employees' appearance, attention to the customer and the way they interact with colleagues. In addition the type and behaviour of other customers affects the servicescape, for example by giving it a 'cool' image or a conventional image.

Some suppliers design separate servicescapes for different types of customer using the same facility; for example some hotels offer executive lounges for the exclusive use of guests booked into executive rooms, and full-service airlines vary the design and layout of each class on board their planes.

Hudson and Hudson (2017) stress the role of servicescape in positioning a tourism organisation relative to competitors and of delivering the experience promised in external marketing. Consistency of physical evidence at each stage of the service delivery process – or the customer journey – is essential because it is used to create expectations and differentiate the product from those of competitors, reinforce a brand image and encourage desirable behaviour amongst consumers.

Physical evidence and the servicescape deliver the augmented product component that Kotler et al. (2017) referred to. For example, a relaxed atmosphere in a holiday hotel may be communicated through soft background music at a low volume in public areas, subdued lighting, soft furnishings, the scent of fresh flowers and a casual style of staff uniform.

Process

Zeithaml et al. (2013: 27) describe the process marketing mix variable as the 'procedures, mechanisms, and flow of activities by which the service is delivered'. The simultaneous production and consumption of services emphasises the process of service delivery and the need for efficient processes and systems that meet customers' needs. Inseparability and heterogeneity make service encounters hard to control and unsatisfactory 'moments of truth' will affect customer satisfaction and loyalty and the image of the company. The management of the service delivery process is therefore particularly important in delivering service quality, in customer satisfaction and retention, and in positive WOM promotion. Some tourism service providers attempt to manage each service encounter through standardising the process.

Standardised service processes

'Standardised service processes' are sequences of activities that do not vary from one customer to the next, therefore each customer experiences the same interaction with employees (Zeithaml et al., 2013). In the tourism industries, some service processes are routine and can be controlled through standards and rules, for example hotel check-in, airport security and transport boarding processes. One approach to standardising the service process is through the use of scripts and automation.

In tourism, many service encounters are remote. For example many airlines and hotels have automated check-in facilities, many attractions and destinations provide recorded information systems, and many suppliers interact with customers via websites to provide availability advice, confirm reservations and send documentation. Many suppliers use smartphone apps to enable check in/check out, lock and unlock the guestroom door, track luggage and send messages and updates throughout the customer journey.

An alternative or complementary way of standardising service encounters is to script the process. Scripted processes determine the sequence of actions, words and equipment to ensure consistent, satisfactory service encounters. Telephone, email and face-to-face service encounters can be scripted to some extent through standard introduction and closing statements that all employees use for every customer. Short and uncomplicated face-to-face encounters can also be scripted, for example in food and beverage services or on-site ticket sales for an attraction, and tour guides can to some degree script their presentation.

Standardisation of the service process may reduce the problem of heterogeneity and reduce the risk of communication errors, but it also reduces the service provider's ability to respond to customers' individual needs and requests (Hoffman et al., 2009). In complex service encounters that involve long interactions and require the service provider to have a clear understanding of the customer's needs, for example a MICE agency, an operator or a tourism destination organisation, scripted processes are not appropriate. Instead, the outcome of complex service encounters relies on the communication skills and emotional intelligence of the staff member involved to customise the process to individual customers through a process of co-creation in which all parties are actively involved (Zeithaml et al., 2013).

One method of understanding and managing the delivery of a service process is by developing a blueprint or map of the service.

Service blueprints

Shostack (1977, cited in Grönroos, 2015: 393) proposed blueprinting service operations through a formal flowchart illustrating the service system and clarifying the roles of those involved in delivering the service. Service blueprints identify:

- all service encounters between the customer and service provider
- the activities of all participants
- the activities that are visible to the customer, and support activities that take place behind the scenes
- the standards for each activity, such as time allowed, information to be gathered or imparted, plus the targets to be met
- the stage in the process where customers are required to wait the longest
- stages in the process where visible moments of truth are vulnerable to service failure
- physical evidence of the quality of service.

The resulting blueprint allows companies to calculate employees' productivity and specifies exactly how the service delivery process should take place.

Service blueprinting identifies the back-stage procedures that are invisible to the customer and considers the implementation of the customer journey from the suppliers' perspective. However, a customer-focused approach to process should also understand and manage the journey from the customer's perspective. A tool known as 'customer journey mapping' facilitates this.

Customer journey mapping

Customer journey mapping, also called 'customer experience mapping', captures the customers' experience of a service from the beginning and at every stage, in order to identify the strengths and weaknesses of processes from the customers' view. Through qualitative research, for example interviewing customers, a map of customers' perceptions, actions, interactions, feelings and emotions at each touch point of the service is developed, showing the high points and the low points of the experience from the customer's perspective. This enables suppliers to empathise with their customers, and redesign stages of the process that cause stress or dissatisfaction.

Process, then, has a crucial role in delivering customer satisfaction, affecting customer loyalty and WOM promotion. At the same time, it also has the potential to deliver customer dissatisfaction, prevent repeat business and encourage negative WOM communication.

An integral part of the process marketing mix variable is the ability to recover from service errors. Grönroos (2015: 146) suggests that a service recovery system should focus on three areas: 'constantly monitor service processes to identify problems, solve problems effectively, and learn from problems and the recovery process.' Following Zemke's research into service recovery (1992, cited in Grönroos, 2015: 146), Grönroos proposes that in the event of a service error, customers expect an apology, empathy, compensation, value-added extras and reliable information about the service recovery.

Some tourism services guarantee their service process and promise satisfaction to their customers; the snapshot below describes how service guarantees are used by the Hampton by Hilton brand.

SNAPSHOT 11.4

Service Guarantees – Hampton by Hilton

Hampton by Hilton property, London

Source: Clare Inkson

Hampton by Hilton is a mid-priced hotel brand with 2,200+ hotels in 19 countries. In 1989, the brand was the first hotel company to introduce an unconditional 100 per cent satisfaction guarantee to its guests. Eventually other hotel companies also introduced service guarantees. In 2017, Hampton by Hilton's guarantee was updated to reflect guests' expectations from a hotel experience.

The new 100 per cent guarantee promises: 'Making you happy makes us happy. So, if we can make your stay better, talk to any member of our team, and we'll make sure you're 100 per cent happy'.

The repetition of 'happy' in the new guarantee emphasises the desired outcome of the stay, and the brand's understanding of the emotional importance of the hotel experience. The strapline encourages guests to communicate disappointment to staff at the time of the consumption of the service, and provides staff with more flexibility in service recovery – any employee can take action. Dissatisfied customers may not require a refund but need changes to be made to meet their requirements during their stay. The new guarantee is also intended to add a competitive advantage to the brand.

Source: Hampton by Hilton (2017)

The extended marketing mix highlights the role of a whole company, and all employees, processes and systems, in delivering customer satisfaction.

Grönroos (2015) suggests that interactive and internal marketing require an approach to marketing that extends beyond the marketing department and involves a company-wide focus on customer satisfaction and developing long-term relationships with customers. He proposes that while marketing is considered to be the function of specialists, rather than an approach that permeates throughout an organisation, service organisations will struggle to remain competitive.

Grönroos (2015) points out that people, physical evidence and processes are usually the responsibility of departments other than the marketing department. For example, where 'people' refers to staff, recruitment and selection is often conducted by HR functions. The 'process' of service delivery is usually the responsibility of operating departments such as reservations, front office, housekeeping, food and beverage, and baggage handling, while decisions about physical evidence may be made by interior designers or individual operating departments. This implies that elements of services marketing are not directly controlled by the marketing department and highlights the role of the whole company in achieving effective marketing. Grönroos stresses Gummesson's (1987, cited in Grönroos, 2015: 374) view of employees outside the marketing department as 'part-time marketers' because of their role in the interactive and internal marketing stages of services marketing.

SUMMARY

We have seen that tourism marketing is a complex task. The characteristics of tourism services create particular challenges in identifying, anticipating and satisfying customer needs. The services marketing triangle concept, and the 7Ps framework, are particularly useful in understanding how these challenges can be overcome.

Large tourism corporations have extensive marketing resources while SMEs are more dependent on the marketing research and promotion carried out by tourism destination organisations. These organisations have a vital role in creating a clear identity for the varied attractions and amenities that exist within most destinations and play a key part in assisting and supplementing the marketing efforts of individual suppliers.

The emergence of online and mobile technologies has transformed the marketing process and in particular has created new opportunities for tourism SMEs and micro-businesses; however, the principles of marketing remain the same.

This chapter has been intended as an introduction to marketing concepts and their application in tourism; the scale of the topic precludes a comprehensive discussion of these in one chapter alone. There are, however, a number of textbooks devoted to tourism marketing and it is recommended that these are consulted for a broader and more detailed discussion of tourism marketing.

SELF-TEST QUESTIONS

1. Consider a tourism service that you have consumed recently – what were its core, facilitating, supporting and augmented product types?

2. Using the main segmentation criteria, describe yourself as a consumer purchasing your most recent tourism experience.

3. How important is social media to you in your tourism experiences? List how you use social media before, during or after a trip.

FURTHER READING

Grönroos, C. (2015) *Service Management and Marketing.* Chichester: Wiley.

Hudson, S. and Hudson, L. (2017) *Marketing for Tourism, Hospitality and Events – A Global and Digital Approach.* London: Sage.

Kotler, P., Bowen, J. T., Makens, J. C. and Baloglu, S. (2017) *Marketing for Hospitality and Tourism.* Harlow: Pearson.

USEFUL WEBSITES

Hampton by Hilton: http://hiltonworldwide.com/portfolio/hampton/

Marriott International: www.marriott.com/marriott/aboutmarriott.mi

Reed Exhibitions (2017) *About World Travel Market*: www.wtm.com/about/

Skift: https://skift.com/

Star Alliance: www.staralliance.com/en/homeTourism Montréal: www.youtube.com/watch?v=7r78rTWZ9tY

Travelmole: www.travelmole.com/

TTG Media: www.ttgmedia.com/

TUI Hotels and Resorts: www.tuigroup.com/en-en/about-us/about-tui-group/our-business/tui-hotels-resorts

12

THE MANAGEMENT OF VISITORS

'The voyage of discovery lies not in finding new landscapes,
but in having new eyes.'

Marcel Proust, 1923: 53

LEARNING OUTCOMES

After reading this chapter you will understand:

- that visitor management is made up of two elements: the needs of the tourism resource (e.g. an attraction, destination, natural area) and the needs of the visitor
- the concepts of carrying capacity and quality management with regard to visitor management
- the different strategies and tools that can be used in visitor management plans, both at the level of the visitor and at the level of the site
- examples of how technology can support visitor management.

The Red Fort in Delhi, India

Source: Sandra Charrasse

INTRODUCTION

The previous chapters have discussed the positive and negative economic, social and environmental impacts tourism development can have on destinations. Visitor management is an area of tourism studies that is specifically aimed towards limiting the negative impacts of visitors on destinations, and ensuring that the visitor has an enjoyable experience. Growing global tourism demand has reinforced the importance of visitor management as it plays a central role in sustainable tourism management, particularly in established and successful tourism destinations where resources may be stretched or over-used due to the volume of tourists that make use of them. Different types of destinations can be vulnerable to the negative impacts of tourists and tourism. Visitor management can be applied to destinations with natural, historic or purpose-built attractions.

In this chapter we discuss the aims of visitor management and how these are implemented in practice, and specify some of the negative impacts that a visitor management plan can aim to limit. One of the aims of visitor management, the safeguarding of quality tourism experiences, will be presented in detail. We also give examples of different visitor management tools and techniques destinations can make use of. Finally, the role of technology in visitor management is examined.

THE NEED FOR VISITOR MANAGEMENT

'The dilemma of visitor attractions is that, generally speaking, the greater the exposure of the site to visitors, the greater is the potential for negative visitor impacts to arise' (Garrod, 2008: 166). Indeed, the previous chapters have shown that tourism can have many positive as well as negative impacts. In many cases, the negative impacts will be felt more strongly when the pressures of tourism, or the volumes of tourists, increase. Visitor management strategies aim to limit the negative impacts of tourism and tourists by balancing the needs of tourists with those of the destination or attraction. The concept therefore consists of two equally important parts: protecting the destination, specific sites and the local population; and ensuring that the tourist is offered a quality experience. This section will mainly concentrate on the first element, the needs of the destination; the following section will discuss the quality of the visitor experience in more detail.

Visitor management plans can address a wide range of pressures that are caused by tourists, and which pressures are included often depends on the type of destination the plan is developed for: natural parks, for example, experience different problems from those of historic cities. Even though this makes it hard to generalise the objectives of visitor management plans, these often include to avoid overcrowding, to influence tourists' behaviour and to address traffic-related problems. Garrod (2008) also mentions objectives to address social impacts and authenticity issues – these concepts are discussed in Chapter 8.

TO AVOID OVERCROWDING

When tourist numbers increase, it is not always possible to increase the space or facilities for these extra tourists at the same rate. Historic cities, for example Bruges or Venice, are often typified by small winding streets. In smaller seaside resorts there

Crowds visiting the Sacré Coeur in Paris

Source: Sandra Charrasse

may be enough parking for residents, but not necessarily for all the extra tourists during the peak season. In these conditions overcrowding may become a problem for the destination or attraction: it may cause negative environmental impacts, reduce the visitor experience, and affect the quality of life of the residents. The overcrowding may occur only in certain areas (e.g. at the entrance of an attraction, near a popular facility) or throughout the destination or attraction. Overcrowding can be a problem at certain times of the year, such as during festivals or in the peak season, or may be a constant problem. What constitutes overcrowding is, up to a certain point, subjective: some tourists like the buzz of a crowd, whereas others would find this rather stressful or unpleasant. It will also depend on the type of destination or attraction and how severe the impacts of overcrowding are: in cities, crowds may not have the same detrimental environmental impacts as in fragile natural environments.

Visitor management techniques can be used to discourage one type of tourist whilst attracting another. As Snapshot 12.1 shows, big groups of day visitors bring many negative impacts to the destination, like overcrowding, but do not always bring many benefits – they tend to spend much less than overnight visitors. To discourage day visitors, destinations may put a range of visitor management techniques in place such as limiting access for coaches or marketing overnight packages.

SNAPSHOT 12.1

Visitor Management in Venice

A typical example of a destination that is faced with overcrowding is Venice. In 2016 it attracted 32 million visitors, in a city that covers just 3 square miles. For many years the government has tried to implement initiatives to reduce the negative impacts of mass-visitation on the built environment of the destination and also on the visitor experience. Mass tourism has also changed the actual fabric of the city: many residents have moved out of Venice because they feel the pressures of tourism are just too overwhelming. Overcrowding thus affects the city on three levels: first, it causes damage to the natural and built environment; second, it reduces the visitor experience and thus damages the appeal of the destination; and third, it threatens to turn Venice from a functioning city into an open-air museum. In November 2010, a resident organisation protested that the city had become a theme park: they handed out Disney-style maps and 'free tickets' to what they ironically called 'Veniceland' (Squires, 2010). Protests have intensified over the years as the permanent population of the city approaches a new low of 50,000 inhabitants, and the city is considering capping the number of tourists that will be allowed to enter the city each day (Condé Nast Traveler, 2017).

TO INFLUENCE TOURISTS' BEHAVIOUR

This refers to general damage that may occur to a destination or attraction due its everyday use by visitors. Visitors do not necessarily aim to do damage to the destination or attraction, but because of the sheer volume of them they can still have a negative impact. Garrod (2008: 168) gives as examples of wear and tear, trampling, handling, humidity, temperature and pilfering:

Trampling refers to when tourists walk on certain areas (usually in more fragile natural areas), damaging vegetation and preventing nature from naturally recuperating.

Handling in this context refers to tourists touching historic artefacts, buildings or plants, and thus causing damage to them.

Humidity and *temperature* can cause damage because visitors, just by being there and breathing, can change the temperature and humidity levels that support the conservation of an attraction or resource. This can have a profound impact on historical sites and artifacts. For example, the thousands of tourists who were breathing every day inside the tombs of the Egyptian kings caused damage to wall carvings and paint. The grave sites of the boy king Tutankhamun and of Queen Nefertari and Seti I had so much humidity that fungus was growing on the walls. In response, the Egyptian authorities closed the tombs to the public in 2014, replacing them with replicas one mile away (Neild, 2014).

Pilfering is used to describe tourists taking home elements of a historic or natural attraction as souvenirs. Usually this is done without malicious intent, but can cause damage to the destination or the attraction. An example is the Italian island of Sardinia, famous for its silky white beaches. One island in the Maddalena archipelago, has sand with a distinctive pink colour. Some tourists, keen to preserve a memory of their trip, take bags of sand, pebbles and shells from the beach. This may not seem like a big problem, but in the summer of 2015 alone, around five tonnes of sand was intercepted at Cagliari Airport. Campaigners have called for information panels to be installed at airports and ports in an attempt to educate tourists about the importance of leaving beaches, bays and coves as they find them (Squires, 2016).

Finally, visitor management techniques may be used to keep visitor groups with different behaviours separate in different areas. Zoning (as discussed in Chapter 12) may be a way to achieve this. One example of zoning policy is that of Leicester Square in London. This area, together with neighbouring Soho, is central to London's nightlife, with a wide variety of bars, clubs, restaurants and cinemas. In the late 1990s, Westminster Council attempted to create a 24-hour economy by creating a nightlife zone and granting licences to many large-scale drinking establishments. This policy created heavy pressures on the area as alcohol-fuelled violence and anti-social behaviour became common. More recently Westminster Council has changed its approach by attempting to turn the area into a more family-friendly entertainment zone. They are encouraging al fresco dining on the square and have insisted at least one family movie is shown every evening. The council has also become more cautious when granting licences to nightclubs and bars (Carmona et al., 2008).

TO REDUCE TRAFFIC-RELATED PROBLEMS

Natural environments or historic sites may not be equipped for the traffic that is generated by tourism. There may be a lack of suitable parking spaces, or the roads may not be suited to heavy usage (e.g. by coaches). Exhaust fumes from motor vehicles can also cause damage and pollution. It is not only the destination or attraction that is at risk: traffic-related problems may also lead to an increased risk of accidents for visitors and staff.

Historic cities often struggle to provide sufficient car parking spaces and coach parking spaces for visitors. There is often a lack of suitable drop-off points for coaches as the streets are usually narrow, so these may need to park rather far away from the city centre. In some destinations, park and ride schemes are used to improve visitor flow, or local 'ambassadors' will provide a welcome to coach groups. The visitor management strategy for the Royal Borough of Windsor and Maidenhead ('Our Vision of 2012 and Beyond') mentions this as a particular weakness of the destination:

> Limited parking and congestion are significant concerns as this can have a negative impact on the visitor experience. The cost of parking varies significantly between different operators and transport links between hotels, town-centre and attractions are inadequate. This encourages visitors to use their cars (53 per cent arrive by car and 23 per cent by rail). Coaches can't get close enough to the castle and the coach drop-off point does not provide a good first impression of the destination. (Royal Borough of Windsor and Maidenhead, 2008: 65)

RESPECTING CARRYING CAPACITY

Visitor management can therefore be defined as the combination of measures that aim to reduce negative impacts such as the above. Alternatively, visitor management can be seen as aiming to establish and respect the *carrying capacity* of a destination or attraction.

Richardson and Fluker (2004) define carrying capacity as the level of tourist activity an area can sustain without lasting economic, social or environmental impacts, or without reducing the quality of the visitor experience. They distinguish between five different types of carrying capacity:

Physical: The maximum number of visitors that can be physically accommodated on site. For some attractions, this is fairly easy to establish: for example in a planetarium the carrying capacity per session is likely to be similar to the number of seats in the theatre, but for other attractions such as national parks, or for whole destinations, this number is often harder to establish precisely. The physical carrying capacity may often be higher than the four other types of carrying capacity that follow below.

Ecological: The number of visitors an attraction or destination can sustain before unacceptable or irreparable damage is done to its ecological resources.

Social: The number of visitors an attraction or destination can sustain before the tolerance of the host community is surpassed.

Psychological/perceptual: The number of visitors an attraction or destination can sustain before the visitor experience declines for the majority of visitors. This type of carrying capacity is most dependent on the tourist: what for one tourist may be an unacceptable number of people, could be for another a pleasant crowd. Nevertheless, one can state that the psychological carrying capacity of a destination or attraction is surpassed when the majority of visitors consider that the number of tourists is affecting their experience negatively.

Economic: The number of visitors an attraction or destination can sustain before other desirable economic activities are squeezed out. This type largely refers to the dependency of certain destinations on tourism, and the fact that it is usually better to rely on a diverse economy with different active sectors than to rely overly on one sector alone.

Of these different types of carrying capacity, the *physical* carrying capacity is usually the higher number. It is likely that many destinations can physically accommodate more people than are suitable on an ecological, social and psychological level. It is also interesting that the concept of *psychological* carrying capacity focuses not on the needs and characteristics of the destination, but on the needs of the visitors and the quality of their experience. The next section will focus further on the quality of the visitor experience and how it can be managed.

QUALITY MANAGEMENT

Williams and Buswell (2003: 19) describe quality management as working towards 'continuous improvement, never being satisfied with what the organisation is delivering, and striving to do "better" to meet customers' needs'. Visitor management is aimed at meeting not only the needs of the destination, but also those of the visitor: a good visitor management policy is able to combine and respect both interests. This section will discuss the concepts of product and service quality and introduce approaches to quality management.

PRODUCT QUALITY

Quality management for tourism is often discussed from the viewpoint of service quality: tourism is, after all, a service sector. This does not mean that product quality is an unimportant concept for tourism. The main tourism product is the destination: the difficulty here is that this product is not delivered by one provider, but by a whole range of stakeholders: hotels, restaurants, taxi-drivers, attractions and natural resources. Many of these destination components offer a tangible product that can be assessed on quality, as well as a service.

Product quality has two aspects: functionality and appearance. On a basic level, products can be seen as lacking in quality when they are not functional – when they do not do what customers expect them to do. A customer, for example, will expect a comfortable night's sleep, but if the bed in the hotel is uncomfortable, or the heating does not work, or the air-conditioning is too loud, then this expectation will not be fulfilled. Customers may also expect a product to be free from blemishes and cosmetic defects. In terms of tourism, this could refer to a tourist expecting a meal that looks appetising, or a beach that is not littered. When their expectations are not met, this is called a 'quality defect' (Twigg-Flessner, 2003). These concepts are usually applied to manufactured products such as cars or washing machines, but can, to a certain extent, also be applied to tourism.

SERVICE QUALITY

If destinations aim to provide tourists with quality and enjoyable experiences, particular attention should be paid to the quality of the service provision. A great meal can easily be spoilt by a rude or unhelpful waiter, and the most beautiful hotel will not be enjoyed much if the staff are unpleasant. Understanding that service quality can be key in customer satisfaction, many businesses now aim to monitor and enhance service quality. The basic principle therefore is often that 'customer perceptions should equal or exceed customer expectations for them to be satisfied with the service provided' (Williams and Buswell, 2003: 178). The extent to which expectations and service performance are similar or different will influence the extent to which customers are satisfied or dissatisfied (Wuest, 2001: 53).

The SERVQUAL model was developed in the 1980s and measures gaps in service delivery based on a number of criteria. The model was originally developed for the financial industries, but later adapted for tourism (Williams and Buswell, 2003). By comparing the expectations of the customer with the actual performance of the organisation at the time of the visit, customer satisfaction can be measured numerically, and areas where service is lacking in quality can be easily identified. Methods that can be used to measure service quality include, amongst others, questionnaires and focus groups.

MANAGING QUALITY

Different theories of and approaches to quality management have developed over time. The most recent approaches tend to focus on quality management as an integrated concept: quality management is not just the duty of the customer service staff or the quality manager, it can only be achieved by the organisation as a whole. This means that the entire organisation has to work together to meet (or surpass) the expectations of the customer. In most tourism organisations, this process is monitored and managed in house: the business sets their own targets and trains their own staff. It is not only in the private sector that quality management is an explicit goal: quality is an increasing priority for the public sector too, where it can be enforced through, for example, tendering processes (Williams and Buswell, 2003).

One of the main tools that can be used in the quality management process is education and training. If quality is seen as the duty and responsibility of the whole organisation and every staff member in it, then staff need to be trained and informed about the standards the organisation is striving to achieve. In many organisations this would happen internally. In-house systems are non-accredited: this means they are developed by the organisation itself and not monitored by external organisations.

Accredited systems, involving training and quality control, have third-party certification (Williams and Buswell, 2003). The quality management process needs to be documented in accordance with the chosen system, and if all the requirements are met this can lead to certification. Organisations may choose to participate in accredited systems because an external quality certification is an objective proof of quality, and this may carry more weight with customers than the internal systems do.

Ezeego1 (www.ezeego1.co.in), India's biggest online travel website, was the first travel portal to be certified using the international quality management standard ISO 9001. This standard 'gives the requirements for quality management systems, and is now firmly established as the globally implemented standard for providing assurance about the ability to satisfy quality requirements and to enhance customer satisfaction in supplier–customer relationships' (International Organization for Standardization, n.d.). The standard lays down the quality requirements a system should meet, but does not dictate how exactly these should be achieved: ISO standards are thus not 'tick the box' lists. The organisation is invited to audit its own quality management systems and may also seek audits from clients or external organisations. The different aspects of quality management for this certification are: customer focus, leadership, the involvement of people, a process approach, a system approach to management, continual improvement, a factual approach to decision making, and mutually beneficial supplier relationships (www.iso.org).

Businesses engage in quality management not only to safeguard the experience of the visitor, but also to maximise their profitability. High-quality products can demand higher prices whilst still maintaining customer satisfaction. Laws (2000: 74) points out that price and quality are closely related in customers' buying decisions, and that the price that is charged for a product affects their quality expectations. At a normal price, a high standard of service and amenities will please the client, but those same standards will only 'satisfy' clients paying premium rates. Customers enjoying normal or superior standards on a holiday for which they paid low prices will be pleased or delighted. In contrast, customers receiving normal levels of service in return for high prices will at best feel exploited, and if standards fall further, they are likely to experience (and express) anger. Low levels of service or amenities are likely to provide negative responses whatever the price paid for them.

VISITOR MANAGEMENT MEASURES AND TECHNIQUES

The previous sections have highlighted how visitor management strategies aim on the one hand to protect the resources (natural, historic and built environment) of an attraction or destination, and on the other hand to safeguard the quality of the visitor experience. In this section we will now concentrate on the practical tools and techniques that can be used to achieve successful visitor management. These can be categorised in different ways. Many authors make a distinction between hard and soft measures – both terms are explained below. Other authors also distinguish between visitor management techniques that impact the site (making physical changes to the site) and those that impact the visitor (changing behaviour).

HARD VERSUS SOFT MEASURES

Richardson and Fluker (2004: 303) give the following definitions of hard and soft visitor management techniques:

> *Hard measures*: Measures that can be enforced, that are firm and binding. Examples are physical restrictions on visiting attractions or destination areas, such as closing at certain times, the declaration of no-go zones, requirements for permits, selective parking, and the prohibition of vehicles in certain areas. There may also be financial restrictions such as entrance fees and pricing policies.

> *Soft measures*: Measures that cannot be enforced as easily and are not as binding – they are, by contrast, persuasive. They may offer incentives for taking some action or sometimes act as a deterrent without the need for actual prohibition. Examples are directional signage, codes of ethics, codes of practice and information sheets.

Soft measures are usually easier to introduce as there is no need for an enforcement mechanism. The idea is that by informing visitors about the impacts of their actions and suggesting low-impact behaviours, they will behave in ways that will cause fewer negative impacts to the attraction or destination. The advantage of soft measures is that they do not come across as being very draconian; the disadvantage may be that one has to rely on visitors' goodwill.

Hard measures, however, need enforcement mechanisms: for example if parking is prohibited in certain areas, this needs to be enforced by parking wardens. Dedicated staff have to be on hand to enforce no-go zones or charge the entrance fee. This makes hard measures more complicated to introduce, but in return the guidelines may be followed more closely.

SNAPSHOT 12.2

Yellowstone National Park

Attractions and destinations can choose to use just hard or just soft measures, or they can combine both. The Yellowstone National Park, for example, adopts a combined approach for the management of visitation in areas that are the habitat of grizzly bears and bison. The purpose of bear management areas is to reduce the human impact on bears in high-density grizzly bear habitats. Grizzly bears can become aggressive when they feel that they or their cubs are under threat, so careful management of both the bears and the humans in their habitat is needed to provide a safe environment. Although incidents are rare (there are more visitors hurt by bison than by bears in Yellowstone), a female grizzly bear attacked three tourists on a campsite in the park in 2011, fatally injuring one. In 2015, several tourists were attacked by bison when they came too close to the animals, or in multiple cases, when they turned their back on them to take a selfie (Miller, 2015). Eliminating human entry disturbance in specific areas prevents human/wildlife conflicts and provides areas where the animals can pursue natural behavioural patterns and other social activities free from human disturbance. Examples of hard measures include area closures and trail closures, and only allowing visitation in daylight hours or on established trails. Examples of soft measures include education and only allowing party sizes of four or more people, which will make more noise and are less likely to surprise bears and bison (National Park Service, n.d.).

VISITOR MANAGEMENT TECHNIQUES

There is a range of visitor management techniques that destinations and attractions can make use of. Often different techniques are combined to effectively address the problems caused by intense visitation. These techniques include: increasing capacity, making capacity more flexible, site hardening, restricting/forbidding access, demarketing, charging/pricing, quota systems and timed entry, queue management and education and interpretation.

Increasing Capacity

In some cases the negative impacts of intensive visitation can be limited by increasing the capacity of an attraction. It may be possible to add a new building to a site, or to build an extension. If, for example, the quality of the visitor experience is reduced due to long queues at the lavatories or the catering facilities, this can be avoided by providing more facilities or making the existing facilities better. This is, of course, not an option for all destination areas or attractions. It may not be suitable for historic buildings to add a modern-day extension, for example; nor is it possible to make a natural park or a lake bigger than it is.

An example of increasing capacity is the Cotai Strip in Macau, China. Macau is a popular gaming destination near Hong Kong, and is made up of three islands: Macau, Coloane and Taipa. To expand the capacity of the destination, the 2.2 square mile sea area between Taipa and Coloane was filled in with reclaimed land, creating the 'Cotai Strip'. The land was used to build luxury hotels and casinos, including The Venetian, Sands Cotai Central and Plaza Macau (Macao Government Tourist Office, n.d.).

In 2009, the Natural History Museum in London increased its capacity by opening the Darwin Centre in a landmark glass extension. The focal point of the extension is a giant cocoon structure, built to house 20 million specimens, encased in a glass box. In the cocoon, visitors can study live specimens such as tarantulas and metre-high plants. There is also a studio for events and a climate change wall (Darwin Centre, 2017). This extra facility has created more space for a popular museum that welcomed over 3,800,000 visitors in 2008/2009.

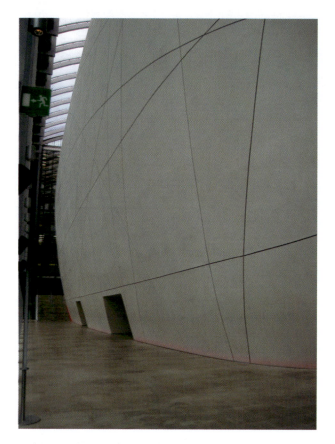

The Darwin Centre at the Natural History Museum in London

Source: Lynn Minnaert

Making Capacity More Flexible

Garrod (2008: 171) provides the following examples of making capacity more flexible so that the negative impacts of tourism can be reduced without negatively affecting the visitor experience:

Extending opening times: This reduces heavy visitor pressures by allowing visitation during a longer period of the day. For example the Louvre museum in Paris is open until 10pm on Wednesdays and Fridays.

Increasing staff levels: Staff, just like space, can be seen as a resource for an attraction or destination. Having more staff available can allow for increased interpretation or support, act as a deterrent against damaging behaviours by visitors, and enhance the visitor experience.

Opening more tills: If queues at tills need to be managed, these can be reduced most easily by constructing or opening extra tills. This may require increased staffing levels. In some cases, automatic ticketing machines where customers can pay via credit card may reduce queues at tills, without the need for extra staff.

Opening additional areas for facilities, such as cafés: At peak times of the year or day visitor pressures on facilities can be reduced by opening up a second area or space. This allows attractions to manage the space flexibly: if there are many visitors, there is extra space; if not, there is no need to staff this extra area. In many zoos, for example, some of the catering facilities are only open during the summer season.

Cross-training staff: By training staff to perform a range of different tasks, the attraction or destination allows for greater flexibility in dealing with overcrowded areas when this is needed.

Managing flows of visitors and offering different routes: If visitors take different routes through a museum, city or natural park, this can improve the general visitor flow and avoid everyone being in the same place at the same time. This can be achieved through maps or signage. The location of toilets, souvenir shops and meeting points at attractions is also an important element in the optimisation of visitor flows.

Site Hardening

Site hardening is often used to protect vulnerable natural environments, such a natural parks, from the negative impacts of tourism. Visitor managers may decide to protect the natural resources of the park by 'constructing a well-designed trail or recreation site, surfacing it with gravel, wood or pavement and adding fencing to keep visitors from trampling sensitive off-trail environments' (Cahill et al., 2008: 233). Trails are likely to have been positioned so as to protect sensitive habitats and vulnerable wildlife; the durable surfacing makes sure that visitors do not destroy vegetation by walking over it. Putting site hardening measures in place 'virtually severs the relationship between the amount of use and its associated resource degradation' (2008: 233). Other benefits are that trails provide a safe passage over inhospitable terrain and can accommodate a range of visitors who would otherwise be less likely or unable to visit the site (Woodland Stewardship, 2011).

Even though site hardening has these benefits, there are also a number of disadvantages attached to this technique. If large numbers of visitors use the trails, for example, they may start walking outside their edges when there is more use, and this can cause muddiness, widening and erosion. Site hardening may also affect the visitor experience: paths and trails may be seen as artificial, ugly or a barrier between the visitor and nature. And because tourists have to stick to set trails, they may feel they are limited in their freedom to explore the landscape (Cahill et al., 2008).

Restricting/Forbidding Access

The most drastic way to stop the negative impacts of tourism is to forbid access to a site, or part of it, altogether. Some commentators feel that tourism is by its nature opposed to conservation and that the needs of the resource are always more important than the needs of the visitor. This point of view reduces visitor management to one of its two functions: although it still protects the building, landscape or destination, the quality of the visitor experience is disregarded as visitation becomes impossible.

Tourism destinations and attractions are often very reluctant to close their doors to tourists altogether, and in practice this rarely happens – other means of achieving better visitor management are opted for. For some attractions, such as natural parks, forbidding access is also very difficult to achieve as these are too large to be cordoned off with fences or other barriers.

Italy's picturesque Cinque Terre, a group of five villages along the Ligurian Sea, is one of the country's most popular sites. In 2016, Italian officials introduced measures to protect the cliffside villages' delicate environments by capping the number of people who are allowed to visit. The maximum number of travelers permitted to visit is 1.5 million per year – a number that may seem high, but is well below the 2.5 million who visited in 2015. Those 1.5 million visitors will have to buy tickets ahead of time, and an app will show the most congested areas in real time (Marcus, 2016).

SNAPSHOT 12.3

The Lascaux II Show Caves

The Lascaux caves are a famous tourist attraction near Montignac in the Dordogne region of France. The caves were discovered in 1940 and contain primitive paintings of large animals from the Upper Palaeolithic era. They were opened in 1948, but by 1955 the paintings had been visibly damaged by the effects of intense visitation – the main cause of the damage was the carbon dioxide in the breath of the visitors. To protect the paintings the caves were closed in 1963 and a replica of two of the cave halls was built about 200 metres away. Lascaux II, as this replica cave was named, opened to the public in 1983. The replica was produced over 10 years, using the same materials and techniques as the original cave painters. Demand for tickets to Lascaux II is high and the number of tickets sold per day is limited to 2,000. Even with these measures in place, the pressures of visitation have started to affect the replica caves: since 2008 the site has been closed several times per year to remove the dust caused by 270,000 visitors annually that covers the walls and damages the paintings (*La Croix*, 2008).

Lascaux II Show Cave

Source: Jack Versloot

Demarketing

'Demarketing' is a term used to describe a form of marketing that reduces the demand of visitors to be more in line with supply by raising prices or reducing advertising. Other strategies that can be used are introducing the need for reservations when tourists want to visit a site, or making the press aware of the negative impacts of tourism on the resources of an attraction or site (Richardson and Fluker, 2004). Demarketing can be used to decrease the overall number of visitors, or can be used to discourage certain types of visitors. It is also an important tool for influencing the expectations and attitudes visitors will bring to a site *before* they visit (Beeton, 2006), thus influencing their behaviour during the visit. 'Demarketing' is also sometimes used to refer to a combination of different visitor management techniques in terms of pricing, entry controls, marketing and behavioural education (Beeton, 2006).

Although the concept of demarketing is sometimes referred to as a 'total halt' in marketing efforts, this rarely happens in practice. In most cases it is the shift from attracting as many visitors as possible via marketing, to attracting the right type of visitors via marketing: that is the key aim. In recent years, for example, Tunisia has repositioned itself as a destination rich in culture and history rather than just a beach destination. The Tunisian National Tourist Office's UK website includes categories about adventure travel, history, culture, and spa and golf tourism. The examples of the promotion campaign for Tunisia below focus on these exact elements, rather than just sun, sea and sand.

Tranquil Tunisia

Source: © Courtesy of the Tunisian National Tourist Office

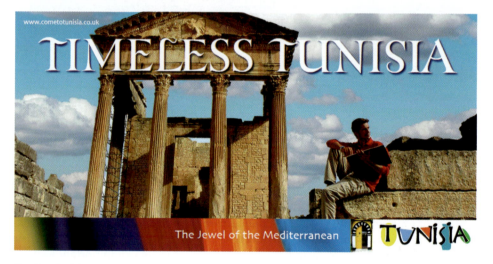

Timeless Tunisia

Source: © Courtesy of the Tunisian National Tourist Office

Charging/Pricing

The demand for a product or service can be directly influenced by pricing. Destinations and attractions that aim to improve visitor flows and reduce the negative impacts of overcrowding can charge fees or increase prices to reduce demand at certain times of the day, week or year. In this case, charging and pricing are used as mechanisms to steer demand away from peak periods, rather than to attract extra visitors in off-peak periods. Many tourism companies operate *seasonal pricing*, whereby prices go up during the peak season. This is apparent in the sector of inclusive holiday packages, where prices are often presented in tables by departure date. In the peak season few discounts are offered because there are enough customers who are willing to pay a premium fare. In the shoulder season the demand may be smaller, but there is an opportunity to stimulate demand via a variety of discounting practices (Laws, 2000: 69).

Pricing strategies may also be used more generally to influence demand: by lowering the price, demand for the tourism product can sometimes be increased; by increasing the price, the demand for the tourism product can sometimes be lowered. Some attractions will decide to apply high entrance fees to reduce overall visitor numbers and thereby reduce the negative impacts of excess visitation. In the case of Bhutan (see the case study below), this principle has even been applied to the destination as a whole.

This approach is not always popular as it is sometimes seen as conflicting with the aim of providing equal access to all layers in society. This means that the higher price will impact much more on visitors with low incomes than on visitors with high incomes who can afford the fee anyway, whereas one group of visitors usually does not cause a more negative impact on the resource than the other. High prices are also sometimes discouraged for economic reasons: the secondary spend (e.g. in a shop and café) may go down if entrance prices go up (Garrod, 2008).

One example of a pricing strategy that could reduce visitor numbers is Angkor Wat temples in Siem Reap, Cambodia. Over two million tourists visit the site each year, leading to concerns about damage to the temple. In response, ticket prices nearly doubled in 2017. From each ticket US$2 will be donated to a charitable foundation running children's hospitals in the region, and a stricter dress code will also be enforced (Marcus, 2017).

The case study of Bhutan (see below) is another example of a destination using pricing to manage visitor numbers.

CASE STUDY 12.1

Visitor Management in Bhutan

The Kingdom of Bhutan is a small, landlocked country in the Himalayas, between India and China. After being cut off from the rest of the world for centuries, it started to open up to outsiders in the 1970s, but is still fiercely guarding its ancient traditions (BBC News, 2017a). It has an exceptional visitor management strategy that relies heavily on hard measures and restrictions on visitor levels which go much further than those of most other destinations in the world.

The unusual nature of Bhutan's visitor management policy is linked to the history of tourism in the country. The tourism industry in Bhutan is still relatively young: the first tourists were allowed in 1974. At first, the tourism sector was fully controlled by the government, but is now increasingly run by operators in the private sector. In 2009, there were nearly 200 private tourism businesses (National Council of Bhutan, 2016).

Bhutan is ranked as one of the poorest countries in the world in terms of GDP and the national poverty rate is estimated at 12 per cent (UNDP, 2017). Instead of striving towards material richness, the Bhutanese monarchy has famously promoted the philosophy of

(Continued)

'gross national happiness' (GNH), which strives to achieve a balance between the spiritual and the material (Plett, 2011).

The country's main tourist attractions are its stunning natural beauty and its ancient Buddhist culture and architecture. Tourism is the main foreign investment sector and an important generator of foreign exchange revenue. However, instead of developing tourism at a rapid rate to maximise the economic benefits, Bhutan has adopted a restrictive, 'low volume, high value' approach to tourism. This is mainly due to the government's concern for the environment and cultural preservation (National Council of Bhutan, 2016). In 2014, just over 133,000 tourists visited the country. Even though visitor numbers are now growing, the rise is limited when it comes to overall visitor numbers. The average spend per visitor is high, as noted in Table 12.1.

TABLE 12.1   Tourist arrivals and revenue in Bhutan

	2012	2013	2014
Arrivals	105,407	116,224	133,480
International	54,685	54,798	68,081
Regional	50,722	63,426	65,399
Gross earnings (from international tourists)	US$62.80m	US$63.49m	US$73.20m
Government commission	US$16.63m	US$16.62m	US$20.20m

Source: Adapted from National Council of Bhutan (2016)

Tourism management is Bhutan is achieved via the following measures.

The country mainly regulates the influx of visitors via its pricing strategy. Bhutan can only be reached by its own national airline, Druk Air. Due to this monopoly, visitors have no choice but to use the rather expensive flights that are on offer. Another form of pricing strategy is the imposing of tourist tariffs on all visitors. Tourists must come to Bhutan on a package tour, organised by a Bhutanese tour operator (foreign companies may not operate in Bhutan itself). The whole itinerary is then organised by this tour operator. The government has set a full inclusive price of US$200 per visitor per day in the low season, and US$250 per visitor per day in the high season – of this price, 10 per cent goes to the foreign travel agent as a commission, 35 per cent goes to the government for education, healthcare and poverty alleviation initiatives, and the rest is paid to the local tour operator. The tariff increases if the visitor wants to travel in a very small group or individually (National Council of Bhutan, 2016).

The second restriction is an administrative restriction. Tourist visas are not available at the airport and need to be arranged before travel, and visa clearance must have been received before a flight ticket to the country can be booked. If the tourist wants to go trekking, a separate permit needs to be requested. This is to ensure that no one route is over-used or new ones are opened without prior approval (Tobgay, 2008).

In terms of demarketing, the country does not market itself on a big scale to attract foreign visitors; rather, targeted marketing is employed.

A number of soft measures are also in place to influence the behaviour of visitors during their trip. For example, visitors are requested not to give sweets to children and not to buy antiques. On national or religious holidays, tours are suspended. The presence of tour guides adds interpretation of these regulations for the tourists and increases understanding of why these guidelines are important. Selling tobacco in Bhutan is forbidden by law.

Visitor numbers in Bhutan and tourism infrastructure have risen in recent years but the rate of growth has been managed carefully because of the regulations mentioned above. The majority of visitors to Bhutan are over 60 years old, university educated, with a middle to high income, and very aware of sustainable tourism (National Council of Bhutan, 2016; Tobgay, 2008).

Reflective Questions

1. Think about the positive and negative social, environmental and economic impacts of tourism. Which ones are maximised and which ones are minimised in Bhutan? Consider the advantages and disadvantages of this protectionist visitor management system.

2. What is the typical visitor profile of tourists in Bhutan? Is this a desirable visitor profile? Why?

Quota Systems and Timed Entry

'Quota systems' refer to the setting of visitor quotas, either daily or over a shorter period of time, that cannot be surpassed. The number of visitors may be limited, or the maximum size of a group may be limited. For attractions, one way of managing a steady flow of visitors throughout the day without surpassing the set quota is by requiring visitors to pre-book a time for their visit. Immediate access is given if the capacity has not been reached, otherwise the entry may be delayed (Richardson and Fluker, 2004). This avoids the attraction being overcrowded at peak times of the day.

Timed tickets are common for popular attractions and also for exhibitions that may only be accessible for a short period of time. They may also be linked to a compulsory guided tour. An example of an attraction that uses this approach is the Courtyard of the Concubines, the harem section of the Topkapi palace in Istanbul. The palace dates from the fifteenth century and is one of the top attractions in the city. Although visitors can explore all the other parts of the palace freely, a visit to the harem needs to be booked in advance and is only possible as part of a guided tour. There is also an extra charge for visiting the harem. There are limited spaces available on this tour and visitors are recommended to book their place early (www.topkapisarayi.gov.tr).

Queue Management

Queues are often linked to tourism experiences: attractions, theme parks, airports and toll booths are examples of tourism settings where queuing often occurs. When this takes a long time or happens often, it can spoil the tourist's experience considerably. Badly managed queues can also become disorganised or disorderly. All this means that visitor managers should pay particular attention to queues when they plan their service provision.

Philip Pearce (1997) points out that it is mainly a lack of control over the situation, and a lack of information, that will cause people in queues to experience stress and negative feelings. Individuals in long queues will often not know how many people

Queues at the Taj Mahal, India

Source: Sandra Charrasse

are before them and how long the queue will take, and usually they cannot easily judge how long they have been in the queue already. They can also get bored because they are passive and not active.

Dawes and Rowley (1996) distinguish two goals in queue management: minimisation of the waiting on the one hand and optimisation of the waiting experience on the other hand. They give the example of Disneyworld as an attraction that has excellent queue management practices. Visitors there will regularly queue for long periods, sometimes even one to two hours for the most popular rides. Minimising the queues, for example by increasing the capacity with extra rides, is not something that can be done easily, so Disneyworld uses a range of techniques to make the waiting time at least *feel* shorter: they snake queues around barriers and corners and hide one section of the queue from another. They also install distractions for visitors to pass the time: there may be screens or displays to look at, or glimpses of the ride can be seen. Distractions can also be in the form of music, entertainment or the screams of people on the rides that can heighten the sense of anticipation. Finally, there are signs that announce how long visitors will have to wait – and usually the time queuing is less than the time advertised. This means that when visitors become aware of the time, it is usually in a positive manner: rather than having to wait one hour for example, they will actually access the ride in 40 minutes.

Some tourism companies have made the reduction of queues a separate product, an option for which the customer can decide to pay a surcharge. Budget airlines like easyJet and Ryanair, for example, offer 'priority boarding' or 'speedy boarding' passes. Passengers pay extra to board the aircraft first, and a guarantee that their cabin luggage will not be moved to the hold. A similar system is operated by several theme parks, where tickets can be bought at an extra cost that will allow visitors to skip the queues for certain rides. The more rides that are included in the ticket, the more expensive the surcharge becomes.

Education and Interpretation

The term 'interpretation' in the context of visitor management refers to the communication process that helps visitors understand the meaning of attractions, exhibits and heritage. Moscardo and Ballantyne (2008) give the examples of guided walks and tours, lectures and audio-visual presentations, signs, panels, guidebooks, pamphlets, brochures and information centres. Cooper (1997) also adds interpretive media such as self-guided trails and reconstructions of the past. A more recent example is applications for electronic devices such as mobile phones and virtual reality devices. An example is the 'Downtown Experience' in New York City, where tourists take tours in theatre-style coaches with side-facing seating and floor-to-ceiling glass windows. The tour is a multimedia 90-minute historical adventure, exploring Downtown Manhattan's most notable landmarks and neighborhoods. Virtual reality technology allows visitors to travel back in time and re-live iconic moments in history along the tour (The Ride, 2017).

Interpretation and education can also be provided by tour guides. Tours can be optional, or attractions can make them obligatory in certain areas or across the whole site. The British Guild of Tourist Guides is a membership organisation for tourist guides across the British Isles. All Blue Badge Tourist Guides have been trained and hold a specific qualification that informs them of the impacts of tourism and the importance of interpretation in the visitor management process.

The provision of interpretation can make the visitor experience more rewarding and increase sustainability as a soft measure; by informing visitors of the negative impacts of tourism, they can be encouraged to behave in a more sustainable fashion. However, simply providing information does not necessarily guarantee these improvements: 'The presence of on-site guardians does not guarantee the effectiveness of visitor management policies, any more than the presence of a guide guarantees that the visitor will receive adequate and appropriate information' (Shackley, 1998: 8).

THE ROLE OF TECHNOLOGY FOR VISITOR MANAGEMENT

Visitor managers can make use of technology in a variety of ways to determine the best strategy for their attraction or destination. As many of the visitor management techniques described above may result in increased staff costs for the organisation (e.g. if opening times are extended or extra facilities need to be provided), automation can help to make processes more effective and keep costs down. The following examples will illustrate how technology can help to count visitors, to monitor and restrict where they go, and to facilitate bookings both on and offline.

COUNTING SYSTEMS

Counting systems can support visitor management by providing an exact overview of the number of visitors that make use of a certain site during a certain time period.

The data that are gathered with counting systems can be helpful in establishing a realistic and sustainable visitor quota and give an idea of the carrying capacity of the facility. By counting how many visitors there are at certain locations at various times of the day, managers can also determine visitor flows and use the data to see where extra staff may be needed. Counting systems come in a variety of forms, from rather basic to the more sophisticated. Visitors can, for example, be counted by having to pass through turnstiles. More sophisticated systems include sensors on walls or near doors, or under carpets. These sensors usually blend in with the surroundings and tend to go unnoticed by visitors, which means they do not affect the visitor experience.

SNAPSHOT 12.4

Mechanical Versus Video Turnstiles

An example of an attraction that successfully uses a mechanical counting system for visitor management is the Sauvabelin Tower in Lausanne, Switzerland. This tower is made completely out of locally sourced wood and offers a panoramic view of the city (www.tour-de-sauvabelin-lausanne.ch). The viewing platform is reached via 302 steps and measures 12 metres in diameter – this attraction can therefore only be used safely by a limited number of visitors, as otherwise congestion would occur on the steps which could make the ascent

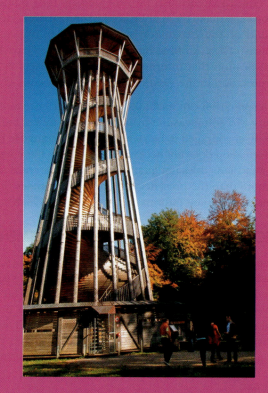

Sauvabelin Tower, Lausanne

Source: © Courtesy of Lausanne Tourisme

or descent dangerous. To avoid accidents or spoiling of the experience, a metal turnstile at the entrance lets through 50 visitors at any one time. If more visitors try to enter, the turnstile will lock; only when one visitor leaves the attraction can another gain access. A mechanical turnstile like this one is highly suitable for the Sauvabelin Tower as this is an unstaffed, free attraction. Staffed attractions can use more advanced counting methods such as video turnstiles, whereby CCTV cameras above entrance doors to attractions, shops and nightclubs are linked to intelligent people-counting systems. In this case there are no physical barriers, but the system counts how many people enter and leave and calculates queues and waiting times. These data can then be used by staff to monitor visitors efficiently.

CAMERAS

CCTV cameras can be used to track where overcrowding usually occurs and where bottlenecks appear. The images need to be monitored and can be used to regulate when extra staff are needed in certain areas or when additional facilities need to be opened. Cameras can also be used as a security measure: they can deter visitors from behaving in an inappropriate manner (e.g. littering, causing damage or pilfering).

CCTV: Closed Circuit Television; this means that the images are not broadcast publicly

One of Scotland's leading tourist attractions, the Falkirk Wheel, has used CCTV cameras to reduce queuing and improve the customer experience. The Falkirk Wheel is the world's only rotating boat lift that provides a connection between two canals. The wheel can carry up to eight boats at a time and visitors can see the structure in action on board one of the specially fitted tourist boats (www.thefalkirkwheel.co.uk). The attraction uses CCTV as a security measure in the retail area, and after opening hours, but also uses the images to supervise boat traffic and manage visitor flows. When bottlenecks form, this allows for a rapid response and a redeployment of staff (*Hi-Tech Security Solutions*, 2004).

VISITOR BADGES

For some forms of tourism, visitor badges may be a useful visitor management tool. In trade shows and exhibitions, for example, badges are commonly used to determine which groups of visitors will have access to certain areas: only important buyers may, for example, have entry to a VIP room, while other areas may be staff-only. Badges may be read through barcodes or **RFID** tags: these are microchips that can trace the movements of an object or person. This technology is mostly used at events, where the information on the badges is often read via portable scanners.

RFID: Radio Frequency Identification

ONLINE RESERVATION SYSTEMS

Another important technological tool is the implementation of advance booking systems. Technology is used to manage reservations in attractions, and increasingly reservations can be made online by the tourists themselves. They may even be able to print off a ticket at home, or collect their tickets at self-service ticket machines. The use of this online technology has a double benefit: on the one hand it avoids overcrowding visitors at peak time and allows a better visitor flow; on the other hand it reduces the queues at entrances or tills because a number of visitors will have printed off their tickets themselves, either on-site or at home.

Madame Tussauds in London is an attraction that encourages visitors to book their tickets online as it avoids long queues and reduces the pressures on staff. When visitors book tickets online in advance, they receive a 10 per cent discount. They are then allocated a half-an-hour time slot and can enter the attraction via a dedicated entrance, so that they do not have to queue needlessly. For the attraction this means that visitors are staggered more evenly during the day (www.madametussauds.com).

SUMMARY

This chapter has discussed visitor management as finding a balance between the needs of the tourism resource and the needs of the visitor. For a tourism resource to achieve sustainable success, it is imperative that the quality of the visitor experience is maintained without putting excessive pressures on the resource, or surpassing its carrying capacity. Visitor managers have a range of tools, techniques and technologies at their disposal, both at the level of the site and at the level of the visitor, which can be used to make sure both needs are met successfully. Success in visitor management refers to minimising the negative environmental, social and economic impacts of tourism, whilst maximising the positive impacts.

SELF-TEST QUESTIONS

1. In destinations like Venice, the large number of day trippers results in high pressures on the natural and built environment, whilst the economic benefits they bring to the destination are often rather small. What can Venice do to manage tourism better while safeguarding the visitor experience?

2. The Abu Dhabi Tourism & Culture Authority achieved the ISO 9001 standard of quality management in 2010. What could be the benefits of having this certification? Are certifications a worthwhile investment for tourism companies?

3. Think of a destination or attraction you have visited, where you feel that you as a visitor or the destination or attraction itself was negatively affected by tourism pressures. What could this destination/attraction do to improve visitor management? What would be the challenges of implementing these ideas?

FURTHER READING

Garrod, B. (2008) 'Managing visitor impacts', in A. Fyall, B. Garrod, A. Leask and S. Wanhill (eds), *Managing Visitor Attractions: New Directions*. Oxford: Butterworth-Heinemann.

Richardson, J. and Fluker, M. (2004) *Understanding and Managing Tourism*. Frenchs Forest: Pearson Education Australia.

Williams, C. and Buswell, J. (2003) *Service Quality in Leisure and Tourism*. Wallingford: CABI.

USEFUL WEBSITES

International Organization for Standardization: www.iso.org

13

PUBLIC SECTOR INVOLVEMENT IN TOURISM

'Everyone has the right to freedom of movement and residence within the borders of each State.

Everyone has the right to leave any country, including his own, and to return to his country.'

Article 13, Universal Declaration of Human Rights

LEARNING OUTCOMES

After reading this chapter you will understand:

- how the public sector can be involved in tourism
- the differences between, and characteristics of, different levels of government involvement in tourism – from international to local
- the role of the public sector in managing, controlling, improving, promoting and branding destinations
- how the public sector can play a role in crisis planning and management in the face of different types of crises that can affect the tourist industry.

Accessible zone at street festival in Montreal, Canada

Source: Lynn Minnaert

INTRODUCTION

Throughout this book, the complex structure of tourism has been emphasised – its fragmentation between generating and destination regions, its range of diverse suppliers and stakeholders, and its potential positive or negative economic, environmental and socio-cultural impacts within destinations. This complexity has created a role for public sector involvement in tourism at international, national, regional and local levels.

The public sector undertakes a broad range of roles in tourism and the extent of their involvement varies between countries. In this chapter we consider the tourism roles of the public sector, the activities of public sector agencies, and how public sector involvement differs at various geographical levels. The discussion of public sector involvement at the local level has been written by Dr Nancy Stevenson, a specialist in the field. We end the chapter by discussing the role of the public sector in managing tourism throughout a crisis.

PUBLIC SECTOR INVOLVEMENT IN TOURISM

In Chapter 5 we explained that the term 'public sector' refers to central and local government and their administrative departments – organisations that are funded by taxation and corporations that are owned by the state.

Elliott (1997) notes that central governments are highly important to the tourism sector: without them, international tourism would not be possible. They have the power to provide the political stability, security and the legal and financial framework that tourism requires and they provide essential services (e.g. issuing passports) and basic infrastructure (e.g. roads and public transport facilities). Moreover, national governments negotiate and make agreements with other governments about issues such as visas, entry requirements and international transit routes. National governments are indeed often highly visible stakeholders in tourism. There is, however, a range of other stakeholders in the public sector that may play a role in the provision and management of tourism. This section will look in more detail at the roles the public sector might play at an international and national level.

TYPES OF GOVERNMENT INVOLVEMENT IN TOURISM

Governments can be involved in tourism in a variety of ways. There are significant differences between countries with regard to how governmental involvement is shaped, which public institution looks after tourism, where the centre of power is situated (locally, regionally, nationally) and the aspirations and goals countries set for their tourism industry. In some settings these tasks are performed by the (central, regional, local) government itself, whereas in other settings there may be a public agency that operates at arm's length from the government but receives financial support from taxation and is responsible to the government for its performance.

In practice this means that the public authority for tourism can lie with a range of different institutions. Tourism may be a part of the responsibilities of the national (or central) government. In this case, tourism can be part of a range of departments, for example in:

- the UK, it is part of the Department of Digital, Culture, Media and Sport
- Germany, it is part of the Department of Economy and Technology
- France, it is part of the Department of Economy, Finance and Industry
- Austria, it is part of the Department of Economy, Family and Youth
- Romania, there is a dedicated Ministry of Tourism.

In some countries, there is no part of the central government that looks after tourism – tourism may be the responsibility of regional authorities. In Belgium, for example, the Flemish and Wallonian regional governments can make autonomous tourism decisions. In many countries, however, regional governments cooperate with the national government in the area of tourism by adapting policies that were designed on a national level to their specific region. The same can apply for local governments, who in their turn may implement plans that were formed at a regional level.

Apart from these different levels of government, there are also organisations active in tourism that operate at arm's length from the government but receive financial support from taxation and are responsible to the government for their performance. National Tourist Organisations are an example of this type of institution. They are usually responsible for the practical implementation of the policy objectives that were set by governments through building partnerships or providing business support, for supporting policy making through research, and/or tourism marketing. Similar organisations may exist on the regional and local level – in the UK examples include VisitBritain, VisitEngland and London & Partners.

Hall (2008) identifies seven broad functions of the public sector: coordination, planning, legislation and regulations, entrepreneurship, promotion, social tourism and protector of the public interest. We will now consider each of these.

Coordination

The tourism sector can be seen as a complex web of different stakeholders, each of which will have their own roles and objectives. It is often the role of the public sector to bring these stakeholders together and try to develop a shared set of goals. These goals can take different forms: the public sector can, for example, be the main driver behind a new tourism brand for a destination, invest in new infrastructure, or work with private partners to develop a new tourism product. Coordination is also important when trying to reduce the negative impacts of tourism as much as possible: the government may put laws and regulations in place to support sustainable tourism development, or might consult and represent the local community when they feel tourism has negative social or cultural impacts.

An example of a coordinating activity is local government involvement in a convention bureau. A convention bureau is a not-for-profit organisation that promotes and supports MICE or business tourism development in a destination. Many convention bureaux are partnerships between the public and the private sector: the local, regional or national government usually works together with hotels, attractions, meeting venues and other companies to bring business to the destination in the form of conferences, meetings and exhibitions. A convention bureau may take the form of a membership organisation, whereby a range of businesses will pay a membership fee to support its activities. In return, these businesses will be promoted by the convention bureau. For example, the Perth Convention Bureau markets Western Australia nationally and internationally as a destination for business tourism. The organisation is coordinated by Tourism Western Australia and the City of Perth as public sector partners, but it also has hundreds of industry partners.

Planning

The public sector is involved in the planning process of tourism when they decide which areas of tourism will be developed in the future, how expansions will be achieved, which steps need to be taken to achieve these, and how success will be measured. The result of this planning activity is usually combined in tourism plans, policies or strategies. These are discussed in more detail later in this chapter. Tourism plans can focus on a range of different goals, for example increasing the volume of tourist arrivals or attracting more high-spending tourists, managing tourists more effectively, or dispersing tourists to a new part of the destination.

There are many different forms of tourism plans, but usually they are formulated to be executed over a number of years, normally between 5 and 10. Some plans are formulated over even longer periods of time: the Kuala Lumpur (Malaysia) tourism plan, for example, is formulated to run for 20 years, from 2000 until 2020. Key objectives of the plan are to make Kuala Lumpur more attractive as a tourism destination and to increase the average length of stay. The city wants to create a distinctive identity to achieve this, based on the promotion of culture and sports, and by creating a tropical garden city and opportunities for eco-tourism (www.dbkl.gov.my/).

On a local level, planning may include decisions on planning permission to construct new hotels or attractions.

Legislation and Regulations

The public sector has legislative and regulative powers which can influence tourism directly or indirectly. Visa policies, for example, enable or restrict access for foreign visitors to the destination. There are also health and safety regulations, environmental regulations and fiscal laws that affect not only the tourism industries, but also many other industries. These laws and regulations have usually not been set with the tourism sector specifically in mind, but still affect tourism indirectly.

An example of a law or regulation that affects tourism indirectly is the Equality Act that was introduced in the UK in 2010. The Act aims to prevent the discrimination disabled people may face in many areas of life. It gives individuals with disabilities rights in the areas of education, employment, and access to goods and services, to name but a few. The access to services includes tourist services such as holiday accommodation, tourist attractions, restaurants and transport providers. The Act states that people with disabilities should receive the same level of service as other service users, even if this means the service provider needs to make certain changes especially for them. Examples of these changes can be providing a low desk for wheelchair users, or having at least one copy of a menu available in Braille, or providing adapted rooms in tourist accommodation.

CASE STUDY 13.1

Government Responses to Airbnb and Short-term Rentals in the USA

Home-sharing and short rental platforms have deeply affected the lodging industry, as well as several communities, in recent years. In response, some governments have introduced regulations and legislation that poses restrictions on rental hosts. The most well-known platform is Airbnb, established in 2008 in San Francisco, California. The home-sharing 'sharing economy' concept of Airbnb has provided personalised and varied cultural experiences for tourists. Since its launch, the company reports that it has a presence in over 65,000 cities, with more than 191 countries and an estimated total of 150 million guests (Airbnb, 2017). A key factor that contributes to the company's success and growth is that it allows guests to 'live like a local' and explore neighbourhoods that do not typically cater to tourists; they achieve this by providing accommodations in a wide variety of locales and by connecting visitors with local residents (Kaplan, 2015: 103).

Home-sharing and short-term rentals can impact local communities positively, as it can provide local residents and businesses with additional income. However, concerns have also been raised about the rapid rise of home sharing. The hotel industry has raised objections, because short-term rental hosts are not subjected to the same tax and safety regulations as the traditional lodging industry. Short-term rentals can also cause neighbourhood problems: the influx of tourists to otherwise residential areas can create an increase in several issues such as noise, traffic and parking problems (Gurran

(Continued)

and Phibbs, 2017: 83). Moreover, areas with a high concentration of short-term rentals may experience a decrease in the permanent rental supply in the area. The decrease in the rental stock can, in turn, force permanent rental rates to skyrocket in the surrounding areas. In the city of Sydney it was found that a total of 1,268 properties, equivalent to 144 per cent of the city's vacant rental stock, are available for holiday rental via Airbnb, which can substantially affect rental availability and costs for locals (Gurran and Phibbs, 2017: 88). In the case of Los Angeles, Lee suggests that Airbnb 'harms neighbourhoods, distorts the housing market, undermines labor unions, and exacerbates Los Angeles's affordable housing crisis' (2016: 1). While tourists and renters are two very different groups of the population with different motives, 64 per cent of the listings on short-term rental platforms like Airbnb are for tourists, and put renters directly in competition with these tourists, thereby distorting the housing market (Lee, 2016: 6).

Because of issues like these, several local governments have started implementing new regulations to cover Airbnb and similar companies in recent years:

Safety: There are many safety concerns related to home rentals. Airbnb rentals are not subjected to the same fire and safety standards as hotel rooms are. Airbnb guests are less familiar with the building they find themselves in, and may therefore be unaware where fire extinguishers and fire exits are located. Many sharing economy units also lack sufficient security mechanisms to regulate guests entering and exiting the buildings, as the units and buildings are designed for permanent tenants only. The Chief of Fire Prevention from the New York City Fire Department, for example, has required that transient occupants' residences have stricter fire protection requirements (design, construction and operation). In November 2014, Nashville, Tennessee implemented stricter regulations for short-term rental hosts, including the requirement to obtain an annual permit and liability insurance coverage (Interian, 2016: 150). Airbnb informs its hosts that they should be aware of and in adherence with the local regulation: 'hosts should understand how the laws work in their respective cities. Some cities have laws that restrict their ability to host paying guests for short periods ... In many cities, hosts must register, get a permit, or obtain a license before listing a property or accepting guests' (Airbnb, n.d. b).

Zoning: Many cities have zoning laws that designate the permitted areas for short-term rental buildings. Airbnb hosts can be fined for violating these zoning laws. For example, the New York State Multiple Dwelling Law (MDL) has been established to maintain building safety, fire protection and other standards. In October 2016, Governor Andrew Cuomo of New York signed a bill to impose significant fines on Airbnb hosts that advertise short-term rentals violating the MDL laws. Fines for violations range from US$1,000 for the first violation, to US$5,000 for the second, to US$7,500 for three or more violations (New York State Multiple Dwelling Law, n.d.). There are similar regulations in other cities, including Santa Monica and Miami. It is likely that other cities may follow this action to limit illegal short-term rentals by enacting similar legislation targeting hosts instead of the platform.

Taxation: Originally, sharing economy platforms and their hosts were not subject to paying taxes similar to hotel occupancy taxes because they were considered to be a company privately contracting accommodations between hosts and guests; for example, Airbnb 'is neither a hotel operator nor a room remarketer'

(Kaplan, 2015: 109). However, Portland (Oregon) amended its transient lodgings tax in August 2014 by including short-term rental housings into the definition of hotels. Chicago and Washington, DC have collected hotel taxes from Airbnb since February 2015 (Interian, 2016: 147–48).

Reflective Questions

1. In your opinion, should Airbnb and similar services be regulated more heavily? If so, which type of regulation would you support (safety regulations, zoning regulations, taxation)?

2. If you support taxation of home sharing services, which party or parties do you believe should be taxed? The hosts, the guests and/or the platform itself?

Entrepreneurship

The public sector may also own and operate tourism ventures. For example, museums, art galleries and parks may be operated by a public body, but be part of the tourist attractions within a destination. The Louvre in Paris, the Van Gogh museum in Amsterdam, and the Prado museum in Madrid are all examples of publicly owned attractions. Some of the hotel provision may be state-owned: this is the case, for

The Louvre, Paris

Source: Sandra Charrasse

example, in China (NUO Hotels), Spain (Paradores) and Portugal (Pousadas). The public sector may also own parts of the transport infrastructure such as the bus network, rail network or airline. State ownership of transport has reduced as a result of the spread of deregulation (see Chapter 5) since the late 1970s, but some airlines are still wholly state owned (Qatar Airways) or partially state owned (Singapore Airlines).

Stimulation/Promotion

The public sector stimulates tourism development in a variety of ways:

Tax concessions: Governments may decide to reduce taxes to encourage certain behaviours or actions, e.g. when the taxes on buying a property are reduced, this may encourage people who rent to buy their own house

- By providing financial incentives to the private sector such as **tax concessions** or low-interest loans. For example, the government of Argentina offered no-interest loans to tourist businesses to help boost domestic tourism in 2008 in response to the global economic crisis.

- By sponsoring research activities and the compilation of relevant statistics. Commissioning market research is often one of the responsibilities of the public sector.

- The public sector may also want to play a role in tourism through promoting and branding (see further in this chapter).

Social Tourism

Social tourism: Social tourism refers to tourism initiatives with a strong moral or ethical dimension: their primary aim is to include groups in tourism who would otherwise be excluded from it

Social tourism refers to initiatives that involve groups in tourism who would otherwise be excluded because of health or financial reasons. Individuals with a disability or illness, for example, may find it difficult to participate in tourism, and individuals on a low income may not have enough discretionary income to pay for a holiday. Many governments in mainland Europe operate schemes that specifically aim to engage these groups in domestic travel. The motive for this may be to support the local economy of a destination, or the belief that participation in tourism is a right that should not be denied to anyone on the basis of income because of the role tourism can play in personal development.

This role of tourism has been highlighted by the European Economic and Social Committee, who linked social tourism to increased citizenship, well-being, the development of beneficiary and host communities, and improved health and employment (Minnaert et al., 2009).

Public social tourism schemes can take a variety of forms. In several countries of mainland Europe, such as France and Hungary, a holiday voucher scheme is in place that can be used by employers as an incentive for their employees. This tends to take the form of a tax-free savings scheme whereby the employee sets aside a small part of his or her wage, which is then supplemented by the employer and paid out in vouchers. The vouchers are accepted in a range of domestic tourism businesses. Whilst the scheme enables people on a low income to travel, it also supports the domestic tourism industry. A disadvantage of the scheme, however, is that people who are unemployed, and often financially unable to travel, cannot access the vouchers since they are not in employment. Other social tourism initiatives can take the form of cooperations between the public and private (and in some cases also social) sectors. The scheme below is an example of this.

SNAPSHOT 13.1

Tourism in Flanders, Belgium

Flanders is the northern, Dutch-speaking region of Belgium. The central organisation in social tourism provision in Flanders is the Holiday Participation Centre, a publicly funded team within Tourism Flanders, the regional Tourist Board. The Centre liaises between the public, private and social sectors. The private tourism sector plays an important role: accommodation providers and private attractions offer voluntary discounts and reduced tariffs for low-income groups. The Holiday Participation Centre communicates these reduced tariffs to the social sector and the holiday makers via their website and yearly brochures. The system is designed as a win–win situation for all the parties involved: the private sector gains access to a new target group and free marketing and can use the initiative as part of their corporate social responsibility policy; the social sector gains access to low-cost holiday opportunities; and the public sector can employ a social intervention method, reaching thousands of low-income and socially excluded citizens, at minimal cost. In 2016, over 110,000 people, most of whom would otherwise have not been able to enjoy a break away or day trip, used the offer of the Holiday Participation Centre to participate in travel (Tourism Flanders, 2017).

Tourism in Flanders

Source: © Courtesy of Ans Brys

Protecting the Public Interest

The public sector has a role in safeguarding the public interest: protecting the public from activity that would be harmful to them. This may mean turning down offers from powerful investors if these are shown to be environmentally or socially unsustainable.

The public sector would also be expected to protect the long-term interest of the community, rather than choosing to support initiatives that would bring only short-term gains. In respect of tourism it is often seen as the task of the government to strive to reduce the negative impacts of tourism on the local community and environment.

In Belfast, Northern Ireland, tourism developments are not granted permission by the local government if the proposed development could be detrimental to:

- the environmental quality of the area or the views
- the character of the area's built heritage or proven archaeological importance
- nature conservation interests or the coast
- road traffic volumes or would cause congestion on the road network.

(www.planningni.gov.uk)

Negative social and environmental impacts are here thus avoided by prohibiting detrimental changes to the built environment. This topic is also discussed in Chapter 9.

TOURISM POLICY

At the centre of government activity in tourism is tourism policy. Hall and Jenkins (1995; Hall and Page, 2002: 138) highlight that a range of definitions of policy exist, and propose that tourism policy is simply whatever governments decide to do or not to do with regard to tourism. Policies may be introduced when the destination is faced with a specific problem or challenge (e.g. in the case of a crisis, see below) or may be part of a more continuous planning process. A range of stakeholders may be involved in policy making, of which the government will be just one. Several groups of people who feel they will be affected by policy decisions may try to influence policy or put pressure on policy makers. Examples of these groups are the tourism businesses, the host community and their leaders in a destination, and pressure groups such as environmental charities and investors.

Tourism policy can be formulated on different levels. Local tourism policies are usually the most specific as they deal with only one destination in great detail. (The involvement of local governments in tourism will be discussed more fully later in this chapter.) Regional and national policies are often more general and may set guidelines for local policy makers. They have to take into account the differences between destinations and set an overall direction for coherent action. The national tourism policy for Germany, for example, has to set principles and guidelines that can apply to nature tourism in mountainous areas in the South, urban and cultural tourism in cities like Berlin and Hamburg, business tourism in cities like Hanover and Frankfurt, and sports tourism in Garmisch-Partenkirchen. Because national tourism products are often diverse and complex, national tourism policies tend to have more generalised objectives than local policies. International tourism policies are rare, for the same reason: if coordinating policy objectives for one country is challenging, than this is even more the case for different countries and regions.

One example of an attempt to internationalise tourism policy is the proposed EU tourism policy. This policy was formulated in 2010 and aims to provide growth for European tourism and the creation of more and better jobs. Sustainability, quality management and competitiveness are other objectives. This will be achieved via stronger regulation and policy coordination between different countries. The policy provides general ideas for national governments to adopt in their tourism policies, but is not prescriptive: the EU does not have the power to enforce this on the member states, but instead aims to influence and steer them. The following section will focus more specifically on international government involvement in tourism.

PUBLIC SECTOR INVOLVEMENT ON AN INTERNATIONAL SCALE

As tourism is a globalised industry, there is a role for public sector involvement in tourism on an international level. Tourism is affected by the following types of organisations, which represent national and regional governments: international trade organisations, international tourism organisations, international conservation organisations and international political organisations.

International Trade Organisations

International trade organisations regulate trade relationships between different countries. These organisations are neither specialised in nor focused on tourism: they treat tourism simply as one of the services that may be traded between countries.

The World Trade Organisation (WTO: not to be confused with UNWTO – see below) is the only global organisation dealing with the rules of trade between nations. It allows governments of different countries to come together and discuss trade problems, maintain or remove trade barriers, and generally regulate how the countries will trade together. Most of these rules are set out in agreements or 'commitments': these are signed between countries that open their markets to each other and regulate how open those markets will be, and what the restrictions for trade must cover. For example, it is common for a nation to allow the consumption of goods or services by foreign nationals (e.g. through tourism) more freely than the supply of these services (e.g. by opening a tourism business in another country). Tourism and travel services are one of the service areas the WTO covers. In this area, commitments have been made between 125 WTO members, which is more than any other services sector. This means that there is a high level of liberalisation in tourism in general (www.wto.org).

The Organisation for Economic Co-operation and Development (OECD) is a trade organisation that represents 35 (mainly European) countries. It provides a setting where governments can compare policy experiences, seek answers to common problems, identify good practice and coordinate domestic and international policies. The OECD gathers economic and social data and uses these to monitor and forecast trends. In terms of tourism, the OECD provides a policy forum to support the sustainable economic growth of tourism (www.oecd.org).

International Tourism Organisations

International tourism organisations, as opposed to international trade organisations, focus fully on international cooperation for tourism. The most important international tourism organisation is the United Nations World Tourism Organization (UNWTO).

This is a specialised agency of the United Nations and the leading international organisation in the field of tourism. It provides training, research and policy advice, and promotes responsible and sustainable tourism. It has a membership of 163 countries and territories and there are also 500 affiliate members who represent the private sector, educational bodies, tourism associations and local tourism authorities. In its statutes, the organisation states its aim as 'the promotion and development of tourism with a view to contributing to economic development, international understanding, peace, prosperity and universal respect for, and observance of, human rights and fundamental freedoms for all without distinction as to race, sex, language or religion' (UNWTO, 2008a).

As an agency it represents the industry in the face of global challenges, for example climate change, health scares (such as Zika), the economic downturn and poverty alleviation. It also makes recommendations to governments regarding these topics to support and develop the tourism industry, with a special focus on supporting tourism in developing countries.

International Conservation Organisations

International conservation organisations have links with tourism via the role of heritage attractions as tourism products. In contrast to international trade or international tourism organisations, they firmly place conservation above economic development. Although international conservation organisations can play an instrumental role in tourism development, it is important not to see their goals as purely tourism-related.

The UNESCO World Heritage Centre (WHC) oversees the implementation of the World Heritage Convention: an agreement made in 1972 setting out the criteria which need to be fulfilled by natural and cultural attractions on the World Heritage list. Countries that have signed the convention can nominate a site for the World Heritage List. The World Heritage Committee then makes the final decision on the application. The sites chosen can apply for funding from the World Heritage Fund. This fund is made up from compulsory contributions from member countries, voluntary contributions and sales of documentation. The money can be used for the provision of experts or the supply of equipment or training. Often the funding is awarded as a low-interest loan. Although the WHC is not a tourism organisation, its activities can have a profound impact on tourism. World Heritage status can increase visitor interest in a destination, or can bring with it a stricter regulation of tourism activity. The WHC provides a tourism management manual for world heritage sites (Pederson, 2002) and aims to help governments support tourism at these sites with appropriate policies and management tools.

International Political Organisations

International political organisations bring together political representatives from different countries and regions and provide a forum for discussing issues that have effects that cross national boundaries. Tourism is usually only one of these, as are issues of environment, trade, customs, justice and defence.

Within the European Commission, tourism falls under the Directorate General Enterprise and Industry. The tourism unit focuses on researching tourism in a pan-European context and the development of competitive and sustainable destinations. The development of high-quality tourism that is accessible to groups who may otherwise find it hard to participate in tourism is also a priority; for instance for individuals with disabilities or those on a low income.

By being a member of the EU, countries can boost their tourism revenues. Not only does accession to the EU enhance a country's image and visibility, it can also reduce trade costs because it now operates in a single market. Being part of the EU can also mean that standards of tourism improve as the country has to conform with European legislation. This may be costly, but EU members can in return apply for EU funding. This funding is usually not specifically tourism-related, but can be applied to tourism projects. European Regional Development Funds (ERDF), for example, support projects that improve the competitiveness and employment levels of a region, through such programmes as knowledge exchange or support for SMEs. The European Maritime and Fisheries Fund (EMFF), the European Social Fund and the European Agricultural Fund for Rural Development (EAFRD) can also be used for tourism projects, although once again none of these are specifically focused on the tourism industry (European Commission, 2015b).

The Organization of American States (OAS) brings together the 35 independent countries of the Americas as a forum to strengthen cooperation between them. The countries are involved in discussions around topics such as public security, social development, financial and legal affairs, trade, culture, science and education. The tourism role of the OAS focuses mainly on tourism development and competitiveness, with a particular emphasis on the role of tourism for poverty alleviation and nature conservation. The OAS tourism section also provides internationally recognised training certification (www.oas.org).

SNAPSHOT 13.2

ASEAN

ASEAN, the Association of Southeast Asian Nations, has 10 member countries: Brunei, Cambodia, Indonesia, Laos, Malaysia, Myanmar, Thailand, the Philippines, Singapore and Vietnam. The organisation is a political and economic alliance for a population of 645.8 million people. With 104 million international arrivals across the region in 2015, ASEAN considers tourism an important driver for economic growth in the region. Similar to the Shengen agreement in the EU, it has proposed visa-free travel between the member states, which has the potential to dramatically increase intra-regional travel. For example, an American citizen can enter Singapore, Indonesia, the Philippines and Thailand visa-free, but if Vietnam or Myanmar are on the itinerary, travellers need a visa. A single visa for the region could encourage visitors to extend their trip, and visit more countries in one trip.

In addition, it has proposed a tourism policy for the different countries in the region, focusing on marketing and promotion, the development of universal standards, product development and attracting investment. ASEAN countries are increasingly focusing on marketing the region as one destination rather than 10 separate destinations. In 2017, as ASEAN's celebrated 50 years of operation, it launched its Golden Celebration campaign, featuring 50 festivals and 50 unique travel experiences across the region.

Source: www.asean.org

THE ROLE OF THE PUBLIC SECTOR AT THE LOCAL LEVEL

By Dr Nancy Stevenson, University of Westminster

Local government is elected to make decisions about geographically defined places. Specific roles vary in different countries but are likely to include areas such as education, economic development and regeneration, housing, transport, land use planning, social and cultural services and environmental services. While many local places attract tourists, they are often not reliant on tourism as their main economic activity. In places where tourism is perceived to be an important element of the local economy, or where it is considered to adversely affect a local area, local government may engage in activities to manage, control and improve tourism in their areas. However, in many places tourism activity is discretionary at the local level, which means that government may or may not choose to engage in tourism management or service provision. Its engagement will depend on a wide range of issues including local political priorities, the importance of tourism to their areas, and the views of local residents.

The Context

The nature of government engagement at the local level will vary and depend upon the wider context or environment. The scope of local government to deliver services, make decisions, and develop and enact policies and projects is prescribed by higher levels of government. In federal systems significant powers will be held at a regional level (e.g. Germany and Brazil), whereas in countries with more central power structures (e.g. the UK) more powers will be held at the national level.

When studying local government involvement in tourism it is important to consider the context in which it is developed. Its role will vary depending on a variety of contextual or environmental considerations including:

- the national policy framework
- the importance of tourism to the national economy
- how tourism policy is defined and its fit with other policy areas
- political considerations such as how power is allocated to decision makers at the local level
- the approaches that have been taken to policy making in the past and approaches that have been perceived to be successful in other areas
- alliances between areas and countries.

Governance and Partnerships

'Governance' is the term used to describe an approach to delivering policies and services in partnership between different organisations. Governance has arisen due to concerns about the role and effectiveness of the state within a rapidly changing and complex environment and seeks to improve efficiency and effectiveness and to focus government away from direct service provision and toward strategic leadership (Giddens, 1998; Stoker, 2004; Stoker and Wilson, 2004). The debates about governance and developing partnerships at the local level are also tied in with ideas about sustainability and the implications that local people need to be more involved in decision making.

Many people hold the view that if local government works in partnership with other stakeholders, it can develop a more effective long-term sustainable vision and deliver better services. Partnership working is seen as a way of:

- bringing in wider expertise and experience about the local area
- making local government more accountable
- getting things done more effectively.

Changes associated with governance mean that local government is likely to work closely with partners to manage and plan for tourism.

The Local Level

Jeffries (2001) refers to the local arena as a place where issues and actions have a coherence. He contrasts this with higher levels of government where policy statements or intentions might be very generalised. One advantage of studying government action and involvement at the local level is that our attention is focused on places which are geographically defined and relatively small scale. This means it is often easier to identify the attributes, opportunities and problems associated with tourism in an area and the major stakeholders and the structures and practices for working together to solve problems. It is possible to investigate questions about what happens in practice and also to see how local and regional initiatives are implemented.

Hall's (2008) seven functions of government are outlined earlier in the chapter. At the local level coordination is particularly important in the context of governance, which means that local government is likely to be involved in setting up, participating in and maintaining partnerships. For example, local government might work with partners to coordinate the marketing and promotion of their areas, to develop new conference facilities, or to stage an event. Many of these partnerships will have an entrepreneurial aspect and involve activity to stimulate development in their areas (Stevenson, 2009). Places will compete with one another for a range of resources including private and public sector investment and specific development projects. Local governments have an increasingly important role in mobilising funds. This involves working in and coordinating partnerships to develop projects and make funding bids.

Local governments may also own and operate local resources which will attract tourists such as parks, museums, art galleries, conference centres, shopping centres and hotels (Stevenson and Lovatt, 2001). They can coordinate the provision of information to tourists as well, sometimes through the provision of Tourist Information Centres or by developing and delivering destination management systems. The latter can provide much wider information functions in terms of information dissemination and collection, reservations and event management (see Chapter 10 for more detail).

Local planning and policy functions are usually designed to achieve longer-term goals, focusing on a mixture of controlling and stimulating development to create lasting benefits. The planning function is often broad-based and developed from a 'strategic vision' about the best way to develop a place. Service delivery around 'place-making' encompasses elements that will attract visitors but are part of a broader objective to attract inward investment and improve people's lives within an area. Some places will have a 'vision' that involves the preparation of a specific tourism plan while in others tourism development objectives will be expressed within broader land use and economic development plans. These may be designed to fit with different activities and uses in an attempt to create places which are vibrant and attractive to residents, visitors and businesses.

Local governments will also often have a regulatory function. For example, they might be responsible for implementing legislation on quality standards in hotels, grading schemes, and inspecting and monitoring bars and restaurants. Local regulations will support and implement the regulatory systems setup at a national and regional level.

Understanding the Role of Government in Managing, Controlling and Improving Supply at the Destination

When setting out to understand the role of government in tourism at the local level it is important to ask a series of questions to find out more about the context within which policies are made and about the nature of tourism policy development and delivery. These might include:

- What is the power structure in the country? Is power centralised or devolved?
- What is the history of government involvement in the management of tourism?
- How is tourism defined and how does it fit with other policy areas?
- How do governments engage in tourism? What do they do? Who do they work with?
- How successful has their involvement been?
- How important is tourism to the area and what are the views of local people and businesses?

DESTINATION PROMOTION

The public sector is often involved in promotion campaigns for tourism destinations. This involves working with partners to identify target markets, developing campaigns to attract them, and deciding which characteristics of the destination to promote. Promotional campaigns may target domestic or international tourists, leisure or business tourists, different demographic groups or niche markets. The following paragraphs will discuss the concept of destination image and how image is different from a destination brand. The role of the government in tourism promotion will also be examined. Finally, different forms of promotion, and the role of technology in them, will be discussed.

Destination Image

Promoting tourism destinations has been compared to selling a dream, particularly when it comes to tourists who have not visited the destination before. The collective ideas, impressions, beliefs and conceptions of tourists about a destination are referred to as the 'destination image'. There are many definitions for this concept (for a list, see e.g. Gallarza et al., 2002), which highlights that the concept is very complex and also fluid: it has evolved strongly over time and is still a very prominent research area for tourism scholars.

A person's image of a destination can be positive, negative or neutral, and is not fixed but can change over time. Gunn (1988) explains that images can be formed on two levels: the organic level and the induced level.

The organic image is developed through an individual's everyday assimilation of information, which may include a wide range of mediums, from geography classes in school over mass media to actual visitation. The induced image is formed through the influence of tourism promotions such as advertising (Pike, 2008: 205). Reports of a terrorist attack in the media can give the destination a more negative image in the mind of many tourists. If the destination hosts an internationally acclaimed event, this can make its image more positive. Media coverage, films, word of mouth, books and pictures can all influence the organic destination image. The image of a destination will probably be different before and after the actual visit, and can still change after every subsequent visit. Promotional campaigns aim to either strengthen the positive image of a destination or turn the negative or neutral image of a destination into a positive one. Via the induced image, campaigns try to reinforce or change the organic image tourists may have already formed in their minds before the campaign.

Destination Branding

The concept of branding is discussed in Chapter 11. By building a brand, a destination's government can send out a clear and uniform message that firmly links the destination to a chosen set of attributes or benefits. Kolb (2006) describes branding as a creative process, involving the formulation of a slogan and designing a symbol or logo. A well designed brand quickly and easily communicates the benefits a tourist will experience from visiting the destination. To reinforce the brand it will need to be integrated into all communications, including brochures, advertisements and billboards.

The role of the public sector in branding a destination is usually one of research, coordination and, in many cases, funding. The tourist destination is a complex amalgam of different attributes and stakeholders and none of these stakeholders will have complete control over the products. This makes it much more difficult to develop a coherent brand for a destination, than, for example, for a soft drink or washing powder. It is usually the task of government to research which type of brand or promotional activity would be useful, and then to bring the various stakeholders together and develop a campaign that most of them will be in agreement with. In many cases, government will then (completely or partly) fund the design and the implementation of the campaign.

Governments will invest in branding for a range of reasons. One of the advantages of a strong brand is that it can encourage **brand loyalty** and repeat purchases. If tourists have had a positive experience of a destination, an unchanging brand will remind them of this and highlight that that positive experience is still available. Rather than communicating the benefits of a visit to new customers, the role of branding has in this case changed to reminding previous customers of the same benefits. Other advantages are that a clear brand can support internet marketing efforts and bring the different stakeholders in the destination together for long-term planning (Middleton et al., 2009).

Brand loyalty: The commitment by a consumer to purchase the same brand again

SNAPSHOT 13.3

Branding Singapore

Singapore is great example of a destination that brands itself in a sophisticated and targeted way. In 2009, the Singapore Tourism Board launched its 'Uniquely Singapore – 2009 Reasons to Visit Singapore' campaign. This global marketing campaign aimed to show visitors that Singapore could offer quality, unique experiences and value for money in terms of pricing. The image challenge for Singapore was that many in the West saw it as a sterile business city. The campaign was part of a S$90 million support package by the Singapore Tourism Board, aimed at helping the tourist industry cope with the effects of the global recession. In 2010, the Uniquely Singapore brand was followed by a campaign entitled 'Your Singapore', which again focused on the colourful vibrancy of the city (Singapore Tourism Board, 2017). The 'Your Singapore' slogan remained in place until 2017, when it was replaced with 'Passion Made Possible'. The Singapore Tourism Board has extended its messaging with customized campaigns in key markets, for example:

India: 'The holiday you take home with you': Indian travellers today possess a more global worldview, and display a strong preference for families to travel and bond together through shared learning experiences. They seek much more out of their holidays and put priority on aspirational, engaging experiences that deliver quality and enrichment, and which suit their passions and interests at the same time.

China: 'New discoveries': Whilst Chinese visitors still come on packaged tours, many are increasingly making their own online bookings and travelling as free and independent travellers. They seek a greater depth of travel experiences that include new, unique ones. The New Discoveries campaign aims to provide Chinese visitors with new, personalised and in-depth experiences. For visitors who have been to

Singapore: Passion Made Possible logo

Source: © Singapore Tourism Board

Singapore before, the campaign will allow them to gain a deeper understanding of Singapore with more reasons to return through the sharing of new discoveries, hidden gems and local insights. For visitors who have not visited Singapore, they will be able to have a more meaningful first trip here that brings them to places beyond the mainstream attractions.

Australia: 'Get lost and find the real Singapore': Most Australians perceived Singapore as a stopover destination, and those who had visited the city in the past three years were pleasantly surprised by the multitude of cultural and heritage gems, diverse food experiences and vibrant nightlife that were interspersed amidst Singapore's eclectic streetscape. They were also delighted at how the city has transformed while retaining the convenient and safe environment that allowed them to experience the city's diverse offerings on their own, an aspect that resonates well with Australians' preferred style of free-and-easy travel.

DESTINATIONS AND CRISIS MANAGEMENT

As discussed in the previous paragraphs, governments have a responsibility in the development, management and marketing of tourism destinations. These responsibilities are severely tested during and in the aftermath of a crisis. In the following sections, different types of crises that can affect the tourism industry are discussed. The role of governments in planning for and responding to crises will also be examined.

Glaesser (2003) and Henderson (2007) researched tourism and crisis management. They identified six forms of crisis that affect tourism: political crises, terrorist attacks, environmental crises, natural disasters, health scares and economic crises.

Political Crises

Political crises come in many forms but in general these include civil war, coups d'état, mass arrests, political assassinations, armed attacks, riots, demonstrations and the threat of war with other countries.

Political unrest and instability have a profound impact on demand for and the image of a tourism destination. When tourists perceive a destination as dangerous, many will choose an alternative destination instead. In the case of persistent or violent political crises, governments may advise their citizens against travelling to a destination. The media attention that political crises attract can also induce a negative image of the destination for years to come, even though political stability may have returned.

The former Yugoslavia was a popular tourist destination for Western and Central Europeans. Croatia was one of the popular tourist areas there, because of its long coastline and several historic cities with a rich cultural heritage. Between 1990 and 1995, the war of independence greatly disturbed the tourist influx and the image of the country. In the first year of the war, tourist arrivals decreased by 70 per cent, and nights spent reduced by 80 per cent compared to the previous year. By the end of the war, many accommodation facilities and much of the supporting infrastructure had been destroyed or damaged during the conflict. Some areas of the country, furthest from where the military forces were based, had managed to keep a minimal level of tourist activity. In the years following the war, Croatia slowly rebuilt its positive image and allure for tourists. Even though the country maintained its political stability after 1995, it took 10 years, until 2005, for the number of nights spent by tourists to reach the same level as before the war. Since then, the country's tourism industry has flourished: in 2016, 14 million tourists visited Croatia (www.htz.hr).

Terrorism

Terrorism, as a form of political crisis, has affected the tourism industry significantly in recent years, particularly when tourists are the target of an attack. Terrorism is not a new phenomenon: the IRA in Northern Ireland and ETA in the Basque region of Spain were notable examples of organisations that employed terrorist acts to achieve their goals. Nationalism and separatism were conventional motivators for terrorism in the 1970s and 1980s; nowadays, religious extremism plays an important role. Terrorist activities tend not only to affect the destination's appeal to tourists, who may now see it as unsafe and decide to visit other destinations instead, terrorist acts can also instil a sense of fear and mistrust more generally, which in turn might discourage people from travelling at all.

Examples of terrorism are bombings, suicide bombings, violent attacks, threats of violence, hijackings, kidnappings, murders and events and demonstrations that are linked to extremism.

Terrorist attacks in a destination have a profound influence on tourist demand for a destination. For example, the 9/11 attacks on New York in 2001 caused a sharp decline in international arrivals and tourist expenditure in New York, and for some the United States in general was instantly seen as dangerous and unsafe. Air travel into/out of and around the USA suffered sharp declines in passenger numbers because of the tarnished image of aviation. US inbound and outbound tourist numbers went down, and domestic tourism was also badly hit, resulting in job losses and bankruptcies.

Hagia Sophia, Istanbul

Source: Lynn Minnaert

More recently, Turkey was rocked by a coup attempt and several terror attacks in Ankara and Istanbul in 2015 and 2016. In addition, Russia banned charter holidays to Turkey after one of its fighter jets was shot down by the Turkish military over the Syrian border in November 2015. Russians accounted for one in 10 of the visitors to Turkey, the second-largest group behind Germans. By May 2016, the number of tourists from Russia had dropped 92 per cent. The number of visitors to Turkey plummeted nearly one-third in 2016 to about 25m – the lowest in nine years. The tourism crisis shaved nearly 1 per cent off Turkey's GDP in that same year, according to the IMF.

Environmental Crises

Fragile natural environments, such as coastlines, mountain areas and lakes, are often popular tourism destinations due to their natural resources. These natural environments can come under threat, sometimes because of tourism itself (see Chapter 9 for a full discussion on the environmental impacts of tourism). But other industries, such as agriculture, fishing, mining, transport and logging, can also have a strong detrimental impact on the environmental conditions in the destination. Environmental crises are events that cause widespread environmental damage in a short timescale, and, as opposed to natural disasters, they are usually connected to human activity.

Examples of environmental crises are oil leaks, oils spills, loss of cargo from ships, polluted smoke from industrial fires, nuclear and radiation accidents, gas leaks, waste water spills and sewage leaks.

In April 2010, the BP *Deepwater Horizon* rig exploded, causing 11 casualties and what is considered to be the largest marine oil spill in history. Estimates are that 4.9 million barrels of oil spilled into the Gulf of Mexico throughout the summer, polluting wetlands and beaches from Texas to Florida. In total, around 1,100 miles of shoreline were polluted. More than one-third of federal waters in the gulf were closed to fishing at the peak of the spill, due to fears of contamination. A study released by the National Oceanic and Atmospheric Administration (NOAA) in April 2016 noted that the spill may have led to historically high death rates and impaired reproductive health for bottlenose dolphins in Louisiana. Tourism operators were worried that the damage to beaches would become permanent; however, the sector recovered fairly swiftly. In July 2015, BP agreed to pay US$18.7 billion in fines, the largest corporate settlement in US history (NPR, n.d.).

Natural Disasters

Many natural locations that are popular with tourists, such as coasts, lakes, riversides and mountains, are at a heightened risk of nature-related disturbances. Some of these can be predicted or occur at particular times of the year, whereas others occur unexpectedly. These disturbances pose a danger to tourists and can cause significant damage to tourism-related infrastructure. Some commentators predict that climate change will increase the likelihood of natural disasters and extreme weather conditions.

Examples of natural disasters are floods, hurricanes, typhoons, earthquakes, blizzards, avalanches, tsunamis, landslides and volcanic eruptions.

On 24 December 2004, dramatic images of a tsunami hitting the shores of South Asia spread around the world. Tsunamis are great displacements of water caused by earthquakes on the sea bed. Large waves form from the epicentre of the earthquake and reach maximum height near coastal areas. Sri Lanka, Thailand, Indonesia and the Maldives were the hardest hit tourism destinations, with much of the coastal tourism infrastructure destroyed. These destinations saw bookings fall: in the rankings of destinations in the affected area, the Maldives was down from first place in 2004 to sixth in 2005, and Thailand fell out of the top 10 (Mintel, 2006). The travel industry in general recovered rapidly after the tsunami, but tourists diverted to other countries, with, for example, an increased interest in the Caribbean. Even though most areas have since recovered, the speed of recovery is greatly dependent on the level of damage and the speed and quality of reconstruction of tourist facilities such as hotels and leisure infrastructure.

More recently, in 2015, a powerful earthquake killed nearly 9,000 people and destroyed more than 824,000 homes in Nepal. The tremor reached 7.8 on the Richter scale, and for months the country was in crisis, with food, energy supplies and infrastructure severely affected. Tourism, one of the major contributors to the country's GDP, collapsed overnight. In 2014, 790,000 visitors came to the country. The following year, when the quake struck, that number plummeted to 539,000 – a loss of almost one-third. In 2016, visitor numbers increased to 753,000 – an indication of how long it can take for a destination to recover from a natural disaster (Carswell, 2017).

Presidential Palace in Port au Price, Haiti after the earthquake in 2010

Source: Valerié Svobodová

Health Scares

Travelling can expose tourists to increased health risks due to the standards of hygiene and exposure to unfamiliar infections and diseases at the destination. Tourists are explicitly warned about infectious diseases like malaria, dengue fever, yellow fever and cholera, for example, when they travel to certain destinations, and for a range of destinations immunisation against certain diseases is part of the entry requirements.

Tourists who engage in sexual activities or drug use during a trip add to the health risks that tourism can represent. Health scares differ from these risks to travel in the sense that they usually concern previously unknown infections or diseases that spread around the world quickly due to international travel. Due to the media attention that often surrounds these diseases a sense of panic can ensue, and governments may decide to put in place travel restrictions and increased vigilance regarding incoming tourists from affected areas.

Examples of health scares in recent years have been SARS, bird flu, foot and mouth disease, mad cow disease (and its human variant Creutzfeldt-Jakob syndrome), legionnaire's disease and swine flu.

SARS, or Severe Acute Respiratory Syndrome, is a potentially fatal respiratory infection. It was first recorded in the Guangdong province of China in 2002. In 2003, due to international air travel, the disease spread around the world. This outbreak led to the deaths of more than 800 people worldwide. It also severely affected tourism in China, Hong Kong, Singapore and Vietnam, where it was estimated about 3 million people lost their jobs. Tourism arrivals also fell by 70 per cent or more in other Asian tourist markets, even those that were not, or hardly, affected by the disease. McKercher and Chon (2004) link this downturn in the general Asian tourism industry to the warnings issued by many governments and the WHO not to travel to Asia unless this was strictly necessary. The movements of Asian tourists were also often restricted through bans, the withholding of visas, and quarantines. Because SARS was an unknown virus, many of these measures were put in place as a first reaction to the health crisis, even though it later transpired that the disease could be controlled by asking departing tourists a few questions and conducting a temperature check.

ADVICE FOR TRAVELLERS GOING TO AREAS AFFECTED BY **INFLUENZA A (H1N1)**

Respiratory diseases such as cold and flu are caused by virus infecting nose, throat and lungs. These coughing or sneezing.

Given that you are travelling to an affected area of influenza A (H1N1), **it is very important to keep in**

ADVICE FOR TRAVELERS **TO** AREAS AFFECTED BY INFLUENZA A

1. Take special car of personal hygiene by washing your hands frequently with warm water a hand cleaner.
2. Don't share food, glasses or cutlery.
3. When coughing or sneezing, cover your mouth and nose with a tissue or with the internal si away in a plastic bag.
4. Avoid touching your eyes, nose or mouth.
5. Do not move around if you feel sick except to seek medical care.
6. Practice good hygiene habits.
7. Avoid close contact with sick people suffering from the following symptoms:
   - Fever ≥ 37,5 °C
     AND

Notice at Valencia airport during the bird flu health crisis

Source: Lynn Minnaert

The Zika virus is a mosquito-borne virus that can be transmitted from pregnant women to fetuses, which can result in birth defects, such as under-developed heads and brain damage. In early 2015, an outbreak of Zika in Brazil spread to the Caribbean, as well as other parts of South America, Texas and Florida. In February 2016, the WHO declared the Zika crisis a Public Health Emergency of International Concern (PHEIC), and advised pregnant women to avoid travel to areas where the transmission of the Zika virus was active. In November 2016, the travel advisory was downgraded: it recommended that women who want to get pregnant in the near future wait at least eight weeks after their last possible exposure to the virus before trying to conceive (WHO, 2016).

Economic Crises

Seeing that level of income is usually a key determinant in participation in leisure travel, the tourism sector is to a large extent dependent on the buoyancy of the overall economy. Economic improvements often go hand in hand with increases in holiday participation and spending: examples are the fast-growing outbound tourism markets of China, India, Russia and Brazil. By contrast, economic slowdowns and crises tend to negatively affect all expenditure that is seen as non-essential, and tourism is usually seen as discretionary spending.

Examples of economic crises are downturns, slow-downs, recessions, depressions, inflation and devaluations of currency.

The tourism industry is largely dependent on the overall state of the economy, as was proven in 2008 in the aftermath of the global economic downturn. Although, overall, the number of international tourist arrivals worldwide grew by 2 per cent compared to 2007, in the second half of the year growth came to a standstill with the number of international arrivals declining slightly. The strongest declines in arrivals were noted in Europe and Asia. A slowdown in tourism-generating countries in advanced economies was also noted, and this started spreading to major emerging markets such as China, India and Brazil at the beginning of 2009. Still, several destinations noted remarkable growth, even in the second half of the year: examples were Honduras, Panama, the Lebanon, Morocco, India, Indonesia and Turkey. Tourism has been described as a resilient economic activity, one that is able to play a key role in economic recovery for many countries and regions (UNWTO, 2009).

CRISIS PLANNING

It is often said that the best way to handle a crisis is to prevent it from occurring. In a time of crisis which disrupts the usual flow of activities and puts pressure on all the stakeholders involved, it is often not possible to call a meeting, get all the stakeholders around the table and discuss possible responses: a crisis demands a swift and effective response, so this should be planned beforehand. However, considering all the things that can potentially go wrong, it is difficult to plan ahead for every possible scenario. Many crisis plans will therefore remain purposely vague: the exact circumstances of a crisis cannot usually be predicted, but the plan must allow destinations to access a frame of reference when this is needed.

It is important that the crisis plan refers clearly to the responsibilities of the different stakeholders in a crisis. Who will be in charge when a crisis occurs? Who will ensure coordination between different stakeholders? Who will speak with the media? To determine these responsibilities, a planning committee or crisis committee should be formed: this committee can include destination managers, public officials, legal advisers, press officers, representatives from the emergency services, external experts, marketing managers and so on. Once responsibilities have been established, communication channels and hierarchies should be put in place, ensuring that everyone has access to the information that will be needed when the time comes.

When this is in place, a number of scenarios or contingencies can be explored, in what is called a 'contingency plan' or an 'emergency plan'. These scenarios can go into a much higher level of detail than the generic crisis plan, and will usually focus on crises that are seen as likely to occur in the destination. The aim of the contingency plan is to prepare the destination as fully as possible for a number of contingencies so that when a crisis occurs, a clear template for the required response will already be in place. It is vital, however, that the plan is actually used in times of crisis; even though these plans may be in place, in the panic that ensues after a crisis, they may be ignored when they are most needed. Regular exercises may be one way to prevent this from happening. It is also important that the plan is easy to follow and not overly complex, so that it is not rejected when a crisis occurs (Glaesser, 2003; Henderson, 2007).

SNAPSHOT 13.4

The National Tourism Incident Response Plan for Australia

The National Tourism Incident Response Plan for Australia was developed after international crises like 9/11, the bomb attacks in Bali and London, and SARS had affected the national tourist industry. The plan was developed by the public sector in close collaboration with the private sector and aims to ensure a coherent national response in crisis situations. It contains detailed flowcharts specifying responsibilities and communication flows. A quick response in the case of more serious crises is ensured by the appointment of a Central Incident Management Group: the plan describes which types of individuals should be in this group and what their key responsibilities should be. The Central Incident Management Groups may convene additional committees in charge of communication, policy making, research and monitoring. General strategies are also suggested in the plan to aid recovery after the crisis in the form of action plans, templates and matrices. The National Tourism Incident Response Plan is always active, but there are different levels of activation: from the lowest level, when there is no threat (blue), to the highest level (red). In response to the swine flu outbreak of 2009, the activation level was raised to amber (incident response required) (Leggat et al., 2009).

CRISIS RECOVERY

When a crisis does occur, the way a destination handles the event can determine how long the negative effects of the crisis will persist and how long the tourist sector will be negatively affected by these. A range of techniques exists for destinations to use in the aftermath of a crisis; these relate to products, price and communication.

In terms of products, it is important that the quality of the tourism facility or service is restored as soon as possible. If there are elements that will endanger a tourist's personal safety, these need to be removed as quickly as possible. When an oil spill has contaminated a beach, for example, and skin contact with the oil constitutes a health risk, then the beach should be closed off and a cleaning programme should be instructed as soon as possible. In the event of substantial damage, restoring this can take considerable time, and the negative effects on the destination's image can last even longer. In this case, Glaesser (2003) suggests a number of short-term strategies based on product diversification to encourage visitation. The destination can, for example, stage an event, such as a concert or festival, attracting the media and diverting attention away from negative connotations. Another strategy, which may be useful for safe destinations in countries that are involved in a political crisis such as a war, may be to focus on domestic and/or regional tourism. These tourists are likely to know the area better and so are less likely to be put off by the negative reputation the political conflict has caused.

The second area for action is price. Businesses in the destination may offer discounts or promote special offers to attract tourists back to the area. Although price is by all means a significant factor in the decision-making process, price promotions are a risky strategy. First, the consumer may get used to the cheaper prices, refusing to pay the higher price later when the crisis is nothing but a distant memory. Second, the crisis is the reason for the price reduction, so by bringing the price down the tourism providers are also highlighting the reason why the product did not sell.

Communication is the third action area in the aftermath of a crisis. A crisis is likely to attract media attention, with images of the destination in crisis being sent throughout the world in many cases, over which the destination itself has little or no control. These images of negative events may influence the image of the destination, as tourists form ideas or misconceptions about the area as a potential holiday destination. As stated before, the negative image of the destination that is thus formed may outlast the crisis, and live on long after its effects have become unnoticeable. It is therefore important that a destination aims to control the damage done to its reputation as soon as possible. This can be done by providing more positive and hopeful messages to the press, for example, or by commissioning an advertising or promotion campaign. The public sector may also encourage businesses in the destination to communicate directly with their customers, informing them of the situation and reassuring them that they do not need to cancel or postpone their holiday. For example, in the aftermath of the suicide bombings in London in 2005, the London Development Agency and the local tourist board, VisitLondon, developed a guide to help tourism businesses manage the first few weeks after the crisis. Below are a number of examples of the guidelines provided:

Websites: We live in an era of instant communication and your customers will use websites to inform themselves. It is important that you review your own website and post some information on there immediately. This can be developed over the next few days but a brief statement reassures customers that you are well prepared.

Be proactive: Review your bookings and identify any that are particularly valuable. Prepare a message for your future bookings in letter, telephone, script and web form. Identify the positive reasons why people should still travel. Contact your customers and tell them that you are looking forward to welcoming them.

Review your offer: In a few days you will have some idea of how badly your business is affected. You will need to act to replace lost customers. In the short term, you will need to offer customers some incentive, and this can be a special offer, some added value, a discounted price, a loyalty bonus, or a new feature.

Positive public relations: In the early days of a crisis it is very easy to believe that there is only bad news. The danger is that this will become a self-fulfilling prophecy – the tourism industry 'talks down' London and therefore visitors stay away. Taking a positive approach means being realistic but optimistic. Try to develop a focus on what visitors will be able to enjoy and emphasise the welcome they will receive from Londoners.

Build your relationships: If you receive business from agents, tour operators or incoming handling agents, get in touch with them. They will be able to give you good market intelligence and you can talk to them about what you can do together to encourage customers.

Review marketing campaigns: You will need to check whether any booked advertising is appropriate. You may decide to cancel some advertising because the message is wrong given the circumstances. Hong Kong tourism experienced an example of this. They had booked colour advertising that featured the slogan 'A breath of fresh air', which was due to run at the height of the SARS outbreak when residents were wearing face masks. The cost of cancelling advertising is better than the bad publicity generated by insensitive messages.

(London Development Agency, 2005)

SUMMARY

This chapter has highlighted the complex and varied nature of government involvement in tourism. It was shown that governments are involved in tourism for different reasons and at different levels: locally, regionally, nationally and even internationally. The roles and responsibilities of governments also vary widely: governments may aim to develop tourism to bring economic benefits to a destination, but at the same time they have to protect the public interest and try to reduce the negative impacts of tourism as much as possible. They play a central role in bringing together a wide range of stakeholders involved in tourism and consult with them to develop policies and regulations. This central role also makes them a key partner in the development, consultation and funding process that underpins tourism promotion and branding.

At a local level, the activities of government are shaped by a range of contextual factors and vary within and between countries. Local governments have a role in creating places which are attractive to people (such as residents, workers and visitors) and they are likely to be involved in bidding for resources for particular projects or events to meet this objective. Local governments are often involved in managing and improving the tourism supply in their areas; however, these tourism initiatives are often integrated within broader objectives to improve the image or attractiveness of certain sites.

Finally, it has been shown that at times when a coordinated response from all stake-holders is most crucial, namely in times of crisis, governments play a central role in planning for crises and managing their effects. Crises can take a wide range of forms and are characterised by their unpredictability; however, a coordinated response can lead the way to a swift recovery.

SELF-TEST QUESTIONS

1. How are international organisations involved in tourism regulation and planning?

2. What sort of activities might be undertaken by local governments?

3. How can destinations respond effectively to crises?

FURTHER READING

Glaesser, D. (2003) *Crisis Management in the Tourism Industry*. Oxford: Elsevier Butterworth-Heinemann.

Hall, C. (2008) *Tourism Planning: Policies, Processes and Relationships*. Harlow: Prentice Hall.

London Development Agency (LDA) (2005) *Business as Usual*. 'Business as usual'. Available at www.lda.avensc.com/documents/Business_as_Usual_PDF.pdf

Minnaert, L., Maitland, R. and Miller, G. (2009) 'Tourism and social policy: the value of social tourism', *Annals of Tourism Research*, 36(2): 316–34.

Mintel (2006) *Holidays, the Impacts of Terrorism and Natural Disasters*. London: Mintel.

Perko, J. and Idaković, M. (2008) *Rise and Fall of Croatian Tourism and the Effects of the War of the 90s* (Statistical Yearbook of the Republic of Croatia). Zagreb: Croatian Bureau of Statistics.

USEFUL WEBSITES

Disability Discrimination Act (2005): www.direct.gov.uk/en/DisabledPeople/RightsAndObligations/DisabilityRights/DG_4001068

European Commission – Guide on EU funding for the tourism sector http://ec.europa.eu/growth/content/guide-eu-funding-tourism-sector-updated-version-0_en

Organization of American States: www.oas.org

The Organisation for Economic Co-operation and Development: www.oecd.org

UN World Tourism Organization: www.unwto.org

World Heritage Convention: whc.unesco.org

World Trade Organization: www.wto.org

PART V
TOURISM AHEAD

CONTENT

14

TOURISM AND THE FUTURE

'The tourism industry offers flexibility, choice and involvement in one of the largest and fastest growing industries in the world. There are more tourism courses available than ever before at different levels, and more people are realising that tourism is an industry they can see themselves working in for years to come.'

V. Reily Collins, 2004b: v

LEARNING OUTCOMES

After reading this chapter you will understand:

- the role of scenario planning in thinking about the future of tourism
- how scenarios are written, and what the advantages and disadvantages are of scenarios
- a number of potential directions in which the tourism of the future could develop
- how to approach planning your own future within tourism
- the types of employers, roles and skills required in tourism employment.

NYU graduation at Yankee Stadium, New York

Source: Lynn Minnaert

INTRODUCTION

Our book has provided a detailed introduction to tourism, tourists, destinations, suppliers and impacts, and given you an understanding of the industries that make up tourism, their influence on each other and how they influence the destinations that attract tourists. We hope that, after reading the previous chapters, we have inspired you to find out more about how tourism demand and destinations are likely to develop in the future, and the opportunities that exist for you within that future. This final chapter is divided along two lines: the future of tourism and your future in tourism.

The future of tourism is of great importance to planners, decision makers and managers in the tourism sector, so what does the future hold for tourism? Will more people travel because of growing prosperity in a number of recently developed countries, such as China and India? How will the Earth and local communities cope with the environmental consequences of this increased demand for tourism? How will we travel when the earth's fossil fuel reserves have been depleted? Questions like these affect tourists, destinations and tourism suppliers alike. They are not easily answered: 'The future is, for the most part, not only unknown: it is unknowable. The decision maker's dilemma, therefore, is how best to commit to a course of action in the absence of knowledge about the future' (Ralston and Wilson, 2006: 3). The first section of this chapter discusses scenarios and scenario planning as a potential way to deal with the insecurities of the future, and how to be prepared for the different courses this future may take.

Your future in tourism focuses on the importance of planning your career and the types of employment opportunities that are available in tourism. The section is intended as an introduction to encourage you to begin considering your career aspirations; detailed information can be found in the texts listed as further reading at the end of the chapter.

SCENARIO PLANNING

The word 'scenario' can be used in a range of different ways. In the world of theatre and film, it refers to a storyline. In a military context, it refers to a detailed contingency plan for different eventualities. Planners and managers use the term in a future-oriented sense, to describe a possible view of the future that allows them to make decisions (Ringland, 2002). Scenario planning is thus a disciplined method for imagining possible futures in detail (Schoemaker, 1995), whereby various possibilities are explored for the opportunities and threats they pose for a business. The following sections define what scenarios are, explore why they are used and how they can be developed, and discuss what their benefits and limitations are.

WHAT ARE SCENARIOS?

There is no single definition for what scenarios are. Instead, different researchers have defined the phenomenon in different ways (see Table 14.1).

TABLE 14.1 Definitions of scenarios

'An internally consistent view of what the future might turn out to be' (Porter, in Lindgren and Bandhold, 2003: 21)
'A tool for ordering one's perceptions about alternative future environments in which one's decision might be played out right' (Schwartz, in Lindgren and Bandhold, 2003: 21)
'A scenario tells a story of how various elements might interact under certain conditions' (Schoemaker, 1995: 26)
'That part of strategic planning which relates to the tools and technologies for managing the uncertainties of the future' (Ringland, in Lindgren and Bandhold, 2003: 21)
'Scenarios are possible views of the world, providing a context in which managers can make decisions' (Ringland, 2002: 2)
'Scenarios are a descriptive narrative of plausible alternative projections of a specific part of the future' (Fahey, 2003: 7)

Ralston and Wilson (2006) argue that all scenarios have the following characteristics:

- They have a *narrative* nature: They have a plot and a storyline, and provide rich detail. Some scenarios are accompanied by quantitative data, such as graphs and tables.
- They are *plural*: Because the future is uncertain, one must consider not just one, but a set of alternative scenarios.
- They are *holistic*: They investigate different elements that together build a complete picture. From this perspective they are different from trend analysis, where one trend is usually investigated at a time.

Scenarios are therefore more than forecasts, in the sense of relatively unsurprising projections of the present. In the traditional sense of the word, forecasts require relatively stable conditions and are constructed over relatively short timeframes. Neither are scenarios visions of a desired future, a 'best-case scenario' (Lindgren and Bandhold, 2003).

The origins of scenario planning can be traced back to 1950s' military planning. Herman Kahn and his associates at the RAND Corporation adapted the meaning and method of theatrical scenarios to war planning. Kahn used scenarios to represent alternative futures; for example he developed four scenarios of how nuclear war might erupt between the US and the Soviet Union (Millett, 2003).

The method was later adapted to new environments. The energy and petrochemical company Shell has used scenario planning since the early 1970s as part of a process for generating and evaluating its strategic options. The company, which is still considered a corporate champion of scenarios today, has been consistently better in its oil forecasts than its competitors (Schoemaker, 1995: 25). In recent decades scenario planning has become an established method, adopted by most major companies and consultancy firms (Lindgren and Bandhold, 2003).

DEVELOPING SCENARIOS

Scenario planning attempts to compensate for two common errors in decision making: under-prediction and over-prediction of change. Under-prediction is the most common error of the two: most people and organisations find it difficult to imagine a future that is very different from the present. A hundred years ago it would have been difficult to predict a world with technologies such as jet planes, the Internet and mobile phones. Yet there are also people who tend to over-predict, expecting levels of change that fail to materialise: space travel, for example, is not yet common, and there is not yet a cure for AIDS. Scenario planning allows managers to steer a middle course between under- and over-prediction (Schoemaker, 1995: 27).

When developing scenarios, we combine the things we think we know about the future with elements about which we are not certain. Some assumptions can be made about the future with relative certainty: we know, for example, that the world population is growing, and that in many developed countries the average age of the population is rising. We also know that new technologies are replacing previous approaches: the popularity of digital music, for example, has reduced the number of CDs that are sold, and the number of tourists booking their holiday online instead of at a travel agency is rising.

Many aspects of the future, however, are still unknown: they are forces that may move in different directions and have significant implications for companies and destinations (Fahey, 2003). The results of elections are one example: if the Green Party, for instance, became a significant partner in government, this would probably lead to increased taxation on polluting activities such as air transport. Oil prices are another example: these are often influenced by political relations between different countries. Rises in oil prices lead to increases in the prices of a range of products and services, from groceries to transport. Higher prices often result in a reduced demand for products, and as many transport providers in tourism (such as airlines and cruise liners) are heavily dependent on oil, this can have a far-reaching effect on their level of business.

When we combine the two elements above – the things we think we know about the future, and a few key uncertainties – we can develop a range of futures. This is usually done via a set of workshops with representatives from different parts of the company or organisation. The further ahead we look, and the more complex the situations we try to predict, the more numerous the options become – hence we need to prepare for not one, but multiple possible futures. At the same time, we cannot explore every possible future. We need to reduce the complexity here in order to handle it. The number of scenarios that are developed can vary widely, and depend on the number of certain trends and uncertainties that are relevant to the organisation.

AIMS

Scenarios can be developed with several purposes in mind. Fahey (2003) discusses three types of aims:

1. Scenarios can foster preparedness. That is, they can allow managers to anticipate a range of potential futures, and to get ready for them before they occur. For example, tourism businesses may use scenarios to consider the consequences of a potential rise in the number of elderly tourists, seeing that this is a population group that is growing in many Western countries.

2. Scenarios also allow managers and planners to consider what they would do if each future were to materialise. In the case of the scenario above, the company could consider the products and services that would be popular with elderly tourists, and the changes the company would have to make to meet their needs.

3. Scenarios can allow managers and planners to develop a new understanding of the present. Although scenario planning is mainly focused on the future, by analysing what this future may look like, the current strengths and weaknesses of the organisation or destination may become apparent. Thinking about the future in a detailed way can also lead to the challenging of tacit beliefs and assumptions in the organisation. We have already explained that organisations often underestimate the changes the future will bring – scenario planning can be a tool to challenge this belief. By thinking in detail about a future with more elderly tourists, the company may challenge existing opinions about the level of accessibility that is needed or the type of new products that should be developed.

BENEFITS AND LIMITATIONS

Scenarios can be powerful instruments for the future planning of an organisation or destination, and bring a number of benefits:

1. They are *easily memorable* and *compatible* with how the human brain works. Because of their narrative format (stories with images), scenarios can be visualised, which often means they are more believable, so that they force the mind to think differently about the future.

2. The format of scenarios *reduces complexity* and is *communicative*. Scenarios are easy to discuss because they reduce the amount of uncertainty to a manageable level. They also provide the organisation with a common language to discuss the future (Lindgren and Bandhold, 2003).

3. Scenario planning requires different teams within the organisation to think together about the future, and can thus encourage *teambuilding.* Developing the scenarios themselves can be a learning process, and allow the participants to build links with other persons in the organisation so that decision making becomes more integrated (Millett, 2003).

Scenario building equally has a number of limitations. Lindgren and Bandhold (2003) name the following:

Uncertainty in conclusions: Scenario planning does not give one single answer about the future. Decision makers who are looking for 'the' answer to their questions about the future may find it a speculative and demanding process. Scenario planning also requires a holistic look at the future, whereas traditionally managers are taught to divide challenges into different smaller parts, and find solutions for each part separately – as such scenario planning may feel counter-intuitive.

Soft methods and soft answers: Although some scenarios include statistics, models and figures, the narrative basis of the scenarios makes them a qualitative rather than a quantitative method. Qualitative methods look for relations, motivations and interactions, whereas quantitative methods look for numerical answers. Many businesses are rather numbers-oriented, and thinking about problems in a more qualitative way may be challenging and new.

Time consuming: Developing scenarios in workshops with representatives from different teams in the organisation is a time-consuming process, and the coordination of the project requires specialist knowledge.

SCENARIOS FOR THE TOURISM OF THE FUTURE

What does the future hold for tourism, and which factors will play a role in how it develops? These are questions addressed by Ian Yeoman in his book *2050 – Tomorrow's Tourism* (2013). Will the world's population keep growing? Will humans keep consuming natural resources at ever increasing rates? Will the number of international tourists keep growing at the rapid pace it does currently? And if so, what impacts would this have on host communities and the environment?

Yeoman (2013) identifies three main factors that will influence tourism (and society) in the decades to come:

Wealth: Tourism demand depends heavily on the economic climate in the major generating markets. Currently, the USA has the world's largest economy; however, that dominance may be about to shift, as China's economy is rapidly growing, according to the World Economic Forum (www.weforum.org). By 2050, PricewaterhouseCoopers predicts that China will be in first place because emerging economies will continue to grow faster than advanced ones. India will rank second, the US will be third, and fourth place is expected to go to Indonesia. The UK could be down to tenth place by 2050, while France could be out of the top 10 and Italy out of the top 20 as they are overtaken by faster-growing emerging economies such as Mexico, Turkey and Vietnam (PwC, 2017).

Technology: Technology has a profound impact on society, and the impacts of automation and AI on the workforce are starting to be felt. Tourism has also been profoundly changed by technology: OTAs have now largely replaced their brick-and-mortar equivalents in many generating regions, and the proliferation of online information has made it much easier for travellers to independently research, plan and book their travel experiences. Same-day bookings via mobile apps make it possible to arrive at the airport and find a hotel before you have cleared passport control. Travellers share travel images and reviews, creating a peer-to-peer information channel that tourism suppliers can no longer control.

Resources: The UN predicts that the world's population is expected to reach 8.6 billion in 2030, 9.8 billion in 2050 and 11.2 billion in 2100. A growing population, combined with increased levels of consumption, raises severe concerns about the availability of resources such as food, water and fossil fuels. As tourism is currently still heavily dependent on oil, a reduction in oil production could be a major threat to destinations, especially those that are more remote (e.g. Hawaii). Climate change, linked to CO_2 consumption, is already affecting societies (and tourism) – how much more consumption can the Earth sustain before irreparable damage is done?

CASE STUDY 14.1

Four Proposed Future Tourism Scenarios

We will now examine how each of the four proposed scenarios will affect a hypothetical family in 2030. The Jones family lives on the outskirts of London. The dad, Mark, works as the manager of a car dealership, while the mum, Jessica, is a part-time medical secretary. They have two children, Adam (10) and Holly (5). What will their travel behaviour look like in the future? These scenarios are based on Yeoman (2013) and previous work by Forum for the Future (2009).

What will tourism look like in the future?

Source: © Ans Brys

(Continued)

Scenario 1: Boom and Bust

Mark Jones is having a good day: it's only Tuesday and already he has sold three new, cell-powered cars this week. Since the UK government has mandated that only electric cars can be sold, business is great. Head office is going to be pleased and there may well be a nice bonus coming his way soon! The UK economy is booming and the Jones family are benefiting from the positive economic climate: the family finances are healthy and Mark's flexible work hours allow the family to spend lots of quality time together. Mark and Jessica love travelling and they take the children with them wherever they go – air travel is affordable, and this year the family has already had a beach break in Australia, a week at the carnival in Rio, and a skiing trip to Hungary. The next trip they would like to take is to the United States, on one of the new cruise ships that can transport up to 7,000 passengers. They are like floating cities!

Transport networks have expanded massively and the world is now the Jones' oyster. They can take a high speed train from London to Barcelona, or fly from their local airport to all five continents. New technologies have reduced the negative environmental impacts of flying to some extent: engines are now more efficient and tourists can pick airlines that fly on 'green fuel' – even though this is often more expensive.

The disadvantage of this booming tourism sector, however, is that some destinations have become very overcrowded. Local communities were protesting against 'over-tourism' – they claim the constant tourist hordes are making life in the city impossible. Many cities, like Barcelona and Venice, have become tourist theme parks: local residents have moved away because the housing stock is increasingly used as sharing economy rentals, and the local stores gradually became replaced by souvenir shops. Last year the Jones family visited Rome, and the city was so crowded that it was at times hard to enjoy attractions like the Coliseum and the Pantheon. Luckily these attractions offered tourists special 3-D glasses that filter out other visitors and hide the degradation of tourism to the buildings. Mark has thought long and hard about a destination where he can take the family where the crowds will be less dense – so next year Antarctica may be the destination of choice. They need to go quickly before tourism spoils that continent too! Or if they win the lottery, they could go on one of the new space tours … Now that certainly would make the neighbours jealous.

Some of Mark and Jessica's friends have commented that the travel lifestyle they lead is not responsible – other industries have had to cut carbon emissions to support the growth of tourism. Mark and Jessica are not sure if what they do is fair … but for now, they enjoy flying around the world every few months.

Scenario 2: Divided Disquiet

Jessica Jones is in a bad mood. The holiday she had booked for her family to Zambia has been cancelled at short notice, due to political unrest in the area. The news reporters said that the same reasons are yet again underlying the unrest: the population of the region has grown dramatically over the last 20 years, and there is just not enough water and food for everyone. Due to the shortages, political conflict in the region has become more pronounced, and terror incidents have occurred in neighbouring countries that make travel there a risky proposition, as it is in many other parts of the world. The Jones family had visited Zambia five years ago, and had found it overcrowded – but at least it was less overcrowded than many other destinations, like those in the Mediterranean area. The pollution and over-development there had now become so bad that the Joneses, like many other families, did not want to go back there anymore.

Cancelled holidays were a recurring problem for Jessica. Last year she had wanted to take the family to the Maldives, but due to rising sea levels the island they were booked to visit was evacuated, and the inhabitants were relocated to India. Two years ago, when they visited Morocco, they were told that due to water shortages in the area they may not be able to go. Luckily, though, the tour operator imported the necessary water in a special tanker ship and the holiday went ahead. However, they did not feel welcome in the destination as local communities protested that tourists were using up the water resources they so desperately needed.

So this year the family are again facing the cancellation of their holiday – Jessica considered her friends' advice to buy one of those 'virtual windows' with the holiday budget instead. These windows allow you to experience any destination in the world in your own living room – she would be able to have lunch with her sister in Atlanta without having to leave the house. Many people were saying tourism was dead, and that it had been a costly mistake of the past, partly responsible for the environmental problems the world was experiencing. Were they right?

Jessica had one last option. Doomsday Tours Ltd offered trips to sites that would soon be ruined forever, such as the Himalayas and Patagonia. Jessica knew it was not the ethical choice: tour operators like these kept developing destinations, regardless of the damage it did. But if she did not book this trip, Holly and Adam would perhaps never get to see these amazing places … She decided to sleep on it, and ask Mark's opinion later.

Scenario 3: Price and Privilege

It is a very special year for the Jones family. After years of carefully saving up, Mark and Jessica are finally able to take the children to the United States. Jessica's sister lives in Atlanta, but because travel is so expensive, Holly and Adam have never met their cousins. This was one of the main reasons why the Jones family received a travel permit – competition for these is fierce, and tourists have to compete against each other to show they are deserving.

Mark and Jessica often think back fondly of when they first met, in 2005, when flying was cheap and they visited foreign destinations several times per year. However, since the cost of oil has risen by 1,000 per cent, flying is only affordable for the very rich. Jessica used to work for a low-cost airline then – none of them exist now though, and all the staff were made redundant.

Luckily for the Jones family, however, the extensive European train network has several hub stations in London. A few years ago they visited Poland by train – it was an enjoyable journey, and due to the latest technological developments it was relatively fast and comfortable. The trains even have humanoid robot butlers, who deliver meals and assist travellers. The technology is still developing, but it is expected that in the coming decades, trains will run without human staff at all!

Mark is a key campaigner in the Right to Fly movement, that campaigns for government support and inclusive legislation to ensure everyone can fly at least once. Mark recognises the severity of climate change, but considers travel to be a key human desire. So far the government has not yet responded to the demands of Right to Fly, but with a growing membership base, the lobbying power of the organisation is increasing.

(Continued)

In the celebrity magazines Jessica reads, there are sometimes reports of the rich and famous who travel to exclusive tropical islands. Jessica often wonders if Holly and Adam will ever be able to experience places like these, and she sometimes asks herself if a different approach to fossil fuels 20 years earlier could have kept travel more inclusive.

Scenario 3: Carbon Clampdown

Jessica has just come back from an afternoon of volunteering at the local care home, and is calculating the carbon credits her volunteering role has earned her so far. Since personal carbon allowances were introduced, the family can do with this credit boost: Mark commutes to work by car, and that takes a big bite out of their carbon allowance as a family – without government and industry support, the electric car movement has not really taken off. The Jones family are saving up carbon emissions for a trip to Atlanta, where Jessica's sister lives. Usually Jessica is rather opposed to travel via air because of the impact it has on the environment, but she wants Adam and Holly to get to know their aunt and cousins, so she is making an exception. The airlines will surely appreciate the business: since personal carbon allowances were introduced they have experienced a large drop in profits.

Usually the Jones family holidays in the UK – they went to Devon last year, and visited the Lake District the year before. In Devon they stayed in an all-inclusive resort that offered lots of activities for when the weather was not so good. In the Lake District they went camping – the kids had a wonderful time! The UK is one of the most carbon-neutral places in the world, and the Jones family like to do their bit to keep it that way. It is also a much cheaper option: Western economies have hardly grown in the past decades, and like many other families, the Jones family need to tighten their budgets.

When Adam and Holly are older, Mark and Jessica hope they will join the Global Peace Corps: an organisation that allows young people to travel around the world to help in humanitarian projects. It's a way to see the planet without ruining it. Holly and Adam have learnt about ecology from a very young age, and for them making green decisions is second nature. Mark and Jessica sometimes think back to how wasteful the tourism sector used to be 20 years ago, and are ashamed of the way they once acted. They are pleased that government regulation has stepped up to the challenge – it took some getting used to, but they are convinced a greener planet is worth it in the end.

Reflective Questions

1. How do you think each of the scenarios above would affect the following businesses:

    *   An airline?
    *   A cross-European rail operator?
    *   A destination in the Mediterranean that is heavily dependent on tourism?

2. Which scenario, if any, is in your opinion most likely to happen? Can you think of other options?

The sample scenarios above can help us imagine what the future of tourism will look like – but what about your own future in tourism? The final section of this book considers career opportunities in tourism.

YOUR FUTURE IN TOURISM

As we have seen throughout this book, the scale and breadth of tourism and its industries are phenomenal; growth is projected to continue long into the future, and the challenges of managing tourism activities in destinations, businesses and organisations are likely to intensify. The availability of a well-educated, professional and passionate workforce is therefore crucial to meet the tourism needs of the future, and the planet's need for tourism to develop sustainably. Reily Collins (2004a) describes the scope of career opportunities in tourism as 'staggering' because of the different types of industries that create, distribute and market tourism products, the involvement of the public, private and voluntary sectors, and the geographic location of tourism organisations and businesses in generating and destination regions. Career opportunities in tourism are offered by a huge variety of industries and in innumerable locations globally. In short, the career opportunities available are vast, and at times overwhelming; it is important that you understand these opportunities and how they can help you to achieve your professional goals.

If you are studying an undergraduate course you have probably heard the term 'employability' used by teaching staff and by your university's career professionals. Employability refers to the skills needed to manage your own professional life; Dibben and Norton (2017) describe the value of employability skills as 'the capacity to have numerous jobs, build a career, for some to start their own business – and certainly to continue to develop as successful individuals in whatever areas they decide to pursue.' Careers in tourism are often described as 'self-directed': that is, that there is no formal career progression in the same way as other sectors such as teaching, medicine or law. This is important because it means that you are responsible for the way in which your professional life unfolds; you will decide the direction you would like your career to develop, the type of roles and industries you would prefer to work in, and you may have to seek out some opportunities yourself. One of the key tenets of employability is career planning, which we discuss now.

CAREER PLANNING

'Career planning' is also known as 'career management' and is an element of personal development planning (PDP). The principle underlying each of these is that individuals can proactively influence their career to reflect their personal goals, interests and aspirations.

Before we consider the role of planning, though, it is useful to define the term 'career'. Arnold (1997: 16) defines it as 'the sequence of employment-related positions, roles, activities and experiences encountered by a person.' This definition avoids interpreting 'career' as an occupation within one industry, or relating it to promotion. Instead, it sees a career as the personal experiences of an individual over time and shows how an individual's roles, responsibilities, skills and interests have changed and evolved. Careers can be influenced by leisure activities, education, domestic tasks and family responsibilities, through the development of new skills and exposure to new experiences. In short, a career is an individual's journey through employment, entrepreneurship or self-employment; it does not necessarily involve promotion to higher levels, and is not confined to one occupation or industry.

Career planning is a structured process that requires you to identify your long-term goals, targets or objectives, plan the most effective route to achieving them, and monitor the success of your plan, making adjustments where necessary (Povey and Oriade, 2009). In other words, you need to clearly define the position and role that you aspire to, your 'dream job', and then plan the steps necessary to acquire the skills, knowledge and experience to progress to that position. Educational qualifications play an important part in this plan, and so too do activities and experiences that demonstrate broader skills and interests; in tourism, a passion for travel, strong interpersonal and communication skills and teamwork ability are prerequisites for many roles, and these can often be demonstrated through leisure activities such as sports, music, drama and so on.

This proactive approach to career planning centres on the individual and stresses the control that you have over your career success. Povey and Oriade (2009) suggest that career development in tourism is largely self-directed, meaning that you must take charge of your employment opportunities, and therefore you must play a key role in directing your career development. Career planning should not start when you are actively seeking your first permanent full-time position, it should be put in place long beforehand to allow you to prepare for securing employment in positions that will contribute to your long-term vision. Povey and Oriade (2009) identify the main elements of the career planning process as:

Self-knowledge: An accurate evaluation of your own skills, attitudes, values, interests, strengths and weaknesses.

Aspiration and expectations: Identifying realistic long-term career goals based on your ability, skills and formal educational achievements.

Planning for success: Your goals must be specific, measurable, achievable, realistic and timed (SMART) in order to monitor your success in achieving them, and may relate to income, responsibility or experiences.

Mobility: Moving between jobs in order to develop the skills, knowledge and experience to progress towards your career goals. This mobility can be achieved through moving between different occupations, to higher levels in the same occupation, and between different industries or different geographical locations.

Employer's role: Supporting and facilitating your career development through training programmes and continuing professional development (CPD) opportunities.

Career planning therefore involves reflecting on your own abilities and aspirations, setting realistic goals, and identifying the skills and abilities you will need, as well as a pathway to your goal through carefully selecting occupations and employers. The career planning process will be on-going throughout your studying and working life, and will include educational achievements as well as skills developed more broadly through work experiences, recreational activities and through community participation. In the UK the Quality Assurance Agency for Higher Education (QAA) requires universities to include elements of career planning as part of PDP on all undergraduate courses, in order to equip students with the skills to understand their abilities, evaluate their performance, and plan and manage their educational, personal and professional development (Cottrell, 2015).

Cottrell (2015) suggests that the kinds of jobs sought by many graduates require a number of skills and qualities that develop over time and demand close support and clear planning; for instance, people skills, self-management, problem solving and project work. People 1st (2016) suggest that the skills required for the tourism managers of the future are changing: whilst the completion of processes remains important, 'motivating teams, engaging with customers and keeping abreast of new technologies and opportunities are becoming increasingly important'. They suggest that the main skills required for managerial positions are:

Organisation skills: The ability to prioritise tasks, manage deadlines and monitor several tasks.

People management: Recruiting, training and motivating staff, and having knowledge of some traditional personnel functions like employment law.

Budget management: Daily financial management and long-term financial planning.

Strategic management and planning: Identifying long-term goals and developing plans to attain them.

Managing the customer experience: Understanding and enhancing service quality.

Delegation skills: Distributing tasks and projects to staff.

Communication skills: The ability to liaise with people at all levels, to write accurately, to negotiate, to be able to react appropriately under pressure.

Increasingly, academic tourism programmes are designed to develop and practise these skills.

TOURISM EDUCATION

There are many opportunities to gain educational qualifications in tourism, ranging from vocational diplomas for ages 14–16, to degrees and postgraduate studies. Some individuals will use education as a starting point for their tourism career development while others may obtain qualifications after gaining industry experience (Povey and Oriade, 2009). Postgraduate qualifications are not essential, but for individuals with industry experience, a postgraduate qualification can develop the skills required to progress to higher levels or to specialise in a management function such as marketing or HR management (Prospects, 2016).

Educational programmes provide an opportunity to develop skills that are not easily acquired during employment. For example, a degree in tourism supplies you with a broad range of transferable skills as well as an in-depth understanding of tourism and tourists, suppliers, intermediaries and impacts and the principles of their effective management. The multi-disciplinary nature of tourism degree programmes also develops strong business management and communication skills, which are equally transferable to other career areas.

Tourism undergraduates acquire and practise skills in leadership, problem-solving, ICT, research, written and verbal communication, presentation, critical analysis, teamwork, organisation, and the ability to work under pressure to deadlines. Degree programmes are structured to enable you to specialise in particular areas of tourism as you progress each year; for example in business or events tourism, aviation or sustainability, in line with your career aspirations and goals, and the final year dissertation gives you the opportunity for in-depth analysis of a tourism topic of your choice that particularly interests you. Many universities also offer modules in entrepreneurship and languages.

Tourism degree programmes provide many opportunities for their students to meet tourism practitioners and find out more about their roles and responsibilities, and to network and build up contacts through guest lecturers, site visits and field trips. Work placements or internships also allow for valuable industry experience; many tourism employers will advertise placements on their websites and through university careers services. Not all opportunities are advertised though, so you should also be proactive by approaching companies speculatively (Christian, 2017).

Some large tourism employers run leadership programmes specifically for graduates; successful applicants are fast-tracked into leadership positions via these programmes. The snapshot below describes TUI Travel's International Graduate Leadership Programme.

SNAPSHOT 14.1

TUI Travel's International Graduate Leadership Programme

TO SHAPE TOMORROW'S TRAVEL WE NEED THE BRIGHTEST MINDS TODAY
TUI Group, a FTSE 100 Company, is currently seeking outstanding graduates for the TUI Group International Graduate Leadership Programme.

This 18 months experience is open to talented and passionate individuals from around the world and will give you amazing exposure within the world's leading travel company. Our objective is to develop future commercial leaders for roles in TUI Group, to develop your business and management skills and provide experience in all aspects of our business.

WHAT YOU WILL BE DOING

- An exciting mix of day-to-day business and project work – enjoy what you do!
- 3 month assignments – working in our different businesses.
- 2 weeks in one of our main holiday destinations as a representative to engage with our customers.
- 8 weeks leadership assignment in a destination – experience leading a team of tour representatives.
- Exceptional experience in all aspects of our organisation, sharing our passion to make travel experiences special.
- Working with senior managers at different locations across the world.

WHAT WE ARE LOOKING FOR

- An innovative, entrepreneurial, motivated professional approach and strong leadership potential.
- Excellent customer focus and strong analytical and communication skills.

- Minimum of 2:1 degree (or equivalent) from a university or a business school.
- Graduated in the last 2 years or by the start of the programme.
- English language skills to business standard and fluency in one other European language.
- Minimum of 3 months international experience (work experience, internship or study).
- Minimum of 6 months commercial work experience (some of which ideally includes dealing with customers).
- Adaptable, emotionally resilient and professional approach suitable for a fast-paced, ever-changing environment.

Source: Courtesy of TUI Group

This snapshot shows the importance not only of education but also of relevant work experience and the particular personal attributes that can be demonstrated through leisure and volunteering activities. Career planning helps you to identify valuable work experience opportunities and to understand how your activities outside education and work can demonstrate a broader range of skills and personal qualities.

A number of sources of advice are available to guide your career planning and find out about career opportunities.

Career Planning Support

Career planning support is provided by careers services, through practical experience and networking.

Careers services available in colleges and universities provide specialist advice about career planning and development, and employment opportunities. They provide guidance on writing effective CVs and application letters, group and individual interview coaching and networking practice, and also arrange regular employer events to provide industry-specific information and recruitment. Many employers advertise their vacancies and graduate recruitment through university careers services. They also advertise part-time and temporary jobs which can be used to expand your industry exposure and provide valuable experience.

There are many opportunities in tourism to supplement your academic development with practical experience, helping you to understand the areas that interest you most and how your skills match practitioner roles, and to test your enjoyment of different tourism industries. The seasonal and part-time nature of many tourism jobs provides students with the opportunity to work part-time during term-time or to take temporary full-time jobs during the long vacations, building up their experience as practitioners. Work experience acquired in hotels, bars, restaurants, tourist attractions, tourist information centres and so on is useful in demonstrating the ability to work successfully in customer-facing roles, in teams or in customer-focused organisations, and to demonstrate a passion for travel.

Networking is a key part of career development (Arnold, 1997; Littleford et al., 2004). Networking involves establishing links and developing relationships with people with whom you share a common interest. Each new contact expands your network and links your network to theirs. Professional networks develop relationships with others and provide potential sources for sharing advice, guidance or business opportunities in the future. Networks can be a valuable source of information, provide support and facilitate your career development. A professional network can be started quite simply by establishing links with colleagues, fellow students, teachers and lecturers, forming a base to which further contacts can be added as your career develops.

In tourism there are many different types of networking opportunities. Trade exhibitions such as World Travel Market and IMEX bring destination organisations, accommodation, transport and attraction suppliers and intermediaries together to showcase products and trends, enabling you to learn about and meet suppliers and potential employers. Membership of professional associations such as your local or national society for tourism professionals or international societies such as Meeting Professionals International (MPI) provides learning opportunities through seminar programmes and conferences, and access to social events that will facilitate networking opportunities. Many professional associations also offer student membership, allowing you to begin establishing your network and develop relationships before entering the job market. Professional networking websites such as www.linkedin.com are very popular as a means of keeping in touch and extending networks. Career services can usually help you to write your LinkedIn profile.

Littleford et al. (2004) suggest that there are a number of basic principles that affect the success of networking, including:

- Recording, storing and updating contacts systematically.
- Keeping in touch and being aware of new opportunities.
- Maintaining relationships by informing contacts of the outcome of their help.
- Creating a positive impression so that contacts have confidence in you – being confident, interested and listening carefully.

In addition to academic qualifications and work experience, other activities also provide evidence of skills, attitudes and personal attributes, for instance membership of societies, volunteering activities, family responsibilities, sport, leadership roles and so on. The self-knowledge stage of the career planning process helps you to identify the skills and attributes developed by your broader experiences and the skills that still need to be developed.

To summarise, your potential to achieve your personal goals through a career in tourism requires you to identify your vision, evaluate your achievements and performance, and plan to develop the required skills and experience. We will now consider the types of employers and common roles within tourism.

TOURISM EMPLOYERS

As we have seen throughout this book, tourism includes a number of distinct industries, and this diversity is reflected in employment. Employers in tourism come from a range of industries as Table 14.2 shows.

TABLE 14.2   Tourism employers

Sector	Service or provision
Accommodation	Hotels – providers of serviced accommodation from budget standard to luxury
	Holiday centres – self-catering accommodation with leisure and entertainment facilities on one site
	Youth backpacker hostels – shared budget accommodation
	Self-catering accommodation – providers of villas, apartments, cottages
Passenger transport and cruise companies	Scheduled and charter coach companies, airlines, rail operators, ferry operators, car rental companies
	River and ocean voyage providers
Events	Suppliers of venues for conferences, conventions, exhibitions, sport, cultural and music events
	Owners of events
Visitor attractions	Leisure parks, theme parks, museums, art galleries, historic attractions, zoos, aquariums, sightseeing tours, activity courses
Travel services	Intermediaries that organise and reserve business and leisure travel products – travel agencies, online travel retailers, foreign exchange providers, sharing economy platforms, tour and MICE operators, wholesalers, travel ticketing
Tourist	Organisations that provide marketing, development and policy support for inbound and domestic tourism – national tourism organisations, regional and local tourism bodies, local government, tourist information centres, tourism partnerships, convention and visitor bureaux

Source: Adapted from People 1st (2010)

While it is possible to specialise and progress within one particular industry, many of the skills required in tourism are transferable and it is possible to develop your career through roles with employers in different tourism industries.

EMPLOYER SIZE

Progression opportunities and recruitment practices often differ substantially between large and small employers, and you should consider this when planning your career development.

Large employers are usually defined as organisations with more than 250 staff. There are many large tourism employers, some with thousands of employees, and often with operations in many locations, and they provide a wide range of career opportunities, for example international airlines, global hotel brands, global attraction operators and international intermediaries. These employers often offer the opportunity to have an international career by transferring between locations. Large companies are usually structured into departments based on a specialist function, for example marketing, finance, HR, and sales and reservations, as well as operations relevant to their industry, and they often recruit specialist staff for each department. Individual departments are usually structured using a hierarchy of responsibilities from entry level, for which few qualifications or little experience are necessary, through to manager and director level, and there are often career progression opportunities within the same organisation.

Large companies often use complex and lengthy recruitment processes, led by their HR department. They may advertise their vacancies on their own website or at recruitment fairs, and use a variety of testing and assessment tools, over a number of stages, to recruit the best staff. For instance, successful online applications may be followed by a telephone interview and then attendance at an assessment centre where skills and competencies are tested through in-depth group and individual exercises. Career services at colleges and universities provide opportunities to practise these tests and exercises. Many large tourism employers, particularly in the hotel and travel organisers' industries, run graduate training programmes to fast-track carefully selected graduates into leadership roles, as the TUI programme in Snapshot 14.1 describes.

Tourism SMEs are less likely to have a formal HR department, and recruitment may be conducted by individual managers or supervisors, or by the owner/general manager. SMEs are unlikely to use complex and lengthy recruitment procedures, and will often advertise their vacancies through the local or trade press, university careers service bulletins, local graduate vacancy listings and through word of mouth. SME employers often offer the advantage of opportunities to become involved in all aspects of the business, and to have close working contacts with colleagues in all roles and at all levels. Small organisations are also less likely to formally provide specialist functions such as finance, marketing and so on, and therefore it is possible to gain a close involvement in all areas and wide experience quite quickly.

Tourism also offers many opportunities for self-employment, for example as tour guides, consultants, home-based travel agencies and business start-ups. There are a growing number of consultants engaged in policy development and research on behalf of tourism companies and organisations. To become established as a consultant, in-depth sector specific knowledge is required, usually gained by professional experience or through research-based knowledge. Graduates who become consultants usually have previous tourism or related experience and a relevant postgraduate qualification.

There are a number of occupations in tourism that are also found in other sectors, for example business functions like marketing, HR management, finance and IT; practitioners have specific skills and knowledge that are transferable between sectors. There are also 'core' occupations that are unique to a specific industry and are not found in other sectors, for example tour guides, travel agents and event organisers. Tourism employers usually require a combination of core and general business functions, although this will vary depending on the size of the organisation, as we explained above.

TOURISM OCCUPATIONS

Tourism occupations are often described by their proximity to the customer: that is, whether they are customer-facing roles or back-office roles.

Tourism is 'inseparable', meaning that the customer is inevitably present when the tourism product or service is produced, and by necessity this frequently involves a face-to-face, telephone or email interaction between staff and customers. Customer-facing roles in tourism are varied and include:

- Reservations staff who interact with customers via phone or email, or in person.

- Front desk employees in accommodation, attraction or transport providers, or tourist information services.

- Operations employees such as aircraft cabin crew, coach drivers, food and beverage employees, resort representatives and tour guides, housekeeping staff.

- Sales staff such as travel agents and account managers of hotel, attraction or transport providers or MICE operators and destination organisations.

Many customer-facing staff will have a high degree of personal contact with customers and will therefore require a high level of interpersonal skills. Some roles will be unsupervised and individual employees will have complete responsibility for the quality of a customer's experience, for example tour guides, tour leaders, sales consultants and account managers.

Customer contact jobs often require a complex range of skills, which Baum (2006) calls 'the skills bundle':

- Technical or professional skills that may require formal training and qualifications, for example the use of specific computer systems such as Galileo or Sabre or tour guiding qualifications.

- General skills such as fluency in other languages, verbal and written communication skills, organisation and administrative skills and IT expertise.

- Personality traits that facilitate the ability to work in conditions that can often be stressful and demanding.

- Interpersonal skills in order to engage effectively with consumers, clients, suppliers and colleagues.

The work of customer contact employees is often described as emotional labour because of the requirement for employees to transmit positive feelings as part of their job, whether contact with consumers is face-to-face or by telephone (Hoffman and Bateson, 2016). Emotional labour involves demonstrating qualities such as friendliness, sincerity, courtesy and reliability, consistently to all customers, who will often be strangers, for the duration of the hours of employment. Cultural and linguistic differences between employees and customers may make this more challenging, and so too will the attitude of the customer, and the occurrence of stressful incidents such as delays, complaints or over-bookings. The ability to use emotional skills is an essential part of a customer contact role and cannot easily be taught in the same way that technical skills can be; consequently many tourism employers will prioritise personality and attitude rather than technical skills in their recruitment process (Baum, 2006).

The breadth of tourism employment creates a range of types of interaction between consumers and frontline staff, which will require different levels of technical and personal skills. Mills and Margulies (1980, in Schlesinger and Heskett, 1991) categorise role types in customer contact tourism employment as follows:

Maintenance interactive: Short interactions with customers that involve limited complexity, for example food and beverage service, ticket desk, housekeeping staff, information desk.

Task interactive: Short interactions that involve quite technical tasks requiring accuracy, for example flight tickets, check-in for a flight or hotel, hotel or holiday reservations.

Personal interactive: Long interactions that involve clarifying and fulfilling the customer's needs, for example MICE sales and operations, event planning, customer account management, travel agency selling holidays, tour guide, resort representative.

The required skills, qualifications, level of education, personality and attitude of staff will vary depending on the type of interaction involved.

There are also a number of occupations within tourism that do not involve direct contact with customers but are essential for the daily operation and long-term success of the organisation. These can be identified as functional roles such as finance, marketing, HR and IT, or operational roles such as security, contracting, housekeeping, scheduling, ticketing and so on, depending on the nature of the industry.

Large companies with multiple sites will usually establish corporate offices from which key business functions for the whole organisation will be provided. For example, Marriott has corporate and regional offices throughout the world that provide functional specialists such as finance and business support, strategy, sales and marketing, brand management, corporate communications and PR, procurement, IT and HR to all of their hotels within the region (Marriott International, 2017c).

The snapshot below presents some of the functional departments within one of the 'disruptor' companies that started up in the first decade of the twenty-first century.

SNAPSHOT 14.2

Careers at Airbnb

Airbnb is based in San Francisco and operates out of more than 15 locations worldwide. It offers an extremely diverse range of career opportunities.

The company is structured into a number of departments as shown in Table 14.3.

TABLE 14.3   Airbnb department structures

Engineering	Data Science and analytics	Finance and accounting	Business development
Customer experience	Design	Employee experience	Information technology
Legal	Operations	Localisation	Marketing and communications
Photography	Product	Public policy	Research
Talent	Trust and safety		

As a technology company, Airbnb's platform relies on engineers and data scientists for its accurate functioning. However, the services that the platform offers depend on professionals with knowledge, expertise and skills in tourism customer experience, destination policy and regulation, tourist and supplier engagement, tourism and services marketing, tourism product development, and new business development.

Tourism courses develop the knowledge and skills to successfully fulfill such roles. In addition, Airbnb seeks imaginative, resourceful and responsible individuals with a positive attitude who continue to learn, and are strong team players.

Source: Airbnb Inc. (n.d. a)

This section on your future in tourism has provided a brief introduction to career planning and to potential roles in tourism. Detailed guidance is available in texts listed at the end of this chapter.

We hope this book has inspired you to learn more about this exciting and transformative sector. We wish you a rewarding and successful career in tourism.

SELF-TEST QUESTIONS

1. Consider your long-term vision – imagine yourself in 10 or 20 years' time – where would you like to be living, what level of workload and stress would be desirable, would you be working alone or in a team, would you be in a leadership role, how much recognition would you like for your work, how important will a high salary be?

2. Having considered the range of industries and sectors that comprise tourism, which ones particularly interest and inspire you?

3. Identify relevant trade and professional associations, events and exhibitions for your chosen industries and sectors, and find out how to join or attend.

FURTHER READING

Burns, J. B. and McInerney, J. A. (2010) *Career Opportunities in Travel and Hospitality*. New York: Infobase Publishing.

Cottrell, S. (2015) *Skills for Success: Personal Development and Employability* Basingstoke: Palgrave Macmillan.

Lindgren, M. and Bandhold, H. (2003) *Scenario Planning: The Link Between Future and Strategy*. Basingstoke: Palgrave Macmillan.

USEFUL WEBSITES

IMEX: www.imex-frankfurt.com

Institute of Travel and Tourism: www.itt.co.uk

Meeting Professionals International: www.mpiweb.org

Prospects – graduate careers website: www.prospects.co.uk

The Tourism Society: www.tourismsociety.org

World Travel Market: www.wtmlondon.com

BIBLIOGRAPHY

Accor Hotels Group (2017) 'Brands'. Available at https://m.accorhotels.com/gb/contact/accor/brands.shtml

AEG Ogden (2017) 'About Us'. Available at www.aegogden.com/About%20Us.aspx (accessed 27/05/17)

Agarwal, S. and Shaw, G. (eds) (2007) *Managing Coastal Tourism Resorts: A Global Perspective (Aspects of Tourism)*. Bristol: Channel View Publications.

Ahmed, M. (2017) 'Accor boosts Onefinestay home-sharing business', *Financial Times*, 26 July. Available at www.ft.com/content/b96ff4c6-708a-11e7-93ff-99f383b09ff9

Airbnb (n.d. a) 'Careers'. Available at www.airbnb.co.uk/careers

Airbnb (n.d. b) 'What legal and regulatory issues should I consider before hosting on Airbnb? Available at www.airbnb.co.uk/help/article/376/what-legal-and-regulatory-issues-should-i-consider-before-hosting-on-airbnb (accessed 20/11/17).

Airbnb (2017) 'Fast Facts'. Available at https://press.atairbnb.com/fast-facts/

Airports Commission (2013) *Airports Commission: Interim Report*, December. London: Airports Commission.

Albrow, M. (2004) 'Travelling beyond local cultures', in F. Lechner and J. Boli (eds), *The Globalisation Reader*. Malden: Blackwell.

Almeida, H. (2016) 'Airbnb finds sweet spot in Lisbon after Berlin and Barcelona struggles in Bloomberg', *Skift*, 7 June. Available at https://skift.com/2016/06/07/airbnb-finds-sweet-spot-in-lisbon-after-berlin-and-barcelona-struggles/

Amadeus (2007) *Commission Cuts – Opportunities and Best Practices for Travel Agencies*. Available at www.amadeus.com/travelagencies/documents/travelagencies/White%20Paper_ForWebUse.pdf

American Express Travel Related Services (2017) 'About American Express global business travel'. Available at www.amexglobalbusinesstravel.com/company-overview/

Andriotis, K. (2016) 'Beggars–tourists' interactions: an unobtrusive typological approach', *Tourism Management, 52*: 64–73.

Ap, J. (1992) 'Residents' perceptions on tourism impacts', *Annals of Tourism Research*, 19(4): 665–90.

Aramberri, J. (2005) 'How global is tourism?', in J. Aramberri and R. Butler (eds), *Tourism Development: Issues for a Vulnerable Industry*. Bristol: Channel View Publications.

ARC and Expedia (2017) '2017 global air travel outlook'. Available at https://www.arccorp.com/email/20161208_ARC_EXPEDIA.pdf

Arduin, J. and Ni, J.(2005) 'French TGV network development', *Japan Railway and Transport Review*, 40: 22–8.

Arnold, J. (1997) *Managing Careers into the 21st Century*. London: Paul Chapman.

Ashley, C., Roe, D. and Goodwin, H. (2001) *Pro-Poor Tourism Strategies: Making Tourism Work For The Poor*. London: Overseas Development Institute.

Ashworth, G. (2003) 'Urban tourism: still an imbalance in attention?', in C. Cooper (ed.), *Classic Reviews in Tourism*. Bristol: Channel View Publications, pp. 143–62.

Asia Adventures (2017) 'Responsible community-based tourism'. Available at http://asia-adventures.com/responsible-tourism.html (accessed 14/11/17).

Association of British Travel Agents (ABTA) (2015a) 'What is a holiday surcharge?' Available at https://abta.com/holiday-help-and-complaints/how-can-we-help-you/what-is-a-holiday-surcharge

Association of British Travel Agents (ABTA) (2015b) 'Membership costs and requirements'. Available at https://abta.com/services-for-business/become-a-member/membership-requirements-and-costs

Association of Leading Visitor Attractions (ALVA) (2010) 'Visits UK leading visitor attractions 2009'. Available at www.alva.org.uk

Augustyn, M. M. and Knowles, T. (2000) 'Performance of tourism partnerships: a focus on York', *Tourism Management*, 21: 341–51.

Australian Bureau of Statistics (2009) *Tourism Satellite Account*. Canberra: Australian Bureau of Statistics.

Backman, K., Backman, S., Uysal, M. and Sunshine, K. (1995) 'Event tourism: an examination of motivations and activities', *Festival Management and Event Tourism*, 3(1): 15–24.

Baggini, J. (2008) *Welcome to Everytown*. London: Granta Books.

Bagwell, P. S. (1974) *The Transport Revolution from 1770*. London: Batsford.

Bain, C. and Wilson, N. (2004) *Lonely Planet: Malta and Gozo*. London: Lonely Planet.

Ballatyne, R. and Packer, J. (2013) *International Handbook on Eco-Tourism*. Cheltenham: Edward Elgar.

Balyozyan, D., Perret, S. and Martin, C. (2017) 'Hotel management contracts in Europe', *HVS*, 24 April. Available at www.hvs.com/article/7993-hotel-management-contracts-in-europe

Baranowski, S. (2007) 'Common ground: linking transport and tourism', *Journal of Transport History*, 28(1): 120–24.

Barbaza, Y. (1970) 'Trois types d'intervention du tourisme dans l'organsiation de l'espace littoral', *Annales de Géographie*, (434): 446–69.

Barker, M. (2004) *Crime and Sports Event Tourism*. Bristol: Channel View Publications.

Barley, M. (2017) 'Soft brand – future opportunities in the Canadian market', *HVS*, 11 May. Available at www.hvs.com/article/8007-soft-brands-future-opportunities-in-the-canadian-market

Barnes, B. (2011) 'Disney report 54% rise in profit', *New York Times*, 8 February. Available at www.nytimes.com/2011/02/09/business/media/09disney.html

Barrett, J. (1958) 'The seaside resort towns of England and Wales'. Unpublished PhD thesis. London: University of London.

Barton, S. (2005) *Working Class Organisations and Popular Tourism 1840–1970*. Manchester: Manchester University Press.

Bateson, J. (1995) *Managing Services Marketing*. Orlando: The Dryden Press.

Baum, T. (2006) *Human Resource Management for Tourism, Hospitality and Leisure: An International Perspective*. Andover: Thomson.

Baum, T. and Lundtorp, S. (2001) *Seasonality in Tourism* (Advances in Tourism Research Series). Oxford: Pergamon.

BBC News (2008) 'Cyprus's water crisis', 16 July. Available at http://news.bbc.co.uk/1/hi/world/europe/7508785.stm (accessed 15/11/17).

BBC News (2017a) 'Bhutan country profile', 13 July. Available at www.bbc.co.uk/news/world-south-asia-12480707 (accessed 20/11/17).BBC (2017b) 'Saudi Arabia plans luxury beach resorts on Red Sea'. Available at www.bbc.co.uk/news/world-middle-east-40795570 (accessed 01/08/17).

BBC (2017b) 'Saudi Arabia plans luxury beach resorts on Red Sea', 1 August. Available at www.bbc.co.uk/news/world-middle-east-40795570 (accessed 05/12/17).

BBC Newsbeat (2017) 'Tonnes of rubbish is being cleared from Mount Everest'. Available at www.bbc.co.uk/newsbeat/article/39442821/tonnes-of-rubbish-is-being-cleared-from-mount-everest

Beard, J. and Ragheb, M. (1983) 'Measuring leisure motivation', *Journal of Leisure Research*, 15: 219–28.

Beaver, A. (2002) *A Dictionary of Travel and Tourism Terminology*. Wallingford: CABI.

Becken, S. and Hay, J. E. (2007) *Tourism and Climate Change: Risks and Opportunities*. Bristol: Channel View Publications.

Becken, S. and Schiff, A. (2011) 'Demand elasticity estimates for New Zealand tourism', *Tourism Management*, (32) 564–75.

Becker, E. (2016) *Overbooked: The Exploding Business of Travel and Tourism*. New York: Simon and Schuster, Chs 10 and 11.

Beech, J. and Chadwick, S. (eds) (2006) *The Business of Tourism Management*. Harlow: Pearson Education.

Beeton, S. (2006) *Community Development through Tourism*. Collingwood: Landlinks Press.

Begg, D., Fisher, S. and Dornbush, R. (1994) *Economics*. London: Mc-Graw-Hill.

Beirman, D. (2003) *Restoring Tourism Destinations in Crisis*. Wallingford: CABI.

Benavides, D. (2002) 'Overcoming poverty in developing countries through self-sustainable international tourism', in B. Rauschelbach, A. Schäfer and B. Steck (eds), *Co-operating for Sustainable Tourism, Proceedings of the Forum International at the Reisepavillion 2002*. Heidelberg: Kasparek.

Benckendorff, P. J., Moscardo, G. and Pendergast, D. (2009) *Tourism and Generation Y*. Wallingford: CABI.

Berry, L. L. (1980) 'Services marketing is different', *Business Magazine* (May–June): 24–9.

Beynon, J. and Dunkerley, D. (eds) (2000) *Globalisation: The Reader*. London: Athlone.

Bianchi, R. (2006) 'Tourism and the globalisation of fear: analysing the politics of risk and (in) security in global travel', *Tourism and Hospitality Research*, 7(1): 64–74.

Bishop, E. (1968) *Questions of Travel*. New York: Farrar, Strauss and Giroux.

Bismart (2017) 'Smart Destination'. Available at https://bismart.com/en/business-intelligence-solutions/smart-destination/

Bisson, J. (1986) 'À l'Origine du Tourisme aux îles Baleares: Vocation Touristique ou Receptivité du Milieu d'Accueuil?' Paper presented at the meeting of the IGU Commission of the Geography of Tourism and Leisure, Palma de Mallorca (mimeo).

Bitner, M. J. (1992) 'Evaluating service encounters: the effects of physical surroundings and employee responses', *Journal of Marketing*, April: 42–50.

Black, M. (1995) *In the Twilight Zone: Child Workers in the Hotel, Tourism and Catering Industry*. Geneva: International Labour Organisation.

Bleasdale, S. and Tapsell, S. (1994) 'Contemporary efforts to expand the tourist industry in Cuba: The Perspective from Britain', in A.V. Seaton (ed.), *Tourism: The state of the art*. Brisbane: Wiley.

Blue Flag (n.d.) 'We bring positive change, we educate, we care'. Available at http://www.blueflag.global/all-bf-sites/ (accessed 05/12/17)

Blewitt, J. (2008) *Understanding Sustainable Development*. London: Earthscan.

BMI Research (2017) 'Oman Tourism Report Q3 2017'. Available at http://web.b.ebscohost.com/ehost/pdfviewer/pdfviewer?vid=2&sid=451f7844-f009-4e2b-8f78-1eee0ff57bdd%40sessionmgr120&hid=123

Boeing (2017) 'Boeing 787'. Available at www.boeing.com/commercial/747/#/design-highlights/economy-performance/speed/

Boer, A., Thomas, R. and Webster, M. (1997) *Small Business Management: A Resource-based Approach for the Hospitality and Tourism Industries*. London: Cassell.

Boissevain, J. (ed.) (1996) *Coping with Tourists: European Reactions to Mass Tourism*. Providence, NY: Berghahn Books.

Bolwell, D. and Weinz, W. (2008) *Reducing Poverty through Tourism* (working document). Geneva: International Labour Organisation.

Bongar, B., Brown, L., Beutler, E. and Zimbardo, P. (2007) *Psychology of Terrorism*. New York: Oxford University Press.

Boniface, B. and Cooper, C. (2005) *Worldwide Destinations Casebook*. Oxford: Butterworth-Heinemann.

Boniface, B. and Cooper, C. (2009) *Worldwide Destinations: The Geography of Travel and Tourism*. London: Elsevier.

Booms, B. H. and Bitner, M. J. (1981) 'Marketing strategies and organisation structures for service firms', in J. Donnelly and W. R. George (eds), *Marketing of Services*. Chicago, IL: American Marketing Association, pp. 47–51.

Borman, E. (2004) 'Health tourism: where healthcare, ethics and the state collide', *British Medical Journal*, 328: 60–61.

Bornhorst, T., Ritchie, J. R. B. and Sheehan, L. (2010) 'Determinants of tourism success for DMOs and destinations: an empirical examination of stakeholders' perspectives', *Tourism Management*, 31(5): 572–89.

Bournemouth Tourism (2010) 'BTMB'. Available at www.bournemouth.co.uk/site/business/btmb

Bournemouth Tourism (2017) 'BTMB'. Available at http://bournemouth.co.uk/btmb/

Bowdin, G., Allen, J., O'Toole, W., Harris, R. and McDonnell, I. (2006) *Events Management*. London: Elsevier.

Bowen, D. and Clarke J. (2009) *Contemporary Tourist Behaviour: Yourself and Others as Tourists*. Wallingford: CABI.

Bradford Council (2002) *Tourism Strategy*. Bradford: Bradford Council.

Bradley, S. (2009) 'Lavaux celebrates its Unesco status in style', *Swissinfo*, 17 November. Available at http://www.swissinfo.ch/eng/lavaux-celebrates-its-unesco-status-in-style/7664614 (accessed 14/11/17).

Bramwell, B. and Lane, B. (eds) (2000) *Tourism Collaboration and Partnerships: Politics, Practice and Sustainability*. Bristol: Channel View Publications.

Brenner, C. and Aguilar, A. G. (2002) 'Luxury tourism and regional economic development in Mexico', *The Professional Geographer*, 54 (4): 500–520.

British Postal Museum and Archive (2005) *The Mail Coach Service*. London: Postal Heritage Trust.

Bromley, D. (1990) *Behavioural Gerontology: Central Issues in the Psychology of Ageing*. Hoboken, NJ: Wiley.

Buckley, M. (1994) *The Structure of Business*. Harlow: Longman.

Buhalis, D. (2000) 'Marketing the competitive destination of the future', *Tourism Management*, 21: 97–116.

Buhalis, D. (2001) 'Tourism distribution channels: practices and processes', in D. Buhalis and E. Laws (eds), *Tourism Distribution Channels: Practices, Issues, and Transformations*. London: Continuum, pp. 7–33.

Buhalis, D. (2003) *eTourism Information Technology for Strategic Tourism Management*. Harlow: Prentice-Hall.

Buhalis, D. and Kaldis, K. (2008) 'eEnabled internet distribution for small and medium sized hotels: the case of Athens', *Tourism Recreation Research*, 33(1): 67–81.

Buhalis, D. and Laws, E. (eds) (2001) *Tourism Distribution Channels: Practices, Issues, and Transformations*. London: Continuum.

Buhalis, D. and Licata, M. C. (2002) 'The future eTourism intermediaries', *Tourism Management*, 23(3): 207–220.

Bureau of Labor Statistics (2016) 'Paid leave benefits, March'. Available at www.bls.gov/ncs/ebs/benefits/2016/benefits_leave.htm

Burke, L. and Maidens, J. (2004) 'Reefs at Risk in the Caribbean'. Available at www.wri.org/publication/reefs-risk-caribbean

Burns, C. (2008) 'Quotable quote', *GWAHS Newsletter* (Greater Western Health Service, Australia), October/November.

Burns, J. B. and McInerney, J. A. (2010) *Career Opportunities in Travel and Hospitality*. New York: Infobase Publishing.

Burns, P. (1998) 'Tourism in Russia: background and structure', *Tourism Management*, 19(6): 555–65.

Business Traveller (2009) 'BA to drop Gatwick–New York route', *Business Traveller*, 29 May. Available at www.businesstraveller.com

Butler, R. (1980) 'The concept of a tourist area cycle of evolution', *The Canadian Geographer*, 24(1): 5–12.

Butler, R. (1993) 'Pre and post impact assessment of tourism developments', in D. Pearce and R. Butler (eds), *Tourism Research: Critiques and Challenges*. London: Routledge.

Butler, R. (2001) 'Seasonality in tourism: issues and implications', in T. Baum and S. Lundtorp (eds), *Seasonality in Tourism*. Oxford: Pergamon, pp. 5–22.

Butler, R. (ed.) (2006a) *The Tourism Area Life Cycle, Vol. 1 Applications and Modifications*. Bristol: Channel View Publications.

Butler, R. (ed.) (2006b) *The Tourism Area Life Cycle, Vol. 2 Conceptual and Theoretical Issues*. Bristol: Channel View Publications.

Butler, R. (2006c) 'The concept of a tourist area life cycle of evolution: implications for management of resources', in R. Butler (ed.), *The Tourism Area Life Cycle, Vol 1 Applications and Modifications*. Bristol: Channel View Publications, Ch. 1.

Cabezas, A. (2008) 'Tropical blues: tourism and social exclusion in the Dominican Republic', *Latin American Perspectives*, 160(35–3): 21–36.

Cahill, K., Marion, J. and Lawson, S. (2008) 'Exploring visitor acceptability for hardening trails to sustain visitation and minimise impacts', *Journal of Sustainable Tourism*, 16(2): 232–45.

Campaign for Rural England (2015) 'Third Heathrow runway would be full frontal assault on Green Belt and tranquillity', 1 July.

Caribbean Tourism Organisation (2014) *Tourist Industry Update 2013*. Richmond: Caribbean Tourism Organisation.

CARICOM (2003) 'Liberalization of air transport services within the Caribbean community'. Available at www.icao.int/sustainability/CaseStudies/StatesReplies/CaricomLib_En.pdf (accessed 11/05/17).

Carmona, M., de Magalhães, C. and Hammond, L. (2008) *Public Space, the Management Dimension*. Oxford: Routledge.

Carr, M. (1997) *New Patterns: Process and Change in Human Geography*. London: Nelson.

Carswell, H. (2017) 'How Nepal's tourist industry is bouncing back two years on from devastating earthquake', *Independent*, 21 April. Available at www.independent.co.uk/travel/asia/nepal-earthquake-tourist-industry-bouncing-back-a7688611.html

Cartwright, R. and Baird, C. (1999) *The Development and Growth of the Cruise Industry*. Oxford: Butterworth-Heinemann.

Casson, L. (1974) *Travel in the Ancient World*. London: George Allen and Unwin.

Causevic, S. (2010) 'Tourism which erases borders: an introspection into Bosnia and Herzegovina', in O. Moufakkir and I. Kelly (eds), *Tourism, Progress and Peace*. Wallingford: CABI.

Ceballos-Lascuráin, H. (1996) *Tourism, Ecotourism and Protected Areas*. Gland: IUCN.

Center on Ecotourism and Sustainable Development (CESD) (2006) *Cruise Tourism in Belize Perceptions of Economic, Social and Environmental Impact*. Washington, DC: CESD.

Chartered Institute of Marketing (2009) *Marketing and the 7Ps: A Brief Summary of Marketing and How it Works*. Maidenhead: CIM Insights.

China National Tourism Administration (CNTA) (2017) 'Top 10 Chinese tourism Destinations for Spring Festival', 13 February. Available at http://en.cnta.gov.cn/News/localnews/201702/t20170213_814620.shtml

China Outbound Tourism Research Institute (COTRI) (2008) 'China outbound on the road'. Available at www.china-outbound.com

Christaller, W. (1963) 'Some considerations of tourism location in Europe: the peripheral regions – underdeveloped countries – recreation areas', *Regional Science Association Papers* XII, Lund Congress, pp. 95–105.

Christian, S. (2017) 'Speculative cover letter, April 2017'. Available at www.prospects.ac.uk/careers-advice/cvs-and-cover-letters/cover-letters/speculative-cover-letter

CITS Group Corporation (2017) 'CITS Group'. Available at www.cits.net/about/cits-group.html

City of Indio (2017) '1.4 million people visit the city of Indio every year!' Available at www.indio.org/civicax/filebank/blobdload.aspx?BlobID=24998 (accessed 10/05/17).

Civil Aviation Authority (CAA) (2010) 'Learn about ATOL'. Available at www.caa.co.uk/default.aspx?catid=1080&pagetype=90

Civil Aviation Authority (CAA) (2015) 'About ATOL'. Available at www.caa.co.uk/ATOL-protection/Consumers/About-ATOL/

Civil Aviation Authority (CAA) (2017) 'Size of UK airports'. Available at www.caa.co.uk/Data-and-analysis/UK-aviation-market/Airports/Datasets/UK-Airport-data/Airport-data-2016/

Clarke, J. and Critcher, C. (1985) *The Devil Makes Work: Leisure in Capitalist Britain*. London: Macmillan.

Clegg, J. (2008) 'Brits holiday more than other Europeans', 4 June. www.ttglive.co.uk

Clift, S. and Forrest, S. (1999) 'Gay men and tourism: destinations and holiday motivations', *Tourism Management* 20: 615–25.

Clover, C. (2007) 'Eathlog: a Spanish tragedy', *Telegraph*, 3 May. Available at www.telegraph.co.uk/earth/earthcomment/charlesclover/3292364/Earthlog.html

Coccossis, H. and Mexa, A. (2004) *The Challenge of Tourism Carrying Capacity Assessment*. Farnham: Ashgate.

Cohen, E. (1972) 'Toward a sociology of international tourism', *Social Research*, 39(1): 164–89.

Cohen, E. (1979) 'A phenomenology of tourist experiences', *Sociology*, 13: 179–201.

Cohen, E. (1984) 'The sociology of tourism: approaches, issues and findings', *Annual Review of Sociology*, 10: 373–92.

Cohen, S. (2010) 'Reconceptualising lifestyle travellers: contemporary "drifters", in K. Hannam and A. Diekmann (eds), *Beyond Backpacker Tourism: Mobilities and Experiences*. Bristol: Channel View Publications.

Cole, S. (2008) *Tourism, Culture and Development: Hopes, Dreams and Realities in East-Indonesia*. Bristol: Channel View Publications.

Cole, S. and Morgan N. (eds) (2010) *Tourism and Inequality: Problems and Prospects*. Wallingford: CABI.

Cole, V. and Sinclair A. (2002) 'Measuring the ecological footprint of a Himalayan tourist centre', *Mountain Research and Development*, 22(2): 132–41.

Collins, S. and Perret, S. (2015) 'Decisions, decisions … which hotel operating model is right for you?', *HVS*, April. Available at www.hvs.com/StaticContent/3672.pdf

Colston, P. (2017) 'Carlson Wagonlit Travel new world sales break $2bn barrier', *Conference and Meeting World*, 9 March. Available at www.c-mw.net/carlson-wagonlit-travel-logs-23-fewer-transactions-new-sales-break-2bn-barrier/

Community Marketing & Insights (CMI) (2016) 'CMI's 21st annual survey on LGBT tourism and hospitality'. Available at www.communitymarketinginc.com/documents/temp/CMI_21st-LGBT-Travel-Study-Report2016.pdf

Community of European Railway and Infrastructure Companies (CER) (2009) 'Railways and the environment: building on the railways' environmental strengths', 20 January. Available at www.cer.be/publications/brochures/railways-and-environment-building-railways-environmental-strengths

Community of European Railway and Infrastructure Companies (CER) (2015) *Rail Transport and Environment: Facts and Figures*. Brussels: CER.

Condé Nast Traveler (2017) 'Venice looks to limit tourist numbers with new measures', 28 April.

Connolly, P. and McGing, G. (2007) 'High performance work practices and competitive advantage in the Irish hospitality sector', *International Journal of Contemporary Hospitality Management*, 19(3): 201–210.

Continental Airlines (2009) '2008 annual report to stockholders'. Available at http://phx.corporate-ir.net/External.File?item=UGFyZW50SUQ9NjQ0OTl8Q2hpbGRJRD0t MXxUeXBlPTM=&t=1

Convention Industry Council (CIC) (2003) 'APEX industry glossary'. Available at http://glossary.convention industry.org

Cooper, C. (1997) 'The technique of interpretation', in S. Medlik (ed.), *Managing Tourism*. Oxford: Butterworth-Heinemann.

Cooper, C. (ed.) (2003) *Classic Reviews in Tourism*. Bristol: Channel View Publications.

Cooper, C. and Hall, M. C. (2008) *Contemporary Tourism: An International Approach*. Oxford: Butterworth-Heinemann.

Cooper, C., Fletcher J., Fyall A., Gilbert, D. and Wanhill, S. (2008) *Tourism Principles and Practice*. Harlow: Pearson Education.

Cottrell, S. (2015) *Skills for Success: Personal Development and Employability*. Basingstoke: Palgrave Macmillan.

Crompton, J. L. (1979) 'Motivations for pleasure vacation', *Annals of Tourism Research* 6(4): 408–424.

Cruiselines International Association (2016) '2017 cruise industry outlook', December. Available at www.cruising.org/docs/default-source/research/clia-2017-state-of-the-industry.pdf?sfvrsn=0

Cruisemapper.com (2015) 'UK cruise ports list 2015'. Available at www.cruisemapper.com/wiki/774-uk-cruise-ports

Cunill, O. M. (2006) *The Growth Strategies of Hotel Chains: Best Business Practices by Leading Companies*. Binghampton, NY: Haworth Hospitality Press.

Daby, D. (2003) 'Effects of seagrass bed removal for tourism purposes in a Mauritian bay', *Environmental Pollution*, 125: 313–24.

Dallen, J., Victor, T. and Teye, B. (2009) *Tourism and the Lodging Sector*. London: Taylor & Francis.

Dann, G. (1977) 'Anomie, ego-enhancement and tourism', *Annals of Tourism Research*, 4(4): 184–94.

Darwin Centre (2017) 'Explore science and nature in the Darwin Centre's Coccoon, meet experts at the daily Attenborough Studio events, and see specimens close up in the Zoology spirit building'. Available at www.nhm.ac.uk/visit/galleries-and-museum-map/darwin-centre.html (accessed 20/11/17)

Davidson, R. (2001) 'Distribution channel analysis for business travel', in D. Buhalis and E. Laws (eds), *Tourism Distribution Channels: Practices, Issues, and Transformations*. London: Continuum, pp. 73–87.

Davidson, R. and Maitland, R. (1997) *Tourism Destinations*. London: Hodder and Stoughton.

Davidson, R. and Rogers, T. (2006) *Marketing Destinations and Venues for Conferences, Conventions and Business Events*. Oxford: Butterworth-Heinemann.

Davidson, T. L. (2005) 'What are travel and tourism – are they really an industry?', in W. F. Theobald (ed.), *Global Tourism*. Burlington, MA: Elsevier, pp. 25–32.

Dawes, J. and Rowley, J. (1996) 'The waiting experience: towards service quality in the leisure industry', *International Journal of Contemporary Hospitality Management*, 8(1): 16–21.

Dawson, S. (2007) 'Working class consumers and the campaign for holidays with pay', *Twentieth-Century British History*, 18: 277–305.

de Botton, A. (2002) *The Art of Travel*. London: Penguin.

De Bruyn P., Bain K.,Vankatraman, N. and Joshi, S. (2008) *Frommer's India*. Hoboken, NJ: Wiley.

Delaney-Smith, P. (1987) 'The tour operator – new and maturing business', in A. Hodgson (ed.), *The Travel and Tourism Industry*. Oxford: Butterworth-Heinemann, pp. 94–106.

Deloitte and Oxford Economics (2013) *The Economic Contribution of the Tourism Economy in the UK*. London: VisitBritain.

Department for Communities and Local Government (DCLG) (2015) 'Promoting the sharing economy in London – policy in short-term use of residential property in London', 9 February. Available at https://www.gov.uk/government/speeches/short-term-use-of-residential-property-in-london (accessed 03/11/17)

Department for Digital, Culture, Media and Sport (DCMS) (2016a) '2015 to 2020 government policy: museums and galleries', 1 June. Available at www.gov.uk/government/uploads/system/uploads/attachment_data/file/529489/2016Updateof2010to2015governmentpolicymuseumsandgalleries-GOV.UK20160425.pdf.pdf

Department for Digital, Culture, Media and Sport (DCMS) (2016b) 'Tourism action plan August 2016'. Available at www.gov.uk/government/publications/tourism-action-plan

Department for Transport (DfT) (2003) *The Future of Air Transport*. London: The Stationery Office.

Destination Think! (2017) 'How will augmented reality support the tourism experience?' Available at https://destinationthink.com/augmented-reality-tourism-experience/

Detroit Historical Society (2017) 'Time line of Detroit'. Available at https://detroithistorical.org/learn/timeline-detroit

Deutsche Messe (n.d.) 'About Us'. Available at www.messe.de/en/company/us/

Dibben, M. and Norton, S. (2017) 'Embedding employability in student programmes – it starts with the right language', *Higher Education Academy*, 2 May. Available at www.heacademy.ac.uk/blog/embedding-employability-student-programmes-%E2%80%93-it-starts-right-language

Dilts, J. C. and Prough, G. E. (1991) 'Travel agent perceptions and responses in a deregulated travel environment', *Journal of Travel Research*, 29: 37–42.

Disney Cruise Line (2017) 'Disney Cruise Line onboard activities'. Available at https://disneycruise.disney.go.com/onboard-activities/overview/

Doganis, R. (1991) *Flying off Course: The Economics of International Airlines*. London: Harper Collins Academic.

Doganis, R. (2009) *Flying Off Course: Airline Economics and Marketing Airlines*. London: Routledge.

Doganis, R. (2012) *Flying off Course: The Economics of International Airlines*. London: Routledge.

Donaghy, G. (2007) 'Convention centres: is the model evolving?', *MICE International*, May–June: 71–72.

Donaldson, J. A. (2007) 'Tourism, development and poverty reduction in Guizhou and Yunnan', *The China Quarterly*, 190: 333–51.

Douglas, N. and Douglas, N. (2004) *The Cruise Experience*. Sydney: Pearson.

Doxey, G. (1975) 'A causation theory of visitor-resident irritants: methodology and research inferences in the impact of tourism', *Sixth Annual Conference Proceedings of the Travel Research Association*, (September): 195–8.

Dredge, D. (2006) 'Policy networks and the local organisation of tourism', *Tourism Management*, 27(2): 269–80.

Dredge, D. and Gyimothy, S. (eds) (2017) *Collaborative Economy and Tourism: Perspectives, Politics, Policies and Prospects (Tourism on the Edge)*. Cham: Springer International.

Dresner, S. (2008) *The Principles of Sustainability*. London: Earthscan.

Drummond, S. and Yeoman, I. (eds) (2001) *Quality Issues in Heritage Visitor Attractions*. Oxford: Butterworth-Heinemann.

Dunn, G. (2016) 'Analysis: The biggest LCCs by traffic and financials in 2015', *Flight Global*, 27 May. Available at: www.flightglobal.com/news/articles/analysis-the-biggest-lccs-by-traffic-and-financials-425117/

Durbarry, R. and Sinclair, M. T. (2002) *The Price Sensitivity of Tourism Demand in Malta*: A *Report for the Malta Tourism Authority.* Nottingham: The Christel DeHaan Tourism and Travel Research Institute, Nottingham University Business School.

Duval, D. (2003) 'When hosts become guests: return visits and diasporic identities in a Commonwealth Eastern Caribbean community', *Current Issues in Tourism*, 6(4): 267–308.

Duval, D. (2007) *Tourism and Transport, Modes, Networks and Flows.* Bristol: Channel View Publications.

Dwyer, L., Forsyth, P. and Dwyer, W. (2010) *Tourism Economics and Policy.* Bristol: Channel View Publications.

DYCD (2017) 'NYC Department of Youth and Community Development'. Available at www1.nyc.gov/site/dycd/index.page (accessed 14/11/17).

easyJet (2010) '2010 annual report'. Available at http://2010annualreport.easyjet.com/easyjet-at-a-glance.asp

Economist (2001) *Globalisation.* London: Profile.

Economist (2015) 'Vatican museums: full to bursting – what to do about overcrowding in holy places'. 12.03.2015 Available at www.economist.com/news/books-and-arts/21646182-what-do-about-overcrowding-holy-places-full-bursting

Ecorys (2009) *Study on the Competitiveness of the EU Tourism Industry – with Specific Focus on the Accommodation and Tour Operator and Travel Agent Industries.* Rotterdam: Ecorys SCS Group.

ECPAT (2016) 'Welcome to ECPAT'. Available at www.ecpat.net (accessed 14/11/17).

Egger, G. (2007) 'Personal carbon trading: a potential "stealth intervention" for obesity reduction?', *Medical Journal of Australia*, 187(3): 185–7.

Egger, R. and Buhalis, D. (2008) *eTourism Case Studies: Management and Marketing Issues in eTourism.* Abingdon: Routledge.

Elliott, J. (1997) *Tourism: Politics and Public Sector Management.* London: Routledge.

EU General Data Protection Regulation (EU GDPR) (2017) 'GDPR key changes'. Available at www.eugdpr.org/key-changes.html

Euromonitor (1988) *The World Package Holidays Market 1980*–1995. London: Euromonitor Publications.

Euromonitor (2006) *Travel and Tourism in Albania.* London: Euromonitor Publications.

Euromonitor International (2008) *Travel and Tourism Country Reports.* London: Euromonitor Publications.

European Commission (2005) *The New SME definition User Guide and Model Declaration.* Luxembourg: Enterprise and Industry Publications.

European Commission (2015a) 'Stronger EU protection for package holidays'. Available at ec.europa.eu/consumers/consumer_rights/.../factsheet_new-package-travel_en.

European Commission (2015b) 'Guide on EU funding for the tourism sector'. Available at http://ec.europa.eu/growth/content/guide-eu-funding-tourism-sector-updated-version-0_en (accessed 05/12/17).

European Competition Network (ECN) (2017) 'Report on the monitoring exercise carried out in the online hotel booking sector by EU competition authorities in 2016'. Available at http://ec.europa.eu/competition/ecn/hotel_monitoring_report_en.pdf

European Environment Agency (2012) *Climate change, impacts and vulnerability in Europe 2012: An indicator-based report*, EEA Report No. 12/2012, European Environment Agency, Copenhagen, Denmark.

European Environment Agency (EEA) (2017) 'Home page'. Available at https://www.eea.europa.eu/ (accessed 06/11/17).

European Tourism Association (ETOA) (2016) 'Fast-forward to 2017: what will the global hotel industry look like?' 25 February. Available at www.etoa.org/media/all-news/news-item/fast-forward-to-2017-what-will-the-global-hotel-industry-look-like-HT

Eurostat (2015) 'Hotels and similar accommodation (NACE Rev.2, I, 55.1) by size class: number of establishments, bedrooms and bed-places (from 2012 onwards)'. Available at http://ec.europa.eu/eurostat/statistics-explained/index.php/Tourism_statistics_-_annual_results_for_the_accommodation_sector

Eurostat (2016) *Panorama on Tourism*. Luxembourg: Eurostat.

Executive Group Travel (2014) 'Our Process'. Available at www.executivegrouptravel.com/our-process

Expedia (2017) 'Infographic – about us'. Available at www.expediainc.com/about/

Experian (2017) 'Mosaic'. Available at www.experian.co.uk/assets/marketing-services/infographics/infographic-new-mosaic-consumer-segmentation.pdf

Facebook (2017) 'Stats'. Available at https://newsroom.fb.com/company-info/

Fahey, L. (2003) 'How corporations learn from scenarios', in R. Randall (ed.), *Integrate Scenario Learning with Decision Making*. Bradford: Emerald.

Faulkner, B. and Tideswell, C. (1997) 'A framework for monitoring community impacts of tourism', *Journal of Sustainable Tourism*, 5(1): 3–28.

FCM Travel Solutions (2017) 'Mobile solutions'. Available at www.us.fcm.travel/solutions/mobile-solutions

Federation of Tour Operators (FTO) (2009) 'Advance planning'. Available at www.fto.co.uk//operators-factfile/advanced-planning/

Fennell, D. A. (2015) *Ecotourism* (4th edn). London: Routledge.

Font, X. and Buckley, R. (2001) *Tourism Ecolabelling: Certification and Promotion of Sustainable Management*. Wallingford: CABI.

Ford, R. (2008) 'Chasing MICE and fellow travellers: a history of the convention and visitor bureau industry', *Journal of Management History*, 14(2): 128–43.

Forsyth, P. (2008) 'Tourism and aviation policy', in A. Graham, A. Papatheodorou and P. Forsyth (eds), *Aviation and Tourism: Implications for Leisure Travel*. Farnham: Ashgate, pp. 73–85.

Forum for the Future (FF) (2009) *Tourism 2023*. London: Forum for the Future.

France, L. (ed.) (1999) *An Earthscan Reader in Sustainable Tourism*. London: Earthscan.

Frechtling, D. (1999) 'The tourism satellite account: foundations, progress and issues', *Tourism Management*, 20: 163–70.

Frechtling, D. (2001) *Forecasting Tourism Demand: Methods and Strategies*. Oxford: Butterworth-Heinemann.

Friends of the Earth (2000) *From Planes to Trains: Realising the Potential from Shifting Short-haul Flights to Rail*. London: Friends of the Earth.

Frochot, I. (2005) 'A benefit segmentation of tourists in rural areas: a Scottish perspective', *Tourism Management*, 26(3): 335-46.

Fuentes, A. (2006) 'Human culture and monkey behavior: assessing the contexts of potential pathogen transmission between macaques and humans', *American Journal of Primatology*, 68: 880–96.

Fyall, A. and Garrod, B. (2005) *Tourism Marketing: A Collaborative Approach*. Bristol: Channel View Publications.

Fyall, A., Garrod, B., Leask, A. and Wanhill, S. (2008) *Managing Visitor Attractions: New Directions*. Oxford: Butterworth-Heinemann.

Gale, T. (2006) 'Mass tourism businesses: tour operators', in J. Beech and S. Chadwick (eds), *The Business of Tourism Management*. Harlow: Pearson Education, pp. 399–413.

Gallarza, M., Saura, I. and Garcia, H. (2002) 'Destination image: towards a conceptual framework', *Annals of Tourism Research*, 29(1): 56–78.

Garcia-Altes, A. (2005) 'The development of health tourism services', *Annals of Tourism Research*, 32(1): 262–6.

Garrod, B. (2008) 'Managing visitor impacts', in A. Fyall, B. Garrod, A. Leask and S. Wanhill (eds), *Managing Visitor Attractions: New Directions*. Oxford: Butterworth-Heinemann.

Gartrell, R. (1994) *Strategic Partnerships: Destination Marketing for Convention and Visitor Bureaux*. Dubuque, IA: Kendall/Hunt, pp. 230–32.

Gatwick Airport (2010) 'Service quality rebate scheme'. Available at www.gatwickairport.com/business/performance/rebate-scheme/

Gelling, N. (2007) 'Before the revolution', *Smithsonian*, 31 July. Available at www.smithsonianmag.com/history/before-the-revolution-159682020/ (accessed 30/03/17)

Getz, D. (2007) *Event Studies: Theory, Research and Policy for Planned Events*. Oxford: Butterworth-Heinemann.

Getz, D. and Page, S. J. (2016) *Event Studies: Theory, Research and Policy for Planned Events*. London: Routledge.

Giddens, A. (1998) *The Third Way: The Renewal of Social Democracy*. Cambridge: Polity Press.

Gilbert, D. (1990) 'Strategic marketing planning for national tourism', *The Tourist Review*, 45(1): 18–27.

Gilbert, D. (1991) 'An examination of the consumer decision process related to tourism', in C. Cooper (ed.), *Progress in Tourism, Recreation and Hospitality Management, Vol. 3*. London: Belhaven.

Gilbert, E. W. (1939) 'The growth of inland and seaside health resorts in England', *Scottish Geographical Magazine*, 55: 16–35.

Gill, R. (2010) 'UK visits abroad fall by 15%', 13 July. Available at www.ttglive.co.uk

Gladstone, D. (2005) *From Pilgrimage to Package Tour: Travel and Tourism in the Third World*. London: Routledge.

Glaesser, D. (2003) *Crisis Management in the Tourism Industry*. Oxford: Elsevier Butterworth-Heinemann.

Glastonbury Festival (2011) 'History'. Available at www.glastonburyfestivals.co.uk/history

Godfrey, K. and Clarke, J. (2000) *The Tourism Development Handbook: A Practical Approach to Planning and Marketing*. London: Thomson Learning.

Goeldner, C. R., Ritchie, J. R. B. and McIntosh, R. W. (2000) *Tourism: Principles, Practices, Philosophies*. Chichester: Wiley.

Gomez-Ibanez, J. A. and de Rus, G. (eds) (2006) *Competition in the Railway Industry: An International Comparative Analysis*. Cheltenham: Edward Elgar.

Gooroochurn, N. and Sinclair, T. (2005) 'Economics of tourism taxation: evidence from Mauritius', *Annals of Tourism Research*, 32(2): 478–98.

Gormsen, E. (1997) 'The impact of tourism on coastal areas', *Geojournal*, 42(1): 39–54.

Government of Canada (2011) 'Transport agreements India', *Canadian Transportation Agency*. Available at https://otc-cta.gc.ca/eng/transport-agreement/india

Government of India (2007) *Incredible India: The Global Healthcare Destination*. Delhi: Ministry of Tourism.

Government of Jamaica (2009) *Team Jamaica* (Tourism Product Development Co. Ltd). Available at www.tpdco.org

Graham, A. and Dennis, N. (2009) 'The impact of low cost airline operations to Malta', *Journal of Air Transport Management*, 15(4): 149–50.

Graham, A., Papatheodorou, A. and Forsyth, P. (eds) (2008) *Aviation and Tourism – Implications for Leisure Travel*. Farnham: Ashgate.

Graham, M. (2009) 'Different models in different spaces or liberalized optimizations? Competitive strategies among budget air carriers', *Journal of Transport Geography*, 17(4): 306–16.

Grant, D. and Mason, S. (2007) *Holiday Law: The Law Relating to Travel and Tourism*. London: Sweet & Maxwell.

Gray, C. (2009) 'Which way for ATOL reform?', *Travel Trade Gazette UK and Ireland*, 17 September.

Greenpeace International (2006) 'Tourism helping to kill the Mediterranean: Concrete stranglehold on the world's largest enclosed sea', 10 July. Available at www.greenpeace. org/international/en/news/features/concrete-stranglehold/ (accessed 05/12/17)

Greff, R. (2015) *China – The Future of Travel*. London: Leyoba.

Grönroos, C. (1978) 'A service-orientated approach to marketing of services', *European Journal of Marketing*, 12(8): 588–601.

Grönroos, C. (2007) *Service Management and Marketing: Customer Management in Service Competition*. Chichester: Wiley.

Grönroos, C. (2015) *Service Management and Marketing: Managing the service profit logic*. Chichester: Wiley.

Gross, S. and Klemmer, L. (2014) *Introduction to Tourism Transport*. Wallingford: CABI.

Guaracino, J. and Salvato, E. (2017) *Handbook of LGBT Tourism and Hospitality*. New York: Harrington Park Press.

Guardian (2013) 'Cuba relaxes travel restrictions', 15 January. Available at www.theguardian.com/world/2013/jan/15/cuba-relaxes-travel-restrictions

Gummesson, E. (1987) 'Marketing revisited: the crucial role of the part-time marketer', *European Journal of* Marketing, 25(2): 60–67.

Gummesson, E. (2008) *Total Relationship Marketing: Rethinking Marketing Management: from 4Pss to 30Rs*. London: Butterworth-Heinemann.

Gunn, C. (1972/1988) *Vacationscape: Designing Tourist Regions*. Austin, TX: University of Texas.

Gunn, C. and Var, T. (2002) *Tourism Planning*. New York: Routledge.

Gupta, V. (1999) 'Sustainable tourism: learning from Indian religious traditions', *International Journal of Contemporary Hospitality Management*, 11(2/3): 91–5.

Gurran, N. and Phibbs, P. (2017) 'When tourists move in: how should urban planners respond to Airbnb', *Journal of the American Planning Association*, 83(1): 80–92.

Hall, C. (2008) *Tourism Planning: Policies, Processes and Relationships*. Harlow: Prentice-Hall.

Hall, C. and Jenkins, J. (1995) *Tourism and Public Policy*. London: Routledge.

Hall, C. M. (2006) 'Introduction', in R. Butler (ed.), *The Tourism Area Life Cycle, Vol. 2 Conceptual and Theoretical Issues*. Bristol: Channel View Publications, pp. xv–xix.

Hall, D., Kirkpatrick, I. and Mitchell, M. (eds) (2005) *Rural Tourism and Sustainable Business*. Bristol: Channel View Publications.

Hall, M. and Page, S. (2002) *The Geography of Tourism and Recreation: Environment, Place and Space*. Abingdon: Routledge.

Hampton by Hilton (2017) 'Hampton by Hilton's new 100% Hampton guarantee', Press release, 19 January. Available at www.hospitalitynet.org/news/4080485.html

Hanlon, P. (2007) *Global Airlines Competition in a Transnational Industry* (3rd edn). Oxford: Butterworth-Heinemann.

Harrington, D. and Lenehan, T. (1998) *Managing Quality in Tourism, Theory and Practice*. Dublin: Oak Tree Press.

Harriott, V., Davis, D. and Banks, S. (1997) 'Recreational diving and its impact in marine protected areas in Eastern Australia', *Ambio*, 26(3): 173–9.

Harris, R., Griffin, T. and Williams, P. (2002) *Sustainable Tourism: A Global Perspective*. Oxford: Butterworth-Heinemann.

Hasler, H. and Ott, J. (2008) 'Diving down the reefs? Intense diving tourism threatens the reefs of the Northern Red Sea', *Marine Pollution Bulletin*, 56: 1788–94.

Haven-Tang, C. and Jones, E. (2005) 'The heterodoxey of tourism SMEs', in E. Jones and C. Haven-Tang (eds), *Tourism SMES: Service Quality and Destination Competitiveness*. Wallingford: CABI, pp. 337–56.

Hawkins, D. E. and Ritchie, J. R. B. (eds) (1991) *World Travel and Tourism Review: Indicators, Trends and Forecasts, Vol. 1*. Wallingford: CABI.

Hazel, N. (2004) 'Holidays for children and families in need: an exploration of the research and policy context for social tourism in the UK', *Children and Society*, 19: 225–36.

Heede, R. (2014) 'Tracing anthropogenic carbon dioxide and methane emissions to fossil fuel and cement producers, 1854–2010', *Climatic Change*, 122(1–2): 229–41.

Henderson, J. (2006) 'Tourism in Dubai: overcoming barriers to tourism development', *International Journal of Tourism Research*, 8: 87–99.

Henderson, J. (2007) *Tourism Crises: Causes, Consequences and Management*. Oxford: Elsevier Butterworth-Heinemann.

Heskett, J., Earl Sasser, Jr, W. and Schlesinger, L. (1997) *The Service Profit Chain: How Leading Companies Link Profit and Growth to Loyalty, Satisfaction and Value*. New York: The Free Press.

Hiel, A. (2012) '13 things you should not buy on your vacation', IFAW, 13 December. Available at www.ifaw.org/united-kingdom/news/13-things-you-should-not-buy-your-vacation (accessed 15/11/17).

Higginbottom, K. (2004) *Wildlife Tourism: Impacts, Management and Planning*. Hamburg: Common Ground.

Higgins-Desbiolles, F. (2006a) 'Reconciliation tourism: on crossing bridges and changing ferries', in P. Burns and M. Novelli (eds), *Tourism and Social Identities*. Oxford: Elsevier.

Higgins-Desbiolles, F. (2006b) 'More than an "industry": the forgotten power of tourism as a social force', *Tourism Management*, 27: 1192–1208.

Hi-Tech Security Solutions (2004) 'Tourist attraction uses CCTV to improve customer experience', July. Available at www.securitysa.com/news.aspx?pklnewsid=14819 (accessed 20/11/17).

Hilling, D. (1996) *Transport and Developing Countries*. London: Routledge.

HM Revenue and Customs (2010) Excise notice 550: Air Passenger Duty', August. Available at http://customs.hmrc.gov.uk/channelsPortalWebApp/channelsPortalWebApp.portal?_nfpb=true&_pageLa'bel=pageExcise_ShowContent&id=HMCE_CL_000505&propertyType=document

HM Treasury (2006) *Pre-Budget Report*. London: HM Treasury.

Hodgson, A. (ed.) (1987) *The Travel and Tourism Industry: Strategies for the Future*. Oxford: Butterworth-Heinemann.

Hoffman, K. D. and Bateson, J. E. G. (2001/2006) *Essentials of Services Marketing: Concepts, Strategies and Cases*. Nashville, TN: South-western College Publishing.

Hoffman, K. D. and Bateson, J. E. G. (2016) *Services Marketing: Concepts, Strategies and Cases*. Boston, MA: Cengage Learning.

Hoffman, K. D., Bateson, J., Wood, E. and Kenyon, A. (2009) *Services Marketing, Concepts, Strategies and Cases*. London: Cengage Learning.

Holden, A. (2003) 'In need of new environmental ethics for tourism?', *Annals of Tourism Research*, 30(1): 94–108.

Holden, A. (2005) *Tourism Studies and the Social Sciences*. London and New York: Routledge.

Holden, A. (2008) *Environment and Tourism*. London and New York: Routledge.

Holden, A. (2016) *Environment and Tourism* (3rd edn). London and New York: Routledge.

Holland, J. and Leslie, D. (2017) *Tour Operators and Operations: Development, Management and Responsibility*. Wallingford: CABI.

Holloway, J. C. (1985/1998/2006) *The Business of Tourism*. Harlow: Prentice-Hall.

Holloway, J. C. (2004) *Marketing for Tourism*. Harlow: Prentice-Hall.

Hope, C. and Klemm, M. (2001) 'Tourism in difficult areas revisited: the case of Bradford', *Tourism Management*, 22(6): 629–35.

Horner, S. and Swarbrooke, J. (1996) *Marketing Tourism Hospitality and Leisure in Europe*. London: Thomson.

Horner, S. and Swarbrooke, J. (2004) *International Cases in Tourism Management*. Oxford: Butterworth-Heinemann.

House, J. (1954) 'Geographical aspects of coastal holiday resorts'. Unpublished PhD thesis. Durham: Kings College.

Howard, S. and Jackman, M. (2014) 'When the seasons change: tourism seasonality in Barbados', *Antilles Economics*, 11 March.

Howie, F. (2003) *Managing the Tourist Destination*. London: Thomson Learning.

Howitt, O. J. A., Revol, V. G. N., Smith, I. J., Rodger, C. J. (2010) 'Carbon emissions from international cruise ship passengers' travel to and from New Zealand', *Energy Policy*, 38(5): 2552–60.

Hudman, L. and Jackson, R. (2002) *Geography of Travel and Tourism*. Florence: Cengage Learning.

Hudson, S. and Hudson, L. (2017) M*arketing for Tourism, Hospitality and Events*: *A Global and Digital Perspective*. London: Sage.

Hughes, H. (2002) 'Marketing gay tourism in Manchester: new market for urban tourism or destruction of "gay space"?', *Journal of Vacation Marketing*, 9(2): 152–63.

Hughes, J. C. and Rog, E. (2006) 'Talent management: a strategy for improving employee recruitment, retention and engagement within hospitality organisations', *International Journal of Contemporary Hospitality Management*, 20: 743–57.

Hughes, M. (2008) 'An open passenger market beckons', *Railway Gazette International*, 19 February.

Humphreys, C. (2006) 'Mass tourism businesses 2: travel agents', in J. Beech and S. Chadwick (eds), *The Business of Tourism Management*. Harlow: Pearson Education, pp. 415–39.

Hunter, C. (1997) 'Sustainable tourism as an adaptive paradigm', *Annals of Tourism Research*, 24(4): 850–67.

Hunter, C. (2004) 'On the need to reconceptualise sustainable tourism development', in S. Williams (ed.), *Tourism: Critical Concepts in the Social Sciences*. London: Taylor & Francis.

Hunziker, W. and Krapf, K. (1942) *Grundriss der Allgemeinen Fremdenverkehrslehre*. Zurich: Polygraphischer.

Icelandic Tourist Board (2017) 'Take the Icelandic Pledge', 19 June. Available at https://www.ferdamalastofa.is/en/moya/news/take-the-icelandic-pledge (accessed 14/11/17).

Inglis, F. (2000) *The Delicious History of the Holiday*. London: Routledge.

Inkpen, G. (1998) *Information Technology for Travel and Tourism*. Harlow: Longman.

Insignia (2015) *Nunavut Visitor Exit Survey*. Toronto: Insignia.

Inskeep, E. (1991) *Tourism Planning: An Integrated and Sustainable Development Approach*. New York: Van Nostrand Reinhold.

Interagency Visitor Use Management Council (n.d.) 'Welcome'. Available at https://visitorusemanagement.nps.gov/ (accessed 05/12/17).

InterContinental Hotels Group (IHG) (2017a) 'HUALUXE hotels and resorts'. Available at www.ihgplc.com/en/our-brands/hualuxe

InterContinental Hotels Group (IHG) (2017b) 'Our global presence'. Available at www.ihgplc.com/en/about-us/our-global-presence (accessed 21/04/17).

Interian, J. (2016) 'Up in the air: harmonizing the sharing economy through Airbnb regulations', *Boston College International & Comparative Law Review*, 39(1): 129–61.

International Air Transport Association (IATA) (2009) 'IATA agency programme'. Available at www.iata.org/pressroom/facts_figures/fact_sheets/Pages/agency.aspx

International Air Transport Association (IATA) (2011) 'Scheduled passenger – kilometres flown', *WATS*, 54th edn. Available at www.iata.org/ps/publications/Pages/wats-passenger-km.aspx

International Air Transport Association (IATA) (2016) 'World air transport statistics summary 2016'. Available at www.iata.org/docx/WATS_2016-infographic.pdf

International Air Transport Association (IATA) (2017) 'Fact Sheet IATA agency program, June 2017'. Available at www.iata.org

International Civil Aviation Organization (ICAO) (2013) 'Developments in the liberalization of international air transport services in the Latin American Region'. Presented at the Worldwide Air Transport Conference (Atconf) Sixth Meeting, Montréal, 18–22 March. Available at: Available at www.icao.int/Meetings/atconf6/Documents/WorkingPapers/ATConf6-ip006_en.pdf

International Civil Aviation Organization (ICAO) (2017) 'Carbon Offsetting and Reduction Scheme for International Aviation (CORSIA)'. Available at www.icao.int/environmental-protection/Pages/market-based-measures.aspx

International Labour Organisation (ILO) (n.d.) 'Fact sheet: rest periods'. Available at www.ilo.org/wcmsp5/groups/public/---ed_protect/---protrav/---travail/documents/publication/wcms_491374.pdf

International Labour Organisation (ILO) (2001) *Human Resources Development, Employment and Globalisation in the Hotel, Catering and Tourism Sector*. Geneva: International Labour Office.

International Labour Organisation (ILO) (2010) *Working Conditions Laws Report*. Geneva: ILO. www.ilo.org/travail

International Labour Organisation (ILO) (2015) 'Working Conditions Laws Database'. Available at www.ilo.org/dyn/travail

International Maritime Organization (IMO) (2014) *Third IMO GHG Study*. London: IMO.

International Organization for Standardization (ISO) (n.d.) 'ISO 9000 – Quality management'. Available at www.iso.org/iso-9001-quality-management.html (accessed 20/11/17).

International Union of Official Travel Organisation (IUOTO) (1963) *Conference on International Travel and Tourism*. Geneva: UN.

Ioannides, D. (2003) 'The economics of tourism in host communities', in S. Singh, J. Dallen and K. Ross (eds), *Tourism in Destination Communities*. Wallingford: CABI.

Jafari, J. (1977) 'Editor's page', *Annals of Tourism Research*, 5(Supplement 1): 6–11.

Jafari, J. (2003) *Encyclopedia of Tourism*. London: Routledge.

Jago, E. and Deery, M. (2002) 'The role of human resource practices in achieving quality enhancement and cost reduction: an investigation of volunteer use in tourism organisations', *International Journal of Contemporary Hospitality Management*, 14(5): 229–36.

James, L. (2006) *The Middle Class: A History*. London: Little, Brown.

Japan Travel Bureau (2011) 'About us'. Available at www.jtbuk.com

Jeffries, D. (2001) *Governments and Tourism*. London: Reed.

Jones, E. and Haven-Tang, C. (2005) *Tourism SMEs: Service Quality and Destination Competitiveness*. Wallingford: CABI.

Juul, M. (2015) *The Sharing Economy and Tourism – Tourist Accommodation*. Brussels: European Parliamentary Research Service

Kaplan, R. (2015) 'Airbnb: a case study in occupancy regulation and taxation', *The University of Chicago Law Review Dialogue*, 82: 103.

Karyopouli, S. (2016) 'The bargaining power of the Republic of Cyprus accommodation providers in contractual and non-contractual negotiations with large European tour operators', Doctoral dissertation. Poole: Bournemouth University.

Kasiev, M. (1971) 'Health protection and the social security of workers in the USSR', *International Social Security Review*, 24(2): 274–83.

KAYAK (2017) 'KAYAK mobile travel report: chatbots in the UK'. Available at www.kayak.co.uk/news/mobile-travel-report-2017/

Kerr, M. (2009) 'Taj Mahal doesn't need a theme park', *Telegraph Travel*, 5 August. Available at www.telegraph.co.uk/travel/destinations/asia/india/5976407/Taj-Mahal-doesnt-need-a-theme-park-India.html (accessed 14/11/17).

Keyser, H. (2002) *Tourism Development*. Oxford: Oxford University Press.

Keyte, M. (2016) 'In this ethical boycott who wins?', *Tourism Concern*, 26 February. Available at https://www.tourismconcern.org.uk/when-an-ethical-boycott-backfires/ (accessed 14/11/17).

Kiley, D. (2016) 'How Detroit plans to become this summer's vacation hotspot', *Fortune*, 31 May. Available at http://fortune.com/2016/05/31/detroit-tourism-vacation/

Kimes, S. (2000) 'Yield management: an overview', in A. Ingold, U. McMahon-Beatty and I. Yeoman (eds), *Yield Management: Strategies for the Service Industries*. London: Cassell.

Klein, A. R. (2002) *Cruise Ship Blues*. Gabriola Island, BC: New Society Publishers.

Knowles, R., Shaw, J. and Docherty, I. (eds) (2008) *Transport Geographies: Mobilities, Flows and Spaces*. Oxford: Blackwell.

Knowles, T. (1996) *Corporate Strategy for Hospitality*. Harlow: Longman.

Kolb, B. (2006) *Tourism Marketing for Cities and Towns: Using Branding and Events to Attract Tourists*. Burlington: Butterworth-Heinemann.

Kotler, P., Bowen, J. T., Makens, J. C. and Baloglu, S. (2017) *Marketing for Hospitality and Tourism*. Harlow: Pearson.

Kotler, P., Haider, D. H. and Rein, I. (1993) *Marketing Places: Attracting Investment, Industry and Tourism to Cities, States and Nations*. New York: Free Press.

Kotler, P., Wong, V., Saunders, J. and Armstrong, G. (2004) *Principles of Marketing: European Edition*. New York: Prentice-Hall.

KPMG (2008) *Climate Changes Your Business*. New York: KPMG International.

Krippendorf, J. (1984) *The Holiday Makers: Understanding the Impact of Leisure and Travel*. Oxford: Butterworth-Heinemann.

Kulic, P. (2004) 'Caribbean hotels and resorts: the seasonality issue', in *HVS International*, 27 February.

Kuniyal, J., Jain, A. and Shannigrahi, A. (2003) 'Solid waste management in Indian Himalayan tourists' treks: a case study in and around the Valley of Flowers and Hemkund Sahib', *Waste Management*, 23: 807–816.

Kuo, I. (2002) 'The effectiveness of environmental interpretation at resource-sensitive tourism destinations', *International Journal of Tourism Research*, 4(2): 87–101.

Kuoni Travel Group (2011) 'Online annual report 2010'. Available at www.kuoni.com

Kweka, J., Morrissey, O. and Blake, A. (2003) 'The economic potential of tourism in Tanzania', *Journal of International* Development, 15: 335–51.

La Croix (2008) 'La réplique de la grotte de Lascaux est, elle aussi, malade', 21 August. Available at www.la-croix.com/Semaine-en-images/La-replique-de-la-grotte-de-Lascaux-est-elle-aussi-malade-_NG_-2008-08-21-675098 (accessed 05/12/17)

Lagiewski, R. M. (2006) 'The application of the TALC model: a literature survey', in R. Butler (ed.), *The Tourism Area Life Cycle, Vol. 1 Applications and Modifications*. Bristol: Channel View Publications, pp. 27–50.

Lane, B. (1994) 'Sustainable rural tourism strategies: a tool for development and conservation', *Journal of Sustainable Tourism*, 2: 102–111.

Lane, B. (2005) 'Sustainable rural tourism strategies: a tool for development and conservation', *RIAT Interamerican Journal of Environment and Tourism*, 1(1): 12–18.

Langer, G. (1996) 'Traffic noise and hotel profits – is there a relationship?', *Tourism Management*, 17(4): 295–305.

Lapunzina, A. (2005) *Architecture of Spain*. Santa Barbara, CA: Greenwood.

Laurance, W. (2007) 'A new initiative to use carbon trading for tropical forest conservation', *Biotropica*, 39(1): 20–24.

Law, C. (1996) *Tourism in Major Cities*. London: International Thomson Business Press.

Law, C. (2003) *Urban Tourism: The Visitor Economy and the Growth of Large Cities*. London: Continuum.

Law, R. (2009) 'Disintermediation of hotel reservations: the perception of different groups of online buyers in Hong Kong', *International Journal of Contemporary Hospitality Management*, 21(6): 766–72.

Law, R., Leung, K. and Wong, J. (2004) 'The impact of the internet on travel agencies', *International Journal of Contemporary Hospitality Management*, 16(2): 101–107.

Laws, E. (1995) *Tourist Destination Management, Issues Analysis and Policies*. London: Routledge.

Laws, E. (1997) *Managing Packaged Tourism: Relationships, Responsibilities and Service Quality in the Inclusive Holiday Industry*. London: Thomson.

Laws, E. (2000) 'Perspectives on pricing decision in the inclusive holiday industry', in A. Ingold, U. McMahon-Beatty and I. Yeoman (eds), *Yield Management: Strategies for the Service Industries*. London: Cassell.

Laws, E. (2001) 'Distribution channel analysis for leisure travel', in D. Buhalis and E. Laws (eds), *Tourism Distribution Channels: Practices, Issues, and Transformations*. London: Continuum, pp. 53–73.

Laws, E., Prideaux B. and Chon K. (2007) *Crisis Management in Tourism*. Wallingford: CABI.

Leask, A. (2008) 'The nature and role of visitor attractions', in A. Fyall, B. Garrod, A. Leask and S. Wanhill (eds), *Managing Visitor Attractions: New Directions*. Oxford: Butterworth-Heinemann, pp. 3–16.

Leatherman, D. (2017) 'China's rural villages offer refreshing authenticity', *The Columbus Dispatch*, 28 May.

Lechner, F. and Boli, J. (2004) *The Globalisation Reader* (2nd edn). Malden: Blackwell.

Lee, D. (2016) 'How Airbnb short-term rentals exacerbate Los Angeles's affordable housing crisis: analysis and policy recommendations', *Harvard Law & Policy Review*, 10: 229.

Lee-Ross, D. (2005) 'Perceived job characteristics and internal work motivation: an exploratory cross-cultural analysis of the motivational antecedents of hotel workers in Mauritius and Australia', *Journal of Management Development*, 24: 253–66.

Leggat, P. A., Speare, R. and Aitken, P. (2009) 'Swine flu and travelers: an Australian perspective', *Journal of Travel Medicine*, 16(6): 373–6.

Leiper, N. (1979) 'The framework of tourism: towards a definition of tourism, tourist and the tourist industry', *Annals of Tourism Research*, 6(4): 390–407.

Leiper, N. (1990a) 'Tourist attraction systems', *Annals of Tourism Research*, 17: 367–84.

Leiper, N. (1990b) 'The partial industrialisation of tourism', *Annals of Tourism Research*, 17: 600–605.

Leslie, D. (2001) 'Urban regeneration and Glasgow's galleries with particular reference to The Burrell Collection', in G. Richards (ed.), *Cultural Attractions and European Tourism*. Wallingford: CABI.

Leslie, D. (ed.) (2012) *Responsible Tourism: Concepts, Theory and Practice*. Wallingford: CABI.

Levitt, T. (1981) 'Marketing intangible products and product intangibles', *Harvard Business Review*, May/June: 37–44.

Li, L. (2007) 'On the road: China on holiday', *The Economic Observer Online*, 26 September. Available at www.eeo.com.cn/ens/Industry/2007/09/26/84236.html

Lindgren, M. and Bandhold, H. (2003) *Scenario Planning: The Link Between Future and Strategy*. Basingstoke: Palgrave Macmillan.

Lindsey, P., Alexander, R. L., Frank, G., Mathieson A. and Romanach S. (2006) 'Potential of trophy hunting to create incentives for wildlife conservation in Africa where alternative wildlife-based land uses may not be viable', *Animal Conservation*, 9: 283–91.

Litteljohn, D. and Baxter, I. (2006) 'The structure of the tourism and travel industry', in J. Beech and S. Chadwick (eds), *The Business of Tourism Management*. Harlow: Pearson Education, pp. 21–39.

Littleford, D., Halstead, J. and Mulraine, C. (2004) *Career Skills: Opening Doors into the Job Market*. Basingstoke: Palgrave Macmillan.

London Development Agency (LDA) (2005) 'Business as usual'. Available at www.lda.avensc.com/documents/Business_as_Usual_PDF.pdf

London Development Agency (LDA) (2009) 'London Tourism Action Plan 2009–13'. www.lda.gov.uk/Documents/London_Tourism_Action_Plan_2009-13_6537.pdf

Lopez, E. and Garcia, F. (2006) 'Agro-tourism, sustainable tourism and ultraperipheral areas: the case of the Canary Islands', *Pasos*, 4(1): 85–97.

Lovelock, C. H. (1983) 'Classifying services to gain strategic marketing insights', *Journal of Marketing*, Summer: 9–20.

Lubbe, B. (2005) 'A new revenue model for travel intermediaries in South Africa: the negotiated approach', *Journal of Retailing and Consumer Services*, 12(6): 385–96.

Lück, M. (2008) *The Encyclopaedia of Tourism and Recreation in Marine Environments*. Wallingford: CABI.

Lumsdon, L. (1997) *Tourism Marketing*. London: International Thomson Business Press.

Lumsdon, L. and Page, S. J. (eds) (2004) *Tourism and Transport Issues: An Agenda for the New Millennium*. Oxford: Elsevier.

Macao Government Tourism Office (n.d.) 'Home page'. Available at http://en.macaotourism.gov.mo/index.php (accessed 20/11/17).

MacCannell, D. (1999) *The Tourist: A New Theory of the Leisure Class*. London: University of California Press.

MacKinnon, D., Pirie, G. and Gather, M. (2008) 'Transport and economic development', in R. Knowles, J. Shaw and I. Docherty (eds), *Transport Geographies: Mobilities, Flows and Spaces*. Oxford: Blackwell, pp. 10–29.

Macleod, D. (2004) *Tourism, Globalisation and Cultural Change: An Island Community Perspective*. Bristol: Channel View Publications.

Mair, J. (2006) 'Eco-tourism: a sustainable trade?' Available at http://news.bbc.co.uk/1/hi/sci/tech/6179901.stm

Mak, J. (2004) *Tourism and the Economy: Understanding the Economics of Tourism*. Honolulu, HI: University of Hawaii Press.

Marcus, L. (2016) 'Italy's Cinque Terre to begin limiting tourists', *CN Traveler*, 17 February. Available at www.cntraveler.com/stories/2016-02-17/italys-cinque-terre-to-begin-limiting-tourists (accessed 20/11/17).

Marcus, L. (2016) 'Angkor Wat nearly doubles its daily ticket prices', 1 February. Available at www.cntraveler.com/stories/2016-03-10/will-angkor-wat-be-the-next-site-to-cap-visitor-numbers (accessed 05/12/17).

Marriott International (2016) 'Marriott International launches M Live Europe, the company's fourth global marketing real-time command centre', 25 July. Available at http://news.marriott.com/2016/07/marriott-international-launches-m-live-europe-companys-fourth-global-marketing-real-time-command-centre/

Marriott International (2017a) '2016 annual report'. Available at http://investor. shareholder.com/mar/marriottAR16/10k-item7-p1.html

Marriott International (2017b) 'Company Overview'. Available at http://investor. shareholder.com/mar/company-overview.cfm

Marriott International (2017c) 'Marriott careers'. Available at www.careers.marriott. com/career-paths/corporate/

Maslow, A. (1954) *Motivation and Personality*. New York: HarperCollins.

Mason, P. (2008) *Tourism Impacts, Planning and Management*. London: Elsevier.

Mathieson, A. and Wall, G. (1982) *Tourism: Economic, Physical and Social Impacts*. London: Longman.

Matley, I. (1976) *The Geography of International Tourism*. Washington, DC: Commission on College Geography, Association of American Geographers.

Mayhew, L. (1987) 'The travel agent – rise or fall?', in A. Hodgson (ed.), *The Travel and Tourism Industry: Strategies for the Future*. Oxford: Butterworth Heinnemann, pp. 49–73.

McCabe, S. (2008) *Marketing Communications in Tourism and Hospitality*. Oxford: Butterworth-Heinemann.

McCabe, V., Poole, B., Weeks, P. and Leiper, N. (2000) *The Business and Management of Conventions*. Jacaranda: Wiley Australia.

McCarthy, E. J. (1981) *Basic Marketing: A Managerial Approach*. New York: Irwin.

McIntosh, R., Goeldner, C. and Ritchie, J. (1995) *Tourism Principles, Practices and Philosophies*. New York: Wiley.

McKercher, B. and Chon, K. (2004) 'The over-reaction to SARS and the collapse of Asian tourism', *Annals of Tourism Research*, 31(3): 716–19.

McLaren, D. (2003) *Rethinking Tourism & Ecotravel*. Boulder, CO: Lynne Rienner.

McLean, F. (1997) *Marketing the Museum*. Abingdon: Routledge.

Meliã Hotels International (2017) 'Talent management'. Available at www. meliahotelsinternational.com/en/employment/talent-management

Mercer (2014) 'UK receives second lowest public holiday entitlement in the world', 9 September. Available at www.mercer.com/newsroom/public-holiday-entitlements.html

Meuller, H. and Kaufmann, E. (2001) 'Wellness tourism: market analysis of a special health tourism segment', *Journal of Vacation Marketing*, 7(1): 5–17.

Micklethwait, J. and Wooldridge, A. (2004) 'The hidden promise: liberty renewed', in F. Lechner and J. Boli (eds), *The Globalisation Reader*. Malden: Blackewell.

Middleton, V. and Clark, J. (2001) *Marketing for Travel and Tourism*. Burlington: Butterworth-Heinemann.

Middleton, V., Fyall, A., Morgan, M. with Ranchhod, A. (2009) *Marketing in Travel and Tourism*. Oxford: Butterworth-Heinemann.

Mihalič, T. (2002) 'Tourism and economic development issues', in R. Sharpley and D. Tefler (eds), *Tourism and Development: Concepts and Issues*. Bristol: Channel View Publications.

Miles, S. J. and Mangold, G. (2004) 'A conceptualisation of the employee branding process', *Journal of Relationship Marketing*, 3(2/3): 65–87.

Miles, S. J. and Mangold, G. (2005) 'Positioning South West Airlines through employee branding', *Business Horizons*, 48: 535–45.

Miller, M. E. (2015) 'Bison selfies are a bad idea: tourist gored in Yellowstone as another photo goes awry', *Washington Post*, 23 July. Available at www.washingtonpost.com/news/morning-mix/wp/2015/07/23/bison-selfies-are-a-bad-idea-tourist-gored-in-yellowstone-as-another-photo-goes-awry/?utm_term=.7d6effc13a47 (accessed 20/11/17).

Millett, S. (2003) 'The future of scenarios: challenges and opportunities', in R. Randall (ed.), *Integrate Scenario Learning with Decision Making*. Bradford: Emerald.

Mills, P. K. and Margulies, N. (1980) 'Toward a core typology of service organisations', *Academy of Management Review*, 5(2): 255–65.

Milner, L., Collins, J., Tashibana, R. and Hiser, R. (2000) 'The Japanese vacation visitor to Alaska', *Journal of Travel and Tourism Marketing*, 9(1–2): 43–56.

Ministry of Business, Innovation and Employment (MBIE) (2017) 'New Zealand tourism forecasts 2017–2023'. Available at www.mbie.govt.nz/info-services/sectors-industries/tourism/tourism-research-data/international-tourism-forecasts/documents-image-library/forecasts-2017-report-final.pdf

Minnaert, L., Maitland, R. and Miller, G. (2009) 'Tourism and social policy: the value of social tourism', *Annals of Tourism Research*, 36(2): 316–34.

Minnaert, L., Quinn, B., Griffen, K. and Stacey, J. (2010) 'Social tourism for low-income groups: benefits in a UK and Irish context', in S. Cole and N. Morgan (eds), *Tourism and Inequality*. Wallingford: CABI.

Mintel (2004) 'Travel and tourism – China', June.

Mintel (2005) 'Travel and tourism – Cuba', February.

Mintel (2006) *Holidays: The Impacts of Terrorism and Natural Disasters*. London: Mintel.

Mintel (2007) 'Travel and Tourism – Saudi Arabia', November.

Mintel (2008) 'Travel and Tourism – India', February.

Mintel (2011) 'Travel and Tourism – Cuba', November.

Mintel (2012) 'Travel and Tourism – Oman', August.

Mintel (2016a) 'Travel and tourism – China', February. Available at http://reports. mintel.com/display/748123

Mintel (2016b) 'Travel and Tourism – Cuba', November. Available at http://reports. mintel.com/display/748371/?__cc=1#

Miossec, J. M. (1977) 'Un modele de l'espace touristique', *L'Espace Geographique*, 6(1): 41–8.

Mook, D. (1996) *Motivation: The Organization of Action* (2nd edn). New York: Norton.

Morris, R. E. (2016) 'Hosts and guests in early Cuba tourism', *Journal of Tourism History*, 8(2): 167–83.

Morrison, A. (2013) *Marketing and Managing Tourism Destinations*. London: Routledge.

Moscardo, G. (ed.) (2004) *Building Community Capacity for Tourism Development*. Wallingford: CABI.

Moscardo, G. and Ballantyne, R. (2008) 'Interpretation and attractions', in A. Fyall, B. Garrod, A. Leask and S. Wanhill (eds), *Managing Visitor Attractions: New Directions*. Oxford: Butterworth-Heinemann.

Moutinho, L. (1987) 'Consumer behaviour in tourism', *European Journal of Marketing*, 21(10): 3–44.

Mowforth, M. and Munt, I. (2003) *Tourism and Sustainability: Development and New Tourism in the Third World*. Oxford: Routledge.

Mowforth, M. and Munt, I. (2008) *Tourism and Sustainability: Development, Globalisation and New Tourism in the Third World*. Abingdon: Routledge.

Munier, N. (2005) *Introduction to Sustainability: Road to a Better Future*. Dordrecht: Springer.

National Aeronautics and Space Administration (NASA) (2017) 'Global climate change: vital signs of the planet'. Available at https://climate.nasa.gov/

National Coastal Tourism Academy (n.d) 'Facts and figures about Bournemouth's visitors'. Available at http://nctastaging.com.gridhosted.co.uk/uploads/Bournemouth_ Facts_and_Figures_pages1.pdf

National Council of Bhutan (2016) *Review Report on Tourism Policy and Strategies*. Thimpu: Tourism Council of Bhutan. Available at www.nationalcouncil.bt/assets/ uploads/files/FINAL%20Tourism%20Policy%20EAC%2016th%20Session.pdf (accessed 20/11/17).

National Fish and Wildlife Foundation (NFWF) (2014) 'Puerto Rico Seagrass Fund'. Available at www.nfwf.org/seagrassfund/Pages/home.aspx (accessed 13/11/17).

National Household Travel Survey (NHTS) (2009) *Our Nation's Travel*. Available at http://nhts.ornl.gov/

National Park Service (n.d.) 'Safety'. Available at www.nps.gov/yell/planyourvisit/ safety.htm (accessed 05/12/17).

National Statistics (2006) *Travel Trends: A Report on the 2005 International Passenger Survey*. London: Office for National Statistics.

National Trading Standards eCrime Team (n.d.) 'Holiday club fraud'. Available at www. tradingstandardsecrime.org.uk/holiday-club-fraud/ (accessed 14/11/17).

Naughton, J. (2014) '25 things you might not know about the web on its 25th birthday', *Observer*, 19 March. Available at www.theguardian.com/technology/2014/mar/09/25-years-web-tim-berners-lee

Neild, B. (2014) 'King Tut replica tomb opens to public in Egypt', 2 May. Available at http://edition.cnn.com/travel/article/tutankhamuns-replica-tomb-egypt/index.html (accessed 20/11/17).

New York State Multiple Dwelling Law (n.d.) 'Article 1'. Available at www1.nyc.gov/assets/buildings/pdf/MultipleDwellingLaw.pdf (accessed 20/11/17).

Noronha, R. (1976) *Review of the Sociological Literature on Tourism*. New York: World Bank.

Noronha, R. (1977) *Social and Cultural Dimensions of Tourism: A Review of the Literature in English*. Washington, DC: World Bank.

NPR (n.d.) 'Stories about bp oil spill'. Available at www.npr.org/tags/127868273/bp-oil-spill (accessed 05/12/17)

Nunavut Bureau of Statistics (n.d.) 'Labour force survey'. Available at www.stats.gov.nu.ca/en/Labour%20survey.aspx (accessed 14/11/17).

Nunavut Tourism (2017) 'Arts, crafts and clothing'. Available at http://nunavuttourism.com/things-to-see-do/arts-crafts-clothing

Nyiri, P. (2006) *Scenic Spots: Chinese Tourism, the State, and Cultural Authority*. Seattle, WA: University of Washington Press.

O'Connor, J. (2000) 'The big squeeze: tourism concern', *Focus*, 36: 4–5.

O'Neil, C. (2017) *Weapons of Math Destruction: How Big Data Increases Inequality and Threatens Democracy*. London: Penguin.

Obiko Pearson, N. (2017) 'Vancouver to limit Airbnb to alleviate housing crunch', *Bloomberg*, cited in *Skift*, 7 May. Available at https://skift.com/2017/05/07/vancouver-to-limit-airbnb-to-alleviate-housing-crunch/

Office for National Statistics (ONS) (2010) 'Travel trends'. Available at www.statistics.gov.uk/downloads/theme_transport/travel-trends-2010.pdf

Office for National Statistics (ONS) (2013) 'Balance of payments'. Available at www.ons.gov.uk/economy/nationalaccounts/balanceofpayments

Office for National Statistics (ONS) (2016) 'IPS 2011–2015 top 50 markets'. Available at www.visitbritain.org/inbound-tourism-trends

Office for National Statistics (2017a) 'International travel survey (IPS)'. Available at www.ons.gov.uk/surveys/informationforhouseholdsandindividuals/household andindividualsurveys/internationalpassengersurveyips (accessed 05/12/17).

Office for National Statistics (2017b) 'Travel trends: 2016'. Available at www.ons.gov.uk/peoplepopulationandcommunity/leisureandtourism/articles/traveltrends/2016

Ogilvie, F.W. (1933) *The Tourism Movement*. London: Staples Press.

Okrant M. and Larson D. (2007) 'Toward a model of balanced tourism development on Baffin Island', Tourism Travel and Research Association International Conference,

Amerherst, MA. Available at http://scholarworks.umass.edu/cgi/viewcontent. cgi?article=1378&context=ttra (accessed 05/11/17).

Oman Economic Review (2017) 'MoT signs agreement for RO256mn Al Nakheel ITC development in Barka', 24 April. Available at http://oeronline.com/news/mot-signs-agreement-for-al-nakheel-itc-development-in-barka.html (accessed 06/11/17).

Orams, M. (2002) 'Feeding wildlife as a tourism attraction: a review of issues and impacts', *Tourism Management*, 23: 281–93.

Orascom Development (2017a) 'Jebel Sifah – Oman'. Available at www.orascomdh. com/en/destinations/operating-destinations/jebel-sifah.html

Orascom Development (2017b) 'Hawana Salalah – Oman'. Available at www.orascomdh. com/en/destinations/operating-destinations/hawana-salalah.html

Organisation for Economic Co-operation and Development (OECD) (2002) *National Tourism Policy Review of Japan*. Paris: OECD.

Organisation for Economic Co-operation and Development (OECD) (2008a) *Measuring the Role of Tourism in OECD economies: The OECD Manual on Tourism Satellite Accounts and Employment*. Paris: OECD.

Organisation for Economic Co-operation and Development (OECD) (2008b) *Tourism in OECD Countries 2008: Trends and Policies*. Paris: OECD.

Organisation for Economic Co-operation and Development (OECD) (2016a) *OECD Economic Surveys: USA 2016* Paris: OECD.

Organisation for Economic Co-operation and Development (OECD) (2016b) OECD *Tourism Trends and Policies 2016*. Paris: OECD.

Page, S. J. (2005) *Transport and Tourism: Global Perspectives*. Harlow: Pearson.

Page, S. J. and Connell J. (2006) *Tourism: A Modern Synthesis*. London: Thomson.

Page, S. J. and Getz, D. (1997) *The Business of Rural Tourism: International Perspectives*. London: International Thomson Business Press.

Page, S. J. and Hall, C. (2003) *Managing Urban Tourism*. Harlow: Prentice-Hall.

Parrinello, G. (1993) 'Motivation and anticipation in post-industrial tourism', *Annals of Tourism Research*, 20: 232–48.

Pearce, D. (1978) 'Tourist development: two processes' *Travel Research Journal*, 43–51.

Pearce, D. (1989) *Tourist Development*. Harlow: Longman.

Pearce, D. G. and Butler, R. W. (eds) (1999) *Contemporary Issues in Tourism Development*. London: Routledge.

Pearce, P. (1997) 'Towards the better management of tourist queues', in S. Medlik (ed.), *Managing Tourism*. Oxford: Butterworth-Heinemann.

Pearce, P. (2005) *Tourist Behaviour: Themes and Conceptual Schemes*. Bristol: Channel View Publications.

Pearce, P. and Lee, U. (2005) 'Developing the travel career approach to tourist motivation', *Journal of Travel Research*, 43: 226–37.

Pearson, M. N. (1996) *Pilgrimage to Mecca: The Indian Experience 1500–1800*. Princeton, NJ: Marcus Wiener.

Pedersen, A. (2002) *Managing Tourism at World Heritage Sites*. Paris: UNESCO World Heritage Centre. Available at http://whc.unesco.org/uploads/activities/documents/activity-113-2.pdf (accessed 20/11/17).

Pender, L. (2001) *Travel Trade and Transport: An Introduction*. London: Continuum.

People 1st (2016) 'Skills and workforce profile: hospitality and tourism'. Available at www.people1st.co.uk/getattachment/Insight-opinion/Latest-insights/Industry-profiles/Hospitality-tourism-skills-and-workforce-profile-2016.pdf/?lang=en-GB

Perko, J. and Idaković, M. (2008) *Rise and Fall of Croatian Tourism and the Effects of the War of the 90s* (Statistical Yearbook of the Republic of Croatia). Zagreb: Croatian Bureau of Statistics.

Phuket Tourism (2010) 'Phuket, Pangnga, Krabi tourism club: welcome to Greater Phuket, Thailand'. Available at www.phukettourism.org/about/index.html

Pike, S. (2008) *Destination Marketing: An Integrated Marketing Communications Approach*. Oxford: Butterworth-Heinemann.

Pimlott, J. A. R. (1947) *The Englishman's Holiday*. London: Faber.

Pine, J. and Gilmore, J. (1999) *The Experience Economy: Work is theater and every business a stage*. Brighton, MS: Harvard Business School Press.

Piozzi, H. (1786) 'Anecdotes of the late Samuel Johnson'. Available at http://books.google.com/books?id=tcIIAAAAQAAJ&printsec=frontcover&source=gbs_ge_summary_r&cad=0#v= onepage&q&f=false

Piznam, A. and Mansfield, Y. (1999) *Consumer Behaviour in Travel and Tourism*. Philadelphia, PA: Haworth Press.

PKF Consulting (2011) 'London Hotel Performance 2007–2009'. Available at www.pkf.co.uk/pkf/publications/hotel_britain_2011&goto=4

Plett, B. (2011) 'Bhutan spreads happiness to UN', *BBC News*, 21 July. Available at www.bbc.co.uk/news/world-14243512 (accessed 20/11/17).

Plog, S. C. (1972) 'Why destination areas rise and fall in popularity'. Paper presented at the Southern California Chapter of the Travel Research Bureau, 10 October.

Plog, S. C. (1974) 'Why destination areas rise and fall in popularity', *Cornell Hotel and Restaurant Administration Quarterly*, 14(4): 55–8.

Plog, S. C. (1991) *Leisure Travel: Making it a Growth Market … Again!* New York: Wiley.

Plog, S. C. (2003) *Leisure Travel: A Marketing Handbook*. Upper Saddle River, NJ: Pearson Education.

Poon, A. (1993) *Tourism, Technology and Competitive Strategies*. Wallingford: CABI.

Povey, G. and Oriade, A. (2009) 'Career development skills and strategies in the travel industry', in P. Robinson (ed.), *Operations Management in the Travel Industry*. Wallingford: CABI.

Priceline Group, The (2017) 'About us'. Available at www.pricelinegroup.com/about/

Prideaux, B. (2000) 'The resort development spectrum: a new approach to modelling resort development', *Tourism Management*, 21: 225–40.

Pritchard, A., Morgan, N., Sedgly, D. and Jenkins, A. (1998) 'Reaching out to the gay tourist: opportunities and threats in an emerging market segment', *Tourism Management*, 19(3): 273–82.

Project: Time Off (2017) 'About us'. Available at www.projecttimeoff.com/about-us

Prospects (2016) 'Should I do a Masters?' Available at www.prospects.ac.uk/postgraduate-study/masters-degrees/should-i-do-a-masters

Proust, M. (1923) *La Prisonnière*. Paris: Grasset.

Prytherch, D. and Huntoon, L. (2005) 'Entrepreneurial regionalist planning in a rescaled Spain: the cases of Bilboa and Valencia', *GeoJournal*, 62: 41–50.

PwC (2016) 'UK Hotels Forecast 2016 Growth is in the air but it's coming down to earth'. Available at www.pwc.co.uk/assets/pdf/uk-hotels-forecast-2016.pdf

PwC (2017) 'The world in 2050'. Available at www.pwc.com/gx/en/issues/economy/the-world-in-2050.html (accessed 20/11/17).

Ralston, B. and Wilson, I. (2006) *The Scenario-Planning Handbook*. Mason, OH: Thomson/South-Western.

Raz, S. S. (2013) 'Kick back on a kibbutz', BBC Travel, 8 March. Available at http://www.bbc.com/travel/story/20130226-kick-back-on-an-israel-kibbutz (accessed 05/12/17)

Reality Tours and Travel (2017) 'Slum Tours'. Available at http://realitytoursandtravel.com/slum-tour.php (accessed 23/03/17).

Reily Collins, V. (2004a) *Working in Tourism: The UK, Europe and Beyond for Seasonal and Permanent Staff*. Oxford: Vacation Work Publications.

Reily Collins, V. (2004b) *Careers and Jobs in Travel and Tourism*. London: Kogan Page.

Reisinger, Y. (2009) *International Tourism: Cultures and Behaviour*. Oxford: Butterworth-Heinemann.

Renshaw, M. B. (1992) *The Travel Agent*. Sunderland: Business Education Publisher.

Responsible Tourism Partnership (2017) 'Overtourism'. Available at http://responsibletourismpartnership.org/overtourism/

Rhoades, D. (2003) *Evolution of International Aviation: Phoenix Rising*. Aldershot: Ashgate.

Richards, D. and Smith M. (2002) *Governance and Public Policy in the UK*. Oxford: Oxford University Press.

Richards, G. (1991) *The UK LA Tourism Survey 1991*. London: Centre for Leisure and Tourism Studies; and Plymouth: British Association of Tourism Officers.

Richards, G. (ed.) (2001) *Cultural Attractions and European Tourism*. Wallingford: CABI.

Richardson, J. and Fluker M. (2004) *Understanding and Managing Tourism*. Frenchs Forest: Pearson Education Australia.

Riley, M. (1996) *Human Resource Management in the Hospitality and Tourism Industry*. Oxford: Butterworth-Heinemann.

Ringland, F. (2002) *Scenarios in Business*. Chichester: Wiley.

Ritchie, J. R. B. and Crouch, G. (2003) *The Competitive Destination: A Sustainable Tourism Perspective*. Wallingford: CABI.

Roberts, K. (1999) *Leisure in Contemporary Society*. Wallingford: CABI.

Robinson, P. (ed.) (2009) *Operations Management in the Travel Industry*. Wallingford: CABI.

Robinson, P., Wales, D. and Dickson, G. (2010) *Events Management.* Wallingford: CABI.

Rogers, C. (1990) 'Responses of coral reefs and reef organisms to sedimentation', *Marine Ecology Progress Series*, 62: 185–202.

Rogers, P., Jalal, K. and Boyd, J. (2008) *An Introduction to Sustainable Development.* London: Earthscan.

Rogers, T. (2013) *Conferences and Conventions: A Global Industry.* London: Routledge.

Roque-Albelo, L., Chauca, E. L. and Gaona, O. C. (2008) 'Dispersal of insect species attracted to ship lights: Conservation implications for Galapagos', Galapagos Report 2007–2008, Charles Darwin Foundation. Available at www.galapagos.org/wp-content/uploads/2012/04/biodiv3-insect-species-dispersal.pdf (accessed 05/12/17).

Rosenbaum, M. and Wong, I. (2008) 'When tourists desire an artificial culture: the Bali Syndrome in Hawaii', in A. Woodside and D. Martin (eds.), *Tourism Management.* Wallingford: CABI.

Rossini, A. (2016) 'State of online travel agencies: Ctrip joins Priceline and Expedia as global giant', *Skift*, 7 July. Available at https://skift.com/2016/07/07/the-state-of-online-travel-agencies-strong-growth-but-big-challenges-ahead/

Royal Borough of Windsor and Maidenhead (2008) 'Our vision for 2012 and beyond'. Available at www.windsor.gov.uk/ebrochure/

Royal Caribbean (2015) 'Blog', 26 August. Available at www.royalcaribbeanblog.com/2015/08/26/royal-caribbean-makes-changes-quantum-of-the-seas-the-chinese-cruise-market

Royal Caribbean International (2017) 'Harmony of the Seas'. Available at www.royalcaribbean.co.uk/our-ships/harmony-of-the-seas/?ship=HM&cid=UKRCBAU_GSHIP_HM_SH&phone=ppcship&gclid=EAIaIQobChMI4Ln1i_OB1gIV6rztCh1WygpUEAAYBCAAEgJs5fD_BwE

Ryan, C. (ed.) (1997, 2002) *The Tourist Experience: A New Introduction* (2nd edn). Andover: Cengage Learning.

Sands Resorts Cotai Strip Macao (2017) 'Home page'. Available at https://en.sandsresortsmacao.com/ (accessed 06/11/17).

Schaal, D. (2016) 'Airbnb flights: should it build, buy or borrow an airline booking service?', *Skift*, 21 December. Available at https://skift.com/2016/12/21/airbnb-flights-should-it-build-buy-or-borrow-an-airline-booking-service/

Schaal, D. (2017) 'Airbnb's buy of Luxury Retreats is latest of a dozen acquisitions', Skift, 16 February. Available at https://skift.com/2017/02/16/airbnbs-buy-of-luxury-retreats-is-latest-of-a-dozen-acquisitions/

Schlesinger, L. A. and Heskett, J. L. (1991) 'Breaking the cycle of failure in services'. *MIT Sloan Management Review*, 15 April. Available at https://sloanreview.mit.edu/article/breaking-the-cycle-of-failure-in-services/

Schoemaker, P. (1995) 'Scenario planning: a tool for strategic thinking', *Sloan Management Review*, 36(2): 25–40.

Schyst Resande & Fair Trade Center (2013) *No Child's Play.* Stockholm: Schyst Resande & Fair Trade Center.

Science Museum (2004) *Crystal Palace and the Great Exhibition.* Available at www.makingthemodernworld.org

Seabrook, J. (2017) 'The mastermind behind Coachella', *New Yorker*, 17 April. Available at www.newyorker.com/magazine/2017/04/17/the-mastermind-behind-coachella

Selin, S. (1999) 'Developing a typology of sustainable tourism partnerships', *Journal of Sustainable Tourism*, 7(3 & 4): 260–73.

Shackley, M. (1998) *Visitor Management: Case Studies from World Heritage Sites*. Oxford: Butterworth-Heinemann.

Shankman, S. (2014) 'Amsterdam legitimises Airbnb with new short-term rental rules', *Skift*, 14 February. Available at https://skift.com/2014/02/14/amsterdam-legitimizes-airbnb-with-new-short-term-rental-rules/

Sharpley, R. and Sharpley, J. (1997) *Rural Tourism: An Introduction*. London: International Thomson Business Press.

Sharpley, R. and Sundaram, P. (2005) 'Tourism, a sacred journey? The case of Ashram tourism, India', *International Journal of Tourism Research*, 7: 161–71.

Sharpley, R. and Telfer, D. (eds) (2002) *Tourism and Development: Concepts and Issues*. Bristol: Channel View Publications.

Shaw, S. (2007) *Airline Marketing and Management*. Farnham: Ashgate Publishing.

Sheldon, J. (1997) *Tourism Information Technology*. Wallingford: CABI.

Shostack, G. L. (1977) 'Breaking free from product marketing', *Journal of Marketing*, 41(April): 73–80.

Shostack, G. L. (1987) 'Service positioning through structural change', *Journal of Marketing*, 51(1): 34–43.

Shoval, N. and Isaacson, M. (2010) *Tourist Mobility and Advanced Tracking Technologies*. London: Routledge.

Singapore Airlines (2017) 'Stock and shareholding information'. Available at www.singaporeair.com/en_UK/gb/about-us/information-for-investors/shareholding-info/

Singapore Tourism Board (2017) 'Marketing Singapore', 7 September. Available at www.stb.gov.sg/about-stb/what-we-do/Pages/Marketing-Singapore.aspx (accessed 20/11/17).

Sky Media (2017) 'Sky AdSmart'. Available at www.skyadsmart.co.uk/

Smith Travel Research (2011) 'Glossary: a guide to our terminology'. Available at www.strglobal.com/Resources/Glossary.aspx

Smith, K. (2016) '44 Twitter statistics for 2016', *Brandwatch*, 17 May. Available at www.brandwatch.com/blog/44-twitter-stats-2016/

Smith, M. (2007) *Tourism, Culture and Regeneration*. Wallingford: CABI.

Smith, M., Macleod, N. and Hart Robertson, M. (2010) *Key Concepts in Tourist Studies*. London: Sage.

Smith, V. L. (1977) *Hosts and Guests: The Anthropology of Tourism*. Philadelphia, PA: University of Pennsylvania Press.

SNCF Group (2017) 'Serving the public'. Available at www.sncf.com/en/meet-sncf/serving-the-public

Sodhi, J. (1999) *A Study of Bundi School of Painting (from the Collection of the National Museum, New Delhi)*. New Delhi: Abhinav Publications.

South African Tourism (2011) 'Highlights of tourism's performance in 2010'. Available at www.southafrica.net/research

South Bank Bid (2017) 'About us'. Available at http://southbankbid.co.uk/about-us/an-area-under-pressure/

Spencer, R. (2016) *Development Tourism – Lessons from Cuba*. London: Routledge.

Squires, N. (2010) 'Protesters invite Venetians to the "Vencieland" theme park in bid to save the city', *Telegraph*, 9 November. Available at http://www.telegraph.co.uk/news/worldnews/europe/italy/8119924/Protesters-invite-Venetians-to-the-Venieceland-theme-park-in-bid-to-save-the-city.html (accessed 20/11/17).

Squires, N. (2016) 'Sand and deliver – Sardinians indignant over tourists stealing sand from beaches as souvenirs', *Telegraph*, 17 July. Available at www.telegraph.co.uk/news/2016/07/17/sand-and-deliver---sardinians-indignant-over-tourists-stealing-s/ (accessed 20/11/17).

Stansfeld, S. and Matheson, M. (2003) 'Noise pollution: non-auditory effects on health', *British Medical Bulletin* 68(1): 243–57.

Stansfield, C. A. (1978) 'Atlantic City and the resort cycle: background to the legalisation of gambling', *Annals of Tourism Research*, 5(2): 238–51.

Star Alliance (2017) 'Background'. Available at www.staralliance.com/en/background

Starin, D. (2008) 'Gambia: on the trail of the green monkey', *Telegraph*, 9 February. Available at www.telegraph.co.uk/travel/destinations/africaandindianocean/gambia/748406/Gambia-on-the-trail-of-the-green-monkey.html (accessed 12/11/17).

Starkie, D. (2008) *Aviation Markets: Studies in Competition and Regulatory Reform*. Farnham: Ashgate.

State of California Department of Justice (2017) 'Seller of travel'. Available at https://oag.ca.gov.travel

Statista (2017a) 'The largest cities in Spain'. Available at www.statista.com/statistics/275361/largest-cities-in-spain/

Statista (2017b) 'International hotel groups by number of hotel rooms worldwide as of December 2016'. Available at www.statista.com/statistics/245690/number-of-hotel-rooms-of-international-hotel-groups/

Statistics Canada (2017a) *Government Revenue Attributable to Tourism, 2016*. Ottawa: Statistics Canada.

Statistics Canada (2017b) *Nunavut Quick Facts*. Ottawa: Statistics Canada.

Statistics Estonia (2017) 'Frontpage'. Available at www.stat.ee/en (accessed 14/11/17).

Steer Davies Geave (2009) *Potential for Modal Shift from Air to Rail for UK Aviation*. London: Steer Davies Geave for Committee on Climate Change.

Stephany, A. (2015) *The Business of Sharing*. Basingstoke: Palgrave Macmillan.

Stevenson, N. (2009) 'The ebbs and flows of tourism policy making', in R. Thomas (ed.), *Managing Regional Tourism: A Case Study of Yorkshire, England*. Ilkley: Great Northern Press.

Stevenson, N. and Lovatt, S. (2001) *The Role of English Local Authorities in Tourism Survey 2000 (Research Report)*. London: University of Westminster.

Stoker, G. (2004) *Transforming Local Governance: From Thatcherism to New Labour*. London: Palgrave Macmillan.

Stoker, G. and Wilson, D. (2004) *British Local Government into the 21st Century*. London: Palgrave Macmillan.

STR Global (2017) 'A guide to our terminology'. Available at http://www.strglobal.com/resources/glossary#A (accessed 11/12/17)

Sultanate of Oman Ministry of Tourism (2017) 'Beauty has an address: FAQs'. Available at www.tourismoman.com.au/travel-info/faqs/ (accessed 05/12/17)Surfers Against Sewage (2017) 'About us'. Available at www.sas.org.uk/about-us/ (accessed 05/12/17)

Swarbrooke, J. (1999) *Sustainable Tourism Management*. Wallingford: CABI.

Swarbrooke, J. and Horner, S. (2001) *Business Travel and Tourism*. Oxford: Butterworth-Heinemann.

Swarbrooke, J. and Horner, S. (2007) *Consumer Behaviour in Tourism*. Oxford: Butterworth-Heinemann.

Swinglehurst, E. (1974) *The Romantic Journey: The Story of Thomas Cook and Victorian Travel*. London: Pica.

Terry, F. (ed.) (2004) *Turning the Corner? A Reader in Contemporary Transport Policy*. Oxford: Blackwell.

Tesone, D. (ed.) (2008) *Handbook of Hospitality Human Resources Management*. Oxford: Butterworth-Heinemann.

The Consulate General of the Sultanate of Oman – Australia (2017) 'Oman's 2040 tourism strategy: RO20bn investments, more than 500,000 jobs'. Available at http://oman.org.au/omans-2040-tourism-strategy-ro20bn-investments-more-than-500000-jobs/

The Dubai Mall (2017) 'About the Dubai Mall'. Available at https://thedubaimall.com/en/about-us/about-the-dubai-mall

The Local (2017) 'Barcelona approves new tourist accommodation cap'. Available at www.thelocal.es/20170127/barcelona-approves-new-tourist-accomodation-cap

The Ride (2017) 'The Downtown Experience – the world's only traveling theatre with virtual reality!'. Available at https://experiencetheride.com/sightseeing-attractions/downtown-experience/ (accessed 20/11/17).

Theobald, W. F. (ed.) (2005a) *Global Tourism* (3rd edn). Burlington, MA: Elsevier-Science.

Theobald, W. F. (2005b) 'The meaning, scope and measurement of travel and tourism', in W. F. Theobald (ed.), *Global Tourism* (3rd edn). Burlington, MA: Elsevier-Science, pp. 3–24.

The Walt Disney Company (2017) 'Walt Disney Company reports fourth quarter earnings full year earning fiscal 2016'. Available at https://thewaltdisneycompany.com/walt-disney-company-reports-fourth-quarter-earnings-full-year-earnings-fiscal-2016/

Thomas Cook Group (2008) 'Thomas Cook history'. Available at www.thomascook.com/about-us/Thomas-cook-history

Thompson Reuters (n.d.) 'Why Thompson Reuters projects?'. Available at https://projects.zawya.com/Omans_MoT_signs_agreement_for_Al_Nakheel_ITC_Development_in_Barka/story/ZAWYA20170424102015/ (accessed 06/11/17).

Thomson (2017) 'Discover your smile become a TUI affiliate'. Available at www.thomson.co.uk/destinations/info/affiliates

Thurot, J. M. (1973) 'Le tourisme tropicale Balneaire: le modele Caraibe et ses extensions'. Thesis, Centre d'Etudes du Tourisme, Aix-en-Provence.

Times Online (2007) 'Briton challenges Kenya tourism scam', 21 June. Available at www.timesonline.co.uk/tol/travel/news/article1962885.ece

Ting, D. (2016a) 'The manifesto for a common sense approach to regulation Airbnb', *Skift*, 1 August. Available at https://skift.com/2016/08/01/the-manifesto-for-a-common-sense-approach-to-regulating-airbnb/

Ting, D. (2016b) 'Airbnb launches Trips, its big tours and activities gamble', *Skift*, 17 November. Available at https://skift.com/2016/11/17/airbnb-launches-trips-its-big-tours-and-activities-gamble/ (accessed 06/11/17).

Ting, D. (2016c) This is how hotels could win the direct booking wars in Skift.com 02/08/2016 Available at https://skift.com/2016/08/02/this-is-how-hotels-could-win-the-direct-booking-wars/

Ting, D. (2017a) 'Airbnb tries to clear away political and legal challenges in New York and San Francisco', *Skift*, 1 May. Available at https://skift.com/2017/05/01/airbnb-tries-to-clear-away-political-and-legal-challenges-in-new-york-and-san-francisco/

Ting, D. (2017b) 'Most hotel CEO's dismiss Airbnb's impact but demand level playing field', *Skift*, 14 June. Available at https://skift.com/2017/06/14/most-hotel-ceos-dismiss-airbnbs-impact-but-demand-level-playing-field/?utm_campaign=Early%20 Time%20Zone%20-%20Skift%20Daily%20Newsletter&utm_source=hs_email&utm_ medium=email&utm_content=53092949&_hsenc=p2ANqtz--XFKvK4_TLjlmIfGD5KT nGeJFHyMIhLtvbkzEEa7iAOCA5MslvkhvCSbuRsd-3GmeK5uG68wMXkDbhp1AfjCi_ eUzN8w&_hsmi=53092949

Ting, D. (2017c) 'Hotel CEOs love direct booking but they have varied views about strategy', *Skift*, 26 June. Available at https://skift.com/2017/06/26/hotel-ceos-love-direct-booking-but-they-have-varied-views-about-strategy/

Tobgay, S. (2008) 'Overview of tourism in Bhutan and how it fits into the general development plans of Bhutan', *Insight: Notes from the Field*, 3.

Tourism Action Club (2017) 'About us'. Available at www.tacjamaica.com/about-us/ (accessed 14/11/17).

Tourism Australia (2016) 'China market profile'. Available at www.tourism.australia.com/content/dam/assets/document/1/6/x/g/p/2002921.pdf

Tourism Australia (2017a) 'Australia's Tourism Satellite Account 2015–2016'. Available at www.abs.gov.au/AUSSTATS/abs@.nsf/MF/5249.0

Tourism Australia (2017b) 'There's nothing like Australia 360 degree footage'. Available at www.tourism.australia.com/en/about/our-campaigns/theres-nothing-like-australia/campaign-assets/360-footage.html

Tourism Australia (2017c) 'Tourism statistics'. Available at www.tourism.australia.com/en/markets-and-research/tourism-statistics.html (accessed 05/12/17)

Tourism Concern (2012) 'Water equity in tourism'. Available at www.tourismconcern.org.uk/wp-content/uploads/2014/10/Water-Equity-Tourism-Report-TC.pdf (accessed 02/12/17)

Tourism Concern (2013) 'Slum tourism'. Available at www.tourismconcern.org.uk/slum-tourism/ (accessed 23/03/17).

Tourism Concern (2017) 'We expose tourism's worst human rights abuses and campaign against them'. Available at https://www.tourismconcern.org.uk/?page=displacement-of-people (accessed 14/11/17).

Tourism Flanders (2017) *Holidays Are for Everyone: Research into the Effects and the Importance of Holidays for People Living in Poverty*. Brussels: Tourism Flanders.

Tourisme Montréal (2016) 'Sorry Toronto! Your neighbour, Montréal', 10 December. Available at www.youtube.com/watch?v=7r78rTWZ9tY (accessed 14/11/17).

Tourisme Montréal (2017) 'Dear neighbour, sorry!', 18 January. Available at www.youtube.com/watch?v=89cSlmaYHDE (accessed 14/11/17).

Tourism New Zealand (2017) 'Markets and stats'. Available at www.tourismnewzealand.com/markets-stats/

Tourism Queensland (2009) 'Best job in the world'. Available at www.islandreefjob.com

Tourism Strategy Group New Zealand (2010) 'New Zealand tourism forecasting methodology 2010–2016'. Available at www.tourismresearch.govt.nz/Documents/Forecasts%20Summary/Forecasts2010-2016/NZ%20Tourism%20Forecasting%20Methodology%202010.pdf

Tourism Thailand (2010) 'Phuket'. Available at www.tourismthailand.org/uk/where-to-go/city-guide/destination/phuket/

Travel Compensation Fund (2010) 'Our role'. Available at www.tcf.org.au/Our_Role.asp?Page=Our_Role

Travel Foundation (2007) 'Maasai village tours'. Available at www.thetravelfoundation.org.uk/index.php?id=112

Travel Trade Gazette (2008) 'XL collapse hits 285,000 customers', 12 September.

Travel Weekly (2008) 'XL failure: the outlook for the travel industry', 18 September.

Travel+SocialGood (2017) 'About us'. Available at www.travelsocialgood.org/ (accessed 14/11/17)/

Tribal Voice Communications (2010) 'Developing and marketing a sustainable Maasai village tourism experience in Kenya'. Available at www.tribal-voice.co.uk/TVC2/PDFS/TVC%20Maasai_Project_Final_Report_1.pdf

Tribe, J. (2005) *The Economics of Leisure, Recreation and Tourism*. Oxford: Elsevier.

Tripadvisor (2011) 'About TripAdvisor Media Group'. Available at www.tripadvisor.co.uk/pages/about_us.html

Trofimyuk, N. A. (1977) 'Social insurance and the trade unions in the USSR', *International Social Security Review*, 30(1): 52–8.

TUI (2010) 'TUI brand launched in Russia and Ukraine', 2 March. Available at www.tuitravelplc.com/content/tui-brand-launched-russia-ukraine

TUI (2016) 'About TUI Group'. Available at www.tuigroup.com/en-en/about-us/about-tui-group (accessed 14/11/17).

Turespana (2013) 'El Hierro becomes the world's first smart island'. Available at http://socialnewsroom.spain.info/el-hierro-becomes-the-world-a-s-first-a-smart-island-a- (accessed 20/03/17)

Twain, M. (1986 [1869]) *The Innocents Abroad*. New York: Hippocrene Books.

Twigg-Flessner, C. (2003) *Consumer Product Guarantees*. Aldershot: Ashgate.

Twitter (2011) 'Twitter is the best way to discover what's new in your world'. Available at http://twitter.com/about

UFI (2008) 'Report on UFI member exhibitions and venue activity'. Available at www.ufi.org

United Nations (UN) (1983) *The Universal Declaration of Human Rights*. Available at www.un.org/en/universal-declaration-human-rights/ (accessed 14/11/17).

United Nations (UN) (1983) *Report of the World Commission on Environment and Development: Our Common Future. Transmitted to the General Assembly as an Annex to Document A/42/427 – Development and International Co-operation: Environment*. Oxford: Oxford University Press.

United Nations (UN) (1994) *Recommendations on Tourism Statistics,* Department for Economic and Social Information and Policy Analysis, Statistical Division, Series M, No 83, United Nations, New York, p. 77.

United Nations (UN) (2010) *International Recommendations for Tourism Statistics 2008*, Department of Economic and Social Affairs Statistics Division. Studies in Methods, Series M No 83/Rev 1. New York: UN.

United Nations Development Programme (UNDP) (2017) 'About Bhutan'. Available at www.undp.org/content/bhutan/en/home/countryinfo.html

United Nations Educational, Scientific and Cultural Organization (UNESCO) (2017a) 'Case study: Galapagos' Available at http://whc.unesco.org/en/activities/615/

United Nations Educational, Scientific and Cultural Organization (UNESCO) World Heritage Centre (2017b) 'Oman'. Available at http://whc.unesco.org/en/statesparties/om

United Nations Educational, Scientific and Cultural Organization (UNESCO) World Heritage Centre (2017c) 'Lavaux, vineyard terraces'. Available at http://whc.unesco.org/en/list/1243 (accessed 05/12/17).

United Nations Environment Programme (UNEP) and United Nations World Tourism Organization (UNWTO) (2005) *Making Tourism More Sustainable – A Guide for Policy Makers*. New York: UNEP and UNWTO.

United Nations Environment Programme (UNEP) (2008) *Climate Change and Tourism: Responding to Global Challenges*. Paris: UNEP.

United Nations Framework Convention on Climate Change (UNFCCC) (2017) 'Paris Agreement: status of ratification'. Available at http://unfccc.int/2860.php

UN Trade Statistics Knowledgebase (2008) 'International recommendations for tourism statistics 2008'. Available at https://unstats.un.org/unsd/tradekb/Knowledgebase/Irts-2008 (accessed 05/12/17).

UNWTO (n.d.) 'Global code of ethics for tourism'. Available at http://ethics.unwto.org/content/global-code-ethics-tourism (accessed 14/11/17).

UNWTO (n.d.) 'FAQ – climate change and tourism'. Available at http://sdt.unwto.org/content/faq-climate-change-and-tourism (accessed 05/12/17).

UNWTO (1991) *International Conference on Travel and Tourism Statistics: Ottawa (Canada), 24–28 June 1991 Resolutions*. Madrid: UNWTO Publications, p. 4.

UNWTO (1996) *International Tourism Overview*. Madrid: UNWTO Publications.

UNWTO (2001) 'Tourism highlights'. Available at www.e-unwto.org/doi/pdf/10.18111/9789284406845

UNWTO (2002) 'Tourism highlights 2002'. Available at www.e-unwto.org/doi/pdf/10.18111/h

UNWTO (2003) 'Chinese outbound tourism'. Available at www.e-unwto.org/doi/book/10.18111/9789284406159

UNWTO (2008a) *Statutes of the World Tourism Organisation*. Madrid: UNWTO Publications.

UNWTO (2008b) 'The conceptual framework for TSA – Tourism Satellite Account: Recommended Methodological Framework (TSA:RMF 2008)'. Available at http://statistics.unwto.org/content/tsarmf2008 (accessed 05/12/17).

UNWTO (2009) 'Impact of the global economic downturn on tourism and the development of a roadmap for resilience: Report on the activities of the Tourism Resilience Committee – CME/32/4(b3)'. Available at www.e-unwto.org/doi/abs/10.18111/unwtorcmme.2009.1.n103w2k855813620?journalCode=unwtorcmme (accessed 05/12/17).

UNWTO (2010a) 'Why tourism: tourism an economic and social phenomenon'. Available at http://unwto.org/en/about/tourism

UNWTO (2010b) *UNWTO Tourism: Highlights Edition 2010*. Madrid: UNWTO Publications.

UNWTO (2011) 'Tourism towards 2030 – global overview'. Available at http://media.unwto.org/sites/all/files/pdf/unwto_2030_ga_2011_korea.pdf (accessed 06/11/17).

UNWTO (2015) 'Tourism and the SDGs'. Available at http://icr.unwto.org/content/tourism-and-sdgs (accessed 06/11/17).

UNWTO (2016a) 'Why tourism'. Available at www.tourism4development2017.org/why-tourism/

UNWTO (2016b) *UNWTO Tourism Highlights: 2016 Edition*. Madrid: UNWTO Publications.

UNWTO (2017a) 'Innovation, technology and sustainability – pillars of Smart Destinations', 21 February. Available at http://media.unwto.org/press-release/2017-02-21/innovation-technology-and-sustainability-pillars-smart-destinations

UNWTO (2017b) 'Why tourism'. Available at www2.unwto.org/content/why-tourism (accessed 14/02/17).

UNWTO (2017c) *UNWTO Tourism Highlights: 2017 Edition*. Madrid: UNWTO Publications.

United States Tour Operators Association (USTOA) (2017) 'USTOA's $1 million travelers assistance program'. Available at www.ustoa.com/travelers-assistance

Urry, J. (2002) *The Tourist Gaze*. London: Sage.

US Department of Justice (2016) 'Princess Cruise Lines to pay largest-ever criminal penalty for deliberate vessel pollution', 1 December. Available at www.justice.gov/opa/pr/princess-cruise-lines-pay-largest-ever-criminal-penalty-deliberate-vessel-pollution (accessed 05/12/17).

US Department of State (2017a) 'Open Skies partners', 7 April. Available at www.state. gov/e/eb/rls/othr/ata/267129.htm (accessed 11/05/17).

US Department of State (2017b) 'US passports and international travel – Cuba'. Available at https://travel.state.gov/content/passports/en/country/cuba.html (accessed 30/03/17).

US Travel Association (2017) 'Project: Time off – the state of American vacation 2017'. Available at www.projecttimeoff.com/

Uthoff, D. (1997) 'Out of the tin crisis into the tourism boom: the transition of the tropical island of Phuket by international tourism', *Applied Geography and Development*, 49: 7–31.

Vail Resorts (2017) 'What we do'. Available at www.vailresorts.com

Vallen, J. J. and Levinson, C. (1989) 'The new Soviet tourism', *Cornell Hotel and Restaurant Quarterly*, 29(4): 72–9.

Vancouver Convention Centre (2011) 'About us'. Available at www.vancouver conventioncentre.com/about-us/fast-facts/

Vanhove, N. (2005) *The Economics of Tourism Destinations*. Oxford: Elsevier.

Virgin Atlantic (2011) 'Codeshare flights'. Available at www.virgin-atlantic.com/en/ gb/customerrelations/customer_charter/codeshareflights.jsp

VisitBritain (2010) 'Luxury research executive summary'. Available at www.visitbritain. org/sites/default/files/vb-corporate/Documents-Library/documents/Luxury_Exec_ Summary.pdf

VisitBritain/Office for National Statistics (2012) 'Foresight: Issue 101', March. Available at www.visitbritain.org/sites/default/files/vb-corporate/Documents-Library/ documents/2012-11%20Global%20Economic%20Outlook.pdf

VisitBritain (2014) 'Russia market and trade profile', January. Available at www. visitbritain.org/sites/default/files/vb-corporate/markets/russia_mp_jan14_0.pdf

VisitBritain (2016a) 'VisitBritain/VisitEngland welcome UK government's tourism action plan'. Available at www.visitbritain.org/visitbritainvisitengland-welcome-uk-government-tourism-action-plan (accessed 25/04/17).

VisitBritain (2016b) 'GB domestic overnight trips summary – all trip purposes 2015'. Available at www.visitbritain.org/gb-tourism-survey-2015-overview

VisitBritain (2016c) 'Inbound tourism trends by market'. Available at www.visitbritain. org/inbound-tourism-trends (accessed 7/3/17).

VisitBritain (2017a) 'Britain's competitiveness'. Available at www.visitbritain.org/ britains-competitiveness (accessed 25/04/17).

VisitBritain (2017b) 'Inbound markets and segments'. Available at www.visitbritain. org/markets-segments

Visit Britain (2017c) 'Inbound tourism trends'. Available at www.visitbritain.org/ inbound-tourism-trends

VisitLondon (2010) 'Event organisers'. Available at http://business.visitlondon.com/ choose_london/entertainment

Wahab, S. and Cooper, C. (2001) *Tourism in the Age of Globalisation*. London: Routledge.

Waitt, G. and Markwell, K. (2006) *Gay Tourism: Culture and Context*. Binghampton, NY: Haworth Hospitality Press.

Wall, G. and Mathieson, A. (2006) *Tourism: Change, Impacts and Opportunities*. Harlow: Pearson Education.

Wang, Y. and Pizam, A. (eds) (2011) *Destination Marketing and Management: Theories and Applications*. Wallingford: CABI.

Wanhill, S. (2008) 'Interpreting the development of the visitor attraction product', in A. Fyall, B. Garrod, A. Leask and S. Wanhill (eds), *Managing Visitor Attractions: New Directions*. Oxford: Butterworth-Heinemann, pp. 16–37.

Weaver, D. (2006) *Sustainable Tourism*. Oxford: Elsevier Butterworth-Heinemann.

Weiss, T. (2004) 'Tourism in America before World War II', *Journal of Economic History*, 64(2): 289–327.

Wel, C. (2017) 'Why isn't California protecting its unique purple corals?', KCET, 13 June. Available at www.kcet.org/shows/earth-focus/why-isnt-california-protecting-its-unique-purple-corals (accessed 05/12/17).

Wheeller, B. (1991) 'Tourism's troubled times: responsible tourism is not the answer', *Tourism Management*, 12(2): 91–6.

Whyte, P. (2017) '6 blockchain takeaways from TUI's hotel initiative', *Skift*, 28 August. Available at https://skift.com/2017/08/28/6-blockchain-takeaways-from-tour-operator-tuis-hotel-initiative/

Williams, A. and Zelinsky, W. (1970) 'On some patterns in international tourist flows', *Economic Geography*, 46(4): 549–67.

Williams, C. and Buswell, J. (2003) *Service Quality in Leisure and Tourism*. Wallingford: CABI.

Wilson, A., Zeithaml, V.A., Bitner, M.J. and Gremler, D.D. (2016) *Services Marketing: Integrating Customer Focus Across the Firm*. London: McGraw Hill Education Europe.

Witt, S. and Witt, C. (1992) *Modelling and Forecasting Demand in Tourism*. London: Academic Press.

Witt, S. and Witt, C. (1995) 'Forecasting tourism demand: a review of empirical research', *International Journal of Forecasting*, 11: 447–75.

Wolfe, R. I. (1952) 'Wasaga Beach – the divorce from the geographic environment', *The Canadian Geographer*, 2: 57–66.

Woodland Stewardship (2011) 'Recreational trail design – online content'. Available at http://woodlandstewardship.org/?page_id=1226http (accessed 05/12/17).

World Animal Protection (2016) 'Exposed: true scale of Thailand's "tiger selfie" tourism', 25 July. Available at www.worldanimalprotection.org/news/exposed-true-scale-thailands-tiger-selfie-tourism (accessed 05/12/17).

World Bank (2017) 'International tourism, number of arrivals'. Available at http://data.worldbank.org/indicator/ST.INT.ARVL

World Health Organization (WHO) (2016) 'Zika virus – fact sheet', September. Available at www.who.int/mediacentre/factsheets/zika/en/ (accessed 06/11/17).

World Travel & Tourism Council (WTTC) (2010) 'Welcome to WTTC'. Available at www.wttc.org

World Travel & Tourism Council (WTTC) (2015) 'WTTC announces 2015 Tourism for Tomorrow Awards winners'. Available at www.wttc.org/media-centre/press-releases/press-releases/2015/wttc-announces-2015-tourism-for-tomorrow-awards-winners/

World Travel & Tourism Council (WTTC) (2016) 'Tourism as a driver of peace: report summary'. Available at http://zh.wttc.org/-/media/files/reports/special-and-periodic-reports/tourism-as-a-driver-of-peace--report-summary-copyrighted.pdf

World Travel & Tourism Council (WTTC) (2017a) 'Travel and tourism economic impact 2017: Cuba'. Available at www.wttc.org/-/media/files/reports/economic-impact-research/countries-2017/cuba2017.pdf (accessed 06/11/17).

World Travel & Tourism Council (WTTC) (2017b) 'Travel and tourism economic impact 2017: United Kingdom'. Available at www.wttc.org/-/media/files/reports/economic-impact-research/countries-2017/unitedkingdom2017.pdf

World Travel & Tourism Council (WTTC) (2017c) 'Travel and tourism economic impact 2017: China'. Available at: Available at www.wttc.org/-/media/files/reports/economic-impact-research/countries-2017/china2017.pdf (accessed 21/04/17).

World Travel & Tourism Council (WTTC) (2017d) 'Welcome to the World Travel & Tourism Council'. Available at www.wttc.org/ (accessed 14/2/17).

World Travel & Tourism Council (WTTC) (2017e) 'Travel and tourism economic impact 2017: Aruba'. Available at www.wttc.org/-/media/files/reports/economic-impact-research/countries-2017/aruba2017.pdf

Worthington, I. and Britton, C. (2006) *The Business Environment*. Harlow: Pearson Education.

Wuest, B. (2001) 'Service quality and dimensions pertinent to tourism, hospitality and leisure services', in J. Kandampully, C. Mok and B. Sparks (eds), *Service Quality Management in Hospitality, Tourism and Leisure*. Binhampton: Hayworth Hospitality Press.

Wunder, S. (1999) 'Promoting forest conservation through ecotourism income? A case study from the Ecuadorian Amazon Region', CIFOR Occasional Paper, 21, Centre for International Forestry Research, Bogor, Indonesia.

Wyndham Worldwide (2015) 'Wyndham marks monumental milestone, becomes first global hospitality company to reach 1,000 hotels in greater China'. Available at www.wyndhamworldwide.com/news-media/press-releases/wyndham-marks-monumental-milestone-becomes-first-global-hospitality (accessed 21/04/17).

Xotels (n.d.) 'Glossary'. Available at www.xotels.com/en/glossary/ (accessed 06/11/17).

Yale, P. (1995) *The Business of Tour Operations*. Harlow: Longman.

Yeoman, I. (2013) *2050 – Tomorrow's Tourism*. Bristol: Channel View Publications.

Yokeno, N. (1968) 'La localisation de l'industrie touristique – application de l'analyse de Thunen-Weber', *Les Cahiers du Tourisme Serie C*, No 9, Aix-en-Provence.

Young, W. B. and Montgomery, R. J. (1998) 'Crisis management and its impact on destination marketing: a guide for convention and visitors bureaus', *Journal of Convention and Exhibition Management*, 1: 3–18.

YouTube (2011) 'Statistics'. Available at www.youtube.com/t/press_statistics

YouTube (2017) *YouTube for Press* https://www.youtube.com/intl/en-GB/yt/about/press/

Zeithaml, V. A. (1981) 'How consumer evaluation processes differ between goods and services', in J. Donnelly and W. R. George (eds), *Marketing of Services*. Chicago, IL: American Marketing Association.

Zeithaml, V. A., Bitner, M. J. and Gremler, D. D. (2013) *Services Marketing: Integrating Customer Focus Across the Firm*. New York: McGraw Hill.

Zeithaml, V. A., Wilson, A., Bitner, M. J. and Gremler, D. D. (2016) *Services Marketing: Integrating Customer Focus Across the Firm* (3rd European edn). London: McGraw Hill Education Europe.

Zemke, R. (1992) 'Supporting service recovery: attributes for excelling at solving customers' problems', in E. E. Sheuing, E. Gummesson and C. H. Little (eds), *Selected Papers from the Second Quality in Services (QUIS 2) Conference*. New York: St John's University and ISQA, International Service Quality Association, pp. 41–6.

Zhang, G. (2003) 'China's tourism since 1978: policies, experiences and lessons learned', in A. Lew, L. Yu, J. Ap and G. Zhang (eds), *Tourism in China*. Binghampton, NY: Haworth Hospitality Press, pp. 13–34.

Zhang, H. Q. and Morrison, A. (2007) 'How can the small to medium sized travel agents stay competitive in China's travel service sector?', *International Journal of Contemporary Hospitality Management*, 19(4): 275–85.

INDEX